KEPT FROM THE HOUR

Biblical Evidence for the
Pretribulational Return of Christ

by

GERALD B. STANTON, TH.D.

"Because thou hast kept the word of my patience,
I also will keep thee from the hour
of temptation which shall come upon all the world,
to try them that dwell upon the earth" (Rev. 3:10).

SCHOETTLE PUBLISHING CO., INC.
P. O. Box 594
Miami Springs, Florida 33166
U.S.A.
1991

To
GOD-FEARING PARENTS
Faithful in prayer
Constant in encouragement
This volume is affectionately dedicated

PREFACE TO THIS FOURTH EDITION

In the midst of present world turmoil and the deepening shadows of a dying age, many of the Lord's people are seriously inquiring if the predicted Tribulation period lies dead ahead. If so, will the Rapture take place first, or will the Church of Jesus Christ go through any portion of that dread hour of human depravity and outpoured divine wrath?

While various answers have been given, it is the firm conviction of this author that the Rapture will be before the Tribulation, and that Christ's true Church will not experience any part of that coming period of judgment.

The timing of the Rapture in its relationship to other future events involves an amazingly large number of Scripture passages, and among students of prophecy many conflicting conclusions have been drawn. For that reason, a third Section has been added to this present edition of *Kept from the Hour* entitled "THE LITERATURE OF THE RAPTURE DEBATE."

Nineteen important volumes have been selected for consideration and review, with major emphasis upon books by Dr. Walvoord and Mr. Rosenthal. Opponents of pretribulationism have been quoted extensively so that they may be represented with accuracy, but the emphasis here is upon the doctrine and not the personality. For each is an honored, premillennial servant of Jesus Christ, and our differences must not be allowed to injure our mutual hope and joy of ultimate union with Him.

May this present volume aid all who "look for that blessed hope" to consider and weigh the many Scriptures and arguments which pertain to the timing of the Rapture. May they find blessing and comfort in knowing that when God's day of grace has run its course, when God deals in wrath and Tribulation judgment falls upon a world that has rejected the Saviour, when eternity's clock has struck and earth's worst hour is ushered in, the people of God will by glorious Rapture experience already be in the presence of Christ their Lord.

GERALD B. STANTON, Th.D

AN INTRODUCTION BY DR. JOHN F. WALVOORD

In the rapidly changing scene of our modern world, the hope of the Lord's return is an anchor to the faith and a bright prospect for the future.

Though Bible scholars have not agreed that this is what the Bible teaches, a careful study of the passages on the rapture reveal that it is an imminent event without any preceding events. This is in sharp contrast to the truth of the second coming of Christ where there are tremendous events leading up to it which are revealed in Revelation 6 – 18. The second coming of Christ to set up His millennial kingdom is by no means an imminent event but is at least seven years away. By contrast, in every passage on the rapture it is presented as an event that could occur any day.

Because the hope of the Lord's return is such a blessing to Christians generally, it is to be regretted that more do not recognize the clear teaching of the Bible on this subject. The hope of the Lord's imminent return is a tremendous encouragement to those who are suffering or in persecution because it assures that this experience may be cut short by the Lord's return.

The hope of the Lord's return is a comfort to those in sorrow because, as Paul wrote the Thessalonians, the hope of the Lord's return means that we may soon be reunited with our loved ones who have preceded us to heaven through death.

The hope of the Lord's return is also a spur to evangelism as the possibility of our life and service being suddenly interrupted by the rapture makes all the more important the time period that remains in which many precious souls need to be won to Christ.

Finally, the hope of the Lord's return is a sanctifying power in the life of a Christian because it calls us to a daily walk with the Lord in keeping with our hope of being with the Lord forever.

As this book presents the many reasons why such a hope is the teaching of the Bible, we trust it will be a blessing to all who share its contents. The author has done an exceedingly careful piece of work in presenting the truth, and it should be received and welcomed by the people of God.

JOHN F. WALVOORD, Th.D., CHANCELLOR
DALLAS THEOLOGICAL SEMINARY

ACKNOWLEDGMENTS

Grateful acknowledgment is expressed to the following publishing concerns and/or authors who have graciously granted permission to quote from their publications:

Scripture Cannot Be Broken by Engelder (Concordia)
Systematic Theology by Chafer
Bibliotheca Sacra articles by Walvoord and others
Matthew 24 and The Revelation by Frost (Wm. B. Eerdmans)
The Second Coming of Christ by Frost (Wm B. Eerdmans)
History of the Christian Church by Schaff (Wm. B. Eerdmans)
Introductory Lectures in Systematic Theology by Thiessen (Eerdmans)
Our Hope articles by English and others
His Coming by Harrison (The Harrison Service)
The End: Re-Thinking the Revelation by Harrison (Harrison Service)
Not Wrath, But Rapture by Ironside (Loizeaux Brothers, Inc.)
Papers on the Lord's Coming by Mackintosh (Loizeaux Brothers, Inc.)
Simplified Classroom Notes on Prophecy by R. Ludwigson
Triumph Through Tribulation by Norman S. McPherson
The Book of the Revelation by Newell (Moody Press)
The Church and the Great Tribulation by Newell (Scripture Press)
Prophecy and the Church by Allis (Presbyterian and Reformed Publ. Co.)
Biblical Doctrines by Warfield (Oxford University Press)
Jesus Is Coming by Blackstone (Fleming H. Revell Company)
Scripture Truth About the Lord's Return by Cameron (Revell)
The Lord's Return by Silver (Fleming H. Revell Company)
Tribulation Till Translation by Rose (Rose Publishing Company)
First the Rapture by J. F. Strombeck
The Four and Twenty Elders by Armerding (Loizeaux Brothers, Inc.)
Protestant Biblical Interpretation by Ramm (W. A. Wilde Company)
Premillennialism or Amillennialism? by Feinberg (Zondervan)
Lectures on the Apocalypse by Seiss (Zondervan Publishing House)
The Basis of Millenial Faith by Hamilton (Wm. B. Eerdmans)
"Parousia," The International Standard Bible Encyclopedia by Erdman
       (Wm. B. Eerdmans Publishing Company)
The Millenial Hope by Case (Copyright 1918, Chicago Univ. Press)
The Calvin Forum "Darbyism vs. the Historical Christian Faith" by A. Pieters
Revelation, "Some Questions About Our Lord's Return" by Barnhouse

Complete information concerning the above titles is given in the bibliography at the end of the book.

CONTENTS

CONTENTS

CONTENTS

CONTENTS

A THEME OF GREAT SIGNIFICANCE

Without question, the Second Coming of Jesus Christ will be the climactic event of human history. For a world torn by hatred and violence, with nations desperately seeking peace where there is no peace, with multitudes living in frustration and sin, nothing will ever surpass the return of the Son of God in power and glory to subdue the nations and reign for ever as King of Kings.

While the Second Coming of Christ is the primary event in the unfolding drama of the last days, it does not stand in isolation. Closely associated are many clearly predicted end-time events, some of which are pivotal in their importance. These include the "blessed hope" of the rapture of the Church, with the resurrection of the dead in Christ and the translation to heaven of the living. The time of trouble and outpoured wrath known as the Tribulation, overshadowed by the dominating presence of Satan's "man of sin," the Antichrist. The splendor and majesty of Christ's return to earth, who will subdue Satan and restore peace and righteousness to a rebellious planet. The conversion of Israel, when "they shall look upon Him whom they have pierced." The judgment of the Gentile nations, separating the righteous from the wicked "as a shepherd separates his sheep from the goats." And of course, the establishment of Christ's millennial Kingdom over all the earth, leading ultimately to the glory of His eternal Kingdom.

Such majestic themes have long captured the interest of God's people, and in recent years have become a major centerpiece of Christian discussion and literature. We are all anxious to learn our future from the sure promises of the Word of God.

Many evangelical Christians consider the Rapture of the Church to be the very next event upon the prophetic timetable of

God. But the Great Tribulation of which the Bible so often speaks is also coming. What is the relationship between the rapture and this predicted time of sorrow and judgment? Will the rapture take place first, or will Christians be required to enter and endure any part of that fearful period?

While there are four main views concerning the time of the Rapture, it is the thesis and conclusion of this volume that the Rapture will be "pretribulational." That is, under no circumstance will the true Church of Jesus Christ go through any portion of the coming Tribulation period. The following pages will review the evidence for that conclusion as well as investigate the alternate positions.

What is the reason for the present revival of interest in our Lord's return? Perhaps it is because so many are convinced that the world is moving toward some ultimate and climactic catastrophe. Perhaps unwittingly the nations are preparing themselves for Armageddon.

With the rise and fall of dictators, many nations are in upheaval. In spite of constant diplomacy, wars and rumors of wars continue, while in the background there exist weapons of sufficient capacity to destroy life from off the face of the earth. Even more, violence rocks our cities and turmoil stirs our homes. These are the chaotic world conditions of the present hour, causing many to wonder if the Tribulation is indeed near at hand. And if so, will the Church pass through any portion of that predicted "time of trouble"?

When this day of grace has run its course, when God deals in wrath and judgment falls upon a world that has little use for the Christ of Calvary, when eternity's clock has struck and earth's worst hour is ushered in, will the people of God remain below, or will they by glorious Rapture experience be ushered into the presence of their Saviour? Within the household of faith, this is one of the most significant and disputed questions of our day.

To find the Scriptural answers to such questions this volume has been written. May this investigation help to put at rest the minds of many of the Lord's people, giving them assurance that before that dark day of judgment breaks Christians shall stand in the light of His countenance!

> Earth, what sorrows lie before thee,
> Unlike it in the shadows past;
> The sharpest throes that ever tore thee,
> Though the briefest and the last!
> I see the shadows of the sunset;
> I see the dread avenger's form;
> I see the Armageddon onset,
> But I shall be above the storm.
> There comes the mourning and the sighing,
> There comes the heart tear's heavy fall,
> The thousand agonies of dying—
> But I shall be above them all!

I. ON THE IMPORTANCE OF PROPHECY

To some minds, every investigation of prophetic subjects is unscholarly and unwise. Since eschatology (the doctrine of future things) is not the *most* vital division of Christian theology, and since minor variations in the understanding of God's prophetic program do not constitute a breach of the faith, some question the wisdom of spending much time and effort unraveling the problems involved. Particularly is this true regarding issues over which genuine and spiritually-minded Bible scholars have been divided. It is always regrettable when controversy and antagonism have been allowed to replace Christian love and understanding and when men forget that, in spite of their differences, they are brethren in Christ. Unfortunately, there are still those who make the order of prophetic events the basis of Christian fellowship rather than the more fundamental issues, such as the glorious Person and the finished work of Christ. The purpose of all investigations on disputed points should be to produce *light* upon the subject. There will be little added light if most of the effort involved goes into the generation of *heat!*

Nevertheless, the investigation of prophetical subjects is of vast importance and it is desirable that evangelical leaders should attain a more united stand, at least on the main outlines of God's future program. The literal fulfillment of Bible prophecy is a striking demonstration to the world of the power and wisdom of God. In the days of Isaiah the prophet, it was the *inability* of the pagan gods to prophesy which actually became one of the chief ways of exposing the fraud of heathen deities (Isa. 41:21-23). The fulfillment of prophecy proves the claim that God knows all things from the beginning. It confirms the claim that the Bible is His Word. It demonstrates the important fact that God has been pleased to reveal something of His future program. Prophecy abounds throughout the Scriptures, and the study of these predictive portions constitutes a fascinating and vital means of gaining insight into the larger purposes of God.

There are additional reasons why all true believers in the Lord Jesus Christ should be interested in prophecy. John 16:13 makes the significant statement that "when he, the Spirit of truth, is come, he will guide you into all truth . . . and he will show you things to come." While there are some who may consider future things unimportant, Spirit-taught believers place great interest on the correct interpretation of prophecy. Then, too, the book of Revelation, which deals almost entirely with future events, is the only book of the Bible to which is attached a special promise of blessing for him who reads and keeps its sayings.

Even more important is the fact that God *does* have a future plan: "Yea, I have spoken it, I will also bring it to pass; I have purposed it, I will also do it" (Isa. 46:11). He has been pleased to reveal this plan; it is evident that what He has revealed, He also means to be understood. It is important to note just how much of the Word of God is predictive in its nature. Feinberg writes:

> From a cursory examination of the entire Word of God it will be found that there are seventeen books strictly prophetic, besides the many portions of eschatological import in other books. Further study will reveal that fully one quarter of the Bible is prophecy, which rightfully includes all that was predictive at the time of its utterance. With such a large place given to eschatology in the Word by the Spirit, it not only deserves, but commands our faithful and prayerful study. It certainly was never in the purpose of God that such a large portion of His Word should be neglected or slighted.[1]

---

[1] Charles L. Feinberg, *Premillennialism or Amillennialism* (1st edition), p. 19.

Because there has been a tremendous revival in the study of prophecy over the course of the past one hundred years, the present interest in the subject can in no wise be attributed to "a passing fancy." A writer from the year 1888 graphically illustrates the vital interest of men of his day when he commences an article with the comment: "The great and increasing interest in eschatology is one of the most conspicuous features of the religious life of our times."[2]

It is this interest in prophecy which has been largely responsible for restoring the doctrine of the second coming of Christ to the Church, and it should not be thought strange that along with this restoration have come differences of opinion as to the time and the order of events. While recognizing the differences, it is still of prime importance that believers should rally around the fundamentals, in order to ward off the advances of liberalism within the church and to counteract effectively the godless forces from without which constantly endeavor to still her testimony. Prophecy should help cement evangelical unity, and must not be allowed to degenerate into a sort of theological football to be tossed to and fro largely for the plaudits of the crowd. In the words of E. Schuyler English: "The study of prophecy is valueless, it is of the flesh, it is but wood, hay, and stubble, unless it is motivated by the holy desire for the consummation of all that will redound to the glory of the Lord, and unless it issues in faithful witness and holy living.[3]

Thus we affirm that Bible prophecy is of tremendous value to the Church, but only as its interpreters endeavor to maintain the unity of the Spirit and cause their findings to be used for the glory of Christ and the ultimate good of His people.

II. THE PROBLEM BEFORE US

One of the most interesting and important problems of

---

[2]S. H. Kellogg, "Premillennialism: Its Relation to Doctrine and Practice," *Bibliotheca Sacra,* VI (April, 1888), 234.

[3]E. Schuyler English, "Re-Thinking the Rapture," *Our Hope,* LVI (November, 1949), 295.

eschatology is that of determining the time of the coming of Christ for His Church in relation to the period most generally known as the Tribulation. It is a vital and determining issue inasmuch as it involves the present comfort and the future hope of the entire Church of Jesus Christ and because it involves one of the leading motives for Christian service and godly living. It deals with the time at which the Church will meet her Lord, and obviously enough, for the generation which is alive at the coming of Christ no question could be more critical, for it determines whether or not they will pass through the horrors of the Tribulation.

This is a problem found within the boundaries of premillennialism. The truth that there will be on earth a literal, visible reign of Christ is so clearly written across the pages of Scripture and has been so adequately defended and substantiated by other writers that it is herein largely presumed.[4] The time of the rapture of the Church will be of little interest to those who deny any future coming of Christ. It will hardly arouse much concern among postmillenarians, who view the second coming to be in the far distant future. It may possibly interest the amillenarian, who generally takes the Tribulation to be an allegorical picture of the persecution which has ever been the lot of the people of God, but chiefly because a premillennial coming is contrary to his whole system.[5] However, for the believer who accepts the premillennial interpretation of Scripture and who believes that the coming of the Lord draws nigh, it immediately becomes of vital interest and importance to determine the time of the rapture of the Church in its relationship to other clearly predicted events. Will the true Church, or any portion of it, go through any part of the coming Tribulation? At this point, there is a sharp cleavage of opinion

---

[4] Chapter VII, however, will demonstrate that the strength of premillennialism and the basic weakness of amillennialism lie in the realm of interpretive methods. See also Section II: "Literal Interpretation, Figurative Language and Prophecy."

[5] The importance of pretribulationalism is admitted by its opponents. Oswald T. Allis (*Prophecy and the Church,* pp. 206-17) is a recent writer who defends the amillennial viewpoint. While attacking pretribulationalism, he nevertheless implies that consistent premillennialists are pretribulational.

among premillennialists, although it must never be forgotten that the differences involved are slight indeed in comparison with that body of truth which is held in conmmon.

There are four major positions among premillennialists as to the time of the rapture of the Church. In brief, these are as follows:

(1) The rapture will precede the Tribulation and no member of the true Church will enter into any part of it. That is, the rapture will be *pretribulational.*

(2) Some members of the Church will be raptured before the Tribulation, but believers who are not spiritually mature, or who are not "ready," or "watching" will be forced to endure all or part of its purifying fires in order that their lives may be purged of all dross. That is, there will be a *partial rapture.*

(3) The Church will bc raptured at a point midway through the Tribulation period, generally associated with the resurrection of the two witnesses and the seventh trumpet of Revelation 11, before "wrath" and "great tribulation" are poured out upon the earth. That is, the rapture will be *midtribulational.*

(4) The Church will go through the entire Tribulation period, the rapture and the revelation of Christ to earth being one simultaneous event at the end of the seven year period. That is, the rapture will be *posttribulational.*

Good and godly men have long been divided over this issue. Much has been written on each point of view,[6] and the problem is still an exceedingly live theme of discussion across the country and in many other parts of the world. It is to be expected if indeed the end of the age is approaching that interest in the coming of the Lord should be on the increase, "and so much the more, as ye see the day approaching" (Heb. 10:25). The question, Will the Church pass through the Tribulation? is no mere detail of eschatology, to be labeled as "controversial" and lightly set to one side. There is hardly a doctrine of Christianity which has not

---

[6]Posttribulational literature is especially plentiful and intolerant. Pretribulationalism also has a wide literature but it is much more scattered, the defense of this position [as of 1956] being largely in pamphlet and periodical form.

in some circles, been so classified. We agree with C. H. Mackintosh when he writes:

> The entire truth of the Church's position and prospect is involved in this question, and this is our reason for urging it so upon the prayerful attention of our readers.
>
> The great object of the enemy is to drag down the Church of God to an earthly level — to set Christians entirely astray as to their divinely appointed hope — to lead them to confound things which God has made to differ, to occupy them with earthly things — to cause them so to mix up the *coming* of Christ for His people, with His *appearing* in judgment upon the world, that they may not be able to cultivate those bridal affections and heavenly aspirations which become them as members of the body of Christ. He would fain have them looking out for various earthly events to come between them and their own proper hope, in order that they may not be — as God would have them — ever on the very tip-toe of expectation, looking out, with ardent desire, for the appearing of "the bright and Morning Star."[7]

Satan is always striving to turn the attention of men from Jesus Christ. Even a doctrine of the Bible or an ordinance of the Church can be used to keep Christians occupied with *things* rather than with their wonderful Lord. During Tribulation days, Satan will instigate his arch deception in the person of the Man of Sin, a counterfeit Messiah ruled by the Devil, and will largely succeed in causing men to worship him rather than turn to God. Can it be that as that day approaches, he would use to turn the eyes of believers from Christ to Antichrist those prophetic schemes which interpose the Tribulation and all of its dread judgment between the Christian and the coming of the Lord? Let us not underestimate the wiles of the Devil. These are difficult days and the outlook is dark, but the uplook is always good. The primary reason for this present investigation is not to raise old and controversial issues, but to re-examine the positive Biblical teachings concerning the time of the coming of the Lord and to point men to Him. It is sincerely hoped that this examination will help, strengthen, and encourage the life and testimony of all who are redeemed by His precious blood, and enable Christians every-

---

[7] C. H. Mackintosh, *Papers on the Lord's Coming,* pp. 31, 32.

where to lift up their eyes, and to look through the fog of our times to see the Man Christ Jesus, whom we love and for whose coming we anxiously wait.

III. WORDS FOR CHRIST'S COMING

During the course of any discussion relative to the second coming of our Lord from heaven, it is unavoidable that certain terms and phrases will constantly recur. Without desiring to burden the reader with all of the technicalities which have their bearing upon the subject, it is still advisable at this early point in the discussion to clarify some of the terms that will be used. Part of the problem of arriving at a conclusion as to the time of the coming of Christ for His saints has been that some authors have used ill-defined terms, or have confused issues by treating dissimilar terms as interchangeable. For example, writers often completely blur over any distinction between "the day of the Lord," "the day of Christ," "the last day," and similar designations, all the while insisting that other terms have a highly technical meaning. For the sake of clarity, the following distinctions are made in this present examination.

The term *rapture* will be used for the coming of Christ for His Church, including the reunion of living saints and their joyful meeting in the air with those who are the "dead in Christ." Unless so designated, *rapture* will signify the pretribulational appearing of Christ. It is recognized, however, that the same term is used by those of midtribulational or posttribulational persuasion at the times which their systems demand.

The term *revelation* will be used to designate the coming of Christ back to the earth to judge His enemies and to set up His millennial kingdom. Postribulationalists merge rapture and revelation into one event, but for all others the two are related but separated by a period of some years."[8]

The term *second coming,* used by some to designate either the rapture or the revelation, will be used here for the return of

---

[8] The primary discussion of these two phases of the return of Christ, together with their distinguishing characteristics, is reserved for Chapter Eleven.

Christ in general, when the above distinctions need not be made. It is believed that the rapture and the revelation, together with the intervening events, are merely different phases of the one second coming of Christ. Pretribulationalists do not believe that there are two second comings, as Allis[9] and others like to imply, but that there is one coming incorporating two separate movements, and certainly only one second coming back to the earth.

The term *Tribulation* will be used to designate the coming seven year period of intense trouble described in the Olivet discourse of Christ, thc Revelation of John, and elsewhere in Scripture. The expression *great tribulation,* often used as a popular designation for the entire Tribulation period, may better be reserved as a description of the suffering of that period, particularly during the last three and one half years following the clear manifestation of Antichrist. In fact, the attempt will be made to distinguish between the Tribulation as a period and the tribulation (suffering, persecution) the saints are called upon to bear in any age, by the simple expedient of capitalizing the former usage. Similarly, the last book of the Bible, the Revelation, while bearing the same name as the coming of Christ to the earth, will not be difficult to distinguish from the *revelation* of the Son of God.

There are in the Greek New Testament three distinct words used for Christ's return. Since they have been the object of considerable confusion, they merit at least brief consideration.

(1) The word most frequently used in Scripture to describe the return of Christ is παρουσία *(parousia).* Its etymology indicates its meaning, *to be near or alongside,* from παρά and εἰμί. Robertson, citing Deissmann on the usage of the word in classical Greek writings, states: "The word *parousia* was the technical word 'for the arrival or visit of the king or emperor' and can be traced from the Ptolemaic period into the second century A.D."[10] The Biblical usage of the word, however, is not so confined. It is used of the

---

[9] Allis, *op. cit.,* pp. 180, 181.

[10] A. T. Robertson, *Word Pictures in the New Testament,* IV, 191, citing Deissmann, *Light from the Ancient East,* p. 368.

"coming of Stephanas and Fortunatus and Achaicus," Paul's friends (I Cor. 16:17), also of "the coming of Titus" (II Cor. 7:6, 7), the coming of Paul (Phil. 1:26), the coming of the lawless one (II Thess. 2:9), and the coming of the day of God (II Pet. 3:12).

The primary meaning seems to be *presence,* rather than mere *coming,* as is further illustrated by II Corinthians 10:10: "For his letters, say they, are weighty and powerful; but his bodily presence *[parousia]* is weak, and his speech contemptible." The eschatological use of the word seems to add the thought of *arrival,* or *advent,* and is not restricted to either phase of the second coming. Some verses using *parousia* clearly refer to the rapture: "they that are Christ's at his coming" (I Cor. 15:23); "Are not even ye in the presence of our Lord Jesus Christ at his coming?" (I Thess. 2:19); "we which are alive and remain unto the coming of the Lord" (I Thess. 4:15).

Other verses which apparently belong to this same group are I Thessalonians 5:23, II Thessalonians 2:1, James 5:7, 8, and I John 2:28.

Still other verses with *parousia* seem to be a clear reference to the revelation of Christ: Matthew 24:3, 27, 37, 39; I Thessalonians 3:13; II Thessalonians 2:8; and II Peter 1:16. There may be some difference of opinion on these verses, but the important thing to note is that *parousia* stresses the coming *bodily presence of Christ* with His people. The varied usage of the word indicates that it is not a technical word used to denote either phase of Christ's coming, nor is it in the least necessary that it should so be used. The term stresses Christ's presence at His coming as against His *absence* now in heaven. It is the opposite of *apousia,* both Greek words appearing in Philippians 2:12, ". . . not in my presence *[parousia]* only, but now much more in my absence *[apousia]*."

(2) The second word for Christ's coming is ἀποκάλυψις *(apokalupsis),* occurring frequently in the New Testament, eighteen times in the noun form, and twenty-six times as a verb. It is made up of ἀπό and καλύπτω, and means *a laying bare, making naked,* or in a broader sense, to *uncover, to unveil,* and hence *reveal.* The title of the last book of the Bible, as indicated in

Revelation 1:1, is this very word. Like *parousia*, it is used for the coming of Christ in the air (I Cor. 1:7; Col. 3:4; and I Pet. 1:7, 13), and for the return of Christ to earth (Luke 17:30; II Thess. 1:7; and I Pet. 4:13). The importance of *apokalupsis* is that it speaks of the *future manifestation of the glory of Christ*, when at the rapture the Church will see Him as He is (I John 3:2), and when at the revelation the world will behold His power and His majesty.

(3) The third word used to describe the coming of Christ is ἐπιφάνεια *(epiphaneia)*, from ἐπί and φανής *to bring forth into the light, to cause to shine, to show,* hence *an appearing.* Polybius, a Greek historian, used *epiphaneia* to express *daybreak* or *dawn.* Other Greek writers used the word for the appearances of deities to those who worshiped. In the New Testament, it is found six times, and each time from the writings of Paul: II Thessalonians 2:8; I Timothy 6:14; II Timothy 1:10; 4:1; 4:8 and Titus 2:13. The verb form is found in Acts 27:20, where it is used of the reappearing of stars that have been hidden by a storm, and in Luke 1:79, where it is used of Christ's incarnation. Of the Pauline passages, I Timothy 6:14 and II Timothy 4:8, at least, refer to the rapture. It has been suggested that Titus 2:13 seems to bring into contrast two expectations of Christ, "the 'blessed hope' of Christ's return for them, and the 'glorious appearing of the great God and our Saviour Jesus Christ,' which will change the 'present world' of Titus 2:12 to millennial conditions."[11] The importance of the word is not in any supposed technical usage, but in the fact that Christ's coming will be a positive manifestation and a visible reality.

As touching the usage of these three Greek words, some pre-tribulationalists have enthusiastically used *parousia* as a technical word for the rapture, and *apokalupsis* and *epiphaneia* as technical words for the revelation, while at the other extreme, posttribula-tionalists have complained that because Paul did *not* use the words in a technical sense, this indicates that rapture and revelation cannot be separated. Neither of these positions is true, nor is it necessary to attempt to settle the time of the rapture on this issue.

---

[11]John F. Walvoord, "New Testament Words for the Lord's Coming" *Bibliotheca Sacra,* CI (July-September, 1944), 288.

The revelation of Scripture is rather to the point that for the Church, the blessed hope is the coming presence of Christ, the unveiling of His glory, and His manifestation as a visible reality. At His second coming, there will be a corresponding revelation. The presence of the Lord will transform the scenes of judgment upon sin into the peace and righteousness of the kingdom upon earth. Christ will be unveiled before the world in His glory, and He will be manifested in such a way that "every eye shall see him." [12]

Before passing to more important matters, one more term should be mentioned, over which posttribulationalists have generated considerable heat, that is, the *secret rapture.* Reese, and others, have poured scorn on the whole idea:

The Secret Coming is so very secret, that John passes it over in silence. . . . The suggestion of Darby, backed by the vigorous efforts of Kelly and others, to prove from this most magnificent passage in I Thessalonians 4 that a secret coming, a secret resurrection, and a secret rapture are portrayed, followed by the *rise* and *reign* of Antichrist, is among the sorriest in the whole history of freak exegesis. [13]

Much of the argument revolves around the verse which all agree speaks of the rapture of the Church: "For the Lord himself shall descend from heaven with a shout, with the voice of the archangel, and with the trump of God: and the dead in Christ shall rise first" (I Thess. 4: 16). All of which led someone to remark that rather than being secret, he thought this was the noisiest chapter in the Bible! This, however, is not exactly the sense in which the word *secret* has been used by its exponents, for secret also means *unexpected* or *unapparent to the world,* and does not necessarily mean *silent.* Even the glorious manifestation of Christ to the world when He comes with ten thousand of His saints is likened to the coming of a *thief:* "Behold, I come as a thief. Blessed is he that watcheth, and keepeth his garments, lest he walk naked, and they see his shame" (Rcv. 16:15), "For when they shall say,

---

[12] Ibid., p. 289.

[13] Alexander Reese, *The Approaching Advent of Christ,* pp. 89, 146. This work by Reese is no doubt the most voluminous and important posttribulational work to date. During the course of this investigation, the opinions of Mr. Reese will often come to the fore, as the leading spokesman for the posttribulational cause.

Peace and safety; then sudden destruction cometh upon them" (I Thess. 5:3).

There are those who think the world will be unaware of the rapture of the Church; she will slip silently away, and the world will hardly know she is gone. Others think that the rapture will not be unknown and "secret," but that the sound of the trump and the voice of the archangel will be heard by all. Possibly, a more intermediate position will prove to be nearer the truth. The world shall hear the shout of His coming, much as those who traveled with Saul on the road to Damascus, who heard the sound of a voice, but evidently did not hear articulate words, and who saw no man (Acts 9:7; 22:9; *cf.* John 12:28, 29; I Cor. 2:14).

The Bible does not say if the graves will be rent asunder and the gravestones overturned by the departure of the "dead in Christ," but silent or noisy, the world will not fail to know of the departure of God's living saints. The important point is that the rapture will be sudden, unexpected, an event which will take the world by surprise, and is not whether it will or will not be *secret*. Pretribulationalism does not need this term, and many do not use it. Some of the opposing brethren, however, seem to think that having dealt with the terminology of Darby and Kelly on the idea of "secrecy," they have met and destroyed the fact of the rapture. That pretribulationalism rests on more solid foundations will be demonstrated again and again in the following chapters.

Chapter Two

NOT APPOINTED UNTO WRATH

One of the most important and interesting themes of prophecy, occupying a large place in both the Old and the New Testament, is that of the great Tribulation. It is a theme which has captivated the attention of a wide segment of God's people, and has resulted in the production of scores of books and thousands of sermons, to say nothing of many fanciful interpretations and much difference of opinion. There are many problems involved which can find no place in this chapter, but it is hoped that enough can be said to demonstrate that when this fearful hour commences upon the earth, the true Church will be with her Saviour. Fortunately, the Scriptures on this subject are plentiful, and sufficiently clear to warrant some definite conclusions, although in every prophetical investigation the words of Fairbairn may be remembered with profit:

> The subject of prophecy is one that peculiarly demands, for its successful treatment, a spirit of careful discrimination. From the very nature of the subject, the want of such a spirit must inevitably lead to mistaken views, and even to dangerous results. . . . For prophecy is by no means uniform, either as regards the manner in which it came, or the form which it assumed. . . . There are portions which are written in language comparatively simple; while others are clothed in the richest imagery, or enveloped in the mystery of symbols.[1]

I. The Tribulation Period in Old Testament Prophecy

The Tribulation period is the subject of much Old Testament prophecy, as a quick review will demonstrate:

> When thou art in tribulation, and all these things are come upon thee, even in the latter days, if thou turn to the Lord thy God, and shalt be obedient unto his voice; . . . he will not for-

---

[1] Patrick Fairbairn, *Prophecy Viewed in Respect to its Distinctive Nature, its Special Function, and Proper Interpretation,* pp. 1, 2.

sake thee, neither destroy thee, nor forget the covenant of thy fathers which he sware unto them (Deut. 4:30, 31).

And they shall go into the holes of the rocks, and into the caves of the earth, for fear of the Lord, and for the glory of his majesty, when he ariseth to shake terribly the earth (Isa. 2:19; cf. 2:21; 4:1, 2).

Come, my people, enter thou into thy chambers, and shut thy doors about thee: hide thyself as it were for a little moment, until the indignation be overpast. For behold, the Lord cometh out of his place to punish the inhabitants of the earth for their iniquity: the earth also shall disclose her blood, and shall no more cover her slain (Isa. 26:20, 21).

Thus saith the Lord of hosts, Behold, evil shall go forth from nation to nation, and a great whirlwind shall be raised up from the coasts of the earth. And the slain of the Lord shall be at that day from one end of the earth even unto the other end of the earth: they shall not be lamented, neither gathered, nor buried (Jer. 25:32, 33; cf. 25:15-38).

For thus saith the Lord; We have heard a voice of trembling, of fear, and not of peace. Ask ye now, and see whether a man doth travail with child? Wherefore do I see every man with his hands on his loins, as a woman in travail, and all faces are turned into paleness? Alas! for that day is great, so that none is like it: it is even the time of Jacob's trouble, but he shall be saved out of it (Jer. 30:5-7).

And he shall confirm the covenant with many for one week: and in the midst of the week he shall cause the sacrifice and the oblation to cease, and for the overspreading of abominations he shall make it desolate, even until the consummation, and that determined shall be poured upon the desolate (Dan. 9:27).

And at that time shall Michael stand up, the great prince which standeth for the children of thy people: and there shall be a time of trouble, such as never was since there was a nation even to that same time: and at that time thy people shall be delivered, every one that shall be found written in the book (Dan. 12:1).

And it shall come to pass, that in all the land, saith the Lord, two parts therein shall be cut off and die; but the third shall be left therein. And I will bring the third part through the fire, and will refine them as silver is refined, and will try them as gold is tried: they shall call on my name, and I will hear them: I will say, It is my people: and they shall say, The Lord is my God (Zech. 13:8, 9).

The prophetic thread continues in the New Testament, as a few verses will serve to illustrate:

> For then shall be great tribulation, such as was not since the beginning of the world to this time, no, nor ever shall be. And except these days should be shortened, there should no flesh be saved: but for the elect's sake those days shall be shortened (Matt. 24:21, 22; cf. Mark 13:19, 20).

> And there shall be signs in the sun, and in the moon, and in the stars; and upon the earth distress of nations, with perplexity; the sea and the waves roaring; Men's hearts failing them for fear, and for looking after those things which are coming on the earth: for the powers of heaven shall be shaken (Luke 21:25, 26).

> And then shall that Wicked [one] be revealed, whom the Lord shall consume with the spirit of his mouth, and shall destroy with the brightness of his coming: Even him, whose coming is after the working of Satan with all power and signs and lying wonders. . . . And for this cause God shall send them strong delusion, that they should believe a lie: That they all might be damned who believed not the truth, but had pleasure in unrighteousness (II Thess. 2:8, 9, 11, 12).

From these passages alone it is not difficult to gather several salient facts concerning the Tribulation:

(1) It is a unique period, for "that day is great, so that none is like it."

(2) It concerns God's judgment upon the godless Gentile nations, with evil going forth "from nation to nation."

(3) It vitally concerns Israel also, for it is "the time of Jacob's trouble." Israel shall suffer greatly, being persecuted by the Beast, but some shall be delivered.

(4) Signs and wonders in the heavens and on earth shall accompany God's judgments.

(5) The Tribulation shall be culminated by the brightness of the coming of the Lord from glory.

One might readily gather additional facts from the passages cited, but it is more important to pass to the question of determining the *duration* of the Tribulation period and whether or not its dread judgments lie yet in the *future*.

In Daniel's important prophecy of the seventy weeks lie the answers to these questions. The text, Daniel 9:24-27, reads as follows:

> Seventy weeks are determined upon thy people and upon thy holy city, to finish the transgression, and to make an end of sins, and to make reconciliation for iniquity and to bring in everlasting righteousness, and to seal up the vision and prophecy, and to anoint the most Holy. Know therefore and understand, that from the going forth of the commandment to restore and to build Jerusalem unto the Messiah the Prince shall be seven weeks, and threescore and two weeks: the street shall be built again, and the wall, even in troublous times. And after threescore and two weeks shall Messiah be cut off, but not for himself: and the people of the prince that shall come shall destroy the city and the sanctuary; and the end thereof shall be with a flood, and unto the end of the war desolations are determined. And he shall confirm the covenant with many for one week: and in the midst of the week he shall cause the sacrifice and the oblation to cease. . . .

In brief, here is the key to the period from the restoration of Israel from her captivity to the death of Christ, the "cutting off of Messiah the Prince," and the key to the duration of Tribulation days. Seventy "weeks" of years are in view. Sir Robert Anderson[2] and other Bible scholars have demonstrated with reasonable agreement and accuracy that the seventy weeks represent 490 years, and that the sixty-nine "weeks" (using a prophetic year of 360 days) began with the decree issued for the rebuilding of Jerusalem given to Nehemiah in 445 B.C. and terminated in 32 A. D., the most probable year for the death of Christ. The last "week" of seven years evidently is to be fulfilled *after* the cutting off of Messiah, and the chronology and literal fulfilling of the details of the sixty-nine weeks gives assurance that the last week will follow the same chronological pattern, and will be as literally fulfilled. The problem is: Is that fulfillment yet future?

At least five theories have been circulated in regard to the fulfillment of this last prophetic week.[3] There are those who find its fulfillment, as they do that of the sixty-nine weeks, in the events of the Maccabean persecution two centuries before Christ. The view of the Jews is that the week was fulfilled in the events which surrounded the destruction of

---

[2] Sir Robert Anderson, *The Coming Prince.*
[3] John F. Walvoord, "Is the Seventieth Week of Daniel Future?" *Bibliotheca Sacra*, CI (January-March, 1944), 30-49.

Jerusalem in 70 A. D. Both of these views reject a literal interpretation of prophecy, and do not attempt to fit the suggested fulfillment to the chronology indicated by Daniel. A third view suggests that the seventieth week is an indefinite period beginning at the death of Christ and extending to the consummation of all things. This view, while extending the fulfillment of the seventieth week into the future, must be rejected on the same basis as the first two views. The death of Christ set the pattern of literal fulfillment for the seventy weeks, and rules out a "spiritualized" interpretation of the final week. However, as Walvoord notes, "while we cannot accept this spiritual interpretation of the passage, it is an interesting confession on the part of those who accept it that history does not record events which correspond with the prophecy of the seventieth week."[4]

The view of Philip Mauro, set forth in his book, *The Seventy Weeks and the Great Tribulation,* is that there can be no break between the fulfillment of the sixty-nine weeks and that of the seventieth week. According to Mauro, the sixty-nine weeks date from the decree of Cyrus in 536 B. C. to the baptism of Christ, even though this entails an error of some eighty years in the chronology. To Mauro, the baptism of Jesus and the accompanying descent of the Holy Spirit fulfills the prophecy "to anoint the most holy," the death of Christ fulfills the Jewish animal sacrifices, thus causing "the sacrifice and the oblation to cease," while the "prince that shall come" is the Roman Titus. While this view cannot be dealt with here in detail, it should be sufficient to note that:

(1) Daniel does not speak of the coming of a prince, but "the people of the prince," while Titus led his army in person;

(2) it is not the first coming, but the second coming of Christ that will "bring in everlasting righteousness";

(3) the death of Christ did not put an end to animal sacrifices, for they were continued unto the actual destruction of the temple in 70 A. D.

(4) Revelation 13 still looks forward to the coming of the

[4] *Ibid.,* p. 36.

Prince, and since this was written after 70 A. D., it cannot be fulfilled in Titus;

(5) if the sixty-nine weeks were weeks of years, and were fulfilled literally at the baptism of Christ, as Mauro contends, the last "week" must be a literal seven years. But seven years from the baptism of Christ does not bring us to 70 A. D. The interpretation is strained at every point.

The only interpretation of the seventy weeks of Daniel's prophecy that makes sense and is self-consistent is that there is a gap in the prophecy (a phenomenon not uncommon to prophetic Scripture) and that while the sixty and nine were fulfilled in Christ, the seventieth week lies yet in the future. In common with the literal interpretation of the former weeks, this "seventieth week" is to be a week of seven actual years. There is no period foreseen in the prophetic Scriptures with which this part of Daniel's vision can harmonize other than the Tribulation, which has been under discussion. This is the same Tribulation period which is described by John in the book of Revelation, there identified also by months and days, and it is not until a future period of seven years of Tribulation is recognized that all these various prophecies fit into a unified pattern. Returning, then, to the characteristics of the Tribulation period, it is concluded that the *duration* of the period will be seven years and that the *time* of the Tribulation is yet in the future. With most of these conclusions, midtribulational and posttribulational brethren will agree. They are being rehearsed at this point as the necessary foundation for discussions which will follow.[5]

Christians are promised tribulation, it is claimed, so naturally God will permit them to go through all or part of the coming Tribulation. Both midtribulationalists and posttribulationalists use this argument and evidently count it as vital to their way of thinking, for they press it to the hilt. But let it not be received

[5] Not all agree, however. George L. Rose, in *Tribulation Till Translation*, p. 247, is a posttribulationalist who finds it convenient to accept the "historical view." Of the pretribulationalists, he says, "Having this supposed seven years on hand they naturally must do something with it, so they join it with the mistaken idea about 'the great tribulation.'" Rose holds that "the seventy weeks were fulfilled more than 1500 years ago."

too hastily, for here is a premise and a conclusion which cannot be made to stand together. First, however, let the opposing brethren speak:

> The ancient prophecies of universal blessing must have their full accomplishment, but that can never be till the Lord takes the dominion manifestly into His own hand. During this dispensation the broad way is thronged by the many, while but few find the narrow; all that will live godly in Christ Jesus must expect persecution, at least in principle.[6]
>
> "Through much tribulation" all must enter into the Kingdom of God. Everywhere in the New Testament it is taught that to suffer for Christ is one of the highest honours Christians can have bestowed upon them. A desire to shirk suffering for Christ is a sign of degeneracy.[7]

All of this is manifestly true, but this is merely a restatement of the promise that Christians are promised tribulation and suffering in this life. McPherson goes further afield when he gives four reasons why he thinks there are so many pretribulationalists:

> A second reason why many have taught the Church will not pass through the Tribulation is an excessive desire to meet a popular demand for the most comforting type of teaching. For example, Dr. H. C. Thiessen closes his book, *Will the Church Pass Through the Tribulation?*, with the words: "We may then comfort one another with the thought that the Church will not pass through the Tribulation." [8]

This, however, is uncharitable, for those of pretribulational persuasion do not gear their ministry to comfortable teachings. Among their number are the most powerful and convicting preachers of sin and judgment and hell, and they preach these things because they are in the Book. The same men preach the comfort of a pretribulational hope, not because it appeals to the flesh, but because this, too, they find in the Word of God. The idea of comforting one another with these truths originated with I Thessalonians 4:18, not with Thiessen, although he loved to proclaim it. McPherson goes on to cite Reese in this connection:

> The very fact of the scheme's being so comforting and pleasing to the flesh is a consideration that reveals its unscriptural charac-

---

[6] S. P. Tregelles, *The Hope of Christ's Second Coming*, p. 30.
[7] Robert Cameron, *Scriptural Truth About the Lord's Return*, p. 18.
[8] Norman S. McPherson, *Triumph Through Tribulation*, pp. 2, 3.

ter: for it is not the way of the scripture to make the path of the saints easy.[9]

Needless to say, Scripture does warn the saint of his daily conflict with the world, the flesh, and the devil, and it is part of the Christlike walk to take up the cross and follow Him. Christ suffered, and the servant is not greater than his Lord. But these sufferings are from without; they originate from the world, from the heat of the battle, and not from any reluctance on the part of Christ or the Scriptures to make the path of the Christian less burdensome. Christ said: "For my yoke is easy, and my burden is light" (Matt. 11:30). Paul told the Gentile believers: "For it seemed good to the Holy Ghost, and to us, to lay upon you no greater burden than these necessary things" (Acts 15:28; cf. Rev. 2:24).

The coming of Christ is to the believer a blessed hope and a comforting hope, and surely it is not engaging in the indolence of the flesh to rest in those things which were meant to give hope and comfort in the midst of the toils of the journey. It would be presumption to do otherwise. Does Reese derive comfort from the truth of the security of the saint and the assurance of heaven? With Christ, the Father has given us freely all good things (Rom. 8:32), yet, using the same reasoning, might not these also be taken from us? Posttribulationalist Scruby writes:

> I am afraid of the doctrine of the Pre-Tribulation Rapture of the Church because it is in accord with the desires of the human heart. The natural inclination is to "follow the line of least resistance," to avoid trial, trouble, suffering, etc. . . .[10]

Scruby is so sold on the proposition that no comfort must come to the Christian that he makes the astounding statement in two of his subtitles: "Post-Tribulation-Rapturism Beneficial Even If It Should Prove To Be Erroneous," and "Pre-Tribulation-Rapturism Injurious Even If True."[11] Let the reader judge these words for himself! Even Reese, speaking of the pretribulational expectation, admits: "It would be a very comforting truth if it were true," but adds, "as it is not, we are safe in discarding it."[12]

[9] Alexander Reese, *The Approaching Advent of Christ*, p. 225.
[10] John J. Scruby, *The Great Tribulation: The Church's Supreme Test*, p. 132.
[11] *Ibid.*, pp. 140, 141.
[12] Reese, *op. cit.*, p. 294.

No one will deny that suffering and tribulation are promised the believer in this life. The Scriptures are explicit and numerous:

> If ye were of the world, the world would love his own: but because ye are not of the world, but I have chosen you out of the world, therefore the world hateth you. Remember the word that I said unto you, The servant is not greater than his lord. If they have persecuted me, they will also persecute you; if they have kept my saying, they will keep yours also (John 15:19, 20).
>
> These things I have spoken unto you, that in me ye might have peace. In the world ye shall have tribulation: but be of good cheer; I have overcome the world (John 16:33).
>
> And they departed from the presence of the council, rejoicing that they were counted worthy to suffer shame for his name (Acts 5:41).
>
> Confirming the souls of the disciples, and exhorting them to continue in the faith, and that we must through much tribulation enter into the kingdom of God (Acts 14:22).
>
> And our hope of you is stedfast, knowing, that as ye are partakers of the sufferings, so shall ye be also of the consolation (II Cor. 1:7).
>
> For unto you it is given in the behalf of Christ, not only to believe on him, but also to suffer for his sake (Phil. 1:29).
>
> Yea, and all that will live godly in Christ Jesus shall suffer persecution (II Tim. 3:12).
>
> But rejoice, inasmuch as ye are partakers of Christ's sufferings; that, when his glory shall be revealed, ye may be glad also with exceeding joy (I Pet. 4:13).

In the verse preceding this last passage, Peter speaks of "the fiery trial which is to try you," and one has but to think of Christians being thrown to the lions in a Roman arena, or Christians being torn on the racks of a Spanish Inquisition, or Christians today being put to death in godless Communistic lands to realize that believers have undergone fiery trials down through the years since the days of the early church. Such persecutions with their untold agony, no matter how severe, are nevertheless not "the great tribulation." If they were, one could hardly read Fox's *Book of Martyrs* without concluding that there have been two or three "great tribulations" every century from the time of Christ!

> Who shall separate us from the love of Christ? shall tribulation, or distress, or persecution, or famine, or nakedness, or peril, or sword? As it is written, For thy sake we are killed all the day

long; we are accounted as sheep for the slaughter. Nay, in all
these things we are more than conquerors through him that loved
us (Rom. 8:35-37).

Down through the centuries, believers have suffered, bled,
and died for their faith in Christ, counting it not loss to seal
their testimony with their blood. It is not assuming too much
that if persecution and fiery trial were to reach some of our
more sheltered lives, those who hold that the rapture will precede the Tribulation would give as good account of their testimony as those who hold a different theological position.

All of this, however, is not directly to the point. The crux
of the problem is that the posttribulationalists hold the tribulation of the coming seven year period to be *the same in kind*
as the sufferings of the saints in this age, differing only in
intensity (although some are not willing to concede even this).
Pretribulationalists hold that the reason this period is especially
designated as "the Tribulation, the great one," is not only that
it is of greater intensity, but also that *it differs in its kind,* in
its essential nature, from anything which has been seen or
experienced heretofore. The Tribulation will not be primarily
a time when the bitter anger of Satan and sinners will afflict
the saints of God, as harsh as their persecution is predicted to
be. Rather, it will be primarily and above all else a period of
judgment from God, a time when the sovereign Lord of the
universe finally speaks forth in awful wrath and His punitive
rod falls upon living nations which have spurned the Son of
His love and rejected the gracious gift of His "so great salvation." Clearly substantiated in Scripture is the fact that the
Tribulation period differs from this present age of grace in its
essential nature. The "great tribulation" of that day is dissimilar in its purpose and source from any "tribulation" which
may be the lot of God's people during this present age of
grace. Or, to put the matter more simply, *sufferings* imposed
by wicked men and *wrath* poured out from an angry God are
in no wise the same thing merely because the Bible designates
them both by the general term "tribulation."

II. FIVE CHARACTERISTICS OF THE TRIBULATION

It will help to clarify this important issue if an examination is given to the distinctive features of the Tribulation period. In fact, it may readily be observed that the Tribulation of that day differs from the sufferings of the Church in at least five particulars, namely its *purpose, extent, duration, intensity,* and *source.*

(1) The *purpose* of the Tribulation. It has been argued again and again by posttribulationalists that since God did not spare His Church of the second and third centuries the bloody persecution of pagan Rome, and again during the Dark Ages the cruel inquisition of papal Rome, that He will not spare the last generation of the Church the sufferings and martyrdoms of the "great tribulation." Scruby even dwells upon the method of execution to be used, saying:

> It is significant that the only form of martyrdom mentioned in connection with the Tribulation is beheading, which is one of the quickest and least painful modes of execution, seeing that it results in instantaneous death; especially when inflicted by the guillotine, as most likely will be the case: following the example set during that miniature Tribulation, the "Reign of Terror" during the time of the French Commune.[13]

All of which may be painfully true, but is hardly calculated to encourage even the most godly believer to look with hope and joy for a coming of Christ which follows such unparalleled suffering. Instead of praying, "Even so, come, Lord Jesus," he would be tempted to say with Barnhouse:

> If the Church is to pass through the Tribulation, then farewell blessed hope, then welcome the coffin, then thrice welcome the undertaker![14]

Posttribulationalists have missed the plainly revealed purposes of the Tribulation period, while dwelling on the supposed fact that God is purifying His Church. The Tribulation does not deal with the Church at all,[15] but with the purification of Israel. It is not the "time of the Church's trouble," but the "time of Jacob's trouble." The emphasis of the Tribulation is

---

13 Scruby, *op. cit.,* pp. 153, 154.
14 Donald Grey Barnhouse, "Some Questions About Our Lord's Return," *Revelation,* XII (November, 1942), 498, 526-28.
15 The church, and the "elect" of Matthew 24 and the book of Revelation, will be discussed in the following chapter.

primarily Jewish. This fact is borne out by Old Testament
Scripture (Deut. 4:30; Jer. 30:7; Ezek. 20:37; Dan. 12:1;
Zech. 13:8,9), by the Olivet Discourse of Christ (Matt. 24:
9-26), and by the book of Revelation itself (Rev. 7:4-8; 12:1,
2,17, etc.). It concerns "Daniel's people," the coming of
"false Messiahs," the preaching of the "gospel of the kingdom,"
flight on the "sabbath," the temple and the "holy place," the
land of Judaea, the city of Jerusalem, the twelve "tribes of
the children of Israel," the "song of Moses," "signs" in the
heavens, the "covenant" with the Beast, the "sanctuary," the
"sacrifice and the oblation" of the temple ritual. These all
speak of Israel and clearly demonstrate that the Tribulation
is largely a time of God's dealing with His ancient people prior
to their entrance into the promised kingdom. The many Old
Testament prophecies yet to be fulfilled for Israel further indicate a future time when God will deal expressly with this
nation (Deut. 30:1-6; Jer. 30:8-10, etc.).

Moreover, it is evident that the Tribulation also concerns
God's judgment upon Christ-rejecting Gentile nations. Babylon,
which "made all nations drink of the wine of the wrath of
her fornication" (Rev. 14:8), shall herself "be utterly burned
with fire: for strong is the Lord God who judgeth her" (Rev.
18:8). The "cities of the nations" shall fall, after which Satan
shall be bound "that he should deceive the nations no more,
till the thousand years should be fulfilled" (Rev. 20:3). God's
judgment falls likewise upon the individual wicked, the kings
of the earth, the great, the rich, and the mighty, every bondman and every free man (Rev. 6:15-17). It falls upon all who
blaspheme the name of God and repent not to give Him glory
(Rev. 16:9). Wicked men, godless nations, suffering Israel —
these may all be found in Revelation 6-18; but one looks in vain
for the Church of Christ, which is His body, until he reaches
the nineteenth chapter. There she is seen as the heavenly
bride of Christ, and when He returns to earth to make His
enemies His footstool, she is seen returning with Him (I Thess.
3:13).

(2) The *extent* of the Tribulation. As it has been indicated,
the Tribulation reaches unto the cities and the nations of the

earth, and will be world-wide in its scope. Luke 17:26-32 compares the Tribulation to God's judgment upon the world in the days of Noah, and upon the cities of the plain in the days of Lot.

(3) The *duration* of the Tribulation. Although there are some who believe there will be an undesignated season of peace and prosperity after the rapture of the Church, during which time Antichrist will have his rise and the Tribulation temple be rebuilt, the actual Tribulation period will be seven years in length. This is in fulfillment of the prophecy of Daniel's seventieth week (Dan. 9:24-27), and any extension of this time is in the realm of conjecture. Daniel 9:27 indicates that the "week" will be divided into two halves, when "in the midst of the week," Antichrist will make the temple desolate with his abominations. Daniel 11:31 is a reference to the act of Antiochus Epiphanes, who entered the holy of holies and sacrificed a sow upon the temple altar, thus becoming the proto-type of the coming man of sin. That the "week" will be divided into two halves of three and one half years is further indicated by the formula "a time, and times, and half a time" (Rev. 12:14; Dan. 12:7); by the measure of "forty and two months" (Rev. 11:2; 13:5); and by the designation of "a thousand two hundred and threescore days" (Rev. 11:3; 12:6). Matthew 24:22 seems to indicate that because of the severity of the Tribulation, the number of its days will be shortened a little.

(4) The *intensity* of the Tribulation. It is needless here to elaborate much upon the severity of the Tribulation judgments. One might start with the mighty plagues called down by Moses upon Egypt, and from there study all the wars, revolutions, persecutions, inquisitions, and the rest of the awful history of the human race down to the gas chambers of modern Dachau, and still not find that with which to compare the judgments of the seals and trumpets and the seven vials of the plagues of God. Revelation 16:2, compared with verse 11, indicates that the plagues continue and are cumulative, God placing His mark upon them which received the mark of the Beast. Revelation 10:4 recounts that the things uttered by the seven

thunders were sealed up. So terrible are they that God in His mercy withholds them. Revelation 16:10 speaks of men who "gnawed their tongues for pain." But why enumerate further? Sufficient unto the day is the evil thereof. It is enough that God's estimate of this awful period is that there shall be "great tribulation, such as was not since the beginning of the world to this time, no, nor ever shall be. And except those days should be shortened, there should no flesh be saved" (Matt. 24:21, 22).

It is one of the peculiar quirks of some of the posttribulational writers, that, having taken the Church into the Tribulation by vehemently insisting that a carnal Church needs to be purged of her dross by tribulation fire, they now labor to dismiss the intensity of its judgments. It is typical of both midtribulational and posttribulational writers that they try to tone down the severity of its plagues, or insist that although the Church is to be in the Tribulation, she has after all very little to do with it. Alexander Fraser writes:

> Much of the scene in Revelation has to do only with God's judgments upon rebellious man and there is no Scriptural reason to believe that God's people will be directly involved in that suffering.[16]

Scruby follows the same pattern:

> Most people think of the Great Tribulation as a period of unparalleled suffering; and in a sense it will be. That is to say: It will be a period of unparalleled suffering on an *international* or world-wide scale. But it does not necessarily follow from this that it will be a period of unparalleled suffering for the *individual* believer.[17]

Note that Scruby is the writer who attempts to make the horror of the Tribulation more vivid by comparing its martyrs to those guillotined during the "reign of terror" of the French Commune. He then completely reverses the force of his argument by going on to illustrate how painless this kind of death might be. It seems that there was a British printer who, supposedly, was cutting paper under a razor-sharp blade. An office girl, by mistake, started the machine. The printer turned to see if any damage had been done to his paper, and "was

---

[16] Alexander Fraser, *Is There But One Return of Christ?*, p. 63.
[17] Scruby, *op. cit.*, p. 152.

astounded to see the severed fingers of his right hand lying across the cutter stick. . . . He had not felt the equivalent of a pin prick when the accident happened."[18] He then goes on to give several even more bizarre illustrations of how the body tends to become numb under torture so that the greatest sufferings result in the greatest reduction of pain! All of which forms a pathetic illustration of the fact that even posttributionalists cannot get away from the thought that it is incongruous for God's children to undergo great tribulation.

Satan's rage will be against the woman — Israel, but God will prepare for her a place of refuge in the wilderness where she will be protected from the face of the serpent (Rev. 12:13-16). If in that same day, the Church, the very body of Christ, were on earth, how much more would she be the object of Satan's attack! How great would his havoc be, for Revelation records no place of refuge for the Church during the days of the Tribulation. Fortunately, she will be in heaven, removed from Satan's wiles (Rev. 12:9). How much more profitable to look with joyous expectancy for the pretribulation rapture of the Church, than to occupy oneself with comparing the "blessed hope" to the French Reign of Terror, or in trying to reconcile the sufferings of that day with the "painless death" of the guillotine! The Tribulation is still the earth's worst hour, no matter how much some try to water it down, and although it is true that God could protect His Church *in* it, He has promised to do that which is far better. He has promised to save His Church *from* it.

(5) The *source* of the Tribulation. Careful consideration at this point is of vital importance. Those who contend that the Church will go through the coming Tribulation claim that the period is one of intensified *persecution*, but not a time of *judgment*. To quote Fraser: "The Great Tribulation is not judgment, but persecution."[19] Frost is of the same mind, for he says:

For the church, therefore, to go into the days of the Antichrist, and to be called upon to endure his hatred and harassments,

18 *Ibid.*, p. 154.
19 Fraser, *op. cit.*, p. 63.

is but for her to pass from one phase of an experience into another, the difference being, not in kind, but in degree.[20]

Those who believe that the Church will not go through the Tribulation, however, hold that the period is primarily a time of judgment. The tribulation inflicted upon the Church in this present age comes from men and from Satan. The tribulation that is to come will be from God. In this age, tribulation comes upon those who bear witness to the Lord Jesus Christ. The tribulation that is to come primarily will be upon those who reject Christ and who will not have God to rule over them. The tribulation of this age can better be called *persecution*. The tribulation of the period to come is rightfully designated as the *wrath of God*. The foremost difference between *persecution* and *wrath* lies in the source from which it comes, and this obvious distinction cancels out the stock posttribulationalist argument that the Church will go through the Tribulation because she has always had tribulation.

To be sure, God will have His saints in the Tribulation—men who repent and secure salvation after the catching up of the Church. This group will be considered more fully at a later point in the discussion. Satan hates these individuals as fully as he hates men of God today, and upon them he will endeavor to pour *his* wrath. Revelation 12:12-17 reveals the wrath of Satan against the Jewish remnant (Isa. 1:9; 10:20; 11:11; 37:32 etc.). Revelation 13:7 records: "And it was given unto him to make war with the saints, and to overcome them: and authority was given him over all kindreds, and tongues, and nations." As would be expected, Reese makes the most of these verses, saying:

> According to Darby and his followers, the Great Tribulation is the wrath of God against the Jewish people for their rejection of Christ. According to Scripture, it is the Devil's wrath against the saints for their rejection of Antichrist, and adherence to Christ.
>
> Let the reader once see the Scripture truth on this point, and the whole Darbyist case will be exposed as a campaign of assumptions, mis-statements, and sentiment.[21]

But Reese overlooks the fact that the God who can make even the *wrath* of men to praise Him; can also use Satan, as He often does in His permissive will (Job 1:12, etc.), to be His

[20] Henry W. Frost, *Matthew Twenty-four and the Revelation*, p. 64.
[21] Reese, *op. cit.*, p. 284.

instrument of punishment or judgment. Many times in the Old Testament, God used pagan nations to scourge Israel and cause her to return unto the Lord. God is still sovereign during Tribulation days, and whereas Satan cannot move one inch beyond what He permits, Satan's wrath against the remnant is used of God to purify her (Zech. 13:9) and drive her from the realm of the Beast to her place of protection. In the whole encounter, Satan is defeated, for the Lord causes the earth to open and swallow up the armies which pursue Israel (Rev. 12:16).

Reese also overlooks the fact that pretribulationalists freely acknowledge the presence of some persecution, all the while maintaining that the primary character of the period is *wrath*. He complains that "Darbyists" cannot be brought to prove that the great Tribulation is the wrath of God, and therefore this "part of their syllogism which they adroitly hurry over is completely false. It is a blunder that the Great Tribulation consists of God's wrath. . . ."[22] Rather than argue the point, it should suffice to look at the Scriptures:

And said to the mountains and rocks, Fall on us, and hide us from the face of him that sitteth on the throne, and from the *wrath of the Lamb*: For the great day of *his wrath* is come; and who shall be able to stand? (Rev. 6:16, 17; *cf.* Deut. 7:9, 10; Hosea 10:8).

Saying with a loud voice, Fear God, and give glory to him; for *the hour of his judgment* is come: and worship him that made heaven, and earth, and the sea, and the fountains of waters (Rev. 14:7).

And the nations were angry, and *thy wrath is come*, and the time of the dead, that they should be judged, and that thou shouldest give reward unto thy servants the prophets, and to the saints, and them that fear thy name, small and great; and shouldest destroy them which destroy the earth (Rev. 11:18).

And the third angel followed them, saying with a loud voice, If any man worship the beast and his image, and receive his mark in his forehead, or in his hand, The same shall drink of the wine of *the wrath of God*, which is poured out without mixture into the cup of his indignation (Rev. 14:9, 10).

And the angel thrust in his sickle into the earth, and gathered the vine of the earth, and cast it into the great winepress of *the wrath of God* (Rev. 14:19).

22 Reese, *op. cit.*, p. 283.

> And I saw another sign in heaven, great and marvellous, seven angels having the seven last plagues; for in them is filled up the *wrath of God* (Rev. 15:1; *cf.* 15:4).
>
> And one of the four beasts gave unto the seven angels seven golden vials full of the *wrath of God,* who liveth for ever and ever (Rev. 15:7).
>
> And I heard a great voice out of the temple saying to the seven angels, Go your ways, and pour out the vials of the *wrath of God* upon the earth (Rev. 16:1; *cf.* 16:7).
>
> And the great city was divided into three parts, and the cities of the nations fell: and great Babylon came in remembrance before God, to give unto her *the cup of the wine of the fierceness of his wrath* (Rev. 16:19).
>
> Standing afar off for the fear of her torment, saying, Alas, alas, that great city Babylon, that mighty city! for in one hour is thy *judgment* come (Rev. 18:10; *cf.* 17:1; 19:2).

These many Scriptures are given here without apology for their number not only because what God has to say is more important than what man may say, but also because they conclusively prove the point: the distinctive character of the Tribulation period is that it is a time of divine wrath. Satan may be given a little leeway before he is chained, but the primary source of wrath in the Tribulation is neither Satan nor wicked men, but God. He pours it out "without mixture." There is not a drop of water to cool its heat. It is not blended with hope or grace. It is God's undiluted wrath on a world that has rejected His own glorious Son.

Reese ignores all these Scriptures, arguing his case only on the basis of Revelation 12:12-17 and 13:7. All of which may serve to illustrate a point: When a clever writer makes a big stir over a weak case, it is good judgment to search the Scriptures independently and to draw one's conclusions directly therefrom. It is here maintained that the persecutions of this age are the endeavors of wicked men to exterminate the Church, while the tribulations of that future period will be primarily the wrath and the judgment of an angry God upon Christ-rejectors. All else is but an incident in the program of God. The *wrath,* the *judgments,* and the *plagues* are from the Lord, and in the words of Hebrews 10:31, it will be "a fearful thing to fall into the hands of the living God."

III. PROMISES OF DELIVERANCE

The Church is expressly promised deliverance from the wrath of God. Of course, the Bible does not come out in so many words and say, "The rapture of the Church will be pre-tribulational." Nor, for example, does the Bible directly say: "Baptism must be by immersion," nor "The representative form of church government is most in accord with the Apostolic Church." Most of the major doctrines of the Bible *are* confirmed by such direct unassailable statements, yet some are not. Many precious Biblical truths do not lie exposed on the immediate surface. Hence, there are differences of opinion even in the ranks of godly Bible students. No doubt the Lord ordained it so in order to keep His people searching the Scriptures.

One must hesitate before being overly dogmatic on subjects concerning which the brethren have agreed to disagree. However, it would seem that in respect to the time of the rapture of the Church, there are enough Scriptures to reach a positive conclusion, opposing brethren failing to agree solely because they have built their conclusions on wrong premises. Fraser is forced to admit that "God may preserve His own from the judgments He sends upon the ungodly,"[23] but argues "It is quite possible, then, for the true Church to go through tribulation without experiencing the judgments of God upon the wicked."[24] This, of course, is true, but beside the point. God *could* take the Church through the whole of the great Tribulation, and all the while shield her from His judgments, even as He protected the Israelites from the great plagues poured out upon Egypt. But the question is not *can God*, but *will God* permit His Church to enter a period manifestly designed as a time of His wrath upon sinners? Scripture, and not speculation, must supply the answer.

It should not be necessary here to prove that Christ provided, through His work on the cross, a complete and eternal salvation for all who will put their trust in Him. The salvation God offers the sinner is *full* (Heb. 7:25); it is *free*

23 Fraser, *op. cit.*, p. 65.
24 *Ibid.*, p. 67.

(Rom. 6:23); it is *forever* (John 10:28). It includes past justification, present sanctification, and future glorification. It redeems and safeguards the believer from the wrath of God in all of its forms.

Romans 8:1 assures that there is no condemnation, or judgment, to them that are in Christ Jesus. Romans 5:9 declares plainly: "Much more then, being now justified by his blood, we shall be *saved from wrath* through him." Here, being saved from wrath refers primarily to salvation from eternal punishment, from hell. But does it not also include deliverance from that time of judgment on earth which is primarily characterized by the pouring out of the vials of the *wrath of God?* I Thessalonians 5:9 confirms the fact that tribulation wrath is in view also, when it speaks of the appearing of Christ for His own in the clouds, and when it declares of those who have put on the helmet of salvation: *"God hath not appointed us to wrath, but to obtain salvation [deliverance] by our Lord Jesus Christ."* *Suffering* is often the portion of the Christian (Rom. 8:17; II Tim. 2:12; Phil. 1:29), but not *wrath!* Wrath is reserved for unbelievers:

> For the wrath of God is revealed from heaven against all ungodliness and unrighteousness of men, who hold the truth in unrighteousness (Rom. 1:18; *cf.* 2:3).
>
> But after thy hardness and impenitent heart treasurest up unto thyself wrath against the day of wrath and revelation of the righteous judgment of God (Rom. 2:5).
>
> But unto them that are contentious, and do not obey the truth, but obey unrighteousness, indignation and wrath, Tribulation and anguish, upon every soul of man that doeth evil, of the Jew first, and also of the Gentile (Rom. 2:8, 9).

Tribulation and vengeance fall upon them that know not God:

> Seeing it is a righteous thing with God to recompense tribulation to them that trouble you; And to you who are troubled rest with us, when the Lord Jesus shall be revealed from heaven with his mighty angels, In flaming fire taking vengeance on them that know not God, and obey not the gospel of our Lord Jesus Christ (II Thess. 1:6-8).

Christians, however, are to serve the living and true God, and "to wait [not for tribulation, but] for his Son from heaven" (I Thess. 1:10). Paul exhorted the Thessalonian believers:

> Brethren, pray for us . . . that we may be delivered from un-reasonable and wicked men: for all men have not faith. But the Lord is faithful, who shall stablish you, and keep you from evil. . . . And the Lord direct your hearts into the love of God, and into the patient waiting for Christ (II Thess. 3:1-5).

Some of the posttribulationalist writers are forced, by the very weight of these Scriptures, to concede that the Church cannot be on the earth during the "day of God's wrath," but because they are not willing to acknowledge that the Church has no place in Revelation 6-18, they are forced to refer the wrath of God to the end of the entire period *after* Christ returns to earth with His saints. This is the position of Rose:

> "The day of Vengeance of Our God" must be interpreted as being different from "The great tribulation." The saints suffer tribulation while Christ is absent from the earth, but when He returns His saints will be delivered; and God will recompense their tribulation with *Wrath* upon the ungodly in The Great Day of Wrath. That wrath will not touch the saints; "for God hath not appointed us unto wrath, but to obtain salvation by our Lord Jesus Christ."[25]

This statement is an unsolicited acknowledgment from a post-tribulationalist writer that I Thessalonians 5:9 speaks of Tribu-lation wrath as well as eternal wrath. Rose's conclusion, how-ever, is definitely in error, for it has already been demonstrated that *wrath* is found in Revelation 6:16,17; 11:18; 14:9,10; 14:19; 15:1,7; 16:1,19, and finds, not its commencement, but its consummation in Revelation 19:15.

Nor should the force of Old Testament typology be missed in connection with God's purpose to save His own from particu-lar seasons of divine wrath. Rahab was saved by Joshua and taken out of Jericho before the city was conquered and destroyed (Josh. 6:16,25; Heb. 11:31). Lot must first be removed from Sodom, before God's wrath could be poured out upon the wicked cities of the plain (Gen. 19:14). Let us recall Abraham's inter-cession before God, when he asked: "Wilt thou also destroy the righteous with the wicked?" and when he received God's re-sponse: "Shall not the Judge of all the earth do right?" (Gen. 18:23,25). God's clear answer is given to Lot by His heavenly messenger: "Haste thee, escape thither; *for I cannot do any*

25 Rose, *op. cit.*, p. 204.

thing till thou be come thither" (Gen. 19:22). So will it be when God prepares to pour out His wrath in great tribulation upon the earth.

It has been objected that God permitted Noah and his family to pass *through* the flood, rather than removing them entirely from the scene of judgment. Noah cannot then be a type of the Church, but rather a type of Israel in the future day of judgment, *in* the Tribulation but protected from the serpent and the flood which he cast out of his mouth (Rev. 12:14, 15). The Church may be prefigured, rather, by Enoch, who was caught up directly into the presence of God *before* the judgment of the flood was poured out upon the earth (Gen. 5:24). That these events were meant to be a sign unto the people of God and a warning to sinners is clearly revealed by the words of Peter:

> For if God spared not the angels that sinned . . . and spared not the old world, but saved Noah the eighth person, a preacher of righteousness, bringing in the flood upon the world of the ungodly; And turning the cities of Sodom and Gomorrha into ashes condemned them with an overthrow, making them an ensample unto those that after should live ungodly; And delivered just Lot, vexed with the filthy conversation of the wicked. (For that righteous man dwelling among them, in seeing and hearing, vexed his righteous soul from day to day with their unlawful deeds;) The Lord knoweth how to deliver the godly out of temptations, and to reserve the unjust unto the day of judgment to be punished (II Peter 2:4-9).

Lot was a man of many imperfections and compromises, yet as a worshiper of the true God, he was considered a "righteous soul." "I cannot do anything," said the angel, "till thou be come thither." Even so will the true Church, in spite of her many imperfections, be caught away as those who are righteous before God. Wrath will not be poured out until she is removed. Because we have been saved from wrath, God will be unable to pour out His vials until the Church is taken out of the way.

One more promise to the Church must be considered before moving along to other matters. It is found in Revelation 3:10, and is part of God's message to the church in Philadelphia: "Because thou hast kept the word of my patience, I also will keep thee from the hour of temptation, which shall come upon

all the world, to try them that dwell upon the earth." In these
words, pretribulationalists find a specific promise that the Church
will be removed before the commencement of the Tribulation.
Reese, however, is quick to point out that the verse has been
otherwise rendered, and quotes with approval the liberal Moffatt
translation: "Because you have kept the word of my patient endurance, *I will keep you safe through the hour of trial* which is
coming upon the whole world to test the dwellers on earth."[26]
Here, then, is the problem: both sides claim Revelation 3:10
as a proof text. Lest hasty readers consider this an impasse, the
following facts are submitted for consideration:

(1) This promise is given to the entire Church of Jesus
Christ, not merely to one local assembly existing in the days
of the Apostle John. These seven letters to the churches have
a manifold significance. They were addressed first of all to
seven existing churches in the western-most province of Asia
Minor, and very probably each letter went to all seven (*cf.*
Rev. 2:29, "what the Spirit saith unto the *churches*"). The
fact that there were seven reveals that the churches were
representative, for there were more than seven local assemblies
in Asia Minor. In like manner, the seven golden candlesticks
seem to be representative of all the churches (Rev. 1:20). These
early assemblies may well reflect seven different kinds of churches
(and also individual Christians) which can be found in any
location in any century. They have been thought to represent
also a prophetic foreview of the course of the visible Church
down through its long and varied history. Thiessen has summarized this last view as follows:

> The characteristics of these churches fit chronologically into their
> respective places in the history of the Church. The Church in
> Ephesus corresponds to the Apostolic Church. The Church in
> Smyrna finds its counterpart in the Martyr Church of the second
> and third centuries. The Church in Pergamos represents the
> State Church, beginning with Constantine and continuing to the
> end. The Church in Thyatira has the features of the Papal Church,
> beginning with Gregory the Great and continuing to the end.
> The Church in Sardis pictures the Reformation Church, begin-
> ning with the sixteenth century. The Church in Philadelphia

[26] Reese, *op. cit.*, p. 201, italics his.

sets forth the characteristics of the Missionary Church, beginning
with the rise of modern missions under William Carey. And the
Church in Laodicea portrays the Apostate Church of the last days.
. . . To the one who believes in the plenary inspiration of the
Scriptures and studies the detailed descriptions, the correspondences
between these churches and the successive periods of church
history seem too marked to be merely incidental. He comes away
with the conviction that when a key fits so completely the several
wards of a lock as do the details in these Letters, he must have
found the right key and the true interpretation.[27]

It is evident that the letter to the church in Philadelphia has
more than local application. If the above interpretation is accepted, it then follows that the message to the Philadelphian
church contains important teaching as to the time of the rapture,
and that the Laodicean Church speaks of an apostate type of
Christendom which will enter the Tribulation after the removal of the true Bride of Christ.

(2) The trial which is promised is not local, for it is to come
"upon the whole world." This fact adds to the conviction that
the Tribulation is yet future, and is not historical. The persecutions of the past, although fearful and revolting, were nevertheless limited to one group, and usually to one country or
area. But in the Tribulation to come, all the world will wonder
after the Beast (Rev. 13:3), and all who worship him will come
under the fierce anger of a righteous God (Rev. 13:8; 14:9-11).

(3) Upon whom is this hour of trial to fall? The text says
that it will come upon "them that dwell on the earth." Concerning these "earth dwellers," Thiessen points out, "It is
significant to note that the word for dwell is not the ordinary
oikeo, but the strengthened form of the word, katoikeo, meaning
those who have settled down upon the earth, who have identified
themselves with it."[28] The word conveys the idea of permanency
and complete identification with the world. As such it would
hardly be suitable if it described or even included the members
of the Church, who upon earth are strangers and pilgrims
(Heb. 11:13) and whose citizenship is in heaven (Phil. 3:20).

(4) It is generally agreed that the Tribulation is in view

[27] Henry C. Thiessen, "Will the Church Pass Through the Tribulation?"
Bibliotheca Sacra, XCII (April-June, 1935), 199, 200.
[28] Henry C. Thiessen, Lectures in Systematic Theology, p. 479.

in Revelation 3:10. The problem is to determine if the words "from the hour of temptation" denote going *through* the Tribulation, or being *taken out* of it? At this point there is a great division of opinion. Reese musters three texts to support his view that the preposition ἐκ permits the translation "through the hour," whereas Pollock writes as emphatically:

> It is remarkable that out of over 890 times the preposition, *ek*, is found in the New Testament, only once, Galatians iii. 8, is it translated *through*, and there the sense is evidently *by*, "God would justify the heathen *through* or by faith." . . .The word is translated dozens and dozens of times by the word, *by*, and many times by the two words, *out of*. But to be "kept *from*," is not being "safe *in*." A child can see the difference between *from* and *in*.[29]

Thiessen cites Alford, Buttmann-Thayer and others to the effect that ἐκ and ἀπό often serve to denote one and the same relation, and that the term τηρεῖν ἐκ may mean either "successful endurance" or "absolute immunity from." Though some may insist on the former connotation, the grammar certainly permits the latter, that the Church is promised complete exemption from this hour of trial. Thiessen seems to carry the weight of the argument when he concludes:

> We should note that the promise is not merely to be kept from the *trial*, but from the *hour* of trial, i.e., it holds out exemption from the period of trial, not only from the trial during that period. And finally, when it would have been so easy to write ἐν τῇ ὡρα, if the writer had meant preservation *in* that hour, why should he write ἐκ τῆς ὡρας, as he did? Surely, this is no accident.[30]

It may be concluded that the grammar, if not conclusive, at least favors *removal from* the hour of trial.[31] This rendering is most in harmony with the context, "the word of my patience," which suggests patient waiting for Christ. The "hour of temptation" is to fall on "earth dwellers," a designation which occurs

[29] A. J. Pollock, *Will the Church Go Through the Great Tribulation?*, p. 11.

[30] Henry C. Thiessen, *Bibliotheca Sacra, op. cit.*, XCII, 202, 203.

[31] Note also that the only other use of τηρεω εκ in the Greek New Testament occurs in John 17:15, where Christ prays for the deliverance of His own from the evil one. The thought is that we shall not be allowed to fall into the clutch of Satan, and not that he shall seize us and cause us to be delivered by force. Similarly, Revelation 3:10 carries no thought of the believer being wrested from the grip of the Tribulation.

constantly throughout the Tribulation portion of the book of
Revelation but which never suggests a heavenly people (Rev.
6:10; 8:13; 11:10; 12:12; 13:8, 12, 14; 14:6; 17:2, 8). In the
words "I come quickly" may be seen the rapture, and the reference to "thy crown" suggests the Bema seat judgment to follow.
"Because thou hast kept the word of my patience, I also will
keep thee from the hour of temptation, which shall come upon
all the world, to try them that dwell upon the earth." Here,
then, is a promise which clearly indicates the pretribulation
rapture of the Church. When it is added to the promises already considered that the Church will never undergo God's
wrath, a strong Scriptural support for the pretribulational position must be admitted.

As to the claim that the Church will pass through the Tribulation because she has always had tribulation, it has been demonstrated that the purpose, extent, duration, intensity, and source
of the tribulation in the period to come differs in almost every
particular from the persecution which in this age still falls in
varying degrees upon God's people. Let the reader judge for
himself the strength and the assurance of these conclusions.
Let him rejoice that the Church is promised, not wrath, but
rapture. Let him consider well that the prospect of the Church
in relation to the Tribulation is accurately expressed by the
Biblical phrase, "Kept from the Hour."

CHAPTER THREE

IS THE CHURCH IN MATTHEW TWENTY-FOUR?

Among Bible students, the fact is well known that in this age there are three distinct groups of people dwelling together. These are the *Jew,* of whom Paul wrote: "My heart's desire and prayer to God for Israel is, that they might be saved" (Rom. 10:1); the *Gentile,* of whom Isaiah spoke when he said: "In his name shall the Gentiles trust" (Matt. 12:21); and the *Christian,* who is no longer seen as Jew or Gentile, but as a "new man" through faith in Christ (Eph. 2:14, 15). All three of these distinct groups are brought together in one verse (I Corinthians 10:32): "Give none offence, neither to the Jews, nor to the Gentiles, nor to the church of God."

These three divisions of the human family, particularly the Jews and the Christians, are the subjects of extended consideration in the Scriptures. Even in the field of prophecy each has its own distinctive program. It is one of the most elementary rules of Bible study and interpretation to determine from the context *to whom* or *of whom* God is speaking, for only by so doing will the reader be enabled to interpret rightly the word of truth (II Tim. 2:15). The popular little chorus, "Every promise in the Book is mine," rightly expresses faith and confidence in the Bible, but the theological implication of the words would be difficult indeed to defend. A better concept and a more accurate principle is expressed in the tenet: "All Scripture is for us, but not all Scripture is about us."

It is the purpose of this chapter to indicate briefly that Israel in the New Testament is not the same as the Church,[1] that each has its own distinctive program in relation to the second coming of Christ, and that the posttribulation rapture theory rests directly upon Scriptures plainly meant for Israel. It has previously been demonstrated from the nature of the Tribulation that one basic premise of posttribulationalism is false. A Scriptural investigation of the nature and program of the Church will reveal additional weaknesses in the foundation upon which this theory has been erected.

I. ISRAEL NOT THE SAME AS THE CHURCH
A. *Israel Stems from Abraham*

Genesis 12:2, 3 records the important Abrahamic covenant in which God made plain His purpose to do a new thing upon the earth: "I will make of thee a great nation, and I will bless thee, and make thy name great; and thou shalt be a blessing: And I will bless them that bless thee, and curse him that curseth thee: and in thee shall all families of the earth be blessed." Whatever Abraham was nationally before being called of God, it is at least certain that his spiritual characteristics were far superior to those of the surrounding heathen, and the Jewish race which found its origin in him has been like-

[1] The chief passage used by those who contend that Israel and the Church are identified in the New Testament is Galatians 6:15, 16: "For in Christ Jesus neither circumcision availeth any thing, nor uncircumcision, but a new creature. And as many as walk according to this rule, peace be on them, and mercy, and upon the Israel of God." In these verses, Paul brings out the contrast between the Jew and the Gentile, which contrast is now of no avail for those who have believed on Christ and so become one "new creature." God's blessing is herein declared to be upon those who "walk according to this rule" (among the Galatians, who were Gentiles) and upon "the Israel of God" (the Jews who have found refuge in Christ). These two classes, joined by the conjunction και, are on the same level and of the same rank in the Church of Jesus Christ. The verse in no wise identifies Israel *as a nation* with the Church, which is Christ's "new creation," as the many contrasts brought forth in the following section will demonstrate. Posttribulationalists lean heavily upon this supposed identification of the Church and the nation Israel. However, one of their number, Howard W. Ferrin, clearly and forcefully refutes such a contention in an address: "Is the Church Ever Called Israel?" published in *The Sure Word of Prophecy*, John W. Bradbury, compiler. Ferrin proves that "Israel" in Galatians 6:16 speaks of "believing Jews," and not Israel as a nation, and concludes: "It is also evident that these Jewish promises have not been fulfilled to the Church. It follows then, that Israel has not been deprived of them ... *the Church is not Israel*" (pp. 160, 161, his italics).

wise unique, both nationally and spiritually. Romans 9:4, 5 records eight special divine favors granted to Israel. However, it is in the great Old Testament covenants made by God with this people that one discovers the five unconditional and eternal promises of Jehovah which constitute Israel's great national heritage. These are:

(1) a national entity (Jer. 31:36)
(2) a land (Gen. 13:15)
(3) a throne (II Sam. 7:16; Ps. 89:36)
(4) a king (Jer. 33:21), and
(5) a kingdom (Dan. 7:14).

The origin of the twelve tribes, the progress of the nation, the kingdoms, the captivities, and the restorations of Israel are familiar matters to any student of the Old Testament. Nor does it require a great deal of searching to discover that Israel enters the New Testament unchanged. It was to Israel that the twelve disciples were commissioned to proclaim their message:

> These twelve Jesus sent forth, and commanded them, saying, Go not into the way of the Gentiles, and into any city of the Samaritans enter ye not: but go rather to the lost sheep of the house of Israel. And as ye go, preach, saying, The kingdom of heaven is at hand (Matt. 10:5-7).

> Now they which were scattered abroad upon the persecution that arose about Stephen travelled as far as Phenice, and Cyprus, and Antioch, preaching the word to none but unto the Jews only (Acts 11:19).

Most of the early church was comprised of converts from among the Jews, and although Paul was commissioned to carry the gospel "far hence unto the Gentiles," he expressed the great burden of his heart in the verse previously mentioned: "Brethren, my heart's desire and prayer to God for Israel is, that they might be saved" (Rom. 10:1). This passage might well be pondered by those who glibly identify Israel and the Church in the New Testament. Israelites who are born anew by the application of the precious blood of Christ enter into the Church which is His body, as do believing Gentiles. Thus is the middle wall of partition broken down, but these are reckoned no longer as Jew and Gentile, but as "one new man, so making peace" (Eph. 2:14-18). Redeemed Jews lose their former identity when they enter the Church of Christ, but Israel as a nation, and Israel as a distinct

religious group, continues unchanged throughout this present
age. They are a nation "scattered and peeled" (Isa. 18:2,7),
a "proverb and a byword among all nations" (Deut. 28:37), yet
God has His hand upon His ancient people and will in Tribulation days purge them (Deut. 4:30,31) and cause them to
recognize and receive His Son (Zech. 12:10; Rom. 11:26).

B. The Origin of the Church Is Pentecost

While those who gloss over the many Biblical distinctions
between Israel and the Church seek to find the origin of the
Church with Abraham, or at some other point in the Old Testament, it is not difficult to prove that the Church originated with
the descent of the Holy Spirit at Pentecost. The statement of
Christ to Peter in Matthew's gospel is alone sufficient to prove
that the Church was not yet formed at the time of the utterance:

> And I say also unto thee, That thou art Peter, and upon
> this rock I will build my church; and the gates of hell shall not
> prevail against it (Matt. 16:18).

Except for the foreview of Matthew 16:18 and 18:17, the Church
is not seen at all until Acts 2:47, which is after Pentecost. It is
true that ἐκκλησία, ekklesia, is used in Acts 7:38 and Hebrews
2:12 of the community of Israel in the sense that in the wilderness they were a "called out body," but this does not place
Israel in the body of Christ any more than it makes the mob in
the Ephesian theater members of the true New Testament
Church (Acts 19:32), for those disorderly worshipers of the
goddess Diana are likewise spoken of as an ἐκκλησία. This word
in its non-technical usage merely indicates a group of people
segregated for a special time or purpose from the general
mass of humanity. The Christian usage of the term is distinct
from both the heathen and the Jewish, the Spirit of God thus
elevating a familiar expression to a new and lofty service,
namely, to designate the people of God during the course of
this present age. The Church did not invent the word at all
but has merely assumed its service, which clearly explains
its presence in Acts 7:38 and 19:32. The employment of
ἐκκλησία at these points in no wise militates against the truth
that the origin of the true New Testament Church was yet

future during the early ministry of the Lord. Chafer has given a concise summary of four reasons why the Church, the body of Christ, had its origin at Pentecost:

> Things cannot be the same in this age as they were in the past age, after the death of Christ has taken place, His resurrection, His ascension, and the advent of the Spirit on Pentecost. In like manner, things cannot be the same in the coming age as they are in this age, after there is brought about the second advent of Christ to reign on the earth, the binding of Satan, the removal of the Church, and the restoration of Israel. Those who see no force in this declaration have hardly considered the measureless meaning of these age-transforming occurrences. In the light of these determining issues, it may be seen (a) that there could be no Church in the world — constituted as she is and distinctive in all her features — until Christ's death; for her relation to that death is not a mere anticipation, but is based wholly on His finished work and she must be purified by His precious blood. (b) There could be no Church until Christ arose from the dead to provide her with resurrection life. (c) There could be no Church until He had ascended up on high to become her Head; for she is a New Creation with a new federal headship in the resurrected Christ. He is, likewise, to her as the head is to the body. Nor could the Church survive for a moment were it not for His intercession and advocacy in heaven. (d) There could be no Church on earth until the advent of the Holy Spirit; for the most basic and fundamental reality respecting the Church is that she is a temple for the habitation of God through the Spirit. She is regenerated, baptized, and sealed by the Spirit. If it be contended that these conditions could have existed before Pentecost, it is easily proved that the Scriptures do not declare that these relationships obtained until *after* Pentecost (cf. John 14:17). A Church without the finished work on which to stand; a Church without resurrection position or life; a Church which is a new humanity, but lacking a federal head; and a Church without Pentecost and all that Pentecost contributes, is only a figment of theological fancy and wholly extraneous to the New Testament.[2]

Here, then, is one clear and vital distinction between Israel and the Church: the time of the origin of each. In addition, there is a marked difference between the two in respect to their calling. Israel's calling is earthly, while that of the Church is heavenly. This in no wise suggests that the one does not receive everlasting salvation and abundant spiritual blessing,

[2] L. S. Chafer, *Systematic Theology*, IV, 45, 46.

or that the other may not on earth receive of the good things God has provided. It does mean, however, that Israel's promises center in the possession of an earthly heritage and kingdom (Gen. 13:14, 15; 17:8; Deut. 11:12; Dan. 7:14, etc.), while the promises to the Church center around "all spiritual blessings in heavenly places" (Eph. 1:3), for theirs is an "heavenly calling" (Heb. 3:1). Israel "shall dwell in their own land" (Jer. 23:7, 8), but the inheritance of the Church is "incorruptible, and undefiled, and that fadeth not away, reserved in heaven" (I Pet. 1:4).

The headship of Israel resides in Abraham, but the Head of the Church is the Lord Jesus Christ (Eph. 5:23). To Israel, Christ is Messiah, Immanuel, and King, but to the Church, He is Lord, Bridegroom, and Head. The Holy Spirit came upon some in Israel, anointing them for unusual service, but He indwells even the weakest member of the Church (I Cor. 6:19, 20). Israel is designated as the servant of Jehovah (Isa. 41:8), but those who compose the Church are members of the family and the household of God (Eph. 2:19). Israel as a nation *had* a priesthood, but the Church of Christ *is* a priesthood (I Pet. 2:5, 9). Israel is revealed as the wife of Jehovah, now untrue but later to be restored, but the Church is spoken of as the spotless bride of Christ (Eph. 5:27; Rev. 19:7-9; 21:9). At least twenty-four distinct contrasts between Israel and the Church have been enumerated,[3] but enough has been said already to indicate that any system of interpretation which merges, blends, and confuses that which God has clearly separated, dishonors the Word and leads the student of Scripture into blind paths of exegetical disharmony and theological error.

II. Do Christ and Paul Disagree?

It is generally safe to assume that when two passages of Scripture, although similar, fail to agree in their important points, that they are speaking of different events and possibly concern different peoples. Seeking to harmonize the Scriptures and to apply to Israel and to the Church those things which particularly

---

[3] *Ibid.*, pp. 47-53. See also Charles L. Feinberg, *Premillennialism or Amillennialism* (1st edition), pp. 187-90.

pertain to each, many Bible students have employed interpretative principles which have come to be called "dispensationalism." Dispensationalists believe that it is neither honest nor proper to claim for the Church all the blessings promised to the nation Israel, meanwhile rejecting all her curses. They believe that the primary interpretation of some sections of the Bible concerns Israel and cannot be appended to Church truth on the basis that "every promise in the Book is mine." They believe that certain relationships the Church sustains to her risen Lord are never true of national Israel. They do not attempt to rend the Word of God, but to honor it and to understand it by rightly interpreting it. As applied to the question at hand, dispensationalists hold that Matthew 24 speaks of Israel in the Tribulation and not of the Church, which they believe to be already raptured (possibly between the eighth and the ninth verses of this chapter). They hold that I Thessalonians 4:13-18 is the primary passage which deals with the rapture of the Church, and that Matthew 24 describes a different event and a different people, namely, the revelation of Christ in respect to Israel following the Tribulation. Posttribulationalists contend that this is to make Christ and Paul disagree; moreover, they back up their claims by loud and often violent attacks upon the entire dispensational principle. While this chapter cannot take an excursus into the dispensational problem (which method has been ably demonstrated by a score or more of prominent writers: Ottman, Gaebelein, Pierson, Ironside, Chafer, to name a few), it will seek to indicate briefly that the Matthew passage contains a heavy Jewish cast and that its details are in contrast to, rather than in harmony with, the passage in I Thessalonians 4.

But first, by way of illustrating their position and attitude, permit a few words from the opposing brethren:

> If we adhere to the simple terminology of our Lord and Paul about "the last day," "the present Age," and "the coming Age," all will be plain, and we shall be saved at the very outset from the danger of getting lost in a labyrinth of dispensational traditions, which lose nothing by comparison with the refinements of the Rabbis.[4]

[4] Reese, *The Approaching Advent of Christ*, p. 56.

We are delivered now from the Judaising system of interpreting the discourses of Christ: instead of handing them over to the semi-converted Jews, ignorant of Christ and redemption, we shall apply them to Christians who know and love Christ, always remembering that there are many passages that pre-suppose the existence of a Jewish Christian Church in Palestine, at a past or future epoch of its history: a Church necessarily under the Law of the land, yet rejoicing only in Christ Jesus as the Saviour and Shepherd of Israel.[5]

Robert Cameron, while allegedly tracing the history of pre-tribulationalism, remarks:

The whole company caught at this solution, cried "eureka" — handed over the Olivet Discourse to a Jewish Remnant, and proclaimed the new dogma to the world.[6]

No part of the New Testament seems safe from their pruning-knife. . . . As Paul is said to be the revealer of the Secret Rapture, his writings have been spared by most, but not by all.

. . . The "Wisdom" of "that old serpent, the devil" is revealed in no better way than in the way in which he enlarged the scope of Modernism by introducing it in the guise of Pre-Tribulation-Rapturism. . . . Thus tens of thousands who perhaps would not listen to a sermon or read an article by such Modernists as Shailer Matthews or Harry Emerson Fosdick, will eagerly swallow this disguised Modernism, and smack their lips over it, when it is presented by a Torrey, a Gray, a Scofield or a Gaebelein on this side of the ocean, or by a Panton, a Marsh, or a Sir Robert Anderson on the other side; and because it has the strong endorsement of such great men, many thousands of evangelists and ministers, who do not know its true character, present it from hundreds of evangelical platforms, and a multitude of professedly evangelical publishing houses turn out multiplied millions of copies of tracts, papers and books containing it. And the same evangelicals will anathematize and excommunicate those other evangelicals whose eyes have been opened to see the delusion, and so will have none of it. "An angel of light"? Yes, Satan can and often does appear as such. "Wise as a serpent"? Yea, verily! Satan is just that.[7]

It seems hardly to occur to these friends who so strongly denounce the dispensational method and confess that their brethren are the tools and dupes of Satan, that perhaps the reason why so many thousands of evangelists and ministers

[5] *Ibid.*, p. 294.
[6] Robert Cameron, *Scriptural Truth About the Lord's Return*, p. 71.
[7] John J. Scruby, *The Great Tribulation: The Church's Supreme Test*, pp. 120, 126, 127, 128.

cannot join the handful "whose eyes have been opened" is that their dispensational convictions are the result of independent and reverent Bible study rather than the product of mass delusion. It is not at all a question of men blindly following the teachings of men, although one might do worse than adopt the conclusions of spiritual giants such as those mentioned in the above citation.

Turning now directly to the chapter in question, Matthew 24, several important factors are immediately apparent: The setting and the cast of the chapter is unmistakably Jewish. The context is the lament over Jerusalem, when Christ wept for the nation Israel which had rejected Him (John 1:11; Acts 7:52). The discourse arises out of a discussion concerning the coming destruction of the temple, as crystalized by the question of the disciples: "Tell us, when shall these things be? and what shall be the sign of thy coming, and of the end of the world?"

It has been noted previously that Jerusalem and Judaea, the worship of the temple, and the desolation of its holy place are in view. The message under consideration is the gospel of the kingdom. The prayer men are commanded to pray is that their flight be not in the winter, neither on the sabbath day. Are posttribulationalists Jews, that when they flee the rage of the beast they should be restricted by the Mosaic legislation over the length of a sabbath day's journey? (Acts 1:12). Do these who insist that the Church is in view put men redeemed by God's grace back under a law which, because of its severity and powerlessness to save, was a curse? (Gal. 3:10). Are Christians bound by a sabbath law which caused even those who lit a fire on the sabbath (Ex. 35:3) or gathered sticks on the sabbath (Num. 15:32-36) to be stoned to death? We think not! How then is this the Church?

Without question, Matthew 24 describes the time of the great Tribulation. The trials and the heavenly signs parallel those of the Revelation; the reference to the "abomination of desolation" (Dan. 9:27; 11:31; 12:11) standing in the holy place is unmistakable; the designation "there shall be great tribulation" is conclusive. The phase of Christ's coming which is in view is the revelation, the return of the Son of Man to the earth. As vital as all this is, it is not the rapture. Where is the Church? Where is there any mention of a resurrection? Posttribulationalists insist that where the rapture is, there will the resurrection be. Where is there any indication that the sixty-nine weeks of Daniel's prophecy should concern Israel alone, as it does, but that the seventieth week should find its fulfillment, not in Israel, but in the Church? It is difficult indeed to see the Church at all in this prophetic picture, whereas in the light of Old Testament predictions, Israel fulfills it perfectly. Is it not *far* more consistent to understand this chapter as a foreview of Israel's place in the Tribulation than to maintain that the Church, the bride of Christ, is purged for seven years before her marriage, with no honeymoon afterwards? The Tribulation is the time of Jacob's sorrow, but the Church, with a perfect standing before God and clothed "in a righteousness so perfect and blessed that even the law of Mount Sinai can find no fault therein," has no need of such purging. Believers in Christ are washed in the blood, accepted in the Beloved, indwelt by the Holy Spirit, and sealed unto the day of redemption. Why then thrust the Church into the Tribulation?

If Matthew 24 is not the rapture, Christ and Paul are not in disagreement. Christ revealed a few things concerning the future Church, but the main body of Church truth is found in the epistles, not in the gospels. Unto Paul was given the privilege of revealing the mystery, in other ages not made known but now revealed by the Spirit, "that the Gentiles should be fellowheirs, and of the same body, and partakers of his promise in Christ by the gospel" (Eph. 3:1-6). Likewise was Paul used to reveal the mystery of the union of Christ with His Church (Eph. 6:32), and the mystery of the indwelling Christ (Col. 1:26-28). It is not strange, therefore, that Paul should be further used to reveal the mystery of the rapture of the Church, a truth previously introduced by Christ (John 14:3), but not developed until the Pauline Epistles. "Behold, I shew you a mystery; We shall not all sleep, but we shall all be changed, In a moment, in the twinkling of an eye, at the last trump: for the trumpet shall sound, and the dead shall be raised incorruptible, and we shall be changed" (I Cor. 15:51, 52). Here, and not in Matthew 24, is revealed the resurrection of the dead in Christ and the rapture of the Church. Here, and in I Thessalonians 4:13-18.

The fact that the Church and her removal finds no mention in Matthew 24 does not argue that there is no rapture any more than it argues that there is no Church. At this time, the rapture is past and the Church is in heaven, and so do not enter into the discussion. It is, of course, argued by the post-tribulationalists that the Church *is* mentioned in the chapter under the name of "elect." "For the elect's sake those days shall be shortened," and false Christs shall attempt to deceive "the very elect" (Matt. 24:22, 24). This is a problem only to those who desire to make it so. Oswald T. Allis is typical of those who believe that these verses speak of the Church, saying "the precious word 'elect' . . . is used everywhere else of Christian believers."[8] But such is not the case, as the Scriptures make abundantly clear. In Isaiah 42:1, the term is used for Christ: "Behold my servant, whom I uphold; mine elect, in whom my soul delighteth." In I Timothy 5:21, the term is used for angels: "I charge thee before God, and the Lord Jesus Christ, and the elect angels. . . ." In Isaiah 45:4, "elect" clearly applies to the Israelites: "For Jacob my servant's sake, and Israel mine elect." This is also true of Isaiah 65:9, 22: "a seed out of Jacob . . . mine elect"; "my people, and my elect." In I Peter 1:2, the same word is used of the Church of Christ: "Elect according to the foreknowledge of God." Christians are exhorted in Colossians 3:12: "Put on therefore, as the elect of God, holy and beloved, bowels of mercies, kindness, humbleness of mind, meekness, longsuffering." To say that the term "elect" speaks *only* of the Church is to ignore the plain testimony of Scripture, and those who use it as a technical term to force the Church into Matthew 24 are indulging in trickery and not exegesis. Barnhouse's remarks are very much to the point:

> There is Biblical authority for calling the elect in Matthew 24:22 a group other than the church of which we are a part. This is by no means a suggestion that anybody can be saved in any other way than by the regenerating work of the Holy Spirit,

[8] Oswald T. Allis, *Prophecy and the Church*, p. 210.

revealing the risen Lord Jesus Christ. In spite of man's weak faith through the ages and the thousands who even today are babes in Christ, we must not be drawn into the false idea that God has only one people and that He has always worked in exactly the same way. . . . We must recognize the fact that . . . God has future purposes which are outside His work in the Church.[9]

A direct comparison between Matthew 24 and I Thessalonians 4 will strengthen the conviction that two different events are in view. There are some similarities, to be sure, both dealing with the general subject of the coming of the Lord. Each speaks of one aspect of Christ's return; in each there is the sound of a trumpet and the gathering of the Lord's people. In each, there is the need for readiness. But here the similarity stops, and if other points of agreement are found, they must be forced to fit a pattern of resemblance. This, Reese proceeds to demonstrate, with the remark that those who disagree "make dark what is clear: complicated, what is simplicity itself; and contradictory, what is beautifully harmonious."[10] But even when the pressure of prejudice is applied, certain factors stubbornly refuse to work into this pattern.

The terminology is not the same. Matthew 24 speaks of the sign of the Son of Man, the name Christ commonly used in His earthly relationships, but in I Thessalonians 4, it is "the Lord himself." In Matthew, there are signs in the heavens, the sun and the moon refusing to shine, the stars falling, and the powers of heavens shaken. These are in keeping with the Jewish content of the passage, for the Jews are a "sign people" (I Cor. 1:22); however, one looks in vain for such signs and marvels in the I Thessalonians passage. In Matthew, there are judgments, warnings of Antichrist, and instructions for escape; in the Thessalonians passage, judgment is not found, Antichrist is not in view, and provision for escape is not mentioned for it is not needed. In Thessalonians, there are no signs preceding the coming, and no personalities or events to detract from "the Lord himself." In the former, the tribes of the earth mourn, for this is Christ's coming to the earth in

---

[9] Donald Grey Barnhouse, "Some Questions About Our Lord's Return," *Revelation*, XII (November, 1942), 527.

[10] Reese, *op. cit.*, p. 258.

judgment. In the latter, however, there is no mourning, no mention of the earth or the tribes of the earth, in fact, no coming to the earth at all, for the meeting is in the air.

The first appearing is public and involves sinners; the second is private, with no judgment, the Church alone being in view. Two classes of men are spoken of in Matthew: the Jewish elect, and the sinful nations. Two classes are mentioned in the Thessalonians passage: "them which are asleep," and "we which are alive"; these together comprise the Church, and neither class corresponds to saved Jews or unsaved nations. In Matthew, there is the sound of a trumpet, but it is blown by an angel; in Thessalonians, a trumpet is sounded, but it is "the trump of God." In the one, angels gather God's elect; in the other, it is Christ Himself. The former implies that time is involved; the latter event is instantaneous.

In Matthew, the Jews are gathered "from the four winds," that is, from the four extremities of the earth, but they are gathered back to Palestine as the prophets so often foretold. In Thessalonians, the saints are gathered unto the Lord, being caught up "to meet the Lord in the air." The first action is explained in Deuteronomy 30:1-6; the second action is explained in John 14:1-3, and the two are vastly different. In the Matthew passage, there is no mention of resurrection, but in Thessalonians, "the dead in Christ shall rise first." In Matthew, rapture is past, but in Thessalonians, the Church is caught up. In Matthew 24:32-44 (unless the theory is accepted that this is a recapitulation, and again speaks concerning the Church) it is a blessing to *remain* for entrance into the Kingdom, the rest being taken away in judgment. In I Thessalonians 4, it is a blessing to be *taken* in rapture, the unsaved being left to go through the Tribulation. (That being taken away in judgment is the probable interpretation of Matthew 24:40,41 is seen by a comparison with the context found in verses 37-39. It was the godless, outside the safety of the ark, that were taken away with the flood into death and judgment.)

Other contrasts might be mentioned between these two passages under consideration, but why look further? All is contrast, and if the two are made to describe the same event, all is confusion. Where is Reese's "simplicity and beautiful harmony"? Wherein does it make dark what is clear, to say that two different aspects of Christ's coming are in view? Pretribulationalists have no desire to complicate the simple, and surely greater simplicity is achieved in the interpretation of these passages by recognizing that Christ and Paul were talking about different events. Complicated indeed is the confusion and contradiction involved when events of such marked contrast are superimposed the one upon the other under the assumption that they are identical. Let it be said in the interest of all that is honest and all that is sensible in the study of the Word of God, that it neither discredits nor complicates the Bible to distinguish between things which are different. The doctrine of the decrees of God, the doctrine of the hypostatic union of the two natures of Christ, the doctrine of election, and even that of redemption, all offer their various complexities.

The Bible presents its truths without apology, and in the understanding of the same the path of over simplification may border perilously close to the rocky pitfalls of unsound doctrine. So it is in the matter of the Lord's return. If the coming of the Lord for His saints, His return to earth with His saints, the day of the Lord, the day of Christ, the resurrection of the just, the judgment of wicked nations, the judgment seat of Christ, the marriage supper of the Lamb, and the other notable events associated with Christ's coming must all occur at one time, and that "in the twinkling of an eye," great is the complexity and confusion of such a proposed program. When, however, it is recognized that the coming of the Lord in its larger context involves two movements on His part, with seven years between to absorb the events which require more time than a fleeting moment, all of the Scriptures involved fit naturally and harmoniously into such a pattern. The many complex wards of the prophetic lock yield to the touch when the rapture of the saints is distinguished from the revelation of Christ upon the earth — proof to the interpreter that he has found and is using the appropriate key.

It is therefore entirely in error to say that belief in a pretribulation rapture causes Christ and Paul to disagree, for the one is speaking primarily to Israel about the great Tribulation and the return of the Son of Man to the earth, while the other is revealing to the saints of this age the hope of the rapture of the Church and the relationship the living will bear to the dead in Christ at His coming. Actually, it is the posttribulation rapture theory which is in deep error at this point, for it is perched insecurely upon a foundation of primarily Jewish Scriptures. When some seek to find the future of the Church in the eschatology of Israel and when they use *elect* as a technical term for the Church in all ages, it is not to be wondered at that their prophetic program is in error. By following the same line of reasoning, the entire Christian Church could be thrown into the lap of Seventh Day Adventism, the modern counterpart of ancient Galatianism. Let Matthew 24 be descriptive of Israel in the Tribulation, culminating in the revelation of Christ, and let I Thessalonians 4 be descriptive of the rapture of Church saints prior to the Tribulation, and the harmony of Scripture for which some profess to seek will become immediately apparent.

III. Tribulation Saints

Posttribulationalists point out and expostulate with great fervor the fairly numerous references to *saints* in the book of Revelation. In Revelation 11:18, reward is given to the saints; in 13:7, there is war with the saints; in 13:10 and 14:12 is mentioned the patience of the saints; 16:6, 17:6, and 18:24 speak of martyrdom, and refer to the blood of the saints; 19:8 is a reference to the righteousness of the saints; while 20:9 records a final rebellion and attack on the camp of the saints. These who are called saints, it is assumed, can be none other than Church saints; *ergo,* the Church is in the Tribulation. Reese adds to Revelation 11:18 his argument on the time of the resurrection,[11] and thinks that if he defeats Kelly at this point every other pretribulationalist will take to his heels.

It is hardly necessary to enter into a detailed analysis of these verses. A few moments spent with a Bible concordance will reveal that Old Testament Jews are called "saints" in upward of two score different Scriptures. *Saint,* like the term

[11] *Ibid.,* pp. 73-80.

elect, is not a technical name for members of the Church, but may be used to designate any of God's people in all ages. There is absolutely nothing to forbid these references in the Revelation from referring to Jewish saints in the end-time. Indeed, since these saints are linked with the prophets, the commandments of God, and the song of Moses, and since Christ is addressed as *King* of saints, it would seem that such an identification has much to commend it. These saints are redeemed; they have "the faith of Jesus"; many of them become martyrs for Christ — they are saved, but they are part of the Jewish remnant of the Tribulation and not part of the Church of this age of grace.

How some posttribulationalists love to multiply epithets and heap up scorn over the "theory of a Jewish remnant." These are the "semi-Christian, semi-converted Jewish Remnant of uncertain standing in the Last Days,"[12] the "two-headed, two-tongued monstrosity in Israel and Christendom at the End-time,"[13] "half-converted Jews, still in their sins,"[14] "an army of half-regenerated . . . Jews"![15] It is hardly worth wasting good paper to comment on such unbecoming scorn. Let it be a sufficient answer to quote Joel's prophecy of this end-time period which clearly indicates that such a remnant shall appear:

> And I will shew wonders in the heavens and in the earth, blood, and fire, and pillars of smoke. The sun shall be turned into darkness, and the moon into blood, before the great and the terrible day of the Lord come. And it shall come to pass, that whosoever shall call on the name of the Lord shall be delivered: for in mount Zion and in Jerusalem shall be deliverance, as the Lord hath said, and *in the remnant whom the Lord shall call* (Joel 2:30-32).

Two groups comprise the "earth-dwellers" of the Tribulation: Gentiles, and Israel. Both of these must find their place in this period in order to fulfill Old Testament prediction, such as that of Isaiah when he writes: "Come near, ye nations, to hear . . . For the indignation of the Lord is upon all

---

[12] *Ibid.,* p. 111.
[13] *Ibid.,* p. 115.
[14] *Ibid.,* p. 269.
[15] *Ibid.,* p. 320.

nations, and his fury upon all their armies . . ." (Isa. 34:1, 2), or that of Ezekiel as he records God's words to *Israel*: "I will . . . gather you out of the countries wherein ye are scattered . . . And I will purge out from among you the rebels, and them that transgress against me" (Ezek. 20:34, 38). However, there is no prophecy that the Church will be so purged.

The epistles, given particularly to guide the Church on her pilgrim pathway, maintain a significant silence as to any purpose God might have in thrusting His Church into such a period. Nor is there any instruction concerning how the Church should act if she were so tested; nor is there any protection promised her from the rage of the Beast. The purpose of the Tribulation, for Israel, is that she should be purified (Mal. 3: 3, 4) and judged for her rejection of Christ (Matt. 27:25). However, the protection of those Jews who will, in that day, turn to the Lord is assured. One hundred forty-four thousand of Israel are sealed of God to protect them from His judgments (Rev. 7:1-8; 9:4). For those who flee the Beast, a refuge in the wilderness has been prepared (Rev. 12:6, 14). Unto the two witnesses, protection is given, for "if any man will hurt them, fire proceedeth out of their mouth, and devoureth their enemies" (Rev. 11:5).

But for the Church, no promise of protection is indicated, no ministry is given them to accomplish, no purpose of God to be fulfilled in them is stated. Such silence is highly significant, and particularly so when God is so explicit when it comes to the nations and to Israel. Then, when it is further noted that in Revelation 2-3 the repeated emphasis is upon "the Church," but from the fourth chapter, through all the plagues, the judgments, the horrors of the Tribulation, the Church is not again mentioned or seen, the conclusion seems obvious that the Church is not present. When finally she reappears in the book of Revelation, the Church is the bride of Christ (Rev. 19:7-9) and in heaven. When Christ descends to judge and to rule the earth, she is seen accompanying Him.

It is a constant accusation by those who deny the pretribulation rapture that such a doctrine appeals to unworthy motives.

To Reese, it is "so comforting and pleasing to the flesh."[16] To
Allis, it is "singularly calculated . . . to appeal to those selfish
and unworthy impulses from which no Christian is wholly immune."[17] It is interesting that Allis implies many objections to
pretribulationalism, listing this as his first, but when it comes
to the demonstration of his objections, this is the only point—
the rest are singularly missing! He has developed this one objection, however:

> In so far as the "any moment!" doctrine of the coming owes its
> popularity to a desire to escape the evils which are to come upon
> all the earth, it is by no means a commendable doctrine. It makes
> its appeal to the human frailty of the Christian, instead of challeng-
> ing him to face the worst of earth's ills courageously.[18]

Now while it must be admitted that the average pretribulationalist has no desire to enter the Tribulation, and has no
ambition to leave his family to starve while he fights a battle
with the Beast and endures a martyr's death, yet it is distinctly
untrue that his motive in all of this is craven cowardice.
Each of these chapters will lend its weight to the assurance
that the rapture will be pretribulational, and his basic reason
will ever be the clear testimony of Scripture and not the supposed weakness of the flesh and the cowardice attributed to him.
He will remember the conclusions of this present chapter, that
Israel is not the Church, that their prophetic programs are not
identical, that the very nature of the Church demands exemption
from the Tribulation, and that posttribulationalism rests pre-
cariously upon Scriptures designated primarily for Israel. Rather
than presumptuously seeking to enter into a period for which
he was not intended, he will gratefully abide by God's program
of rapture before Tribulation, and in it all his prime motive will
not be fear but a sincere desire to be governed only by the
revelation God has given.

But now, suppose for an instant that the Church does enter
the Tribulation, should she add her witness to that of redeemed
Israel? When before did God ever have two separate witnessing
bodies upon earth? God is not a God of confusion. Does He

[16] *Ibid.*, p. 225.
[17] Allis., *op. cit.*, p. 207.
[18] *Ibid.*, p. 208.

not terminate a former course of action before establishing a new one? To whom would the saved Jews of that period belong: to the 144,000 who are Jews, or to the Church, where there is no such distinction? For whom would God answer prayer in that day? The Church is instructed to pray for her enemies (I Tim. 2:1; Rom. 12:17-21; Matt. 5: 44; 6:12) and to speak evil of no man. Israel in the Tribulation, however, will cry unto God to judge her enemies and avenge her blood on them that dwell on the earth (Rev. 6:10). Under such circumstances to whom would God listen, and which prayer should He answer? We need not put God in such a dilemma.

CHAPTER FOUR

THE DAY OF THE LORD

There are several specific "days" mentioned in Scripture, and for the most part they have to do with prophetic themes. A particularly heavy emphasis upon the Day of the Lord is found in both Testaments and as it will become evident, the correct understanding of this "day" enters into the problem of the time of the rapture.

I. VARIOUS DAYS OF SCRIPTURE

A. *Creative Days*

Genesis 1:3-2:3 gives the account of the six days of creation, followed by a seventh day of rest. Scholarship has long been divided as to whether these were literal successive days of twenty-four hours each, or vast epochs of time during which God created all things. Those who accept literal days stress the ability of God to create instantaneously as an act of sovereign will (Psalm 8:3), while those who favor epochs of time point out that nature herself reveals that considerable time has elapsed since the creation of material things. In either event, the term *day* may be used of a period of longer than twenty-four hours, for the entire act of creation is spoken of as one day:

> These are the generations of the heavens and of the earth when they were created, in the day that the Lord God made the earth and the heavens (Gen. 2:4).

B. *Sabbath Day*

One of the requirements of the law of God for Israel was that they should set aside the last day of the week as a day of rest, when all labor and secular activity should cease. Every seventh year was a sabbatic period when it was required that the land should rest and not be cultivated. The sabbath is a distinctive mark of Judaism, and it is not by accident that it is mentioned in connection with those who will be on earth during the Tribulation (Matt. 24:20).

C. *The Lord's Day*

This is the designation used for the Christian day of rest and worship, which is the first day of the week in commemoration of the resurrection of our Lord. The Sabbath day speaks of a finished creation; the Lord's Day speaks of a finished redemption. The former is a day of legal obligation; the latter is a day of voluntary worship and service. The designation "Lord's day" is not found in Scripture, unless it be in Revelation 1:10, but the first day of the week as the day of Christian worship is clearly substantiated (Acts 20:7; I Cor. 16:2).

D. *The Day of the Lord*

This is one of the great themes of Old Testament prophecy, as will shortly be demonstrated. It is likewise mentioned repeatedly in the New Testament, and was still future when the Thessalonian epistles were written (I Thess. 5:1,2; II Thess. 2:1-3). The Authorized Version of II Thessalonians 2:2 contains a notable error: the correct rendering (margin) is the Day of the Lord, rather than the Day of Christ.

E. *The Day of Christ*

The Day of the Lord in Scripture is always associated with the wrath and the judgment of God, while the Day of Christ is distinguished by the fact that it is universally spoken of as a time of blessing. Nothing is predicted as having to take place before the Day of Christ shall come, but the coming of the Day of the Lord is marked by signs in the heavens and notable events upon the earth. The Day of Christ concerns the Church and is to be looked forward to with anticipation.

> So that ye come behind in no gift; waiting for the coming of our Lord Jesus Christ: Who shall also confirm you unto the end, that ye may be blameless in the day of our Lord Jesus Christ (I Cor. 1:7, 8).

> To deliver such an one unto Satan for the destruction of the flesh, that the spirit may be saved in the day of the Lord Jesus (I Cor. 5:5).

> As also ye have acknowledged us in part, that we are your rejoicing, even as ye also are our's in the day of the Lord Jesus (II Cor. 1:14).

> Being confident of this very thing, that he which hath begun a good work in you will perform it until the day of Jesus Christ (Phil. 1:6).
>
> That ye may approve things that are excellent; that ye may be sincere and without offense till the day of Christ (Phil. 1:10).
>
> Holding forth the word of life; that I may rejoice in the day of Christ, that I have not run in vain, neither laboured in vain (Phil. 2:16).

The Day of Christ evidently is the termination of the Church's pilgrim journey upon the earth. It is the time of the coming of our Lord Jesus Christ (I Cor. 1:7), the time when He will catch up His redeemed people "to meet the Lord in the air" (I Thess. 4:17), the time of which He spoke when He promised "to come again, and receive you unto myself; that where I am, there ye may be also" (John 14:3). It is the time when our salvation will be completed, when we shall be with our blessed Lord, and "shall be like him; for we shall see him as he is" (I John 3:2). The Day of Christ has to do with Church saints; it starts at the rapture and probably includes the seven years spent with Christ in glory before the return to earth at the revelation, embracing the judgment seat of Christ (II Cor. 5:10) and the marriage of the Lamb (Rev. 19:7,8). It is a day of glad anticipation and is in contrast at almost every point with the Day of the Lord, which is a day of wrath and darkness and judgment. Yet in spite of the obvious difference between the two "days," posttribulationalism requires that they be made identical. Reese maintains that:

> To most minds no doubt will remain from a consideration of Paul's use of "the Day," "in that Day," "the Day of the Lord," and "Messiah's Day," that *all are synonymous expressions* for the day of the Parousia, which closes the present Age, and ushers in the Age to Come; it is the day of resurrection, of reward, of rest for the saints; but of judgment and condemnation for the impenitent.[1]

Reese prefers to call the Day of Christ "Messiah's Day," which helps his argument that "it is the day when Messiah comes forth in glory to set up His Kingdom in the Future Age."[2] But such an inference completely ignores the fact that Christ is Messiah of Israel, not the Church, and blurs over any dis-

---

[1] Alexander Reese, *The Approaching Advent of Christ*, p. 179. Italics added.
[2] *Ibid.*, p. 171.

tinctive meaning the Day of Christ may have for the Church in her relationship to her coming Lord. While these two days under consideration do roughly parallel each other in point of time, one applies to the Church and finds its fulfillment in heaven, while the other applies to Israel and the nations in the Tribulation and finds its fulfillment upon the earth. Any premise which makes these two days synonymous, both applicable to the Church upon earth, must completely ignore the characteristics of each as displayed in Scripture. It hardly needs to be said that conclusions based upon faulty premises are likewise in error and must be rejected.

F. *Other Days*

John 6:40, 44, 54 speak of the dead in Christ being raised "at the last day," and evidently is a reference to the final day of the Church on earth before the rapture. Other Scriptures speak of the "last days" for the Church, and give the general characteristics of the end time (II Tim. 3:1-5; I Tim. 4:1-5; II Pet. 3:3). Still other Scriptures refer to the "last days" for Israel, which carry over into the Tribulation and on into the millennial kingdom (Isa. 2:2-5). II Corinthians 6:2 speaks of the *day of salvation*, identical with this present age of grace, and II Peter 3:12 speaks of the *day of God*, which is evidently a designation of the eternal state after the creation of the new heavens and the new earth. Although some of these days herein summarized do not directly concern the present discussion, it is well to remember the words of Peter: "Wherefore, beloved, seeing that ye look for such things, be diligent that ye may be found of him in peace, without spot, and blameless" (II Pet. 3:14).

II. DAY USED FOR A PERIOD OF TIME

As already implied, the word *day* is used in Scripture in a number of different ways. It is used to speak of a period of twenty-four hours. This may well be the import of the repeated phrase of Genesis 1: "And the evening and the morning were the first [second, etc.] day." It is employed likewise to designate that part of the twenty-four hour period which is light, in contrast to the time of darkness, which is *night* (Psalm 22:2). *Day* and *night* are also used with a symbolic meaning to designate the saved and the unsaved, the "children of light" and the "children of darkness" (I Thess. 5:5-8).

However, the term *day* is clearly used in another sense, to designate a period of time, whether long or short, in which certain events are to take place. Paul writes in II Corinthians 6:2: "Behold, now is the accepted time; behold, now is the *day of salvation*." This *day* was in progress when Paul wrote, and at the present hour nineteen hundred years later it is still in progress. It corresponds to this entire age of grace, yet God calls this long period of time a "day" (*cf.* II Pet. 3:8).

It has been indicated that the Day of Christ speaks of the period the Church spends in heaven with Christ between rapture and revelation, and that the Day of God designates the entire eternal state. The Scriptures of the following section will prove that the Day of the Lord is not one single event, nor one twenty-four hour day, but likewise a definite period of time, and that upon the earth. The Day of the Lord, seen as a period, upsets completely the posttribulational view at this point, although Reese finds it more advantageous to launch his attack upon Darby's interpretation and dismisses the more normal pretribulational position with sarcasm but without investigation.

> Messrs. Hogg and Vine in *Touching the Coming* have discovered that the expressions "Day of Christ," "Day of Jesus Christ," and "Day of the Lord Jesus" are a *period of time* beginning with the Rapture and ending with the Glorious Advent. . . . And the proof of this latest dispensational novelty? None but the requirements of their own fantastic programme; they make what they would prove, the presupposition of their exegesis. . . . One must sorrowfully remark that the defence of these false theories throws up sophistry that can give points and a beating to the Rabbis in Israel.[3]

Thus, Reese dismisses unconsidered the very answer to his whole argument, as set forth in the chapter, "Messiah's Day." He does say that there are scores of texts against this position, but mentions only one, namely I Corinthians 1:7. It is most difficult to see how this verse damages in any way the claim that the Day of Christ and the Day of the Lord are periods of time: "So that ye come behind in no gift; waiting for the coming of our

[3] *Ibid.,* p. 183.

Lord Jesus Christ." Reese evidently was counting, at this point, on the tendency among readers not to look up references which are given without the text, and hoping that his allusion to "scores of others"[4] would carry the day.

III. THE DAY OF THE LORD, AND THE GREAT TRIBULATION

There has been a great deal of confusion over the location of the Day of the Lord. Some writers have placed it at the time of the rapture, others at the time of the revelation, and still others, as a bridge which spans the two. Posttribulational writers make the Day of the Lord synonymous with the Day of Christ, both of which are equal to the *parousia* and fall on the same day as the joint *rapture* and *revelation,* although they have yet to explain why God calls the same thing by so many different names. They hardly seem to recognize that the Holy Spirit, the divine Author of the Scriptures, never uses terms indiscriminately. They dismiss with a wave of the hand any possibility that such terms, although related, are none the less distinguishable the one from the other. Reese laments that "those of us who still assert that the Day *of Christ* and the Day *of the Lord* are the same, are looked upon as benighted people."[5] However, it is warmly contended that those who do *not* teach that these expressions are interchangeable are misleading and false teachers, and that any distinction between the two "is another one of the many meaningless and confusing hair-splittings which characterize the dispensational school."[6]

It has already been demonstrated that the Day of Christ is a time of great expectation for the Church, and is associated with rapture and reward. Even a cursory examination and comparison of the following Scriptures should be sufficient to convince any open minded reader that the Day of the Lord, in both Testaments, does not concern the Church but is the time of God's wrath and judgment upon the world. It is not a twenty-four hour day, or one single event, but a period of time

---

[4] *Loc. cit.*

[5] *Ibid.,* p. 182.

[6] Posttribulationalism thus joins forces with amillennial theology, both in its attack against dispensationalism and in its identification of the Day of Christ with the Day of the Lord. See Oswald T. Allis, *Prophecy and the Church,* pp. 188-90 for the similarities of the amillennial view at this point.

which starts after the rapture of the Church and incorporates the entirety of the Tribulation period. The remarkable parallelism of the following verses concerning the Day of the Lord and the coming Tribulation hardly calls for comment. Italics are added to emphasize leading points of comparison.

"The word of the Lord came again unto me, saying, Son of man, prophesy and say, Thus saith the Lord God; Howl ye, Woe worth the day! For the day is near, even the day of the Lord is near, a *cloudy day;* it shall be the time of the *heathen*" (Ezekiel 30:1-3).

"Alas for the day! for the day of the Lord is at hand, and as a *destruction from the Almighty* shall it come" (Joel 1:15).

"For this is the day of the Lord God of hosts, a *day of vengeance . . .*" (Jer. 46:10; Isa. 61:2).

"Come near, ye nations, to hear; and hearken, ye people . . . For the *indignation of the Lord* is upon *all nations,* and his fury upon *all their armies:* he hath utterly destroyed them, he hath delivered them to the *slaughter. . . .* For it is the day of the Lord's *vengeance . . .*" (Isa. 34:1, 2, 8; 66:15, 16).

> And he gathered them together into a place called in the Hebrew tongue Armageddon (Rev. 16:16).
> The same shall drink of the wine of the *wrath of God,* which is poured out without mixture into the *cup of his indignation;* . . . And the angel thrust in his sickle into the earth, and gathered the vine of the earth, and cast it into the great winepress of the *wrath of God* (Rev. 14:10, 19).
> And I saw the beast, and the *kings of the earth,* and *their armies,* gathered together to make war against him that sat on the horse, and against his army. And the beast was taken . . . and the remnant were slain with the sword of him that sat upon the horse, which sword proceeded out of his mouth: and all the fowls were filled with their flesh (Rev. 19:19-21).

"Let the *heathen* be awakened, and come up to the valley of Jehoshaphat: for there will I sit to *judge all the heathen* round about. *Put in the sickle, for the harvest is ripe:* come, get you down; for *the press is full,* the fats overflow; for their wickedness is great. Multitudes, multitudes in the valley of decision: for the *day of the Lord* is near in the valley of decision" (Joel 3:12-14).

And another angel came out of the temple, crying with a loud voice to him that sat on the cloud, Thrust in *thy sickle, and reap: for the time is come for thee to reap; for the harvest of the earth is ripe.* And he that sat on the cloud thrust in his sickle on the earth; and the earth was reaped. . . . The great *winepress* of the wrath of God . . . was trodden without the city . . . (Rev. 14: 14-20).

"For the *day of the Lord* is near upon all the *heathen* . . ." (Obad. 1:15).

"Behold, the day of the Lord cometh. . . . For I will gather *all nations* against *Jerusalem* to battle. . . . Then shall the Lord go forth, and *fight against those nations,* as when he fought in the day of battle" (Zech. 14:1-3).

"For, behold, the day cometh, that shall *burn as an oven; and all the proud,* yea, and *all that do wickedly,* shall be stubble: and the day that cometh shall *burn them up,* saith the Lord of hosts, that it shall leave them neither root nor branch" (Mal. 4:1).

And he saith unto me, The waters which thou sawest, where the whore sitteth, are *peoples,* and *multitudes,* and *nations,* and *tongues* (Rev. 17:15).

Therefore shall her plagues come in one day, *death,* and *mourning,* and famine; and she shall be utterly *burned with fire:* for strong is *the Lord God who judgeth her* (Rev. 18:8).

And out of his mouth goeth a sharp sword, that with it he should *smite the nations:* and he shall rule them with a rod of iron: and *he treadeth the winepress of the fierceness and wrath of Almighty God* (Rev. 19:15).

And the fourth angel poured out his vial upon the sun; and power was given unto him to *scorch men with fire.* And men were *scorched with great heat,* and blasphemed the name of God, which hath power over these plagues: and they repented not to give him glory (Rev. 16:8, 9). [These judgments do not turn men back to the Lord, as the tribulationalists claim, for they "blasphemed" and "repented not."]

"For the day of the Lord of hosts shall be upon every one that is *proud and lofty,* and upon every one that is lifted up; and *he shall be brought low.* . . . And *they shall go into the holes of the rocks, and into the caves of the earth, for fear of the Lord,* and for the glory of his majesty, when he ariseth to shake terribly the earth" (Isa. 2:12, 19).

And the *kings of the earth,* and the *great men,* and the *rich men,* and the *chief captains,* and the *mighty men,* and every bondman, and every free man, hid themselves *in the dens and in the rocks of the mountains;* And said to the mountains and rocks, Fall on us, and hide us from the face of him that sitteth on the throne, and from *the wrath of the Lamb* (Rev. 6:15, 16).

"Behold, the day of the Lord cometh, *cruel* both with *wrath and fierce anger,* to lay the land desolate; and he shall *destroy* the *sinners* thereof out of it" (Isa. 13:9).

"The great day of the Lord is near, it is near, and hasteth greatly, even the voice of the day of the Lord: the *mighty men shall* cry there bitterly. That day is a *day of wrath,* a *day of trouble and distress,* a day of *wasteness* and *desolation,* a day of *darkness* and *gloominess,* a day of clouds and thick darkness. . . . And I will bring *distress upon men,* that they shall walk like blind men, because they have sinned against the Lord" (Zeph. 1:14, 15, 17).

For the *great day of his wrath is come;* and who shall be able to stand? (Rev. 6:17; 14:10, 19).

And I saw another sign in heaven, great and marvellous, seven angels having the seven last plagues; for in them is filled up the *wrath of God* (Rev. 15:1).

Woe unto you that desire the day of the Lord! to what end is it for you? *the day of the Lord is darkness, and not light* . . . even *very dark,* and no brightness in it? (Amos 5:18, 20).

"Behold, the day of the Lord cometh, cruel both with *wrath* and *fierce anger,* to lay the land desolate: and he shall destroy the sinners thereof out of it. For the *stars of heaven* and the constellations thereof *shall not give their light:* the *sun shall be darkened* in his going forth, and the *moon shall not cause her light to shine.* And I will punish the world for their evil, and the wicked for their iniquity; and I will cause the arrogancy of the proud to cease, and will lay low the haughtiness of the terrible" (Isa. 13:9-11).

"Blow ye the trumpet in Zion, and sound an *alarm* in my holy mountain: let all the inhabitants of the land *tremble:* for the day of the Lord cometh . . . A *day of darkness* and of *gloominess,* a day of clouds and of *thick darkness*" (Joel 2:1, 2).

"And I will shew *wonders in the heavens and in the earth,* blood, and fire, and pillars of smoke. The *sun shall be turned into darkness,* and the *moon into blood,* before the great and the terrible day of the Lord come" (Joel 2:30, 31).

> And the fourth angel sounded, and the third part of the *sun was smitten,* and the third part of the *moon,* and the third part of the *stars;* so as the third part of them was *darkened,* and the *day shone not* for a third part of it, and the night likewise (Rev. 8:12).

> And I beheld when he had opened the sixth seal, and, lo, there was a great *earthquake;* and the *sun became black as sackcloth* of hair, and the *moon became as blood;* And the *stars of heaven* fell unto the earth . . . (Rev. 6:12, 13).

"Behold, I will make *Jerusalem a cup of trembling* unto all the people round about. . . . I will make Jerusalem a burdensome stone for all people: all that burden themselves with it shall be cut in pieces, though all the people of the earth be gathered together against it. . . . And it shall come to pass in that day, that I will seek to destroy all the nations that come against Jerusalem" (Zech. 12:2, 3, 9).

> And their dead bodies shall lie in the street of *the great city* . . . *where also our Lord was crucified* . . . And the same hour there was a *great earthquake,* and the tenth part of the city fell, and in the earthquake were slain of men seven thousand (Rev. 11:8, 13).

A day of *darkness* and of *gloominess,* a day of clouds and of thick darkness . . . *there hath not been ever the like, neither shall be any more* after it, even to the years of many generations (Joel 2:2).

> For then shall be great tribulation, *such as was not since the beginning* of the world to this time, no, *nor ever shall be.* And except those days should be shortened, there should no flesh be saved: but for the elect's sake those days shall be shortened (Matt. 24:21, 22).

"The sun and the moon shall be darkened, and the stars shall withdraw their shining. The Lord also shall roar out of Zion, and utter his voice from Jerusalem; and the heavens and the earth shall shake: but the Lord will be *the hope of his people, and the strength of the children of Israel*" (Joel 3:15, 16).

"Come, my people, enter thou into thy chambers, and shut thy doors about thee; *hide thyself as it were for a little moment,* until the indignation be overpast. For, behold, the Lord cometh out of his place to punish the inhabitants of the earth for their iniquity" (Isa. 26:20, 21).

"And it shall come to pass, that whosoever shall call on the name of the Lord *shall be delivered:* for in mount Zion and in Jerusalem shall be deliverance, as the Lord hath said, and *in the remnant whom the Lord shall call"* (Joel 2:32).

Saying, Hurt not the earth, neither the sea, nor the trees, till we have *sealed the servants of our God* in their foreheads. And I heard the number of them which were sealed: and there were sealed an hundred and forty and four thousand of all the tribes of the *children of Israel* (Rev. 7:3, 4).

And the woman [Israel] fled into the wilderness, where she hath *a place prepared of God,* that they should feed her there a thousand two hundred and threescore days . . . into the wilderness, into her place . . . from the face of the serpent. . . . And the dragon was wroth with the woman, and went to make war with *the remnant of her seed,* which keep the commandments of God, and have the testimony of Jesus Christ (Rev. 12:6, 13-17).

"And his feet shall stand in that day upon the mount of Olives, which is before Jerusalem on the east, and the mount of Olives shall cleave in the midst thereof toward the east and toward the west . . . and the *Lord my God shall come, and all the saints* with thee. . . . And the Lord shall be *king over all the earth:* in that day shall there be *one Lord,* and his name one" (Zech. 14:4, 5, 9).

And I saw heaven opened, and behold a white horse: and he that sat upon him was called Faithful and True, and in righteousness he doth *judge and make war.* . . . And the *armies which were in heaven followed him* upon white horses, clothed in fine linen, white and clean. And out of his mouth goeth a *sharp sword,* that with it he should *smite the nations:* and he treadeth the winepress of the fierceness and wrath of Almighty God. And he hath on his vesture and on his thigh a name written, *KING OF KINGS, AND LORD OF LORDS* (Rev. 19:11, 14-16).

On this issue of the Day of the Lord, it would seem that certain conclusions are inevitable — let the reader check the Scriptures for himself.

(1) The message of the Day of the Lord is predominately one of woe, wrath, and darkness. It contrasts at every point with what is said of the Day of Christ, no matter how diligently posttribulationalists attempt to identify the two.

(2) The events of the Day of the Lord occur over a *period of time*, and cannot be synonymous, as Reese asserts, with "Messiah's Day" and with "the day of the Parousia, which closes the present Age, and ushers in the Age to Come."[7]

(3) As a period, the Day of the Lord includes the Tribulation, and in most of these texts, is synonymous with the Tribulation. II Peter 3:8, 10, however, gives a good indication that the Day of the Lord extends even beyond and includes the entire millennial kingdom, up to the creation of a new heaven and a new earth:

> But, beloved, be not ignorant of this one thing, that one day is with the Lord as a thousand years, and a thousand years as one day. . . . But the day of the Lord will come as a thief in the night; in the which the heavens shall pass away with a great noise, and the elements shall melt with fervent heat, the earth also and the works that are therein shall be burned up.

(4) The Day of the Lord does not mention and has no application whatsoever to the Church saints. It concerns Israel and the nations of earth, but not the redeemed of the Lord which now comprise the body of Christ. The only way in which the Church is involved at all with the Day of the Lord is that when Christ comes back to earth to consummate the judgment of the wicked, the saints appear as part of the "armies which are in heaven." They come to earth with Christ, and the fact that they have been *in heaven* and must come *from heaven* shows that this event sustains the pretribulational position. Certainly, it is not in accord with any theory which maintains that the Church has not yet been taken *to heaven*.

(5) Posttribulationalists are quick to attempt the identification of the rapture and the Day of the Lord on the basis of I Thessalonians 5:2: "For yourselves know perfectly that the day of the Lord so cometh as a thief in the night." Fraser puts the assumption this way:

> But here, too, is a clear identification of "the coming of the Lord" *for* His saints in I Thessalonians 4:13-18 with "the day of the Lord," when He comes *with* His saints in judgment as indicated in Chapter 5:2. The first part of the fifth chapter is definitely a continuation of the discussion of the same scene as

[7] Reese, *op. cit.*, p. 179.

portrayed in the last verses of the fourth chapter. Only, a new aspect of this blessed event is dealt with.[8]

It must be conceded that there are no chapter divisions in the original manuscripts, but there all agreement stops. It is most difficult to imagine how a Bible teacher could call the Day of the Lord, whose judgments have been described in the verses considered above, "a new aspect of this blessed event," referring to the rapture experience. Reese, who reaches similar conclusions with Fraser, has involved himself in the same difficulty:

> Beginning to exhort them touching the *Coming* of the Lord, he proceeds to speak of the *Day* of the Lord. Is not this a remarkable circumstance? It is a convincing proof that the two things were synchronous in Paul's mind, and not separated by a period of years as the theorists assert.[9]

Again, we must concede that a partial truth has been spoken. Those who made the Day of the Lord a twenty-four hour day and identified it only with the return of Christ in judgment, were manifestly in error. But as usual, Reese attacks extremes, rather than the more normal pretribulational interpretation. It is here maintained that the rapture precedes and falls in no part of the Day of the Lord. The two follow in close sequence, which would explain the order of events set forth in I Thessalonians 4 and 5, but when that dread day breaks, the Church of Jesus Christ will be with her Lord.

Reese, setting forth the posttribulational position, lumps together a number of major events and places them on the day of Christ's return to the earth. The revelation thus becomes the same as the Day of the Lord; the resurrection of Old Testament saints is in the Day of the Lord;[10] the first resurrection, that of the Christian dead, and the rapture, likewise, are in the Day of the Lord.[11] Evidently the Bema seat judgment of Christ, the judgments upon the nations, and the marriage of the Lamb all fall within the same day. No doubt a busy twenty-four hours! Such a view has many objectionable features. The lumping together of prophetic events may at first seem to lead to

---

[8] Alexander Fraser, *Is There But One Return of Christ*, pp. 56, 57.
[9] Reese, *op. cit.*, p. 178.
[10] *Ibid.*, p. 72.
[11] *Ibid.*, p. 81.

simplification, but the end result is confusion. Among other things, such a view makes the rapture of the Church utterly unimportant, a mere incident in the midst of greater, fast-moving events.

> It is a *sentimental delusion that a secret Rapture,* or a pretribulation Rapture, *is the hope of the Church.* Scripture, on the contrary, asserts in the clearest manner that the Glorious Appearing of Christ is the definite hope of Christians (Tit. 2:13) and with terrible inconvenience for theorists, locates it at the Day of the Lord. [No proof is offered for this statement. He is evidently building upon his interpretation of I Thessalonians 5:2. Note the following.] . . . The Rapture is *a mere incident of the Appearing,* spoken of in order to show the relation of the sleeping to the living saints at the one Advent in glory, and especially that the saints who survive till the Advent will have no advantage at all over the dead in Christ. It is a stupid obsession to make the Rapture the touchstone of everything.[12]

However, when the Day of the Lord is given its rightful and Scriptural place as a period starting after the rapture, the first years of which correspond to the Tribulation, all the end time events drop into their proper place and the pretribulation position is confirmed rather than injured. The Day of the Lord may well be spoken of in close conjunction with the rapture, for it is next in sequence after that event, but it is gross assumption to identify the two. The judgments of the revelation of Christ are rightfully connected with the Day of the Lord, for they fall within that period. When properly related all the Scriptures harmonize. It is only when interpretation is strained by false premises that conflicts arise and theological delusions appear.

IV. I THESSALONIANS 4 AND 5

It is recognized by most Bible students that I Thessalonians 4:13-18 is the primary passage of the Word of God on the subject of the rapture of the Church. It is likewise apparent that I Thessalonians 5:1-11 is one of the central passages from which an attempt is made to prove a posttribulational rapture. Paul begins this section by saying: "I would not have you to be ignorant, brethren." These are all good reasons for examining the entire passage closely.

---

[12] *Ibid.,* p. 266. Italics added.

A. *1 Thessalonians 4:13-18*

This paragraph has much to contribute toward the right understanding of God's future program for His Church. Paul would
not have us ignorant (Greek: *agnostic*) and of doubtful persuasion about so vital an issue. It is evident that the Thessalonian
Christians previously had some instruction concerning the coming of the Lord, but during the interval since the apostle had
left Thessalonica, one or more of the converts had died. Also,
the Thessalonians had received a letter, purporting to be from
Paul, which implied that the Day of the Lord was already upon
them. The Thessalonian letters were written to counteract these
two fears: first, that the dead saints have no part in the coming
of Christ for His own, and second, that the living saints were
already in the Day of the Lord and would have to make their
way through its judgments.

Paul writes in this section concerning "them which are asleep"
(or, "them that fall asleep from time to time"). Now, *sleep*
is the softened word used in Scripture for the death of a believer, as when Jesus said: "Our friend Lazarus sleepeth; but
I go, that I may awake him out of sleep" (John 11:11). The
sleep of death will have its conclusion at the resurrection. The
word cemetery comes from the Greek *dormitory,* or "sleeping
place." It is said that the following words were found inscribed
upon one of the tombs at Thessalonica:

> When our life on earth is past,
> We enter into eternal sleep.

Christians, however, look past the sleep of death to physical
resurrection and glorious reunion, and therefore are not "as
others which have no hope."

> Thus Theocritus, a Greek poet of the 3rd century B.C., writes:
> "Hopes are among the living, the dead are without hope"; and
> Moschus, his contemporary, speaking of the plants that perish in
> the garden: "Alas! Alas! . . . these live and spring again in an-
> other year; but we . . . when we die, deaf to all sound in the
> hollow earth, sleep a long, long, endless sleep that knows no
> waking." The Roman poets of the last century B.C. speak in
> similar strain; thus Catullus: "Suns may set and rise again, but
> we, when once our brief light goes down, must sleep an endless
> night"; and Lucretius: "No one awakes and arises who has once

been overtaken by the chilling end of life." These sorrowed with a double sorrow: first for the loss they themselves sustained, then for the loss suffered by the departed. Such was the gloom which Greek and Roman philosophy had failed to pierce, and which the gospel came to dispel.[13]

Unbelievers who fall into the sleep of death have *no hope*, but in contrast, believers in Christ share the *blessed hope* of His return, at which time the Christian dead shall be raised.

> For if we believe that Jesus died and rose again, even so them also which sleep in Jesus will God bring with him. For this we say unto you by the word of the Lord, that we which are alive and remain unto the coming of the Lord shall not prevent them [precede them] which are asleep (I Thess. 4:14, 15).

The victory of the Christian over death rests securely upon the two cardinal pillars of the Christian faith: Christ *died* for our sins and *rose* again (I Cor. 15:3, 4). The doctrine of the rapture of the Church is similarly undergirded, for it is "by the word of the Lord." The latter part of verse 14 refers either to the coming of Christ at the revelation, when He returns "with all his saints" (I Thess. 3:13), or to the rapture when the souls of the Christian dead are united with their resurrection bodies (II Cor. 5:1-4). In either event, those who sleep shall be raised, and the living will not *precede*, or go on before. All of this was evidently given to Paul by direct revelation, the *word of the Lord*, its "mystery" character (I Cor. 15:51) indicating that it was never a topic of Old Testament revelation. Christ had taught the simple fact that He would come again for His own (John 14:3), but until the time of Paul's writing there had been no pointed revelation as to the relationship of the living and the dead at the coming of Christ. The phraseology seems to suggest that a special revelation was granted to meet the perplexity that had arisen at Thessalonica: The living shall in no wise attain an advantage over the dead!

> For the Lord himself shall descend from heaven with a shout, with the voice of the archangel, and with the trump of God: and the dead in Christ shall rise first: Then we which are alive and remain shall be caught up together with them in the clouds, to meet the Lord in the air: and so shall we ever be with the Lord.

[13] C. F. Hogg and W. E. Vine, *The Epistles of Paul the Apostle to the Thessalonians*, p. 132.

Wherefore comfort one another with these words (I Thess. 4: 16-18).

Behold, I shew you a mystery; We shall not all sleep, but we shall *all* be changed, in a moment, in the twinkling of an eye, at the last trump: for the trumpet shall sound, and the dead shall be raised incorruptible, and we shall be changed (I Cor. 15:51, 52).

Christ will not send an angel for us; it is to be the *Lord Himself*, the same One who died and rose again. (These words, in the Greek, are in the emphatic position: emphasizing that it will be a personal return. None other will do to meet the Bride than the Bridegroom Himself, who has redeemed her.)

Three sounds herald His coming, the first of which is a *shout*. Posttribulationalists make this the triumphant cry of Christ, the military command of one who gathers his armies about him, and apply it to Christ's glorious appearing on earth following the Tribulation. It is true that the word is a command, military or other, but it does not say that Christ utters the shout. The only other Biblical usage is in the Septuagint version of Proverbs 30:27, where it refers to the signal used by locusts. Thayer's *Lexicon* gives the meaning from classical Greek as the cry of charioteers to their horses, of hunters to their hounds, or of a captain to the rowers of his vessel. It may mean the cry of a captain to his soldiers, but Reese reads far too much into the text when he makes it descriptive of the "triumphant arrival of our Lord as King, assembling His hosts for the conflict with the powers of this world and the rescue of the Elect. This is the Day of the Lord."[14]

It is sufficient, rather to understand this "shout" simply as a signal cry, heard only by the Church, and accompanied by the *voice* of the archangel (possibly Michael: Jude 1:9) and the *trump* of God. This may indeed be descriptive of only *one* great signal from heaven, as it has been paraphrased: "a shout in the archangel's voice, even with the voice of the trump of God."[15] It is a signal to the Church, both dead and living, and if it is heard by the world at all, it will not be understood and will engender no response. This is a *catching up*, not a *coming down*: it is the Day of Christ, not the Day of the Lord.

[14] Reese, *op. cit.*, p. 175.
[15] Hogg and Vine, *op. cit.*, p. 143.

There are several parts to the glad anticipation of verses 16 and 17. There is *resurrection:* "the dead in Christ shall rise first." This is evidently not a general resurrection of the saints from both Testaments. Israel, though redeemed, is never said to be "in Christ," nor is her eschatology identical with that of the Christian. Such distinctions are glossed over by those who identify rapture with revelation, for their view requires that Israel and the Church be raised at the same time. There is *rapture:* those that are alive and remain are caught up. There is glad *reunion:* for both groups come together in the clouds (not "clouds of saints," as a comparison with Acts 1:9 will demonstrate).

> The great family of believers whose bodies are sleeping will rise "first." The apostle is showing how unfounded is the despairing grief of those in Thessalonica, for instead of being at a disadvantage, the sleeping believers will be the first to experience the power of resurrection life.[16]

With reunion, there will be *recognition* of loved ones who have died and gone before, but even more important will be the *rejoicing* of meeting the Lord in the air. So will be fulfilled the prayer of Christ recorded in John 17:24: "Father, I will that they also, whom thou hast given me, be with me where I am; that they may behold my glory, which thou hast given me." Paul then adds the words so freighted with meaning and happy anticipation: "and so shall we ever be with the Lord." This last phrase suggests the prospect of *rewards,* and later, of *reigning* with Him. The text does not read: "we which live through the tribulation shall be caught up," but "we which are alive and remain." Therefore, Paul is able to conclude this wonderful revelation of coming rapture, not with "scare one another," but with "comfort one another with these words." The whole passage is one of encouragement, whereas it would never encourage persecuted saints to tell them that worse things were in store. The pretribulation rapture is woven into the very warp and woof of this cardinal Scripture.

[16] Arthur B. Whiting, "The Rapture of the Church," *Bibliotheca Sacra*, CII (July-September, 1945), 369.

B. *I Thessalonians 5:1-11*

Here is the passage that posttribulationalists use in their attempt to prove that Paul links the Day of the Lord "with the hope and final salvation of the Church."[17] It is not difficult to show that their exegesis is in error at this point.

The immediate context of this chapter comprises a clear reference to the rapture of the Church. It is a message of comfort and contains absolutely no hint that Tribulation must first be endured, during which time many who are "alive and remain" will be forced to endure a martyr's death. I Thessalonians 4:11, 12, with the command "study to be quiet and to do your own business" would hardly be suitable for persons enduring a raging persecution. In fact, the whole context implies that the Thessalonian saints had been expecting imminent rapture, rather than wrath, for it took a special revelation to comfort them concerning those who had by death, as they assumed, missed the rapture experience.

Moreover the language of I Thessalonians 5:1,2 carries the definite implication that the subject of the rapture was a recent revelation, not found in the Old Testament and only now being clarified as to its details. "But of the times and seasons, brethren, ye have *no need that I write unto you*. For yourselves *know perfectly* that the day of the Lord so cometh as a thief in the night." The believers knew about the Day of the Lord because, as it has been demonstrated, the Old Testament Scriptures which were in their possession were full of this teaching. Joel, for example, had written extensively about the Day of the Lord. Christ also had discoursed on the subject (Matt. 24:27-31), and Paul himself had evidently given some teaching along the same line (II Thess. 2:1-5). "Remember ye not, that, when I was yet with you, I told you these things?" The Day of the Lord was familiar to those at Thessalonica: "no need that I write" for ye "know perfectly" these things. How different as touching the rapture: "I would not have you to be ignorant, brethren!" Rather than being identical, the two subjects are worlds apart, and this in the very passage by which posttribulationalists would prove their identity.

[17] Reese, *op. cit.*, p. 172.

Also, the careful use Paul makes of his pronouns throughout this section renders conclusive evidence that the Church is a distinct group from those who enter the Day of the Lord. "*Ye,* brethren, are not in darkness . . . *ye* are all the children of light, and the children of the day: *we* are not of the night . . . let *us* not sleep, as do others, but let *us* watch and be sober." "Let *us,* who are of the day, be sober . . . for God hath not appointed *us* to wrath, but to obtain salvation [deliverance] by *our* Lord Jesus Christ. Who died for *us,* that . . . *we* should live together with him. Wherefore comfort *yourselves* together . . ."

Contrast, from the same passage: "Then sudden destruction cometh upon *them,* as travail upon a woman with child [*cf.* Isa. 13:8; Jer. 30:6]; and *they* shall not escape." "*They* that sleep sleep in the night; and *they* that be drunken are drunken in the night." The children of light *watch,* but the children of darkness are *drunken* and *sleep.* If language means anything, Paul is here distinguishing carefully between those who are ready for the rapture, and those who have not put on the helmet of salvation at all, and so must enter into the tribulation of the Day of the Lord.

Lastly, it is a common teaching of Scripture that unbelievers have "no hope, and [are] without God in the world" (Eph. 2:12), but believers are to look with expectation for the "blessed hope" of Christ's coming. It is significant that in this I Thessalonians passage, believers are spoken of as having "the *hope* of deliverance," and are assured that they are "not appointed to *wrath.*" These are idle words if, in this context, deliverance from Tribulation is not included along with assurance of present salvation.

Although I Thessalonians 5 is not the strongest passage for establishing a pretribulational rapture, enough has been said to show that it is in harmony with that position, and not without some evidence for its support. Posttribulationalism, however, empties the passage of its obviously intended meaning in a vain attempt to establish the idea that the rapture falls on the Day of the Lord. Everything points to the contrary, and the only connection between the two is that they happen to occur in close sequence.

It might be well to close this discussion of the Day of the Lord with a summary of the two principle viewpoints involved. The posttribulational line of reasoning seems to be as follows: The Day of the Lord refers specifically to the very day when Christ returns to the earth to rule and reign. Since it is admitted by all that I Thessalonians 4 is the cardinal passage on the rapture of the saints, and since Paul turns immediately in chapter five to a contemplation of the Day of the Lord, rapture and revelation must fall upon the same day and comprise one single event. Therefore, according to this line of reasoning, the rapture must follow the Tribulation.

The burden of this chapter has been to analyze these issues and to consider the important Scriptures which have been used to sustain the posttribulational contention. From this study the following conclusions fairly may be drawn:

(1) Although the Bible speaks of a number of different days, the term *day* is not in every case limited to a twenty-four hour period.

(2) The Day of Christ commences with the rapture and evidently refers to the entire period the Church will be with her Lord prior to her return with Him to set up the millennial kingdom. It is a day of great blessing and is awaited with anticipation, which places it in marked contrast with the Day of the Lord.

(3) The Day of the Lord is likewise a period of time, but it commences after the rapture and comprehends the entire Tribulation period on earth, as the detailed comparison of Old and New Testament Scriptures at this point have abundantly demonstrated. This "day" involves Israel and the godless nations, wrath and judgment from Almighty God, but nothing by way of application to the Church of Jesus Christ.

(4) The cardinal Scripture involved, namely I Thessalonians 4, 5, lends no support to posttribulationalism. The rapture of chapter four is a new mystery-revelation and must not be confused with a time of judgment clearly predicted in the Old Testament. The resurrection spoken of applies only to those who are "in Christ," and the whole passage is one of encouragement and comfort rather than warning and alarm. As for chapter five, it has been demonstrated from the personal pronouns used that

the Church saints are held in contrast with those who enter the Day of the Lord. Here again the rapture is spoken of as a new revelation, and here also is recorded the promise that the believers are appointed unto deliverance rather than wrath. The rapture is found in the same general context with the Day of the Lord only because of its proximity to it. But proximity is not identity, particularly when all of the evidence indicates the contrary.

(5) The pretribulational view places the rapture of Church saints in the position of prominence which the New Testament emphasis upon that doctrine requires. On the other hand, post-tribulationalism is guilty of lumping together a large number of end-time events, in which the rapture becomes an utterly unimportant and almost meaningless detail.

Thus, rather than destroying the pretribulational view, the study of the Day of the Lord and its related subjects adds yet another confirmation to the position that the Church will be spared this time of God's wrath.

Chapter Five

WHO IS "THE RESTRAINER"?

One of the interesting problems connected with Paul's second epistle to the Thessalonians is that of identifying the "restrainer," who will be taken out of the way before the manifestation of the "lawless one." The passage is a familiar one, although somewhat confusing in the Authorized Version due to the use of the old English term "let," meaning *hinder*. The passage is reproduced here from the American Revised Version for greater clarity:

> Now we beseech you, brethren, touching the coming of our Lord Jesus Christ, and our gathering together unto him, to the end that ye be not quickly shaken from your mind, nor yet be troubled, either by spirit, or by word, or by epistle as from us, as that the day of the Lord is just at hand; let no man beguile you in any wise: for it will not be, except the falling away come first, and the man of sin be revealed, the son of perdition, he that opposeth and exalteth himself against all that is called God or that is worshipped; so that he sitteth in the temple of God, setting himself forth as God. Remember ye not, that, when I was yet with you, I told you these things? And now ye know that which restraineth, to the end that he may be revealed in his own season. For the mystery of lawlessness doth already work: only there is one that restraineth now, until he be taken out of the way. And then shall be revealed the lawless one, whom the Lord Jesus shall slay with the breath of his mouth, and bring to nought by the manifestation of his coming; even he, whose coming is according to the working of Satan with all power and signs and lying wonders, and with all deceit of unrighteousness for them that perish; because they received not the love of the truth, that they might be saved. And for this cause God sendeth them a working of error, that they should believe a lie: that they all might be judged who believed not the truth, but had pleasure in unrighteousness (II Thess. 2:1-12).

These verses are not particularly difficult. Paul writes concerning the coming of the Lord and deals with the false report that the Day of the Lord had already come. To remove this fear, assurance is given that this day will not come until the final falling away, or apostasy, and the revelation of the Antichrist, the "lawless one" who works by the "activity of Satan." There is in the world today, moreover, a restraining person or influence which holds unrighteousness in check, and Antichrist cannot be revealed until this "restrainer" be taken out of the way. It is at this point that expositors differ widely, and wonder at "Paul's mysterious words in 2 Thess. ii. 6-7."[1] For those who reject the removal of the Church prior to the revelation of Antichrist, it is of little wonder that these are mysterious words. However, since "all scripture is given by inspiration of God and profitable" (II Tim. 3:16), it should not be assumed that a solution is impossible, or that the identity of the "restrainer" cannot be determined.

It is immediately evident that the passage deals with the Tribulation, even the Day of the Lord, and with the manifestation of Antichrist as foretold in Daniel 9:27 and Revelation 13. It is also evident that the Wicked One cannot be revealed and that present iniquity cannot reach its peak until a "restrainer" be taken out of the way. It seems obvious that if the identity of the restrainer can be established, much light will be shed upon the commencement and the character of the Tribulation period. Actually, this passage bears so vitally upon the future of the Church that it may become a major factor in determining the relationship of the Church to the great Tribulation.

I. ATTEMPTED IDENTIFICATIONS

Many widely divergent answers have been proposed for the identity of the restrainer, including groups or agencies such as the Roman Empire or the Jewish State, and individuals such as James, or even Satan. These attempts at identifying the restrainer must be briefly examined.

A. *The Roman Empire*

It is argued that the restrainer could not be a person, for the use of the neuter "that which restraineth" favors identification with an agency, force, or group of people.

---

[1] Alexander Reese, *The Approaching Advent of Christ*, p. 244.

Some of the early fathers thought the hinderer was the Roman Empire, and that Paul dared not put upon paper just what was in his mind, lest he expose the Christians to the charge of plotting the downfall of the existing government.[2]

Such is the view of Reese, who says:

The oldest and best interpretation is that Paul hesitated to set down in words what he meant, because he had in mind the Roman Empire. The impersonal influence was the magnificent system of law and justice throughout the Roman world; this held lawlessness and the Man of Lawlessness in check. Then the line of emperors, in spite of wicked individuals, had the same influence.[3]

Response to this theory might be made in his own words: "This is ingenious, but it is a mere conjecture, and precarious at that."[4] The Roman Empire has not existed down through the present age as the power which has held evil in check. The Roman government of that day was exceedingly corrupt and was of little consequence in holding back the tides of iniquity throughout the empire and the world. History clearly records the tragic failure and decline of the Roman Empire. Far from restraining the evil present in the world, Rome fell under the very weight of her own iniquity. She has long since ceased to exist as an empire, and still Antichrist has not been revealed. Anticipating these objections, Reese adds:

Roman law and Roman justice are still a barrier, and the Emperors live on in the Papacy. . . . "And if a man consider the origin of this great ecclesiastical dominion, he will easily perceive that the Papacy is no other than the ghost of the deceased Roman Empire sitting crowned on the grave thereof."[5]

Reese himself says that the Roman Empire was swept away and will not be revived. How then will it restrain Antichrist and godless forces in the last day? Did it ever restrain evil, even when the empire was at its height? It is well to inquire further with Pollock:

Was the Roman Empire the restraining influence when the Coliseum of Rome, built by 30,000 Jews taken captive by Titus at the siege of Jerusalem, holding 80,000 people, echoed with the cry, "Throw the Christians to the lions?" Was it witnessed by 575 miles of amazing Catacombs at Rome, where the Christians were

[2] Henry A. Ironside, *Not Wrath But Rapture,* p. 27.
[3] Reese, *op. cit.,* p. 246.
[4] *Ibid.,* p. 245.
[5] *Ibid.,* p. 247.

driven underground to worship and to bury their dead to the number, it is said, of 4,000,000?[6]

As for the idea that Roman "restraint" of evil lives on in the Papacy, as the "ghost of the deceased Roman empire," when one remembers that down through the centuries the Roman Church has ever been the most aggressive opponent of evangelical Christianity and has been guilty of spilling rivers of Protestant blood, the whole idea is nauseating to the extreme. As to the claim that Paul did not speak more clearly lest Christians be charged with plotting the downfall of the empire, this has long been the charge of the enemies of Christ, and the Saviour Himself was so accused: "We found this fellow perverting the nation, and forbidding to give tribute to Caesar" (Luke 23:2). No need for Paul to keep silence at this point, as if he ever was silent for fear of men, or from lack of faith that God could care for His own![7] The idea that the restrainer of II Thessalonians 2 is the Roman Empire is fraught with such difficulties and dangers and has so little to commend it that the theory may unhesitatingly be called false.

B. The Jewish State

This hypothesis is suggested by Warfield:

> For the continued existence of the Jewish state was both graciously and naturally a protection to Christianity, and hence a restraint on the revelation of the persecuting power. Graciously, it was God's plan to develop Christianity under the protection of Judaism for a short time, with the double purpose of keeping the door of salvation open to the Jews until all of their elect of that generation should be gathered in and the apostasy of the nation should be rendered doubly and trebly without excuse, and of hiding the tender infancy of the Church within the canopy of a protecting sheath until it should grow strong enough to withstand all storms.[8]

Two objections to this theory immediately stand out, and it is to be wondered how a theologian of Warfield's stature could have missed them: First, the early church did not have years of "tender infancy," but was from its inception on the day of Pente-

[6] A. J. Pollock, *Will the Church Go Through the Great Tribulation?*, p. 36.
[7] If Paul is guilty of any vagueness at all at this point, it is because: "Remember . . . when I was with you, I told you these things" (II Thess. 2:5, 15).
[8] B. B. Warfield, "The Prophecies of St. Paul," *Biblical Doctrines*, p. 611.

cost (when three thousand were saved and added to the disciples) a sturdy, vigorous body, so that it was said of its members, "These that have turned the world upside down are come hither also" (Acts 17:6). Second, the Jewish State never functioned as a "protecting sheath" about the early Christian testimony, but to the contrary, Saul and other Jews "made havoc of the church." Witness Paul's testimony before Agrippa:

> Many of the saints also did I shut up in prison, having received authority from the chief priests; and when they were put to death, I gave my voice against them. And I punished them oft in every synagogue, and compelled them to blaspheme; and being exceedingly mad against them, I persecuted them even unto strange cities (Acts 26:10, 11).

At no point does the Jewish State prove to be the solution to the problem of identifying the restrainer. Nor does Warfield himself seem wholly satisfied with his own suggestion, for he offers an alternate:

> If the masculine form of "the restrainer" in verse 7 demands interpretation as a person — which we more than doubt — it might possibly be referred without too great pressure to James of Jerusalem, God's chosen instrument in keeping the door of Christianity open for the Jews and by so doing continuing and completing their probation. Thus he may be said to have been the upholder of the restraining power, the savour of the salt that preserved the Christians from persecution, and so in a high sense the restrainer.[9]

As valuable as James may have been to the Early Church, it is utterly impossible for him to be the restrainer. No man is able to restrain all the evil within his own heart, to say nothing of doing so throughout the world until the end of the age. Christians are to exert a preserving influence in this world as "the salt of the earth," but it is also true that any success James, or any other believer, is given must be by the power of the indwelling Spirit of God. *James* provides no solution to the problem of identifying the restrainer, although the idea is not as bad as the proposal of another that the Man of Sin is *Nero,* and the restrainer the wise *Seneca,* his tutor, whose death he ultimately procured.

---

[9] *Ibid.,* p. 612.

C. *Human Government or Gentile Dominion*

Hogg and Vine, although pretribulationalists, seem to favor this view, citing the words of Daniel 2:37-44.

> In due time the Babylonian Empire, to whose king the words were spoken, was succeeded by the Persian, that by the Grecian, and that again by the Roman, which flourished in the Apostle's day. . . . The laws under which these states maintain their existence were inherited from Rome as Rome inherited them from the Empire that preceded her. Thus the existing authorities are ordained of God . . . constituted authority is intended to act in restraint of lawlessness.[10]

Yet even here it is admitted that "the Roman Emperors . . . presented some of the characteristics of the Antichrist. Themselves the representatives of the law, they were yet at heart lawless. . . ."[11]

It is true that "the powers that be are ordained of God" (Rom. 13:1), and that rulers are ministers of God in the sense that they derive their authority from Him. But it is likewise true that civil government or authority vested in Gentile rulers cannot avail in itself to resist the forces of evil. These can become channels of blessing to the world when the rulers are godly, but human government which spurns the sovereignty of God and depends upon its own resources becomes itself lawless, with corruption in high places. One has only to dip into history, or, it might be suggested, into the daily newspapers, to have it impressed on him that governments have availed little in checking the evil of the age and have been lawless themselves both before God and society. Then, when it is remembered that the restrainer must be caught away before the revelation of the Man of Sin, and that Gentile dominion and human government go on into the Tribulation unchanged, eventually to be seized by the Beast himself, it will be obvious that such agencies in no wise correspond to that which is required of the restrainer.

D. *Satan*

A strange suggestion, yet not without a following among posttribulationalists, is that which is made for the identity of the restrainer by Mrs. George C. Needham:

> Why should every one conclude that this hinderer must be

[10] C. F. Hogg and W. E. Vine, *The Epistles of Paul the Apostle to the Thessalonians*, pp. 259, 260.
[11] *Loc. cit.*

some good thing? May not this restraining power be Satan himself? Has he not a plan for the manifestation of the Son of Perdition, as truly as God had a time appointed for the incarnation of His divine Son?[12]

The obvious answer is that Satan never restrains evil, but is everywhere in the Bible presented as the author and instigator of it. He would not oppose his own program, for:

If a house be divided against itself, that house cannot stand. And if Satan rise up against himself, and be divided, he cannot stand, but hath an end (Mark 3:25, 26).

The Scriptures represent the restrainer as holding the whole course of iniquity in check, not just withholding Antichrist until the time appointed. Also, Satan is not removed from the scene before the disclosure of his false Christ; rather, he is ejected from the heavenly sphere and cast down upon the earth, together with his unholy angels (Rev. 12:9). The earth will be no new sphere for Satan's working, but then he will be in full control. Satan is never the restrainer of evil. He is rather the deceiver of the whole world. This has ever been his objective and occupation.

E. *The Church*

The suggestion that the restrainer of iniquity may be the Church, the redeemed of this age, has far more to commend it than any suggestion considered thus far. Like salt, Christians are a true preservative in a civilization which is corrupt and marked for death. As lights, they are to shine in a world of darkness; as ambassadors, they witness for Christ and show forth their heavenly citizenship. Yet, the Church is at best an imperfect organism, perfect in standing before God, to be sure, but experimentally before men, not always blameless, not always beyond reproach. Similar to human government, the Church is being used of God to hinder the full manifestation of the Evil One in this present age, but He who effectively restrains is certainly not the believer himself, but the One who empowers the believer, even the indwelling Holy Spirit (John 16:7; I Cor. 6:19). Apart from His presence, neither Church nor government would avail to hinder the program and power of Satan.

It is doubtful if the Church is in view in II Thessalonians

[12] Mrs. George C. Needham, *The Anti-Christ*, p. 94.

2:6, 7. The restraining force of verse six is referred to in the neuter, *that which,* while the person of the restrainer in verse seven is in the masculine. Since the Greek word for church, *ekklesia,* is a first declension noun and always used in the feminine gender, any attempted identification of the Church as the restrainer would seem precarious. Even so, the Church has more to commend itself in the role of restrainer than any suggestion previously considered. It should not go unnoticed that if the Church *is* the restrainer, she will be "taken out of the midst" before the coming of the "lawless one," which would mean that the Church could not first pass through the Tribulation.

II. The Holy Spirit as Restrainer

There are a number of factors which unite to provide a positive identification that the restrainer of II Thessalonians 2:6, 7 is none other than the Holy Spirit. Posttribulationalist Scruby writes: "I believe, but cannot prove, that Paul did mean the Holy Spirit."[13] Perhaps the following discussion will help others of like doubtful persuasion to see the issues involved and the evidence for making such an identification.

A. *Reasons for This Identification*

The following reasons are suggestive, rather than exhaustive, in their treatment:

(1) By mere elimination, the Holy Spirit must be the restrainer. All other possibilities fall far short of meeting the requirements of one who is to hold in check the forces of evil until the manifestation of Antichrist. Some of the alternate suggestions are out of harmony with the basic text itself.

(2) The Wicked One is a personality, and his operations include the realm of the spiritual. The restrainer must likewise be a personality and of a spiritual order, to resist the wiles of the Devil and to hold Antichrist in check until the time of his revealing. Mere agencies or impersonal spiritual forces would be inadequate. Moreover, the masculine gender of II Thessalonians 2:7 requires the restrainer to be a person.

(3) To achieve all that is to be accomplished, the restrainer must be a member of the Godhead. He must be stronger than

13 John J. Scruby, *The Great Tribulation: The Church's Supreme Test,* p. 194.

the Man of Sin, and stronger than Satan. In order to restrain evil down through the course of the age, the restrainer must be eternal, for Satan and his workers of iniquity have made their influence felt throughout the entire history of the Church. Likewise, the theater of sin is the whole world, making it imperative that the restrainer be one who is not limited by time or space. Such a one is the Holy Spirit of God, for He is omnipotent, eternal, and omnipresent throughout the universe, and therefore preeminently qualified to hold in check all of the Satanic forces of darkness.

(4) This present age is in a particular sense the "dispensation of the Spirit," for He works in a way uncommon to other ages as an abiding Presence within the children of God. While Christ dwelt among men for the space of thirty-three years, the Spirit is the only member of the Trinity to have an earthly abode throughout the age (John 16:7; Acts 1:5; 2:4; I Cor. 3:16; 6:19, etc.). As part of His present ministry, believers are *regenerated* by the Spirit (John 3:5,6), *baptized* by the Spirit (I Cor. 12:12, 13), *indwelt* by the Spirit (Rom. 8:9; I Cor. 6:19, 20), and *sealed* by the Spirit (Eph. 1:13; 4:30). It is God's will that they should be *filled* with the Spirit (Eph. 5:18).

The Church age commenced with the advent of the Spirit at Pentecost, and will close with a reversal of Pentecost, the removal of the Spirit. This does not mean that He will no longer be operative in the world, but only that He will no longer be resident upon the earth.

(5) The work of the Spirit since His advent has included the restraint of evil. The Spirit is God's righteous Agent for the age, and there are many reasons to be grateful for His restraining hand upon this world's iniquity. None but the Lawful One could restrain the workings of Satan, the lawless one. The book of Revelation reveals how awful this world will be without the hand of the Spirit, when the power of Satan will be unleashed with none to rebuke, and when sin will know no restraint. Meanwhile, the Spirit does restrain, for this is part of the work He came to do.

It is expedient for you that I go away: for if I go not away, the Comforter will not come unto you; but if I depart, I will send him unto you. And when he is come, he will reprove the world of sin, and of righteousness, and of judgment: Of sin, because they believe not on me . . . of judgment, because the prince of this world is judged (John 16:7-11).

Of inestimable value is the quiet work of the Spirit in behalf of those who are Christ's, guiding believers into all truth (John 16:13), empowering for witness (Acts 1:8), convicting of sin (Eph. 4:30), and assisting believers in their stand against the wiles of the Devil (Eph. 6:11, 17, 18). When Christians are exhorted to overcome the spirit of Antichrist, they are reminded that the Holy Spirit is greater than Satan. "Ye are of God, little children, and have overcome them [that have the spirit of antichrist]: because greater is he [the Spirit] that is in you, than he [Satan] that is in the world" (I John 4:4). How different it will be in the Tribulation when many of these gracious influences will be removed. How manifestly impossible for the Church to go into the Tribulation once the Spirit has been caught away from the earth. As Strombeck well says:

> Then there would be no Comforter (John 14:16) during those awful days of torment. But this is contrary to God's promise: "I will never leave thee, nor forsake thee." There would be none to show the believer the things of Christ (John 16:14). There would be none to teach all things (John 14:26) during those bewildering years. There would be a Church without power to resist Satan during the time that He is cast out from heaven upon the earth. There would be an impotent Church during the most terrible days of the entire human history.[14]

(6) It is not difficult to establish that although the Spirit was not resident on earth during Old Testament days, whatever restraint was exerted was by the Spirit. Isaiah testified: "When the enemy shall come in like a flood, the Spirit of the Lord shall lift up a standard against him" (Isa. 59:19). Another important passage concerns the days of Noah and conditions which existed before the judgment of the flood. The wickedness of Noah's day and the fact that life went on as usual in blindness to impending destruction is used of the Spirit in vivid portrayal of careless and wicked men upon whom Tribulation judgments shall fall.

> As it was in the days of Noe, so shall it be also in the days of the Son of man. They did eat, they drank, they married wives,

14 J. F. Strombeck, *First the Rapture,* p. 104.

they were given in marriage, until the day that Noe entered into
the ark, and the flood came, and destroyed them all (Luke 17:
26, 27).

In the light of this Scriptural parallel, it is exceedingly significant that in the days immediately preceding the destruction of
the flood, the restraining work of the Spirit is emphasized. God
saw that the wickedness of man was great in the earth, and to
the people of that day the warning of Jehovah was clearly given:
"My spirit shall not always strive with man" (Gen. 6:3).
Couched within that warning was the implication that the
restraint of the Spirit would be removed, after which God would
act in righteous judgment. Even so, just prior to Tribulation
judgment, the restraining hand of the Spirit shall be removed
from the earth. Then will the wrath of God be poured out and
the Man of Sin be revealed.

The similarity between this event, so early in earth's history,
and the removal of the Spirit at the end of the age is most
striking. Evidently in all ages, although more particularly in this
age, the Spirit has held back the flood tides of evil and checked
the activities of the principalities and powers of darkness. Christians should be everlastingly grateful that such a restraining
ministry is part of the work of God in their behalf. How pitifully
weak are all human efforts to rebuke Satanic agencies and to
bind the Strong One (Jude 9)! The very fact that during the
Tribulation, Satan, the Antichrist, and the False Prophet—that
great trinity of evil—shall be on earth and be permitted full
sway, argues strongly that the Holy Spirit of God will no longer
be resident in the earthly sphere. It would seem that the pretribulation removal of the Spirit fits well into the broad Biblical
pattern. It is corroborated by II Thessalonians 2:6, 7, but is
not dependent upon this one passage for its sole support.

B. *Objections to This View*

(1) The fact that the neuter gender, "that which restraineth,"
is used in verse 6 gives the impression that Paul is speaking of
an impersonal force or agency. It is affirmed that the neuter
would be most unsuitable if the Holy Spirit were in view.
Verse 7 shifts to the masculine gender, "he who restrains," implying personality. Therefore, some have maintained that verse
7 speaks of the Spirit, but that verse 6 speaks of the Church as

the agent of the Spirit. While this position is not objectionable and is still perfectly in harmony with the pretribulational interpretation of the passage, it is not necessary for the sake of gender to deny that both verses speak of the Spirit. The passage, of course, is Pauline, and the use of the neuter to apply to the Spirit is not uncommon to his writings. In Romans 8:16 and 26, there are two clear references to the Spirit, both in the neuter gender. This very fact strengthens more than it weakens the argument that the restrainer of II Thessalonians 2:6, recorded as it is by the same author, is indeed the Holy Spirit. Thiessen, an authority on the Greek New Testament, confirms this point:

> The writer holds . . . that that which "withholdeth" (neuter, ver. 6) and "he who letteth" (hindereth) (masculine, ver. 7), is none other than the Holy Spirit.[15]

Surely, there is no reason from the Pauline use of the neuter gender for departing from this conclusion.

(2) It is held by some that the phrase ἐκ μέσου γένηται cannot be translated "taken out of the way" because the verb γίνομαι seems quite incapable of the translation "removed," or "be taken." Thayer's *Lexicon* is often referred to as the authority, where the first definition of γίνομαι is *to become, to come into existence, begin to be, receive being.* The same verb is used of the incarnation of Christ, when "the Word was made flesh" (John 1:14), so that II Thessalonians 2:7 is said not to be the removal of the Holy Spirit from the earth but the *coming into being* from the midst of the earth of Antichrist, who has been withholding himself until the time is ripe for open manifestation. However, as English has pointed out:

> *Ginomai* alone has many meanings. We have traced through the New Testament to find that the word is used, in various forms, 621 times, and is translated in 49 different ways. . . . It is rather difficult, therefore, to determine with finality its exact meaning. Yet practically every translater of the New Testament gives the connotation, with *ek mesou*, of *to be taken out of the way,* or *to be removed.*[16]

Thayer's *Lexicon* does give several meanings to the verb γίνομαι, but it must not be overlooked that when it comes to this

15 Henry C. Thiessen, *Will the Church Pass Through the Tribulation?*, p. 41.
16 E. Schuyler English, "Re-Thinking the Rapture," *Our Hope*, LVI (June, 1950), 753.

passage, it clearly states: "*γίνεσθαι ἐκ μέσου, to be taken out of the way*, 2 Th. ii. 7."[17] The verb γίνομαι is exceedingly flexible and not infrequently suggests a change from one state to another, as in John 1:14: "the Word *became* flesh"; Matthew 4:3: "command that these stones *be made* bread"; and Matthew 21:42: "the stone which the builders rejected, the same *is become* the head of the corner." As for the final clause of II Thessalonians 2:7, it is rendered "until he be taken out of the way" by the Authorized, Revised, American Standard, Douay Versions, and others. In the face of such substantiation, one might judge a hasty change to some other rendering of the passage unwarranted and precarious.

(3) The third major objection against the removal of the Holy Spirit as the restrainer of evil is based on the false notion that the Spirit would then have no place or ministry during the Tribulation, and that the saints of that day would be left to their own resources.

> It would seem to be incredible that those who will be witnesses for God against the Antichrist will be left to their own resources in coping with the delusions and awful persecutions of that hour, without the aid of the Holy Spirit.[18]

Added to this is the objection that a Jewish remnant could not be saved, yet alone evangelize the world, without the Holy Spirit. Reese in particular has heaped scorn and abuse upon such an idea, and seems never to tire of expressing his contempt for such "half-converted Jews."

> Their exegesis now, instead of adhering to the main emphasis of Scripture, and basing itself on careful and obvious deductions from clear texts, was shot to pieces by idle speculation, by the adoption of innovations like the Secret Rapture, and the prodigious missionary tour of the world in 1,260 days, by an army of half-converted Jews, still in their sins. Preachers without life, without forgiveness, and without the Holy Ghost in the soul, will do in 1,260 days what the whole Christian Church has been unable to do in 1,900 years — evangelize the world. . . . This at a time when, *ex hypothesi*, the Holy Spirit is in heaven, Antichrist is

[17] Joseph Thayer, *A Greek-English Lexicon of the New Testament*, p. 117.
[18] Robert Cameron, *Scriptural Truth About the Lord's Return*, p. 120.

raging here below, and the elect evangelists are torn between the Imprecatory Psalms and the Sermon on the Mount![19]

Here indeed is a creed that no one will profess. It is but a poor caricature of the pretribulational position, a veritable "straw man" set up only to be knocked down again. Yet the underlying criticism is clear, for it questions what will be the saving and enabling power during the Tribulation if the Spirit of God is removed. As always, the answer lies in the Scriptures.

It is believed by many that the Jews will do a large share of the evangelism during the Tribulation period, but it is hardly fair to characterize them as without life or forgiveness, "half-converted Jews still in their sins." In the Tribulation, Israel is to be purged (Deut. 4:30, 31; Zech. 13:8, 9) and there will be a national turning to God (Ezek. 20:33-44; Rom. 11:26). The 144,000 of Israel are sealed of the Lord, and expressly called "servants of our God" (Rev. 7:3). The martyrs of that day will be "beheaded for the witness of Jesus" (Rev. 20:4), and will overcome Satan by "the word of their testimony" (Rev. 12:11). There need be no doubt at all about these being redeemed men, while the vital character of their testimony is demonstrated by the fact that they seal their witness with their blood. Their evangelism, coupled with the unique ministry of God's especially appointed two witnesses (Rev. 11:3-12), will no doubt be most effective in turning many unto God.

Nor can it be said that these witnesses will work without the convicting power of the Spirit. How men have stumbled over this simple problem! The work of empowering and convicting during the Tribulation is still that of the Holy Spirit. Because He is God, the Spirit is omnipresent, and in that sense, He is present among men and operative in every age. But it is only since Pentecost that His place of *residence* has been on the earth, indwelling the members of the true Church. When He, as restrainer, is removed, there will be a reversal of Pentecost, which will mean that the Spirit will minister from heaven as during the Old Testament economy. He will be present, but not resident; operating, but no longer indwelling. He will save

[19] Reese, *op. cit.*, p. 269. On page 208, Reese further characterizes these tribulation Jews: "half-converted, half-Christian, Jewish Remnant (unconverted, un-Christian would fit the facts better)"!

souls, but no longer baptize them into the body of Christ, for the Church will be complete and in heaven.

Removal of residence does not mean loss of omnipresence or of power to save. The Spirit has various ministries, and because He no longer restrains does not mean that He no longer draws men to Christ. This procedure should not amaze any who are acquainted at all with their Bibles. Did not Christ dwell in the heavenly sphere throughout the Old Testament period, only to come to earth at His incarnation (John 1:14), and to return to the Father at the ascension? Christ had several particular ministries to perform while on earth, but He did not cease to save souls when He was caught up into glory. In like manner, there is no reason for saying that if the Holy Spirit is the restrainer, no one could be saved after He is taken out of the way.

Was Jonah a "half-converted Jew still in his sin" when he preached the shortest sermon on record and saw the mighty city of Nineveh repent in sackcloth? Did not the Spirit convict in power when the land was swept by a mighty revival during the days of Josiah? Yet the Holy Spirit sustained the same relationship to the earth in those days as will exist during the Tribulation. Although He will not indwell His servants in the same sense that the Church is now indwelt, yet He will come upon them with enabling power sufficient for all the mighty works which will characterize that day.

Having reached this point of the discussion, it would seem that the identity of the restrainer is sufficiently established. He who now restrains and will be taken away before the manifestation of the Man of Sin is undoubtedly the Holy Spirit. He alone could fulfill all that is required of the restrainer of evil; all other suggestions fall far short of satisfactory identification. Indeed, the Church has reason to be thankful that He who is the Comforter, He who indwells those that are Christ's, He who intercedes with groanings that cannot be uttered and has baptized and sealed God's children until the day of redemption, also has His hand upon the course of the age, restraining iniquity, holding back the Evil One, detaining the apostasy of the last days, and assisting the members of the body of Christ in the task of living the Christian life in the midst of a wicked and adulterous generation.

One more ministry of the Spirit must receive mention, and that in connection with the rapture of the Church. Even as the servant of Abraham brought home to Isaac a bride, chosen of God, so will the Spirit lead home the Bride of Christ. When the Spirit is removed, then the Church must also be snatched away. To say otherwise is to make void the promise of Christ: "And I will pray the Father, and he shall give you another Comforter, *that he may abide with you for ever:* Even the Spirit of truth . . ." (John 14:16). The removal of the Spirit takes place before the Wicked One shall be revealed, and this removal sets the time for the rapture of the Church. Thus II Thessalonians 2:6, 7 adds a considerable weight of evidence to the teaching of other Scriptures that the rapture of the Church is clearly pretribulational.

Chapter Six

THE IMMINENCY OF THE COMING OF CHRIST
FOR THE CHURCH

In the most plain and concise language, the New Testament Scriptures set forth the coming of the Lord Jesus Christ as the hope, encouragement, and comfort of God's pilgrim people. It is for His appearing that they are instructed to watch and to wait. It is by the expectation of His soon return that they are encouraged to live in all purity. It is with the knowledge that reunion will be made with departed ones at the return of Christ that they are exhorted to comfort one another. The fact that Christ will come again and that His coming may be very soon has long been the prime hope of the people of God.

It is likewise clear from Scripture that no man can know the day, nor the hour, of Christ's return. To many Christians, as they study the Word, it is equally clear that no prophesied, or clearly scheduled, event stands between the present hour and the catching away of the Church at the rapture. They do not look for the earthly kingdom of Christ, nor for the revelation of the Antichrist and the awful years of the Tribulation. They look for Christ Himself, believing that His coming is the next major event upon the calendar of heaven.

In so believing, many Christians affirm that the coming of Christ is *imminent*, which does not mean that this glad event must be immediate, but rather that it is *overhanging*, that it *may occur* at any moment. The word *imminent*, if used of an evil event, might be rendered *impending*, for it is always threatening to come to pass. An imminent event is one that hangs suspended, possibly for an indefinite period of time, but the final occurrence is certain. As applied to the coming of the Lord, imminency consists of three things: the certainty that He may come at any moment, the uncertainty of the time of that arrival, and the fact that no prophesied event stands between the believer and that hour.

The purpose of such imminency is that the Church may be in a constant state of expectancy, always looking for and waiting for the coming of her Lord from heaven. Not only is the hope of His return a source of comfort and encouragement to the believer, but also it is a very definite incentive for service and for holy living. By the very nature of the case, if the exact time of the rapture had been revealed, none but the final generation of Christians would have cause to look for the return of their Saviour, and for every other generation this vital hope and incentive would then have been lost. Such is the mischief caused when any known event, such as the Tribulation, the coming of Antichrist, or the Millennium, is thrust between the Church and the coming of Christ for His own. Arthur T. Pierson writes:

> The imminence of the second advent is destroyed the moment that we locate between the first and second coming of our Lord any such definite period of time, whether it be one hundred years or a thousand; for how can one look for an event as imminent which he knows is not to take place for a definite time to come?[1]

The placing of even a seven year period such as the Tribulation, with its impressive personages and clearly scheduled events, between the present hour and the rapture just as certainly destroys the Biblical concept of an imminent return. Yet this is the position of posttribulational brethren, who vehemently defend the hypothesis that the Church must pass through the entire Tribulation period. Indeed, the denial of imminency as applied to the coming of Christ is one of their main contentions, as illustrated by Robert Cameron, who fills approximately one third of his book with this very argument.[2]

Since the return of Christ for His Church is a very precious hope to Christians everywhere, since there is involved no small amount of comfort, encouragement, and incentive to right living, and since much of this advantage is lost by any denial of the imminency of that coming, it is important to give the subject a thorough re-examination. Little has been written in its defence, but the charges hurled against it are many. The following pages will demonstrate, it is believed, that the charges are

---

[1] Arthur T. Pierson, *The Coming of the Lord*, p. 53.
[2] Robert Cameron, *Scriptural Truth About the Lord's Return*, pp. 21-69.

false and that the doctrine stands firm. First to be considered are the various arguments against imminency, after which the large Scriptural support for the doctrine will be indicated.

I. The Case Against Imminency

Robert Cameron, because of his heavy emphasis upon this particular problem, may well be chosen as the spokesman for the case against imminency. Certainly, his approach is thorough, and it is also ambitious, for he writes "to show that such teaching is opposed to the whole of the New Testament."[3] In common with others who deny the imminent return of Christ, Cameron enumerates a number of basic objections:

The fact that Christ promised the coming of the Comforter, the Holy Spirit, seems to indicate that a period of time must occur between Christ's departure and His return, and an imminent return would make the coming of the Spirit "a fool's errand."[4] So also, the promise of Christ to Peter (John 21: 18, 19) that he would live until old age would preclude the possibility of early Christians looking for Christ at any moment. Peter also wrote of "mockers," who would say, in after years, "Where is the promise of his coming?" Likewise, the parables of Matthew 13 were intended to reveal truths, previously not made known, concerning the period between the rejection of Christ by Israel and His return. Claiming that these parables set forth the course of this entire age, Cameron implies that a long time must elapse before their completion.

> Time, labour, many years of toil, growth and development, in the history of Christendom *must precede* the Advent.[5]

This same thought he finds in the parable of the nobleman who went into a far country to receive for himself a kingdom, then returned. Before the return, his servants must have ample time to trade and to increase the number of their talents. Even more definite, according to Cameron, is the parable of the talents in Matthew 25:14-30, where it is distinctly said, "after a long time the Lord of these servants cometh and maketh a reckoning with them."

[3] *Ibid.*, p. 21.
[4] *Ibid.*, p. 23.
[5] *Ibid.*, p. 29.

Now, while no definite period is named, by no juggling of words can a *"long time"* be turned into a *short time*, much less into a moment. By virtue of the terms of this Parable, harmonizing with the teaching of all other Parables, the "imminent," or "any moment" Advent of the Lord was an unthinkable possibility.[6]

Cameron argues further that the Great Commission of Matthew 28:19, 20 implies a long interval of time, and that there is not the slightest reason for assuming that an "un-named Jewish company," converted after the rapture but before the Millennium, could complete the accomplishment of this task. Still more definite, it is argued, Paul evidently did not expect the Lord to come during his lifetime, for he records in II Timothy 4:6-8, "the time of my departure has come." Also, he wrote the church at Rome of his proposed journey to Jerusalem, then to Rome, and after that, to Spain (Rom. 15:22-25, 30, 31). "If he had any thought of Christ coming immediately, could he have written this?"[7]

Another posttribulationalist, Edmund Shackleton, sums up the further details of this argument as well as any, when he says:

Prophets too, speaking by the Spirit, had told him that bonds and afflictions awaited him. In bidding farewell to the elders at Miletus, he told them of evils that would arise after his departing from them; and these things would take a little time to develop. Then when Paul had been cast into prison at Jerusalem, the Lord stood by him at night and told him that he must bear witness also at Rome (Acts xxiii.11). Again, when writing to the Philippians from prison, he speaks of his desire to depart, or the alternative, that he might be liberated and pay them another visit. In both his Epistles to Timothy, he foretells spiritual dangers of a time still in the future.[8]

It is further argued by Cameron that Christ prophesied concerning the fall of Jerusalem, Paul predicted perilous times in the last days, and numerous other predicted events are to be found in the New Testament, all of which are used to demonstrate that the return of Christ could not have been expected in that day. In other words, the second coming of Christ must

[6] *Ibid.*, p. 30.
[7] *Ibid.*, p. 41.
[8] Edmund Shackleton, *Will the Church Escape the Great Tribulation?*, pp. 31, 32, cited by Reese, *The Approaching Advent of Christ*, p. 231.

follow well-defined events of unfulfilled prophecy and therefore can not be imminent.

II. These Objections Answered

Although this present treatment of Cameron's arguments can in no wise rival in length the fifty pages he fills with objections to imminency, it is believed that a brief analysis of the chief issues will suffice to reveal the general weakness of his presentation and open the way for Bible students who desire to pursue the subject in greater detail. The following divisions follow the order of the objections set forth in the preceding section.

A. *The Promise of the Comforter*

Surely the promise that the disciples would be "baptized with the Holy Ghost not many days hence" (Acts 1:5) was no indication of any appreciable time which had to elapse before the Spirit could come. Actually, Pentecost took place a mere ten days after the ascension of Christ. It must constantly be kept in mind throughout this discussion that *imminent* does not mean *immediate,* and the fact that there was a brief interval before Pentecost does not prove that it formed any barrier to the disciples' faith in the Lord's soon return. In fact, when Christ does return, it will be for His *Church,* and the Church was not instituted until the time of the descent of the Spirit. It is difficult to see how Pentecost, before which the Church, as such, did not exist, could have been any kind of obstacle to faith in the imminent return of Christ for the members of that Church.

B. *The Promise to Peter*

Lest it be said that the posttribulational argument against imminency carries no weight, and that the events predicted concerning Peter and Paul have little bearing on one's belief in the imminent return of Christ, the following citation from Oswald Smith, pastor of the People's Church of Toronto, is significant. Setting forth his reasons for forsaking the pretribulation view, he writes:

> Then when I remembered that the death of Peter, his prediction of corruption and apostasy after his decease, the death of

Paul, and many other events had to occur before the Rapture, my "any moment" theory took wings and flew.[9]

It is the belief of this present investigator that such a "flight" from a confident hope in the imminent return of Christ was an unnecessary departure, and that the former position was more tenable than the latter. No doubt many a busy pastor, and many an earnest saint, have been so mislead by some clever writer pursuing a proselyting campaign for posttribulationalism.

The argument concerning Peter is that, on the basis of John 21:18, 19, Peter knew he would grow old and die, and therefore, for him at least, the coming of Christ could not be imminent. However, it is not clear that Peter so understood the Lord on this point. Certainly he encouraged the believers of his day to look for the coming of the Lord. Also, he knew that he might die suddenly (II Pet. 1:14), and although it is not stated whether he expected death, Herod had just killed with the sword James, the brother of John, and had seized Peter with the same intention (Acts 12:1-3). At least, it is certain that the believers expected Peter's death, for when Rhoda bore the news of his release, they said unto her, "Thou art mad," and when they saw Peter, "they were astonished" (Acts 12:15, 16). It is most doubtful if Peter had assurance that his death must precede the coming of his Lord, and it is obvious that the people had no concept that his would be a long life. The actual passage in question, John 21:18, with the apostle's explanation in the following verse, was not written until twenty or more years after the death of Peter. In the same context, verses 20-23, there is found a clear indication that the believers of that day expected the return of Christ within the lifetime of John. In contemplating Christ's coming, Peter, at least, was not a factor in the thinking of the early church. As they looked for the Saviour, they did not run around asking, "I wonder if Peter is dead yet?" Peter could have died suddenly without most people knowing it. Even if the promise of Christ were known throughout the Church, and interpreted in the strictest sense that Peter's death must precede Christ's coming, there was no reason for the Church

---

[9] Oswald Smith, *God's Future Program: Will the Church Escape the Tribulation?* cited by John J. Scruby, *The Great Tribulation: The Church's Supreme Test,* p. 75.

to reject her belief in the imminent return on that basis. Judging from their spirit of expectancy, it is evident that they did not. This whole objection strikes one as being foolish and unnecessary, and it is dealt with here only because it seems to occupy so much posttribulational thinking.

Concerning the statement of Peter that in the last days, men should scoff at the promise of Christ's coming (II Pet. 3:3-5), and the kindred predictions by Paul of "perilous times" (II Tim. 3:1-5) and departure from the faith (I Tim. 4:1-3), these conditions had a near, as well as a far, fulfillment. Such predictions were never an obstacle in the minds of believers of apostolic days, again evident from the fact that Christ's return was expected by the Early Church. Thiessen aptly harmonized these verses when he commented:

> The writers of these prophecies did not think of them as lying in the remote future, but spoke of them as already present, at least in their beginnings, in their own day. They intended their statements to be a warning to the very people to whom they wrote, and not simply to us who live in the twentieth century.[10]

C. The Problem of Christ's Parables

Cameron rightfully holds the position that the seven parables of Christ, set forth in Matthew 13, picture the course of this present age between the rejection of Christ by Israel and His return to reign. He then defends his posttribulational view on the basis that both tares and wheat grow together until the time of harvest, and that there is a long time of sowing before the whole world is reached. Moreover:

> The other six parables harmonize with this one, and a *long time* must elapse before the world could be sown; before the tares and wheat (Christendom) could mature; before the leaven of evil could spread through the whole meal of truth and before the drag net could be filled and the separation made.[11]

Hence, the tares will first be disposed of and the rapture cannot precede the judgment; also since a long time is involved in the fulfillment of these parables, the rapture is not imminent.

Similarly, it is argued, the parable of the nobleman who gave his servants the ten pounds was a rebuke to those who "thought

---

[10] Henry C. Thiessen, "Will the Church Pass Through the Tribulation?" *Bibliotheca Sacra,* XCII (July-September, 1935), 310.
[11] Cameron, *op. cit.,* pp. 28, 29.

that the kingdom of God should immediately appear," and the parable of the talents in Matthew 25 clearly records that it was only after "a long time" that the lord of those servants came and made his reckoning with them. On the basis of such passages of Scripture, the posttribulationalists build an argument against imminency which they unhesitatingly label "unanswerable."

Yet a fair and reasonable answer is not difficult to find. The question is not whether God foresaw the entirety of the Church age when He gave these Scriptures, for that fact is obvious. Nor does the question inquire whether the entire age is pictured in sufficient clarity for *twentieth century* believers to visualize in these parables the long history of Christendom. We have the advantage of the *backward* look, the historical perspective, and must concede from our vantage point that these parables do describe something of the task of the Church and the progress of the age.

The issue rather is whether or not *first century* Christians saw and understood in these parables enough of God's future purposes to reject the imminency of Christ's coming. We believe they did not. Since the very disciples of Christ failed so long to understand even the most basic issues of God's *redemptive* program, notably, that Christ must go to the cross and on the third day rise again (Matt. 16:21-23; 17:22, 23; 26:69-75; Luke 24:21, 25; John 20:25, etc.), it is difficult indeed to see how early Christians in general could have comprehended God's prophetic program to the point of rejecting the imminent return of Him for whose coming they had been instructed to watch. This is particularly true, clothed as the predictions were — in the language of parables. To the contrary, the whole apostolic Church and the Christians of the following two centuries[12] were characterized by the fact that they did look for the soon return of Christ. While it is admitted that a general outline of the development of Christendom is to be found pictured in the parables of the kingdom, it must be recognized that there was also a simultaneous, local application of these same parables. "All the conditions described in the parables exist simultaneously in all

12 The hope of Christ's coming in the first three centuries will be discussed in chapter 10.

periods of the Church's history, and yet there is a progressive fulfillment as well."[13] It is most probable that the early Christians saw only the preliminary fulfillment of their own day and had no true concept of the full development of the age. Was not the gospel soon carried to the furthermost parts of the then-known world? Did not apostasy immediately set in, with unbelievers scoffing at the promise of Christ's coming? Apostasy has been present throughout the age, although it will reach its peak after the Church and the restraint of the Spirit have been removed. It is safe to conclude then, that the parabolic teachings of Christ constituted no obstacle to the hope of the apostolic Church in His imminent return.

It is said that the seven churches of Revelation 1-3 picture the course of the age, and therefore early Christians could not have held to the doctrine under consideration. While it is true that these churches bear a marked resemblance to the various periods of church history, and while granting that this is a legitimate application, it must not be forgotten that John was writing to seven existing, although representative, congregations. All these varying shades of Christian testimony, or of departure from, were present in John's day throughout the early church. John saw no need for projecting the second coming into the far distant future, for he was himself one of the chief witnesses to the soon coming of Christ, the closing words penned in the book of Revelation being "Surely I come quickly [ταχύ, speedily, as quickly as possible]. Even so, come, Lord Jesus" (Rev. 22: 20). Paul also rejoiced that the Thessalonians "turned to God from idols . . . and to wait for his Son from heaven."

In direct contradiction to the idea that certain parables would have led the early church to reject the hope of an imminent return, there is indication that some had actually ceased to work on the grounds that Christ might come at any moment (I Thess. 4:11; II Thess. 3:10-12), and that others were growing restless at the seeming delay and had to be exhorted to patience (James 5:7,8). There can therefore be no doubt that the apostolic church viewed the coming of Christ as imminent. Christ had comforted His disciples with the fact that He would come again,

[13] Thiessen, *op. cit.,* p. 310.

and there is much throughout the entire New Testament to encourage in the believer a spirit of daily expectation. Simultaneously, the too common error of fixing dates for the time of His return is carefully guarded against.

Now to deal more directly with the parables under discussion. The parable of the wheat and the tares indicates the nature of the present age, declaring that the godly and the wicked will live side by side until the return of Christ. But this can hardly mean that no believers or unbelievers at all will leave the earth before God's final harvest, for representatives of both groups are being removed by death almost every moment of the day. The parable merely presents the fact that both wheat and tares will continue on earth until the end, at which time separation will be made. Thus is explained the problem of why God permits the wicked to flourish with the righteous. He is aware of their seeming prosperity, but the time of separation has not yet come.

The parable, then, in no wise excludes the possibility of rapture before judgment, in which case the "wheat" of that final day will consist of those saved after the rapture, even the Jewish remnant and the many converts from among Gentile nations. And if, as posttribulationalists insist, this parable sets the order of the harvest, even their system is not immune to difficulty, for the parable declares, "First, the tares."

While Cameron urges that this passage proves "time, labour, many years of toil, growth and development, in the history of Christendom *must precede* the Advent,"[14] who can deny that tares were flourishing in the midst of the wheat, even in the early church? Paul warned the elders of the spiritual Ephesian assembly that after his departing, "grievous wolves" should enter in among them and tear the flock (Acts 20:29). It would have been difficult indeed to persuade these elders that Christ could not come at any moment, on the grounds that the tares had not yet a sufficient time to flourish in the midst of the wheat! Although apostasy will reach its climax in the end time, it has marked the professing Church in every century of her existence.

[14] Cameron, *op. cit.*, p. 29.

The Early Church was not so immune that lack of apostasy would have kept them from anticipating the coming of Christ.

The purpose of the parable of the nobleman is clearly explained in Luke 19:11. Christ's followers were looking for the earthly kingdom of Messiah, and "because he was nigh to Jerusalem . . . they thought that the kingdom of God should immediately appear." As yet, they did not comprehend that Christ would leave them, or that He must die, or that the setting up of the visible kingdom must await a second advent. Christ gave this parable to correct their thinking and to instruct them to "carry on business" for Him after His departure. He did not say how long He would be gone, but He did promise to return in such a manner that service should be rendered in the spirit of expectancy. We must "occupy" *till He comes,* even as in the Lord's Supper, we "do shew the Lord's death till he come" (I Cor. 11:26). These expressions emphasize the imminency of the return of Christ, rather than denying it.

This is also true of the parable of the talents. An adult who has already achieved possession of a home, money, and servants, takes a journey, having first committed his goods into the hands of his servants. The length of his journey is not revealed, but the "long time" was not so many months or years that the owner did not find them all living upon his return, so that they might be held responsible. The parable was given to illustrate the need for watchfulness and not to establish the extent of the absence. If any impression was made at all concerning the time of the return, it must have been that the arrival would be within the lifetime of the servants. There is absolutely nothing to indicate, as Cameron pleads, that this parable makes the imminent return of the Lord "an unthinkable possibility."[15]

D. The Great Commission

Matthew 28:18-20 records the last command of Christ to His followers prior to His ascension. The passage is generally referred to as the "Great Commission," or the "marching orders of the church." Here is set forth the parting instruction of our Lord to carry the gospel to every creature and to teach all nations those things which He has commanded (*cf.* Mark 16:15, 16). Accord-

15 Cameron, *loc. cit.*

ing to Cameron, Jesus is here setting forth a vast program for this present age, and since many centuries have passed and still "all nations, and peoples, and kindreds, and tongues" have not yet been reached by the gospel, the idea of an imminent return of Christ "is absurd!"[16]

It must be remembered once more that it is not a matter of God's knowing and recording His advance program, but rather this question: "Would such a Scripture have caused the disciples to realize the extent of the coming age and so have forced them to give up any personal belief in the imminent return of Christ?" When the vitality and zeal of Paul and other early converts, with their world-shaking testimony (Acts 17:6), is remembered, together with the size of the then-inhabited world (grown yet smaller by the unifying influence of Roman rule and Roman roads), it must be confessed that world evangelism was a greater possibility in Paul's day than in ours. Nor was it the intent of the Great Commission that Paul and his successors should attempt to convert the world, although post-millennialists have strained to read this into the text. It is most evident that the disciples did not so understand the Lord. When Peter addressed the council at Jerusalem, he did not say that all the Gentiles were going to be saved during this age, but that God would visit the Gentiles "to take *out of them* a people for his name" (Acts 15:14). Thiessen has commented:

> What the Lord asked the disciples to do was to witness to all nations (Acts 1:8), and to make disciples of such as believed. That is, the Great Commission points out the *destination* of the gospel, but makes no prediction as to the *success* of the gospel.[17]

When the Great Commission says "all nations," it cannot mean that the entirety of the world's population must be saved before Christ can come. On such a basis, no generation would witness the Lord's coming from glory, for hundreds are being born into the world for every new convert to Christ. But if it means that all nations must have an opportunity to hear the gospel, that fact alone largely explains the incentive and the tremendous mission-ary impetus of the early church. That this is the correct con-

[16] *Ibid.,* p. 34.
[17] Thiessen, *Will the Church Pass Through the Tribulation?,* p. 52.

clusion and was the view of early Christians, is borne out by the words of Paul to the Colossians:

> . . . the gospel, which is come unto you, as it is in all the world . . . and be not moved away from the hope of the gospel, which ye have heard, and which was preached to every creature which is under heaven: whereof I Paul am made a minister (Col. 1:6, 23).

In the light of this overwhelming success granted to the missionary program of the early church, there is absolutely no indication that Matthew 28:18-20 was a barrier to their expectation that the Lord could have returned in their day.[18]

E. *The Statements of Paul*

Prominent in the case against imminency is the contention that the Apostle Paul did not, and could not, expect Christ to return in his lifetime. There seem to be three major objections to the idea that Paul viewed the coming of Christ as imminent. The first of these is that Paul wrote to Timothy concerning "latter times [when] some shall depart from the faith" (I Tim. 4:1-3), and of "last days [when] perilous times shall come" (II Tim. 3:1-5), men having "a form of godliness" but denying the power thereof. Although this is now recognized to be a picture of the end of the age, the sins listed are universal. Beyond any reasonable doubt, Christians of every century have found these verses applicable to the times in which they lived at least sufficiently so that they did not view the prophecy as yet awaiting fulfillment before the Lord could come. As has been noted, apostasy set in extremely early (Gal. 1:6; 3:1; 4:11; Acts 15:1, ff.). While it is true that Paul's predictions of final apostasy imply a development greater than any attained in his generation, Scripture does not declare that the consummation of apostasy must occur *before* the rapture. II Thessalonians 2:3 speaks of a "falling away," and the revelation of the Man of Sin, but the Tribulation is

---

[18] Reese, *op. cit.*, writes a chapter entitled "The Great Missionary Commission and Its Fulfillment," pp. 108-19. The entire effort is an attack on Darby and some of his followers who applied the Great Commission to the evangelistic zeal of the Jewish remnant during the Tribulation period. Reese attempts to pin this admittedly ultra-dispensational interpretation to pretribulationalism as a whole, and then proceeds to refute the view with sarcasm and ridicule. While it may be a clever debater's device to give the impression that the opponent's position is unsound by attributing to it, and then attacking, an extreme view on a minor point, the value of such misrepresentation is questionable.

here in view and not conditions of the Church age. The apostasy in its final form will reach its climax only under the Satan-inspired leadership of the Antichrist during the great Tribulation.

The second objection is that Paul was distinctly promised a long career as an apostle, and that he wrote under inspiration that he would travel to far off lands. At his conversion and baptism, he was told that he would bear the name of Christ "before the Gentiles, and kings, and the children of Israel" (Acts 9:15). He completed three missionary journeys. He visited Ephesus and promised to return. He planned to visit the saints at Jerusalem, visit Rome, and journey on into Spain (Rom. 15:23-25). How could all these things be fulfilled if Paul viewed the coming of Christ as an imminent event?

The answer to the problem lies in the fact that Paul served the Lord in the spirit of the exhortation, "Occupy till I come" (Luke 19:13). All of his plans, including these proposed journeys, were contingent on the Lord's leading and the further revelation of God's will for his life. Thus it was that he conditioned his promise to the Ephesians, "But I will return again unto you, *if God will*" (Acts 18:21). To the Christians at Rome he expressed his desire that "I might have a prosperous journey *by the will of God* to come unto you." Often he had purposed to come unto them but had been hindered (Rom. 1:9, 10, 13). He wrote plainly to the Corinthians: "But I will come to you shortly, *if the Lord will*" (I Cor. 4:19).

Few men have served as well or suffered more for the cause of Christ than Paul, yet along with his service he ever expressed himself as one who believed the Lord might come at any time. To the Philippians, he wrote: "For our conversation [citizenship] is in heaven; from whence also we look for the Saviour, the Lord Jesus Christ" (Phil. 3:20). He prayed for the Thessalonian Christians that their "whole spirit and soul and body be preserved blameless until the coming of our Lord Jesus Christ" (I Thess. 5:23). Likewise, he commended them for turning "to God from idols to serve the living and true God; and to wait for his Son from heaven" (I Thess. 1:9, 10). Such an attitude is a far cry from that attributed to him by posttribulationist Cameron:

He did not look for the "imminent" coming of the Lord. He had been too well instructed by the Prince of teachers that he did not make such a glaring mistake.[19]

The third part of the argument based on the life of Paul is not only that he would go "far hence unto the Gentiles" (Acts 22:21), but also that he would enjoy great length of years as the apostle to the Gentiles. This being the case, it is assured, Christ could not have returned in his lifetime. But it has been seen that it did not take long for Paul to reach the Gentiles; in fact, he had already been to the Macedonians (Acts 16). Carrying the gospel unto uttermost parts was rapidly accomplished (Col. 1:6, 23). As to the length of his life, Paul testified in I Corinthians 15:30: "Why stand we in jeopardy every hour?" Of his own suffering he recorded:

> Of the Jews five times received I forty stripes save one. Thrice was I beaten with rods, once was I stoned, thrice I suffered shipwreck, a night and a day I have been in the deep. . . .

As one reads these and the following verses of II Corinthians 11:23-28, he can scarcely conclude that Paul enjoyed great assurance of a long and healthy life. His purpose was not necessarily to live, but merely to magnify Christ Jesus the Lord in his body "whether it be by life, or by death" (Phil. 1:20, 21). For Paul, length of life was not contingent on his being the apostle to the Gentiles but upon his doing the will of God, and that very attitude enabled him to live and serve in the hope of an imminent return of Christ.[20]

F. Why This Attack on Imminency?

What is Cameron, and the many who follow his example, attempting to prove by his long and laborious arguments? What is the purpose of this detailed and supposedly unanswerable case which he strives so diligently to establish? Surely he has a deeper motive than trying to prove that first century saints were not

[19] Cameron, op. cit., p. 50.

[20] In addition to these major objections to an early belief in the imminency of Christ's appearing, one or two other trifling objections are brought forward, such as the promised destruction of Jerusalem. Luke 21:20-24 records this prediction of Christ, and it is argued that here was another known and clearly prophesied event which separated early Christians from any hope of being in the rapture. When, however, it is noted that the time of this destruction was not foretold — it might have come much earlier than 70 A.D. — and when it is realized that the destruction might have been part of the time of trouble after the rapture, this objection is robbed of all its force.

looking for their Lord from glory. At the end of his argument, the motive is finally stated:

> Thus, we find that the Apostles looked for *intervening events* between them and the Coming of the Lord. This attitude did not make His coming any less precious to their hearts. We are certainly in good company when we share the same faith and feeling, and it is still the blessed hope to our hearts.[21]

In other words, Cameron is attempting to prove that the second coming of Christ was a precious hope to the apostles, but not on the basis that they thought His coming was imminent, or that they might share in the rapture experience. What actually did make His coming a precious hope to them, when first they must look for the death of Peter and the death of Paul, and await the coming of the Spirit, the fall of Jerusalem, and the fulfillment of the Great Commission, giving time for the gospel to reach Spain and for the tares to grow up with the wheat, Cameron and his friends do not care to indicate. Can it be that the coming of Christ was a source of comfort and encouragement to the early church because, in spite of other predictions, they held it to be imminent? Assuredly, this is the truth of the case.

The doctrine of the imminent return of Christ is not under attack, however, because of its application to the early church. If this were a question which influenced only that one generation of believers, it might be easier to dismiss the entire matter. The posttribulational view robs every generation of an imminent, and consequently of a comforting and purifying hope. It argues that, because the rapture was not imminent in the first century, it is not imminent in any century, and it cannot be imminent *now*. Antichrist and the great Tribulation are ahead, and there is no basis for expecting Christ to come before such clearly scheduled events. It is unscriptural to say that "perhaps tonight the Lord will come." It is erroneous to take hope that *this* may be the year of *His* return. Even though He were to come in this generation, Tribulation and martyrdom are brought that much closer. No need to watch for Christ; watch for Antichrist — he will be here first! This is posttribulationalism!

The doctrine of the imminent return of Christ is absolutely

21 Cameron, *op. cit.*, p. 68.

fatal to such a posttribulational philosophy. Therefore, they press the attack against imminency and labor so hard to discount the doctrine. It may be concluded from the very weakness of the arguments by their chief spokesman that their task has not been accomplished, for they can be met and defeated on their own ground. Thus far, the consideration has been negative; the actual strength of the doctrine of imminency will be demonstrated more conclusively by the positive approach: the testimony of the Scriptures to the actual hope of the apostles and the attitude of the early church.

III. The Hope of the Early Church

The confidence of the apostles concerning the possibility of an early advent has been touched on in the previous section and needs but a brief summary at this point. A consideration of the Scriptures involved will be sufficient to convince the average reader that the hope of Christ's coming was shared by the early church.

A. *Testimony from Scripture*

Among the words spoken by Christ to His disciples in the intimacy of the passover chamber were those which promised a heavenly mansion and a certain return of Christ for His own: "I go to prepare a place for you. And . . . I will come again, and receive you unto myself; that where I am, there ye may be also" (John 14:2, 3). To this promise, the angels add their testimony: "This same Jesus . . . shall so come in like manner as ye have seen him go into heaven" (Acts 1:11). There is every indication that the apostles received such promises as applying directly unto themselves. In his letter to the Christians at Corinth, Paul writes words applicable to the entire Church throughout the present age: "We shall not all sleep, but we shall all be changed, In a moment, in the twinkling of an eye . . ." (I Cor. 15:51, 52), and who can prove that Paul himself did not cherish the hope of being included among those that shall not "sleep"? When he wrote the Philippians, he reminded them of citizenship in heaven: "from whence also we look for the Saviour" (Phil. 3:20).

When he wrote to the Colossians, part of his theme was: "When Christ, who is our life, shall appear, then shall ye also appear with him in glory" (Col. 3:4). When he wrote to the Thessalonians, he commended them that they had "turned to God from idols to serve the living and true God; And to wait for his Son from heaven" (I Thess. 1:9, 10). Paul instructed his son in the faith, Timothy, and exhorted him to "keep this commandment without spot, unrebukable, until the appearing of our Lord Jesus Christ" (I Tim. 6:14).

Jewish converts were reminded that "yet a little while, and he that shall come will come, and will not tarry" (Heb. 10:37). James exhorts those to whom he wrote: "Be ye also patient; stablish your hearts: for the coming of the Lord draweth nigh" (James 5:8). Peter remarks that those who scoff at the coming of the Lord are "willingly ignorant" (II Pet. 3:4, 5), while John concludes the Revelation and closes the canon of Scripture with the glad cry: "He which testifieth these things saith, Surely I come quickly. Amen. Even so, come, Lord Jesus" (Rev. 22: 20). Here is testimony indeed to the hope of the early church!

It is fully recognized that these, and like precious promises, were given through the apostles and prophets to the entire church, and for the entire age. This alone is sufficient ground to prove that all generations during the church age have had the right to consider the coming of Christ as imminent. But those New Testament writings were sent to living people and real places, sent to answer actual problems in existing local churches, and it is undeniable that the generation which received the original autographs believed that they had a right to take these promises unto themselves. Nor did Paul rebuke the Thessalonian Christians for waiting "for his Son from heaven" on the grounds that Peter was not yet dead, or that Jerusalem was not yet destroyed!

The coming of Christ was just as imminent in the first century as it is today, by which is meant that from the viewpoint of the believer, Christ could have come in that generation. From the same Scriptures, men today look for His appearing. The promises are so worded that every age may view the coming as imminent and receive the blessing and comfort of such a hope, without any age or generation being able to say emphatically: "Christ *will* come in our day."

B. *The Hope of the First Three Centuries*

Not only may it be demonstrated that the New Testament church held the coming of Christ to be imminent, but the same conclusion is reached from the writings of men of God in subsequent generations. Silver says of the Apostolic Fathers that "they expected the return of the Lord in their day. . . . They believed the time was imminent because their Lord had taught them to live in a watchful attitude."[22] Concerning the Ante-Nicene Fathers, he says: "By tradition they knew the faith of the Apostles. They taught the doctrine of the imminent and premillennial return of the Lord."[23] Something of the evidence for these claims will be presented at a later point, under the consideration of the "historical problem" in chapter 10. Many authors can be cited to prove that a belief in the soon return of Christ existed throughout the first three centuries. Although a member of the liberal theological school, out of sheer honesty as a historian, A. Harnack writes:

> In the history of Christianity three main forces are found to have acted as auxiliaries to the gospel. They have elicited the ardent enthusiasm of men whom the bare preaching of the gospel would never have made decided converts. These are a belief in the speedy return of Christ and in His glorious reign on earth. . . . First in point of time came the faith in the nearness of Christ's second advent and the establishing of His reign of glory on the earth. Indeed it appears so early that it might be questioned whether it ought not to be regarded as an essential part of the Christian religion.[24]

The weight of evidence from the writings of the apostles and from the faith of the early church on into the third century is solidly behind the claim that the Bible teaches the imminency of the return of Christ.

---

[22] Jesse Forest Silver, *The Lord's Return: Seen in History and in Scripture as Premillennial and Imminent*, pp. 62, 63.

[23] *Ibid.*, p. 64.

[24] A. Harnack, "Millennium," *Encyclopaedia Britannica* (ninth edition), XVI, 314.

IV. The New Testament Exhortations

There is in the New Testament a body of truth which rightfully belongs under the heading, "The hope of the early church," yct it is sufficiently extensive to warrant separate treatment. It consists of the apostolic exhortations to *look, watch, wait,* and *be ready* for the coming of the Saviour. Herein lies additional positive and Scriptural proof for the imminency of His return. The argument, in brief, is as follows:

In Philippians 3:20, Paul speaks of citizenship in heaven, "from whence also we *look* for the Saviour." Hebrews 9:28 records, "unto them that *look* for him shall he appear the second time without sin unto salvation." According to Titus 2:13, believers are to be *"looking* for that blessed hope, and the glorious appearing of the great God and our Saviour Jesus Christ."

> Paul . . . does not ask us to look for the Tribulation, or the Antichrist, or for persecution and martyrdom, or for death, but for the return of Christ. If any of these events must precede the Rapture, then how can we help looking for them rather than the Lord's coming? Such a view of the coming of the Lord can at best only induce a very general interest in the "blessed hope."[25]

The very fact that all generations of Christians have looked for and are exhorted to keep looking for the coming of the Lord, gives witness to the fact that Christ may come at any time. Yet, some have lost sight of this fact and have followed the philosophy of those servants who said: "My Lord delays his coming" (Matt. 24:48).

> The fact that, according to an Act of Parliament adopted in 1752, the Episcopal *Book of Common Prayer* gives directions for calculating the feasts of the Church year as far ahead as A.D. 8500, was not calculated to convince Darby and his associates a century ago that the bishops and other clergy of the Established Church were living in eager expectancy of the advent. It indicated rather that they regarded the Church of England as firmly established on earth and expected it to remain there almost "world without end."[26]

To the exhortations to *look* for the return of Christ are added the similar exhortations to *watch.* This command is given to the Church in view of the rapture in I Thessalonians 5:6. "There-

---

[25] Thiessen, *Bibliotheca Sacra,* XCII (July-September, 1935), 307.
[26] Oswald T. Allis, *Prophecy and the Church,* p. 167.

fore let us not sleep, as do others; but let us *watch* and be sober."
The same exhortation is given to the church at Sardis, in Revelation 3:3. "If therefore thou shalt not *watch*, I will come on
thee as a thief, and thou shalt not know what hour I will come
upon thee." A similar command to watch is given to believers,
particularly Israel, who will be under the persecution of the
Beast during the great Tribulation. "Watch therefore: for ye
know not what hour your Lord doth come" (Matt. 24:42; *cf*,
25:13; Rev. 16:15). "Blessed are those servants, whom the Lord
when he cometh shall find watching" (Luke 12:37; *cf*. 21:36).
Thus, the attitude of watchfulness is becoming to any believer
in Christ, and the exhortation to watch seems to be applied to
the second coming as a whole. Certainly, the language of
Mark 13:32-37, although given in the setting of the Lord's
return to earth, may be used by application as a general exhortation to all saints through the course of the entire age:

> But of that day and that hour knoweth no man, no, not the
> angels which are in heaven, neither the Son, but the Father. Take
> ye heed, watch and pray: for ye know not when the time is. For
> the Son of man is as a man taking a far journey, who left his
> house, and gave authority to his servants, and to every man his
> work, and commanded the porter to watch. Watch ye therefore:
> for ye know not when the master of the house cometh, at even,
> or at midnight, or at the cockcrowing, or in the morning: Lest
> coming suddenly he find you sleeping. And what I say unto you
> I say unto all, Watch.

For these many years, believers have been looking and watching for their Lord from glory. They have believed that, while
His coming might not be immediate, nor necessarily in their
lifetime, His coming could be very soon. Weary from the
presence of sin or in pain from the presence of sickness, in the
morning they have said, "Perhaps today!" and in the evening
they have whispered, "Perhaps tonight!" They have "loved
his appearing," viewing it as imminent, and so have watched
for the return of the Saviour. Yet, with it all, they have lived
in accord with that other most practical exhortation, "Occupy
till I come." As Blackstone well says:

> True watching is an attitude of mind and heart which would
> joyfully and quickly turn from any occupation to meet our Be-

loved, rapturously exclaiming "this is the Lord; we have waited for Him."[27]

Needless to say, the posttribulational view discredits and robs the Biblical exhortations to watchfulness of any real and significant meaning. This was clearly seen by the honored James H. Brookes:

> If the Church must pass through the tribulation, it is useless to watch for Him daily. According to this view the apostasy must first set in like a flood, and sweep away the great mass of professing Christianity, the Antichrist in his proud lawlessness is to be developed, and the Jews restored in unbelief to their own land. None of these things have occurred [the latter yet only in part]: and hence it is impossible for those who hold the error, here condemned, to heed the Saviour's admonition, "Watch ye therefore, and pray always," uttering the cry of the longing apostle, "Even so, come, Lord Jesus," Rev. xxii:20. They put themselves out of sympathy with the mind of the Master, for they postpone his advent at least for some years.[28]

The third exhortation in view of the second coming of Christ is to *wait*. Such is the attitude of believers who wait for the redemption of their bodies (Rom. 8:23). Those at Corinth came behind in no gift, "waiting for the coming of our Lord Jesus Christ" (I Cor. 1:7), while the Thessalonian believers served the living and true God and were waiting for His Son from heaven (I Thess. 1:10; *cf.* II Thess. 3:5). Certainly, this is a normal attitude for redeemed men who view the coming of their Lord as imminent. One might expect that the command to wait (Luke 12:36) and to be ready (Luke 12:40; Matt. 24:44) should be given prophetically to men in the great Tribulation who have refused the mark of the Beast which would seal their doom (Rev. 14:9, 10). These will be waiting and eagerly watching for the One who will destroy their enemies with the brightness of His appearing (II Thess. 2:8). It is not to be expected, however, that these same exhortations should be given generally to the Church, as they are, unless it is intended for every generation of believers to be characterized by an attitude of watchful expectancy, viewing the coming of Christ for His Church as imminent throughout the age.

[27] W. E. Blackstone, *Jesus Is Coming*, p. 65.
[28] James H. Brookes, "Kept Out of the Hour," *Our Hope*, VI (November, 1899), 154.

It is not necessary for these commands to *watch, wait,* and *be ready* to be technical words used only of the rapture, or of the revelation. It has been demonstrated that these exhortations were given to the first century Church and are applicable to the whole age, which in itself supports the doctrine of imminency. It is only when the believer realizes that Christ's coming may be very soon, and must be before the unveiling of Antichrist and the day of God's outpoured wrath, that he can express the hope:

I am waiting for the dawning, Of the bright and blessed day:
When the darksome night of sorrow, Shall have vanished far away:
When forever with the Saviour, Far beyond this vale of tears,
I shall swell the song of worship, Through the everlasting years.

I am looking at the brightness, (See, it shineth from afar,)
Of the clear and joyous beaming, Of the "Bright and Morning Star";
Through the dark grey mist of morning, Do I see its glorious light;
Then away with every shadow, Of this sad and weary night.

I am waiting for the coming, Of the Lord who died for me;
Oh! His words have thrilled my spirit: "I will come again for thee."
I can almost hear his footfall, On the threshold of the door,
And my heart, my heart is longing, To be His for evermore!

To avoid the full force of the argument for imminency from these exhortations to look, to watch, and to wait, posttribulationalists have tried to prove by illustration that scheduled events before the coming do not keep us from watching for Christ Himself. When you stand at the station awaiting a train which bears a beloved friend, it is argued, you watch the signals. As long as the semaphore stands at right angles, you know the train has not passed the last station, but you are watching, not for the dropping of the semaphore, but for your friend who is near.[29] Similarly, you wait for the royal parade and for the sight of the king. In the distance, you hear the band which leads the parade, but as you watch for the first sight of the band, in reality you look, not for the band, but for the king himself.

From these illustrations, posttribulationalists would have the Christian believe that Antichrist, Tribulation and wrath from

[29] Cameron, *op. cit.,* p. 107.

God do not prevent them from looking beyond for the coming of the King. These other events are but the "band" which precedes the royal carriage.

However, it is the native responsibility of an illustration to at least resemble the thing illustrated. Waiting for a signal to drop is certainly a harmless activity, but hardly illustrative of seven years of horror such as the world never before has known, when men shall seek for death and shall not find it, when they shall gnaw their tongues in pain and cry for the mountains to fall upon them to hide them from the wrath of the One who sits upon His throne. The tuneful band which gayly precedes the royal monarch scarcely exemplifies the prospect of war and famine, of unparalleled death and destruction, of conflict with the great Beast and a martyr's grave at the end. Such illustrations, typical of posttribulational argument, do not illustrate but *hide* the truth. The only thing illustrated is the tendency of those who reject an "any moment" rapture, whether they be posttribulationalists or amillennialists, to spiritualize away any true significance to the Tribulation period, making it the equivalent of any other time of persecution endured by the people of God. By their clutching at such straws for their illustrations, the truth of imminency is not injured. It is rather vindicated.

The Scriptures couple with the exhortations to *look*, *watch* and to *wait* three distinct characteristics of the rapture which further indicate that this event must precede the Tribulation. For the Christian in this age, the coming of Christ is a "blessed hope," a "comforting hope," and a "purifying hope." Those who love the Lord are constrained to look for "that *blessed hope*, and the glorious appearing of the great God and our Saviour Jesus Christ" (Titus 2:13). They are not to sorrow over loved ones who are "asleep" as men which have no hope, for Christ shall raise them also, "and so shall we ever be with the Lord. Wherefore *comfort one another* with these words" (I Thess. 4:13-18). Indeed, the first comfort given to the bewildered disciples who beheld their Lord ascend into heaven and who then stood gazing into the skies, was: "This same Jesus . . . shall so come in like manner" (Acts 1:11). Previously, they had been comforted by the same hope: "Let not your heart be troubled . . . I go and prepare a place for you. And . . . I will come again and receive you unto myself" (John 14:1,3). This return of the Lord is later signified by John as a purifying hope when he said: "And every man that hath this hope in him *purifieth himself,* even as he is pure" (I John 3:3; *cf.* 2:28; II Pet. 3:14). Paul himself exhorted: "Let your moderation be known unto all men. The Lord is at hand" (Phil. 4:5).

There is not a little wrong with any system of interpretation which destroys the force of exhortations such as these, painting over the bright hues of the hope of an imminent return of Christ with the somber shades of impending Tribulation. Yet Frost introduces his chapter entitled "The Coming Posttribulational" with these words:

> My purpose now, will be to indicate that *the second advent,* according to the Scripture, *may not momentarily be expected,* as it will not take place until God has fulfilled certain large purposes of His and has brought to pass the last great testing and purifying of His people in the midst of furnace fires. As touching this last aspect of our subject, let me frankly admit that *it is not an inviting one,* for all of us shrink from suffering of any kind. But let me add that we must not evade prophetical presentations simply because they are *dark* and *sinister.*[80]

Now it is freely admitted that the Tribulation will be "dark and sinister." There is nothing attractive about the rider on the pale horse, called Death, who is followed by another called Hell, both of whom kill with the sword and with hunger, with death and the beasts of the earth. There is nothing attractive about the torment of hellish locusts, nor the vile rivers of waters turned to blood, nor the plagues of grievous sores upon the bodies of men, nor the great hail out of heaven nor the winepress of the wrath of almighty God!

Neither is there anything particularly attractive about a system of interpretation which substitutes the expectation of these trials for the blessed hope of God's people. It is not amiss to ask those who mistakenly would take the Church, Christ's bride, into the time of "Jacob's trouble," if for them these sorrows comprise the "blessed hope." Is it for death and hell and wrath that one must watch? Does the prospect of grievous sores and

---

[80] Henry W. Frost, *The Second Coming of Christ,* p. 202. Italics added.

hellish pestilence comprise the prelude to the "comforting hope" of the Church? Can the Christian fully rejoice in the knowledge of His soon coming, believing that those who share the rapture experience must first endure the greatest hour of torment in earth's history and that, at best, the privilege of rapture awaits *only the few* who escape the Beast's rage and a martyr's death? The pretribulational interpretation of prophecy may have some difficulties, but none so grave and far-reaching as these!

The very fact that the primary passage on the rapture of the Church (I Thessalonians 4:13-18) declares that this message is one of comfort, makes a posttribulational rapture incredible. Looking forward to seven years of intense suffering, the "purifying of His people in the midst of furnace fires," as Frost puts it, is a doubtful source of hope or comfort. It is of no solace or encouragement to tell suffering saints that far worse things are in store for them! There is all the difference in the world between looking for the Lord and looking for the Antichrist, the Devil's counterfeit Messiah. The plainly intended meaning of the Thessalonians passage is that saints should be *comforted* by the prospect of Christ's coming. There is not the slightest hint that distressed saints must endure still greater distress in the Tribulation. Rather than enter that period of anguish and torment, it would be *far better to die*, for to be absent from the body means to be gloriously present with the Lord (II Cor. 5:8). Death is a defeated enemy, having lost its sting by Christ's victory over the grave (I Cor. 15:54-57), but it is an enemy nevertheless, and as such is of doubtful comfort. Yet death is far to be preferred to the great Tribulation.

Only one position does honor to the Scriptures which speak of hope and comfort, and only one interpretation makes sense in view of the exhortations to look, wait, and watch for the Lord from glory. This is to understand and to be assured that God will not thrust His Church into the Tribulation period. Others may declare these prophetic portions "dark and sinister." Still others may try to harmonize life and death, blessing and cursing, comfort and the prospect of martyr blood, but the instructed Christian will encourage himself in the Lord and in the hope of His imminent, pretribulational return. With this hope, Christians will cheer and sustain one another, and in the light of such a hope they will serve Him, purifying their lives in order to have confidence and not be ashamed before Him at His coming.

> Oh joy! Oh delight! Should we go without dying:
> No sickness, no sadness, no pain, and no crying!
> Caught up in the clouds with the Lord into glory,
> When Jesus receives His own!

V. The Imminent Return: An Incentive to Holiness

Not only does the doctrine of the imminent return of Christ keep the promises and exhortations connected with His coming in their proper and Scriptural perspective, but also this truth is one of the greatest incentives to the Church for vitality of service and holiness of life. Charles R. Erdman has stated the case clearly:

> The fact of the Parousia has been, in all ages of the Church, a source of inspiration and cheer. Upon it are based exhortations to purity, fidelity, holiness, hope, and practically all the virtues of a Christian life.[31]

Gibbon, the author of the immense work, "The Decline and Fall of the Roman Empire," and himself a bitter critic of all things pertaining to Christianity, is forced to admit as he writes concerning the coming of Christ:

> Those who understood in their literal sense the discourses of Christ Himself were obliged to expect the Second and glorious Coming of the Son of Man before that generation was totally extinguished. . . . As long as for wise purposes this error was permitted to exist in the Church, it was productive of the most salutary effects on the faith and practice of Christians who lived in the awful expectation of that moment.[32]

It stands to reason that Christians, who believe that Christ may return and snatch away His own at almost any moment and that their reward at the Bema seat judgment is determined by their behavior and service before the rapture experience, have a tremendous ever-present incentive to live well pleasing in the sight of the Lord. Now it is true that the doctrine of the second coming is not the only (and may not even be the chief) guide

---

[31] Charles R. Erdman, "Parousia," *The International Standard Bible Encyclopaedia*, IV, 2251-F.

[32] Cited by I. M. Haldeman, *The History of the Doctrine of Our Lord's Return*, p. 17.

for Christian behavior. We have the whole Word of God and must be led by its plain and direct instructions for Christian living. Nevertheless, belief in the imminent return of the Lord does provide a tremendous incentive for right behavior, which may well explain why the Spirit gave the second coming promises in such a way that they have been appropriated by believers of every generation. It is the evil servant, who is persuaded in his heart: "My lord delayeth his coming," who proceeds to smite his fellow servants and to eat and drink with the drunken (Matt. 24:49-51). Such is the ill effect upon the behavior of men who do not look for the Master's return.

It has been seen that the coming of Christ for His own is a "purifying hope." In Titus 2:12, 13, looking for Christ is linked with living *soberly, righteously,* and *godly.* In I Thessalonians 5:6, the second coming issues in *sobriety*; James 5:7, 8, in *patience*; Philippians 1:10, in *sincerity*; I John 3:3, in *purity*; I Thessalonians 3:12, 13, in *brotherly love* and *holiness,* and so forth. Blackstone lists forty uses made of the doctrine of the second coming in the New Testament, and concludes:

> It is employed to arm the appeals, to point the arguments, and to enforce the exhortations. What is there more PRACTICAL in any other doctrine? [33]

The value of the truth of imminency in the life and outlook of the saints is well summarized by Brookes:

> If we heartily and practically believe that the Lord may come for His people at any moment, it must separate from the world, and kill selfishness, and blast the roots of personal ambition, and increase brotherly love, and intensify zeal, and deepen concern for the salvation of the lost, and give comfort in affliction, and put us in a state of preparedness for the great interview, like a bride arraying herself to meet her bridegroom. Oh, there is no truth in the Bible that can bring greater blessing to the soul, when received in the power of the Holy Ghost, but this blessing is largely hindered if we are taught to expect that our gathering together unto him lies beyond the appalling tribulation that shall come upon all the world.[34]

From the standpoint of a pastor or evangelist, the value of teaching and preaching the imminency of the return of Christ

[33] Blackstone, *op. cit.,* p. 181.
[34] Brookes, *op. cit.,* p. 157.

is plainly marked. Preach that the coming of Christ from glory is an imminent event, that it may transpire even in our day, and the people are blessed and hearts throb with a joyful anticipation. Teach that the Church must face the fires of the great Tribulation, and you send people back to their homes in despondency and dismay. Preach the posttribulational view to believers who hope and look for His return, and discord and heartache is sown in the midst. Multiplied examples that this is true could readily be cited. Teach the imminent return of Christ and people are renewed in hope and courage, despite the surrounding gloom.

It is important to remember that in teaching the doctrine of the second coming, the main theme and center of attraction must be Christ Himself, and not merely a human desire to escape Tribulation, or even the holy desire of gaining heaven. Christ is the central theme of the Bible. He is the One of whom prophets and apostles wrote and to whom angels and redeemed hosts ascribe praise and glory and honor. Christ, and Christ alone, must be our hope — not the glory of the coming, not the joy and benefit His coming will bring, but Christ alone! Our desire is unto Him. Our vision must be clarified and our ears must be attuned for the sight and sound of Him who promised, "Surely, I come quickly." The next thing for the Church, that long-promised event which is nearest and is therefore imminent, is *His coming*. May the hearts of all who read these lines be stirred afresh to answer, "Even so, come, Lord Jesus."

VI. Summary and Appeal

It is sincerely hoped that those who have pursued this argument for pretribulationalism thus far, including those who may not be in full agreement with the position herein presented, may be caused to rejoice in the *fact* and the *assurance* of Christ's coming. May personal spiritual values not be lost in the interest of drawing theological distinctions!

As for the discussion at hand, the arguments of Robert Cameron, as spokesman for the case against imminency, have been presented and, it is believed, fairly and conclusively answered. Not only did the early church look for the return of Christ, she was exhorted and encouraged by the apostles to do so. It is said that a common salutation between Christians in the early days of the Church was "Maranatha!" — Our Lord is coming! Predictions concerning the death of Peter or Paul, and so forth, never seemed to be a hindrance to first century belief in the Lord's imminent return, and most certainly have been no obstacle since that century.

It has been established from the New Testament that the coming of Christ was the hope of the early church, and to those Scriptures was added the weight of the constant exhortations to look, watch, and wait for the Lord's return. It has been seen that the posttribulation rapture theory is incongruous with the fact that the rapture comprises the blessed hope, the comforting hope, and the purifying hope of the Church. It has been demonstrated that Christ's coming for His own is to the Church one of her great incentives to holiness and service, and that this attains full force only when the rapture is viewed as pretribulational. Thus, the New Testament Scriptures widely testify to the truth and practical value of the imminent return of our Lord from glory. Since, then, Christians look for Christ and not for Antichrist, and for the joy of His coming rather than for Tribulation wrath and despair, let them be careful to serve Christ faithfully, trimming their lamps to shine more brightly, walking the path of this life with many an upward glance to Him whose coming is their hope.

> These days of toil — what matters it?
> So short this life of tears and pain;
> Lift up thy face! What dost thou fear?
> Thou hast not given thine all in vain.
> Soon thou shalt walk with Him in white;
> Who knoweth? Perhaps — tonight!

CHAPTER SEVEN

THE GOLDEN RULE OF BIBLICAL INTERPRETATION

There is no doubt about it. The basic issue in settling problems pertaining to the Bible is to determine the method of interpretation to be used. Without a clear and consistent guiding principle, the student of divine revelation will drift helplessly as a rudderless vessel upon a vast ocean, and will lose his way as an explorer who ventures too deep into an unknown labyrinth without a light or a compass. He will seek to unlock the mysteries of God, but shall not enter therein if he has no key.

The fact that God has given an extensive revelation of Himself and of His dealings with men, has caused such revelation to be recorded accurately in a Book, and has emplanted within His own a thirst for God and a Holy Spirit to minister to that need, argues indisputably that the Bible is meant to be understood by every Christian.

The idea that God's children should find their spiritual sustenance by feeding upon the Word of God is not new. This truth antedates the prophets. It is older than Moses. No doubt its earliest written expression is found in the testimony of Job, who said, "I have esteemed the words of his mouth more than my necessary food" (Job 23:12). It is repeated in the command of Christ to search the Scriptures (John 5:39) and in the exhortation of Paul to Timothy: "Study to show thyself approved unto God" (II Tim. 2:15). Even so difficult a book as the Revelation gives the promise of special blessing to those who keep its sayings (Rev. 22:7), and leaves the reader with the distinct impression that all of the Word of God is to be read with benefit by all of the people of God.

Yet, in spite of the express injunction to study the Word and the natural craving of the human heart for fellowship with God, the Bible is a highly neglected Book. Food there is in abundance, but the people do not eat. Even those who are members of the household of God through faith in Christ are, for the most part, spiritually impoverished. Why, then, these jaded appetites for the things of God? Why these careless attitudes and sinful lives? Why this sweeping indifference toward the one Book which can purify hearts, sweeten testimonies, and bring one the unsurpassed joy of the knowledge of the Lord?

Is not much of the answer in the realm of understanding? Inquire of the average church member, or press the man on the street for his answer, and he will invariably explain his ignorance of spiritual things on the basis that the Bible is so difficult he cannot understand it. Or, similarly, there are so very many different interpretations of the Bible that he is confused. How is he to know which interpretation is true or what he is to believe? Now these are not good excuses, to be sure. They will in no wise satisfy God or explain a wilful neglect of His precious Word, but do they not suggest the root difficulty of all Bible study? The very basic problem in understanding the Word of God is the matter of *interpretation*.

Even the most casual observer must be aware of the fact that Catholics, liberal or orthodox Jews, and Protestants of every theological stripe and denomination claim equally to find the basis for their convictions within the Bible. The following account of a conversation between a Christian minister and a Jew may serve to illustrate this situation, and point out that the key to the whole problem concerns the *literal* versus the *figurative* interpretation of that which has been written:

> Taking a New Testament and opening it at Luke 1:32, the Jew asked: "Do you believe that what is here written shall be literally accomplished,— The Lord God shall give unto Him the throne of His father, David; and He shall reign over the house of Jacob forever?" "I do not," answered the clergyman, "but rather take it to be figurative language, descriptive of Christ's spiritual reign over the Church."
>
> "Then," replied the Jew, "neither do I believe literally the words preceding, which say that this Son of David should be born of a virgin; but take them to be merely a figurative manner of describing the remarkable character for purity of him who is the

subject of the prophecy." "But why," continued the Jew, "do you refuse to believe literally verses 32 and 33, while you believe implicitly the far more incredible statement of verse 31?" "I believe it," replied the clergyman, "because it is a fact." "Ah!" exclaimed the Jew, with an inexpressible air of scorn and triumph. "*You* believe the Scripture because it is a fact; I believe it because it is the *Word of God*."[1]

I. Literal Interpretation and Its Significance

The science and art of interpreting the Scriptures of God is called *hermeneutics*. Its various laws have been designed to prevent the spread of false doctrine and to determine accurately the meaning of divine revelation. Correct hermeneutical procedures are of prime importance, for it is "little good for us if God has spoken, and we do not know what He has said."[2] However, since God has spoken and has placed His Word within the hands of men, they are duty bound to interpret it properly. This is for their own good, that they might be rightly related to God and know how to live acceptably before their fellow men.

It is not the purpose of this chapter to attempt a survey of the entire field of hermeneutics or to give even a brief digest of its laws. The purpose, rather, is to examine the one central, most basic issue of that science, namely: Is the Bible to be interpreted *literally*? Or, to state the problem from the opposing viewpoint: "To what extent is the *spiritualizing* of Scripture permissible, and what is the relationship between the literal method and the interpretation of prophecy?" With the Bible abounding in figures of speech and with prophecy full of symbolism, can the rule of literal interpretation be held consistently? For the serious Bible student, the importance of questions such as these would be hard to exaggerate. It will be demonstrated that the *sine qua non*, the one thing indispensable to the premillennial viewpoint — indeed, to orthodoxy itself — is that the Scriptures of God be understood in a normal, grammatical, literal fashion. It will then be demonstrated that both midtribulationalists and posttribulationalists violate this principle whenever their systems demand it, thus throwing open the door to a spiritualizing or allegorizing method which has fostered modernism and which

[1] W. E. Blackstone, *Jesus Is Coming*, pp. 20, 21.
[2] Bernard Ramm, *Protestant Biblical Interpretation*, p. 1.

violates a consistent premillennial theology. However, since even the most ardent literalist must recognize the presence of figures of speech in the Bible, and symbolic language in the prophetical sections, something of the application of the literal method to these areas will find a place in the discussion also. As a whole, the chapter purposes to forward the argument for pretribulationalism in two ways: by demonstrating the solid interpretive ground upon which it rests, and by illustrating the insecure footing of other schools of thought which would take the Church of Jesus Christ into or through the coming hour of trial.

A. Definition of Terms

When one speaks of the literal interpretation of the Bible, it is not to be assumed that every word and every line is to be taken at its "dead level" meaning. As indicated, some parts of the Bible are highly figurative; the Hebrew of the Old Testament in particular abounds with figures of speech and poetic descriptions of every kind. But when advocates of the literal method freely recognize this element in the composition of the Bible, it must be remembered that "this is no concession to those who deny the inspiration of the Word, since a figure or parable may be just as much inspired as a rigid syllogism."[3] Now it is true that one's understanding of the Bible is rendered more difficult because of the presence of figurative language, but this does not militate against the fact that the basic rule of Bible interpretation is literal interpretation. Special rules governing the use of figures of speech enable these to be interpreted in full harmony with the basic rule without any violation being involved.

To interpret the Scriptures *literally* means to interpret them *grammatically*, that is, according to the normal use of the words and the accepted rules of grammar. The terms *literal* and *grammatical* are essentially the same, and are generally used interchangeably. The same is true, on the other hand, of *figurative* and *tropical*. The first pair is derived from the Latin *litera* and from the Greek γράμμα, both denoting that the sense of the word is "according to the letter," the meaning it bears in its ordinary, primary usage.

---

[3] Charles Ellicott and W. J. Harsha, *Biblical Hermeneutics*, p. 142.

"But when a word, originally appropriated to one thing, comes to be applied to another, which bears some real or fancied resemblance to it, as there is then a τρόπος or turning of it to a new use, so the meaning is called *tropical*, or, if we prefer the Latin form of expression, figurative. . . ."[4] When the figurative meaning of a passage of Scripture is taken in preference to the ordinary "literal" meaning, the passage is often said to be *spiritualized*, the implication being that a deeper, more spiritual understanding of the passage has been reached by the recognition of the hidden figurative interpretation. While these terms, *literal* and *spiritual*, are not the best which could be used to designate the two methods of interpretation under investigation,[5] they have been utilized so widely that a change of terminology seems unwarranted at this point.

It is necessary to understand, however, that the advocate of literal interpretation does not exclude from his method the proper use of Biblical figures. Nor are the results of his exegesis to be considered in any respect less "spiritual" than those of men who are heavily inclined to follow a more figurative interpretation. Excessive spiritualization of the Sacred Text is likewise often called *allegorizing*, and whereas some have denied that the two

---

[4] Patrick Fairbairn, *Hermeneutical Manual*, p. 137.

[5] Craven appends this helpful note to Lange's commentary, *The Revelation of John*, p. 98: "No terms could have been chosen more unfit to designate the two great schools of prophetical exegetes than *literal and spiritual*. These terms are not antithetical, nor are they in any proper sense significant of the peculiarities of the respective systems they are employed to characterize. They are positively misleading and confusing. *Literal* is opposed not to *spiritual* but to *figurative*; *spiritual* is in antithesis on the one hand to material, on the other to *carnal* (in a bad sense). The Literalist (so called) is not one who denies that *figurative* language, that symbols, are used in prophecy, nor does he deny that great *spiritual* truths are set forth therein; his position is, simply, that the prophecies are to be *normally* interpreted (i.e. according to the received laws of language) as any other utterances are interpreted — that which is manifestly literal being regarded as literal, that which is manifestly figurative being so regarded. The position of the Spiritualists (so called) is not that which is properly indicated by the term. He is one who holds that whilst certain portions of the prophecies are to be *normally* interpreted, other portions are to be regarded as having a *mystical* (i.e. involving some secret meaning) sense. Thus, for instance, Spiritualists (so called) do not deny that when the Messiah is spoken of as "a man of sorrows and acquainted with grief," the prophecy is to be *normally* interpreted; they affirm, however, that when He is spoken of as coming "in the clouds of heaven" the language is to be "spiritually" (mystically) interpreted. . . . The terms properly expressive of the schools are *normal* and *mystical*.

are the same, others (like Allis[6]) freely admit their identity. The significance of this terminology will become more apparent in the discussion which follows.

B. *The Importance of the Literal Method*

The extent to which a man spiritualizes the Scriptures will largely determine his doctrinal position. The basic difference between a liberal and a conservative interpreter may be traced directly to the fact that the liberal spiritualizes away the obvious meaning of cardinal doctrines. Liberal, or reformed, Jews spiritualize the Messianic portions of the Old Testament and so have ceased to look for any literal Messiah. Indeed, some have held the absurd doctrine that the "nineteenth century is the Messiah."[7]

By the same failure to accept the literal sense of the plain testimony of Scripture, some interpreters have stolen away the foundations of every cardinal Christian doctrine and left the Church to drift into liberalism and infidelity. The difference, then, between the liberal and the conservative evangelical lies squarely in the system of hermeneutics employed. Conservatives find that the literal interpretation of the Bible is a natural corollary to the truth of verbal inspiration, and the denial of the one constitutes a definite step toward the denial of the other. Most liberals are emphatic about their denial of both.

Moreover, the basic difference between the amillennial and the premillennial viewpoints is essentially whether one is to interpret the kingdom prophecies figuratively or literally. That this is the main issue has been clearly pointed out by Albertus Pieters:

> The question whether the Old Testament prophecies concerning the people of God must be interpreted in their ordinary sense, as other Scriptures are interpreted, or can properly be applied to the Christian Church, is called the question of the spiritualization of prophecy. This is one of the major problems in Biblical interpretation, and confronts everyone who makes a serious study

---

[6] Oswald T. Allis, *Prophecy and the Church*, p. 18: "Whether the figurative or 'spiritual' interpretation of a given passage is justified or not depends solely upon whether it gives the true meaning. If it is used to empty words of their plain and obvious meaning, to read out of them what is clearly intended by them, then *allegorizing* or *spiritualizing* is a term of reproach which is well merited." Italics added.

[7] Blackstone, *op. cit.*, p. 22.

of the Word of God. It is one of the chief keys to the difference
of opinion between Premillenarians and the mass of Christian
scholars. The former reject such spiritualization, the latter employ it; and as long as there is no agreement on this point the
debate is interminable and fruitless.[8]

Amillennialist Rutgers also sees that this is the main issue,
when he observes: "I regard their interpretation of Scripture as
the fundamental error."[9] Likewise, Adolf Harnack admits that
the premillennial system is rooted in the literal method of interpretation, when he notes that in recent times a "mild type of
'academic' chiliasm has been developed from a belief in the verbal inspiration of the Bible."[10] From these citations, it is evident
that one's millennial position is determined directly by the interpretative method he employs.

In like manner, this issue is raised even within the ranks of
premillennial men in the familiar controversy between covenant
and dispensational theology. That the dispensationalists are
more consistent in adhering to those principles of interpretation
which have sheltered them from liberalism's errors and amillennial vagaries can be seen from the following terse analysis of
the covenant position:

> The major objections to the covenant view can only be stated.
> Covenant theology is built upon a spiritualizing method of inter-
> preting the Scriptures. In order to make the various covenants
> of the Old Testament conform to the pattern of the covenant of
> grace it is necessary to interpret them in other than their literal
> sense. . . .
>
> The covenant theory allows no place for literal fulfillment of
> Israel's national and racial promises and either cancels them on
> the ground that Israel failed to meet the necessary conditions, or
> transfers them to the saints in general. From the dispensational
> and literal standpoint, this is misappropriation of Scriptural
> promises. . . .
>
> The dispensational view of Scripture taken as a whole is far
> more satisfactory as it allows for the literal and natural interpreta-
> tion of the great covenants of Scripture, in particular those with
> Abraham, Moses, David, and with Israel as a whole, and explains

[8] Albertus Pieters, *The Leader*, September 5, 1934, as cited by Gerrit H.
Hospers, *The Principle of Spiritualizing in Hermeneutics*, p. 5.
[9] William H. Rutgers, *Premillennialism in America*, p. 263.
[10] Adolf Harnack, "Millennium," *Encyclopaedia Britannica*, 14th edition,
XV, 497.

them in the light of their own historical and prophetical context without attempting to conform them to a theological concept to which they are mostly unsuited.[11]

Further comment is hardly necessary to underline the importance of determining which method shall be the basic rule for the interpretation of Scripture. Nor is there any issue more pertinent to this analysis of the time of the rapture in relation to the Tribulation. There are very few problems raised in connection with the study of prophetic subjects where one can avoid asking himself the question: "Is this passage to be taken literally?" It remains to be demonstrated that one of the fundamental weaknesses of both the midtribulational and posttribulational systems is their marked propensity to spiritualize away the purpose and severity of the Tribulation period.

II. HISTORICAL BACKGROUNDS

It is hardly necessary here to trace the long history of Biblical interpretation from early Old Testament days until this present hour. Such a study, although not without interest and value, would be lengthy and extraneous to the present purpose. However, a brief historical survey of the backgrounds of the two hermeneutical methods being discussed may well clarify some of the issues involved in the modern conflict, and grant the necessary perspective for a wise treatment of the eschatological problem under consideration.

A. *The Allegorical School of Interpretation*

The allegorizing method of interpretation had its origin with the Alexandrian Jews of about two centuries before Christ, although it is claimed that the Greeks applied the method to their own religious poets at a still earlier date. At least, the Alexandrian Jews were the first to apply the principle to the Old Testament Scriptures as a whole. Farrar notes that "by a singular concurrence of circumstances, the Homeric studies of Pagan philosophers suggested first to Jews and then, through them, to Christians, a method of Scriptural interpretation before unheard

[11] John F. Walvoord, "Amillennial Soteriology," *Bibliotheca Sacra*, CVII (July-September, 1950), 287, 289.

of which remained unshaken for more than fifteen hundred years."[12]

It is generally conceded that Aristobulus (160 B. C.) was the first of the Alexandrian school. It was his conviction that Greek philosophy was borrowed from the Old Testament, and that, by reading between the lines, all the tenets of the Greek philosophers (especially Aristotle) are to be found in Moses and the prophets.

> In answer to a question of Ptolemy, Aristobulus told him that Scripture was not to be literally understood. The "hand" of God means His might; the "speech" of God means the organization and immovable stability of the world. The "coming down" of God has nothing to do with time or space. The "fire" and the "trumpet" of Sinai are pure metaphors corresponding to nothing external. The six days' creation merely implied continuous development. The seventh day indicates the cycle of hebdomads which prevails among all living things — whatever that piece of Pythagorean mysticism may chance to mean.[18]

Philo, next, contended that every passage of Scripture has two meanings: a literal and an allegorical. The literal was for the weakminded, while the allegorical was for the advanced.[14] "To him the Bible furnished not so much a text for criticism as a pretext for theory. Instead of elucidating the literal sense he transforms it into a philosophical symbol."[15] In these early Jews is clearly indicated the heart of the allegorical method: the literal sense of the text of Scripture is regarded merely as the vehicle which carries, to those who look for it, the more spiritual and profound sense. Philo held to the most rigid views of the inspiration of Scripture, but when he came to their explanation and application, he became vague and contradictory, much like allegorizers of this present day.

With conservative interpretation, an allegory is a legitimate figure of speech, found occasionally in the Bible as in the famous allegory of Paul recorded in Galatians 4:21-31. But here, the literal is in no wise set aside, for Abraham and Sarah are real people, and Jerusalem and Sinai are literal geographical

---

[12] F. W. Farrar, *History of Interpretation*, p. 135.

[13] *Ibid*, pp. 130, 131.

[14] Ramm, *op. cit.*, p. 23.

[15] Farrar, *op. cit.*, p. 139.

locations. Far different is the method of the allegorizers, who give an entirely new and different meaning to accounts which were never intended to be allegorical. Farrar comments:

> St. Paul borrows an incidental illustration from the methods of the Rabbis, without for a moment disturbing the literal sense; Origen borrows from heathen Platonists and from Jewish philosophers a method which converts the whole of Scripture, alike the New and Old Testament, into a series of clumsy, varying, and incredible enigmas. Allegory helped him to get rid of Chiliasm and superstitious literalism and the "antitheses" of the Gnostics, but it opened the door for deadlier evils.[16]

Among Christians, the allegorical method was unknown through the first century and well until the end of the second. Pantaenus (180 A. D.) was the first to adopt the system, followed by Clement, who said that the literal sense of Scripture was milk, and the allegorical, meat. It remained for Origen to fashion the teachings of the New Testament as a whole into the allegorical mold, and it is to him that this form of interpretation, among Christians, is generally traced.

> Origen was the first to lay down, in connection with the allegorical method of the Jewish Platonist, Philo, a formal theory of interpretation, which he carried out in a long series of exegetical works remarkable for industry and ingenuity, but meagre in solid results. He considered the Bible a living organism, consisting of three elements which answer to the body, soul, and spirit of man, after the Platonic psychology. Accordingly, he attributed to the scriptures a threefold sense: (1) a somatic, literal, or historical sense, furnished immediately by the meaning of the words, but only serving as a veil for a higher idea; (2) a psychic or moral sense, animating the first, and serving for general edification; (3) a pneumatic or mystic and ideal sense, for those who stand on the high ground of philosophical knowledge. In the application of this theory he shows the same tendency as Philo, to spiritualize away the letter of scripture . . . ; and instead of simply bringing out the sense of the Bible, he puts into it all sorts of foreign ideas and irrelevant fancies. But this allegorizing suited the taste of the age, and, with his fertile mind and imposing learning, Origen was the exegetical oracle of the early Church, till his orthodoxy fell into disrepute.[17]

In the hands of Origen the entire body of Christian doctrine suffered, and because of his method of interpretation the funda-

---

[16] Farrar, op. cit., p. 196.
[17] Philip Schaff, History of the Christian Church, p. 521.

mentals of the faith were weakened to the point that Origen's views were branded as heretical. It hardly needs to be said, therefore, that most of the Reformers rejected the validity of the allegorical method. Among these, and in no uncertain terms, spoke Luther. Said he:

> An interpreter . . . must as much as possible avoid allegory, that he may not wander in idle dreams. . . . Origen's allegories are not worth so much dirt. . . . Allegories are empty speculations, and as it were the scum of Holy Scripture. . . . To allegorize is to juggle with Scripture. . . . Allegories are awkward, absurd, invented, obsolete, loose rags . . . mere spangles and pretty ornaments, but nothing more.[18]

Certainly, the unsavory history of the allegorical method will cause thoughtful Bible students to look with suspicion upon all theological schemes that display allegorizing tendencies. In the words of Farrar, "allegory by no means sprang from spontaneous piety, but was the child of Rationalism which owed its birth to the heathen theories of Plato. It deserved its name, for it made Scripture say something else . . . than it really meant."[19] Ramm sums up the weakness of this school of interpretation when he says:

> The great curse of the allegorical method is that it obscures the true meaning of the Word of God. There are no controls on the imagination of the interpreter, so the Bible becomes putty in the hands of each interpreter. As a result different doctrinal systems could well arise within the sanction of the allegorical method, yet no way exists for breaking the deadlock within the allegorical system. The only retreat is to the literal meaning of the Bible. . . .[20]

With the Reformation, all but the most liberal theologians rejected the allegorizing method for most areas of Christian doctrine. It remained for Augustine to modify the spiritualizing principle *by applying it to the interpretation of prophecy only,* while holding that the historical and doctrinal sections should be interpreted by normal "historical-grammatical" literal methods.

> This was a decided improvement as far as theology as a whole was concerned, even if it left the millennial issue unsolved and at the mercy of the allegorical school. Because of the weight of

18 Farrar, *op. cit.,* p. 328.
19 *Ibid.,* pp. 193, 194.
20 Ramm, *op. cit.,* p. 24.

Augustine in other major issues of theology where he was in the main correct, Augustine became the model for the Protestant Reformers who accepted his amillennialism along with his other teachings.[21]

This should be sufficient, at this point, to introduce the fact that many modern interpreters, while basically conservative because of their adherence to the literal method, nevertheless cling to the allegorizing principle in the area of eschatology. It is not diffcult to demonstrate that such a concession to the interpretive methods of liberalism is entirely unwarranted.

B. *The School of Literal Interpretation*

It was one of the distinct advantages of the Jewish people "that unto them were committed the oracles of God" (Rom. 3:2). To them pertained the covenants and the promises, the giving of the law, and the service of God (Rom. 9:4), but for generations the law was slighted and broken, and for many years of captivity and exile the Scriptures which they possessed lay hidden and ignored in the dust of a broken temple. But while yet in the land of exile, a young priest by the name of Ezra, a direct descendant of Aaron, "prepared his heart to seek the law of the Lord, and to do it, and to teach in Israel statutes and judgments" (Ezra 7:10). In person, he led a group of Jews from the land of their captivity back to Jerusalem and rejoiced that the Lord God had permitted a remnant to escape, giving "a little reviving in our bondage" (Ezra 9:8). Later, after the rebuilding of the city walls, directed by Nehemiah and the register of the remnant returned from captivity, the people "spake unto Ezra the scribe to bring the book of the law of Moses. . . . So they read in the book in the law of God distinctly, and gave the sense, and caused them to understand the reading" (Neh. 8:1, 8). Here, then, was Bible exposition, the purpose of which was to seek the reformation of Israel by calling the people to the obedience of the words and commandments of God. "We may, accordingly, date the beginning of formal exposition of the Scriptures in the time of Ezra."[22]

---

[21] Walvoord, "Amillennialism As a Method of Interpretation," *Bibliotheca Sacra*, CVII (January-March, 1950), p. 43.

[22] Milton S. Terry, *Biblical Hermeneutics*, p. 32.

Ezra is generally considered the first of the Jewish interpreters, and the ultimate source of the Jewish-Palestinian-Hyperliteralist school. The Jews, in the Babylonian Captivity, soon replaced their native tongue with the Aramaic. This created a gap between their minds and the language of the Scriptures. It was the task of Ezra to give the meaning of the Scriptures from the Hebrew to the Aramaic, and this is generally considered the first case of Biblical hermeneutics in history.[23]

Under the scribes of the period following Ezra and Nehemiah, much of the value of this noble beginning was lost, for they set about to make a hedge around the Sacred Writings by setting a value to the very letters of the law, counting their letters and guarding the manuscripts with a zeal which bordered on fanaticism.

The net result of a good movement started by Ezra was a degenerative-literalistic interpretation that was current among the Jews in the days of Jesus and Paul. The Jewish literalistic school is literalism at its worst. It is the exaltation of the letter to the point that all true sense is lost. It grossly exaggerates the incidental and accidental and ignores and misses the essential.[24]

Farrar gives a digest of Rabbinic tradition, and sums up the period by saying: "The age of the Rabbis lost itself in worthless trivialities, and suffocated the warmth and light of Scripture under the white ashes of ceremonial discussion, yet in preserving the text of the Old Testament it rendered services of inestimable value."[25]

Literal interpretation, although employed by devout students of the Scripture down through the intervening years (Matt. 2:4,5; Luke 2:29-32, etc.), is next seen as a school in the Syrian School of Antioch. It is said to be the first Protestant school of hermeneutics, and was founded by Lucian and established by Diodorus of Tarsus (393 A.D.). It was "a school of literalists with little or no patience for allegorism, and it produced the most competent Bible expositors for a thousand years. . . . In many of their interpretations they anticipated modern expositors by more than a millennium. It was tragic that such good sense was lost to the Church."[26]

[23] Ramm, op. cit., p. 27.
[24] Ibid., p. 28.
[25] Farrar, op. cit., p. 15.
[26] Ramm, op cit., p. 29.

The literal interpretation of the Scriptures next came to the front with the Protestant Reformation, which was in a real sense a hermeneutical revolt before it was either theological or ecclesiastical.[27] With this revolt, the mind of Germany and other European countries tore itself away from the bonds of ignorance and superstition imposed by the Roman church. Priestly absolution of sin was exchanged for the Biblical doctrine of justification by faith, and carnal tradition was exposed by appealing to the Holy Scriptures as the only infallible revelation of God. The great commanding voice which directed this remarkable revolution was that of Martin Luther, who, in October of the year 1517, nailed his famous theses to the door of the Schlosskirche of Wittenberg, and five years later performed one of the most valuable services of his life when he gave his translation of the New Testament to the German people "in the simple, idiomatic, and racy language of common life, and enabled them to read for themselves the teachings of Christ and the apostles."[28] Although Protestants may not fully agree with all that Luther said and did, it must be admitted that his teachings and his stand against carnal ecclesiasticism formed the charter of Christian liberty for all Protestant people and for all who exalt the Word of God above the word of man. It is therefore highly significant to examine that system of interpretation which taught Luther his doctrines and fired him for his task.

Luther rejected allegorizing interpretations in no uncertain terms. Farrar outlines four distinct stages to Luther's spiritual advance, and indicates that only in the fourth stage did he gain a clear grasp of the principles which all Reformed and Lutheran churches have since steadily recognized in the proper interpretation of Scripture. Among these principles are:

(1) The supreme and final authority of Scripture, apart from all ecclesiastical authority or interference.

(2) Not only the supreme authority, but also the *sufficiency* of Scripture.

> I ask for Scripture, and Eck offers me the Fathers. I ask for the sun, and he shows me his lanterns. I ask, "Where is your

[27] *Ibid.*, p. 30.
[28] Terry, *op. cit.*, p. 47.

Scripture proof?" and he adduces Ambrose and Cyril. . . . With all due respect to the Fathers, I prefer the authority of Scripture.[29]

(3) The literal sense of the passage to be interpreted is the true sense. "The literal sense of Scripture alone is the whole essence of faith and Christian theology. . . . Each passage has one clear, definite, and true sense of its own. All others are but doubtful and uncertain opinions."[30] In taking this stand Luther was, like other Reformers, setting aside the dreary fiction of the "fourfold sense" of the former era, and was, in this respect, in advance of Erasmus, who thought that the Holy Spirit meant the words of Scripture to be taken in various senses. Said Luther:

> I have observed this, that all heresies and errors have originated, not from the simple words of Scripture, as is so universally asserted, but from *neglecting* the simple words of Scripture, and from the affectation of purely subjective tropes and inferences. In the schools of theologians it is a well-known rule that Scripture is to be understood in four ways, literal, allegoric, moral, anagogic. But if we wish to handle Scripture aright, our one effort will be to obtain *unum, simplicem, germanum, et certum sensus literalem.*[31]

Other principles outlined by Luther included the rejection of the allegorical method, faith in the perspicuity (the sufficient clarity) of Scripture, and the right of private judgment.

No doubt the greatest exegete and theologian of the Reformation was John Calvin. Farrar says that in spite of his "hard expressions and injurious declamations," he is one of the greatest interpreters of Scripture who ever lived.[32] His vigorous intellect, his logical mind, his classic training and wide knowledge, his deep religious feeling, his careful attention to the entire scope and context of every passage, and the fact that he has commented on almost the whole of the Bible, these and many other traits combine to make him tower above the great majority of men who have written on the Holy Scriptures.

Like Luther, Calvin rejected the fourfold sense and the whole scholasticism system of allegorical interpretation. He was a literalist and a grammarian, and in the preface of his commentary

---

[29] Farrar, *op. cit.*, p. 327.
[30] Farrar, *op. cit.*, p. 327.
[31] *Loc. cit.*
[32] *Ibid.*, p. 343.

on the book of Romans, he laid down his golden rule, that "it is the first business of an interpreter to let his author say what he does say, instead of attributing to him what we think he ought to say."[33] Whether or not we agree with all of Calvin's conclusions, we must at least recognize that he rejected the spiritualizing method of interpretation. His authoritative voice speaks strongly in favor of the truth and historicity of the literal method. "Let us know then," said he, "that the true meaning of Scripture is the natural and obvious meaning; and let us embrace and abide by it resolutely."[34] Schaff, an historian, writes his own conclusion in the matter:

> Calvin is the founder of grammatico-historical exegesis. He affirmed and carried out the sound hermeneutical principle the Biblical authors, like all sensible writers, wished to convey to their readers — one definite thought in words which they could understand. A passage may have a literal or a figurative sense; but cannot have two senses at once. The Word of God is inexhaustible and applicable to all times, but there is a difference between explanation and application, and application must be consistent with explanation.[35]

In defense and support of the literal principle as the basic rule of Biblical interpretation, many voices yet clamor to be heard. Scholars, both ancient and modern, rise up to add their testimony. Before passing from this investigation of historical backgrounds, several more representative scholars should be allowed to speak, with as little added comment as possible.

Maresius declares:

> A single sense of Scripture, viz., the grammatical is to be allowed, and then it may be expressed in any terms whether proper, or tropical and figurative.[36]

Speaking on the interpretation of the "first resurrection" of the Revelation, Dean Alford, Greek scholar, writes:

> I cannot consent to distort words from their plain sense and chronological place in the prophecy, on account of any consideration of difficulty, or any risk of abuses which the doctrine of the millennium may bring with it. Those who lived next to the

---

[33] *Ibid.*, p. 347.
[34] John Calvin, *Commentary on the Epistle of Paul to the Galatians*, p. 136, cited by Hospers, *op. cit.*, p. 11.
[35] Cited by Hospers, *op. cit.*, p. 12.
[36] *Ibid.*, p. 11.

apostles, and the whole Church for 300 years understood them in the plain literal sense; and it is a strange sight in these days to see expositors who are among the first in reverence of antiquity, complacently casting aside the most cogent instance of consensus which primitive antiquity presents. . . . If the first resurrection is spiritual, then so is the second, which I suppose none will be hardy enough to maintain: but if the second is literal, then so is the first, which in common with the whole primitive Church and many of the best modern expositors, I maintain, and receive as an article of faith and hope.[37]

Probably the most factual and voluminous written defense of the premillennial system is the three volume *Theocratic Kingdom*, by George N. H. Peters. One of the early and fundamental propositions of this work concerns the adherence to the literal, grammatical interpretation of Scripture:

We unhesitatingly plant ourselves upon the famous maxim of the able Hooker: "I hold for a most infallible rule in expositions of the Sacred Scriptures, that where a literal construction will stand, the furthest from the letter is commonly the worst. There is nothing more dangerous than this licentious and deluding art, which changes the meaning of words, as alchemy doth, or would do, the substance of metals, making of anything what it pleases, and bringing in the end all truth to nothing." The primitive Church occupied this position, and Irenaeus . . . gives us the general sentiment when . . . "he says of the Holy Scriptures: that what the understanding can daily make use of, what it can easily know, is that which lies before our eyes, unambiguously, literally, and clearly in Holy Writ." . . . Thus Luther remarks: "I have grounded my preaching upon the literal word; he that pleases may follow me, he that will not may stay."

When employing the word "literal," we are to be comprehended as also fully acknowledging the figurative sense, the beautiful ornaments of language; we cordially accept all that is *natural* to language itself, its naked strength and its charming adornments, but object to *additionally* forcing on it a *foreign* element, and enclosing it in a garb that hides its just proportions.[38]

Silver remarks that there is safety in literal interpretation, in the faith of that childlike simplicity which takes the Scriptures to mean what they say. He quotes the statement of Seiss:

[37] Dean Alford, *Greek Testament*, IV, 732, 733.
[38] George N. H. Peters, *Theocratic Kingdom*, pp. 47, 48.

Christ knew what He wished to say, and how to say what He meant, and I find myself bound to understand Him to mean just what He says.[39]

Feinberg mentions two more scholars who have a right to be heard before bringing this section to a close:

Sir Isaac Newton with great insight and foresight foretold that about the time of the end certain men would arise who would devote their energies to prophetic studies and "insist upon their literal interpretation in the midst of much clamor and opposition." Probably as valuable a testimony as any that could be offered was given by Dr. Horatius Bonar. When speaking of the results of fifty years of the study of prophecy, he concluded with the statement that first of all, he had gained assurance as to the authority and inspiration of the Scriptures. Secondly, he felt more certain than ever that the literal interpretation of the Word is the best. Said he: " 'Literal, if possible,' is, I believe the only maxim that will carry you right through the Word of God from Genesis to Revelation."[40]

In this study, the allegorical method of interpretation has been traced from its origin among pagan philosophers, through the vague interpretations of Philo and the Alexandrian Jews, to Origen, who first applied the principle to the entire body of Christian doctrine, and whose writings were publically condemned and burned because of the heresy into which he fell.

The school of literal interpretation has been traced from the interpretative methods of Ezra, through the excessive literalism of the Rabbinic period, through the school of Lucian, unto the clear commitment of the Protestant Reformation and the acknowledgment of leading Christian scholars since that day. It is self evident which school of interpretation has best served God and honored the Word which He has commited unto men.

III. THE RIGHT USE OF THE LITERAL METHOD

An old Scotch minister said that in visiting his congregation he found three great evils: a misunderstanding of Scripture, a misapplication of Scripture, and a dislocation of Scripture. It is hardly necessary to note that these three hermeneutical evils are still present, and if one is to judge by what he hears from

[39] Joseph A. Seiss, *Last Times,* p. 116, cited by Jesse Forest Silver, *The Lord's Return,* pp. 212, 213.

[40] Charles L. Feinberg, *Premillennialism or Amillennialism* (first edition), p. 51.

modern pulpits and reads from the religious press, the clergy is even more sadly afflicted than those to whom they minister. The idea is abroad that the Bible is no longer the final word in matters pertaining to redemption and Christian ethics. Under constant attack is the principle of literal interpretation, and widespread is the philosophy that the Bible need not mean exactly what it appears to say. The Gospel must be "released from literal bondage to old categories and set free to do its work in modern terms of thought." So says modernist Harry Emerson Fosdick.[41] "Christian liberty," says M. G. G. Sherer, "knows how to distinguish between Scripture and Scripture, between the chaff and the wheat."[42] "The hue and cry is: 'The enslaving legalism of the letter!' We will not have this 'fetter,' this 'handicap,' these 'clamps and chains,' this 'straight jacket' of literalism put on us."[43]

The fact is entirely ignored that Bible believing Christians do not hold themselves slaves to the letter of the law, nor do they require that every single passage be interpreted literally in the strictest sense of the term. Most certainly do they recognize types and figures of many kinds in the structure of the Word of God. That they do not allow their imagination and interpretation to run wild is not due to a literalistic "straight jacket," but to a simple recognition of and an obedience to certain basic hermeneutical principles. They believe that correct processes alone bring correct results, and that loose and erroneous interpretations stem from wrong processes and dishonor the God who gave the Scriptures.

The proof that adherents to the literal method do not, as they are so often accused, slavishly follow the method to the point of disparaging the presence of figurative language in the Bible is clearly seen in the way they have formulated orderly rules for the interpretation of Biblical figures and symbols. The literalist rightfully contends that the presence of figurative language does not injure the literal method. Figures are a normal ingredient of any language, and particularly do they abound in the Hebrew of the Old Testament, while prophetic portions are

---

[41] Cited by Th. Engelder, *Scripture Cannot Be Broken*, p. 372.
[42] *Ibid.*, p. 373.
[43] *Ibid.*, p. 375.

noted for their profusion of types and symbols. The literalist contends, rather, that even a figure of speech must be framed out of basic literal elements such as persons, places, and events, and that within the figure is a literal concept the author intended to make more graphic by the use of that figure. In this way, figurative language has a rightful place in the literal method of interpretation, and the presence of figures of speech in the Bible in no wise justifies a departure from that method.

The two outstanding arguments against the consistent use of the literal method are those of the liberals, who contend that the presence of Biblical types and figures make literal interpretation an impossible theory, and of the amillennialists, who argue that the literal method cannot apply to the prophetic areas of the Bible, even though the principle be valid for the historical and didactic portions. On the supposed strength of these objections, the amillenarian allegorizes those Scriptures which teach a glorious, visible reign of Christ upon the earth for one thousand years, while the liberal carries the allegorizing principle into the more cardinal areas of the Christian faith to such an extent that no doctrine is entirely safe from attack or outright denial.

This twofold assault upon the literal method demands a response and an answer. It is, however, hardly within the scope of this present discussion to pursue these issues further, as vital as they are to the defense of the evangelical, premillennial heritage. It is not the purpose of this chapter to give a complete argument for literal interpretation, but to introduce this vital principle to the reader with enough by way of historical backgrounds and contemporary significance to indicate the danger involved when men unwittingly turn to the spiritualizing method in order to sustain some favored theological theory. We are about to see that both midtribulationalists and posttribulationalists are guilty of most flagrant departures from the literal method, particularly in respect to the severity of the coming Tribulation, and that only upon the demands of their systems. If such a departure can be demonstrated, the very weakness of the opposing systems will strengthen the argument for pretribulationalism. Those who believe the coming of Christ will precede the time of His wrath stand alone in their literal interpretation of the true nature of the Tribulation period. In this respect, pretribulationalists alone are consistent premillennialists.

No doubt there will be readers sufficiently interested in this foundation stone of premillennial interpretation to want to probe more deeply into its methods and problems. May such readers be referred to Section Two, "Literal Interpretation, Figurative Language and Prophecy," which shows how our interpretive method applies to the whole range of Bible prophecy. There are three major parts to that discussion:

(1) *The problem of interpreting figurative language.* In this section, the figures of speech of the Bible are classified and illustrated, with rules given for their interpretation in accord with the literal method.

(2) *Special rules for the interpretation of prophecy.* The spiritualizing principle, once admitted into the area of prophetic interpretation, may readily spread to other areas of doctrine and endanger the faith. The peculiar problems raised in the interpretation of prophecy call for specialized rules within the literal method, but do not warrant a complete departure from that method after the fashion of the amillennialists.

(3) *The symbolism of the book of Revelation.* It is demonstrated that the symbols of the book do not hide its meaning but illustrate it, and even in this much disputed portion of the Word of God, symbolism, with its attendant problems, presents no adequate cause for any departure from the basic method of literal interpretation. The study of prophecy offers few more interesting and significant issues than these. It is believed that the discussion [in appendix] will bring to the attention of the reader sufficient evidence to vindicate the literal method at those very points where it is confronted with the harshest criticism. Important literature bearing on the subject will be indicated, while some original material will be set forth with the hope that it may make some small contribution to premillennial doctrine. This present chapter, however, must now return to deal more directly with the issue of the rapture and the Tribulation.

IV. LITERAL INTERPRETATION AND THE TIME OF THE RAPTURE

Having seen that the spiritualizing, allegorical method of interpretation stands historically and doctrinally condemned, it now is necessary to see that there is a very definite application of these issues to the problem of the time of the rapture.

The basic philosophy of amillennialism is that there will be no literal earthly Millennium; all the Scriptures which promise such are spiritualized and made to apply to the program of God in the present age. The Scriptures which pertain to the Tribulation suffer the same treatment.

> Reformed theologians who follow the amillennial interpretation usually minimize and spiritualize the time of tribulation preceding the second advent, particularly in such passages as Revelation 6-19. Amillenarians often find the tribulation being fulfilled in contemporary events, and interpret Revelation 6-19 as history. While interpreting the second advent literally, they spiritualize the tribulation.[44]

Although posttribulationalists do not completely spiritualize the Tribulation, it is not difficult to detect a strong inclination in that direction, as the following citations will indicate. They minimize its severity and try to tone down its judgments to the point that the Tribulation is no longer a unique period of unprecedented wrath, but merely another period of persecution upon the people of God and that no more severe than previous times of suffering. McPherson writes:

> Surely the Church has been permitted to pass through many other periods of suffering and anguish so acute that if those who went through them should have to go through the Tribulation, they would not feel they had missed anything during their first period of trial.[45]

Posttribulationalists labor to prove that a carnal church needs the purging and purifying fires of the great Tribulation, and then must labor to protect her from the worst of its wrath. Reese avers:

> It is possible to reject the pleasing delusion of a rapture some years before the Day of wrath, without accepting the error that the Church will partake of the wrath. It never seems to occur to these writers that, immediately before the wrath of the Day

---

[44] Walvoord, "Amillennial Eschatology," op. cit., p. 11.
[45] Norman S. McPherson, Triumph Through Tribulation, p. 22.

of the Lord falls, God can call His saints to Himself, without the necessity of an additional advent a generation earlier.[46]

Likewise, it never seems to occur to posttribulationalists the inconsistency of having the Church both purged and protected at the same time, or that wrath starts at Revelation 6:16 and not at 19:15, or that if God did not want His Church to go through this time of wrath He would have taken them out of the way before its commencement. In Fraser's opinion:

> Much of the scene in Revelation has to do only with God's judgments upon rebellious man and there is no Scriptural reason to believe that God's people will be directly involved in that suffering. *The Great Tribulation is not judgment, but persecution.*[47]

Without going into the fact that Fraser fails to say what the Church is doing in the midst of God's judgments at all, let it be noticed that here is a clear example of posttribulational attempts to water down the severity of the Tribulation, if not to change its nature altogether. "The great Tribulation is not judgment, but persecution"! Let the reader give thoughtful attention to the Old Testament prophecy of the Day of the Lord in the light of that statement, then read slowly and thoughtfully Revelation 6-19, and he will be forced to conclude that either posttribulationalists are guilty of flagrant spiritualization in these sections, or else that they wrest the Scriptures and ignore large portions of it in the interest of their theory.

John Scruby goes so far as to say that the Tribulation may be a "punishment for the sinner," but that it will be a "privilege for the saint":

> Yet when it comes to the Great Tribulation . . . to be found in it will be . . . an opportunity for greater achievements in "the good fight of faith," and therefore for the attaining of still greater rewards. . . . Yet I dare to say that if the belief that the Church will go into the Tribulation is an error, it is a beneficial error.[48]

To Scruby, there are various "small rivers of trial" that flow across the path of the Christian, and the Great Tribulation is

---

[46] Alexander Reese, *The Approaching Advent of Christ*, p. 212.

[47] Alexander Fraser, *Is There But One Return of Christ?* p. 63. Italics added.

[48] John J. Scruby, *The Great Tribulation: The Church's Supreme Test*, pp. 132, 133.

merely "the swelling of the Jordan."[49] He says that "it is an honor to be in the great tribulation,"[50] although most Christians would be disposed to decline such an honor. Again, it is affirmed that the Great Tribulation will have nothing to offer in excess of the sufferings of this present age:

> If one may believe one-half the stories which have come out of Soviet Russia, then many of the saints there have already had to face as "great tribulation" as any saint will be called upon to face during the Great Tribulation itself.[51]

All of this is nothing more or less than the flagrant spiritualization of Scripture and is in direct contradiction to passages such as Matthew 24:21, 22: "For then shall be great tribulation, such as was not since the beginning of the world to this time, no, nor ever shall be. And except those days should be shortened, there should no flesh be saved. . . ."

Posttribulationalists accept the literal interpretation of the Bible for the fundamentals of the faith, and the literal interpretation of prophecy as the necessary basis of their premillennial hope, which is most commendable. But when it comes to the Tribulation, all has gone to pieces, all has changed, spiritualization has become the order of the day, and this only in the interest of saving a theory which cannot be made to harmonize with the literal interpretation of Tribulation passages.

Nor can *midtribulationalists* escape the same indictment. When they place the time of the rapture in the eleventh chapter of the book of Revelation, largely on the basis of a surface similarity between the trumpet of that chapter and another found in I Corinthians 15, and then cooly proceed to spiritualize five and one half chapters filled with the direct judgments of God, they are equally guilty. A quick review will illustrate in graphic form the nature of the judgments which must precede the sounding of the seventh trump: peace taken from the earth — famine — Death and Hell, with power to kill the fourth part of the earth — heavens darkened and earth quaking — men hiding in the caves of the earth and crying for the mountains to fall upon them to

[49] *Ibid.*, p. 137.
[50] *Ibid.*, p. 142.
[51] *Ibid.*, p. 150.

hide them from the awful wrath of God—a multitude of
martyred saints—hail and fire mingled with blood—trees and
grass burnt up—the third of the creatures in the sea destroyed—
many dying because of the waters which are made bitter—sun,
moon, and stars smitten—hellish locusts who torment men with
their stings for five months—men seeking death, and not able
to find it—a godless host which kills the third part of those who
yet live—murders, fornication, and theft—seven thunders, with
judgment too terrible to utter—two witnesses, who devour their
enemies with fire and who smite the earth with drought and
plagues—waters turned into blood—seven thousand men slain
in one earthquake. Could any judgments be more devastating?
Could any torments be more fearful? Could any fact be more
obvious, that here is the awful heart of the Great Tribulation,
so designated at Revelation 7:14? Consider now the doctrine
of midtribulationalism, as set forth by one of its leading advocates
(italics are added):

> We will find that the Trumpets, at least the last three, reach
> only *to* the Great Tribulation. . . . Moreover, at the sounding
> of the seventh the Church is caught away to escape that wrath.
> Nothing, therefore, in these six Trumpets can rightfully and
> Scripturally be considered "wrath" or "judgment," *however closely
> they may resemble it.*[52]

> If, as we have been constrained to believe for many years, in
> Matt. 24:7 our Lord Jesus invisioned the World War of 1914-18
> with its accompaniments and the forces that lead on irresistibly
> into the Great Tribulation, then we are confirmed beyond question
> in our position, namely, that the *Seals series does its work while
> the Church is still here; and the Seals are not part of the Tribu-
> lation,* but that they lead on into it; that the seals are *not judg-
> ments, but man's folly* brought to its fearful finality.[53]

> These experiences, though so very severe, are *not judgments.*
> Commentators invariably call them Trumpet Judgments. God
> never does, and He ought to know.[54]

> The first half of the week, or period of seven years, was a
> *"sweet" anticipation* to John, as it is to them; under treaty pro-
> tection, they will be *"sitting pretty,"* as we say. . . . We know of

[52] Norman B. Harrison, *The End: Re-thinking the Revelation,* p. 105.
[53] *Ibid.,* p. 94.
[54] *Ibid.,* p. 104.

no justification for thinking of the first half of Israel's future "week" as being anything but "sweet" to them.[55]

This is most certainly spiritualization! This business of making sweet what is bitter — ordinary what is unique — mere persecution what is judgment — a privilege what is a curse — beneficial, enjoyable, and desirable what is clearly the wrath of Almighty God — this twisting and wrenching of Scripture in the vain attempt of making it say something other than what it does say — this is a return to the methods of Plato and Origen and constitutes a dangerous departure from conservative Biblical interpretation, which is literal interpretation. It is a departure which endangers all for which fundamental, premillennial men stand. Liberalism spiritualizes cardinal doctrines; amillennialism spiritualizes the Millennium; midtribulationalism and posttribulationalism spiritualize the Tribulation — but the root error throughout is the same. Nor is it impossible for a premillennial conservative, having once given up his basic defense of literal interpretation, to retreat to posttribulationalism, then to amillennialism, then on to liberalism in other areas. There are men who have trodden this pathway, although fortunately, most are arrested in their course and do not reach the apostasy which is the natural outgrowth of the principle of interpretation they have adopted.

It is most probable that some of the brethren who minimize the severity of the Tribulation judgments do so in the enthusiasm of their argument without being consciously aware of having fallen into the snare of the spiritualizing method. Nevertheless, when a doctrinal point which involves the blessed hope of the Church is under consideration, and when men are forced to turn in defense of their theory to the interpretive methods of the enemies of the faith, it is time to call a halt and issue a word of warning. When men fail to see that the Church of Jesus Christ differs in its essential nature, as well as its eschatology, from ancient Israel — when they miss the obvious fact that the Tribulation is primarily a time of God's wrath upon the enemies of His Son — and when they explain away every

[55] *Ibid.*, pp. 111, 112. Harrison makes the eating of the "little book" (Rev 10:9, 10) symbolic of the two halves of the Tribulation period, the first part of which is *"enjoyable* and *desirable"* (p. 111).

divine promise to save the Church from wrath to come — these are errors of important magnitude.

But, when they fail to let the Scriptures speak and reverse the meaning of what God has been pleased to reveal concerning the coming time of trouble — when, in a word, they resort to the process of spiritualizing the Bible whenever and wherever their systems demand it — then they are involved in a clear and dangerous departure from that very method of interpretation upon which their conservative, premillennial faith is founded.

Whether historically or in the laboratory of twentieth century exegesis, pretribulationalism alone is consistent fundamentalism and consistent premillennialism, for it alone is based on a clear commitment to the vital keynote doctrine — the golden rule of Biblical interpretation — which is literal interpretation.

CHAPTER EIGHT

THE PARTIAL-RAPTURE THEORY

The fourth chapter of II Timothy is a favorite portion of the Word of God with any minister of the Gospel who takes seriously his high calling. Those who would lead men into a knowledge of the Lord are solemnly charged to "preach the word," the direct implication being that they are to be occupied primarily with a positive declaration of the Scriptures of God. However, when error arises in the church, the minister must also stand ready to "reprove, rebuke, exhort with all longsuffering and doctrine." In order that the believers might "henceforth be no more children . . . carried about with every wind of doctrine" (Eph. 4:14), he must speak the truth in love, and when the need arises, "exhort and rebuke with all authority" (Titus 2:15). Only by so doing will purity of doctrine and order in the churches be maintained.

Since an important part of the presentation of truth consists of a rebuke and correction of error, and since one line of interpretation is not fully established until at least the principle tenets of opposing schemes have been refuted, it is now necessary to turn from the more positive approach to an examination of the three alternate theories concerning the time of the rapture. It is sincerely hoped that *truth* will be spoken with *love,* remembering that all these with · whom a difference of opinion is found are brethren in Christ, not a few being faithful preachers of the saving grace of God. When the need arises to mention by name individuals with whom the author differs, it must be remembered that *this work is in no sense an attack upon their person.* It is the *doctrinal position,* and not the *personality,* that is in view. The sincerity of these men is not disputed, but when their views permeate the Church and rend the unity of the body of Christ, it is high time to take a stand for the truth which includes the vigorous denunciation of error.

Under consideration in this chapter is the view that only zealous Christians, faithful to the Lord and watching for His return, will be caught up before the Tribulation. Weaker brethren, who are not actively *waiting* for Christ, or who, because of the manner of their lives, are not counted as *overcomers*, will be forced to go through part or all of its purifying fires. This *"partial-rapture"* theory attempts to distinguish between devout Christians and worldly Christians who neither are ready nor are anticipating the call of the Bridegroom. Adherents include G. H. Pember, J. A. Seiss, D. M. Panton, and many other great and good men. They contend that all believers "go home on the same train," but not "all on the first section." Some, like Bengel, hold that there will be a series of raptures, believers being caught up as they become ready. Illustrative of the partial rapture view in general are the words of Hubbard:

> Are you, reader, among the lukewarm whom the Lord will spew out of His mouth to pass through the tribulation, or the loyal who are faithfully performing the tasks and utilizing the privileges of grace, thus showing yourself "worthy to escape it?"
> . . . The great tribulation is the chastening fires, over which the Lord sits as the refiner of silver, watching, guarding these imperfect, unfit, unworthy but loved ones, until the dross has been purged and they are ready to reign with Him and to "offer unto the Lord an offering in righteousness" (Mal. 3:3).[1]

Such a view has been adopted by a small minority of the Church on the basis of verses which seem to condition rapture on "readiness." I John 2:28 states that some will be ashamed before Christ at His coming. Hebrews 9:28 seems to imply that Christ will appear only to those who "look for him." Philippians 3:11 and I Corinthians 9:27 seem to imply that Paul wondered at his own status at the time of the resurrection. Luke 21:36, taken by itself, seems to imply that only the worthy will escape the Tribulation. Do these verses justify belief in a partial rapture? There are some major objections to such a conclusion.

The partial rapture theory conditions the privilege of rapture

[1] W. H. Hubbard, *Does the Church Go Through the Great Tribulation?* pp. 18, 22.

upon human works, and as such is a co-mingling of *legalism* with *grace.* It must never be forgotten that salvation stems from the death of Christ, the merits of which are applied to the sinner by God's grace and not in answer to human works or supposed worthiness (Eph. 2:8,9). Moreover, the Christian is to live under the same grace principle: "Sin shall not have dominion over you: for ye are not under the law, but under grace" (Rom. 6:14). The grace of God not only "bringeth salvation," but also teaches us to "live soberly, righteously, and godly in this present world" (Titus 2:11,12). Grace, not fear of the Tribulation, is the motive and the power for right conduct. Paul writes the Galatians: "Are ye so foolish? having begun in the Spirit, are ye now made perfect by the flesh?" (Gal. 3:3).

Underlying the entire life in grace is the fact that the Christian possesses no merit in himself, nothing at all which might possibly fit him for the presence of God. Nor is such merit necessary, for the work of Christ on Calvary is a finished redemption (John 17:4; 19:30), sufficient to make even His enemies a new creation, unblamable in His sight (II Cor. 5:17; Col. 1:20-22). Even the present continuation of salvation depends, not on us, but on His resurrection life (Rom. 5:10), while its consummation likewise rests upon Christ's work rather than upon man's faithfulness (Phil. 3:20,21). The salvation spoken of in I Thessalonians 5:9,10 is a future deliverance, referring to the believer's change and translation at the Lord's coming.

Adding human responsibility to the grace principle in any aspect of salvation borders dangerously upon the Galatian heresy of attempting to live under law, while in reality, having entered into life by grace alone.

> The last chapter of the story of salvation is to be written by the pen of unmerited grace, as truly as the first. When Jesus comes to save us out of this world, and to save our bodies from their present condition, it will not be because of His grace and our merit; nor, the grace of God and our faithfulness; nor the grace of God and our watchfulness. It is pure, unmixed grace that brought salvation in the past (Titus 2:11), and it is the same unmixed, unmerited grace that will bring salvation in the future (I Peter 1:5, 13).[2]

[2] H. P. Barker, "A Partial Rapture," *Prophetic Digest,* February 1952, pp. 229, 230.

D. M. Panton himself conditioned readiness for the coming of Christ upon "spiritual maturity," by comparing believers to wheat, ripening gradually for the harvest:

> Earth-removal depends, for the servant of God, on spiritual maturity, as exactly and as inevitably as harvesting is dated, not by the farmer, but by the grain. . . . Wheat which never ripens would be a blasted field; for the Church of God cannot be a blighted crop; sooner or later, all mature, all are reaped, all are gathered into the Heavenly Garner.[3]

But if translation depends upon spiritual maturity, on readiness, or upon "watching," it then becomes necessary to ask: Just *how ready* must the believer be? What degree of spiritual maturity will God require? What degree of perfection must the believer attain before he is assured a place in the rapture? Must his watching be an eager expectancy or merely a general attitude of heart? Needless to say, these questions are not answered by the proponents of this theory. In fact, one is made to wonder who shall enter heaven at all when Christ comes for His own, for, on the basis of Philippians 3, Pember writes that Paul, "devoted as he was to his Master . . . had as yet no absolute certainty of attaining to the First Resurrection."[4]

> His aim was to be numbered with those blessed and holy ones who shall have part in the First Resurrection (Rev. xx. 6). But we must note, that he had, at the time, no certain assurance that he would compass the desire of his heart. . . . Just before his death, however, it was graciously revealed to him that he was one of the approved. . . . But, at the time when he was writing to the Philippians, he could not speak with such confidence.[5]

If spiritual maturity be the condition for translation at the rapture of the saints, and if the Apostle Paul himself had "no certain assurance" of attaining to the first resurrection, who then will be worthy? All those who hold the partial rapture theory assume that they are among the "ready,"[6] but if rapture is so conditioned upon personal merit, who else would dare make such a claim? Is it not more desirable, and far more Scriptural,

---

[3] D. M. Panton, "The Removal of the Church from the Earth," *The Dawn*, December 15, 1927, p. 393.

[4] G. H. Pember, *The Great Prophecies of the Centuries*, p. 211.

[5] *Ibid.*, p. 210.

[6] As one has well said: "Partial rapturists expect to be taken up in 'bunches,' but I have never met one yet who did not expect to be taken up in the first 'bunch.' "

to rest solely upon the grace and the goodness of God for a place in the host of translated saints, rather than on the doubtful merit of human faithfulness?

Marsh relates the following experience:

> Some years since, I was talking with our beloved and esteemed brother, Dr. Neatby, about the subject before us, and I asked him, "Doctor, do you expect to be saved from the great tribulation on the ground of your personal holiness, moral fitness, or watchfulness?" He replied in his characteristic way, "I am quite sure that if I am saved from the great tribulation by virtue of any personal fitness, I shall go through it." Yes, and so says every one who knows anything of his own unworthiness, and his own unfitness as seen in the light of the holiness of God. Grace, grace, grace, and grace alone must be the basis of our being in the glory with Christ.[7]

It is commendable that the adherents of the partial-rapture theory do stress holy living, and it is most certainly true that the expectation of Christ's return is a purifying hope (I John 3:3), but this in no wise warrants mingling human works with divine grace as the grounds of resurrection privilege. None were more carnal than the Corinthian Christians, but they were, nonethe-less, part of the temple of God (I Cor. 3:16; 6:19). To them, Paul wrote of the coming of Christ: "We shall not all sleep, but we shall *all* be changed" (I Cor. 15:51). Had the words of the Gospel song been written in their day, the Corinthian believers would surely have joined in singing:

> 'Twas grace that taught my heart to fear,
>   And grace my fears relieved;
> How precious did that grace appear
>   The hour I first believed!
>
> Thro' many dangers, toils and snares,
>   I have already come;
> 'Tis grace hath bro't me safe thus far,
>   And *grace will lead me home.*

The partial-rapture theory confuses the Biblical doctrine of rewards. Hubbard declares "that to escape the great tribulation and be able to stand before the Son of Man, are not

[7] F. E. Marsh, *Will the Church or Any Part of It Go Through the Great Tribulation?*, p. 30.

unconditioned gifts of love or grace, but rewards and privileges
for those who are accounted worthy of them."[8] A contributor to
The Dawn magazine writes: "We believe that the frequent
exhortations in the Scriptures to watch, to be faithful, to be
ready for Christ's coming, to live Spirit-filled lives, all suggest
that translation is a reward."[9]

No one will deny that the Bible promises a reward to him
who runs well the Christian race (I Cor. 9:24, 25) and adorns
the walls of his life with gold, silver, and precious stones (I
Cor. 3:11-15). When one is saved, the Lord asks that person
to live for Him, and it is typical of His grace that He should
reward him for doing what normally should be expected in a
redeemed life. But it must be emphatically denied that the
privilege of translation is in itself a reward for godly living.
According to II Corinthians 5:10, the time of reward is not
at the translation of the saints, but when they stand before
what is generally known as the Bema Seat of Christ. "For
we must all appear before the judgment seat of Christ; that
every one may receive the things done in his body, according
to that he hath done, whether it be good or bad." In that day,
the believer's works must stand the test of fire (I Cor. 3:13),
not the test of translation. It is highly significant, also, that
among the rewards which are promised believers there are *five
crowns*: the *crown of life* (Rev. 2:10; James 1:12), the *crown
of rejoicing* (I Thess. 2:19; Phil. 4:1), the *incorruptible crown*
(I Cor. 9:25), the *crown of glory* (I Peter 5:4), and the *crown
of righteousness* (II Tim. 4:8). Paul wrote concerning this last
crown:

> Henceforth there is laid up for me a crown of righteousness,
> which the Lord, the righteous judge, shall give me at that day:
> and not to me only, but unto all them also that love his ap-
> pearing.

Other crowns are designated for those who have served well
and suffered much for Christ, but the crown of righteousness is
especially designated as the reward for those who have loved
His appearing. Partial-rapturists are entirely right in anticipating

---

[8] Hubbard, *op. cit.*, p. 25.
[9] Ira E. David, "Translation: When Does It Occur?" *The Dawn*, Nov. 15,
1935, pp. 358, 359.

rewards for the virtues they enumerate, but in the clear light of Scripture they are *entirely wrong* in saying that the privilege of translation is itself that reward. God has designated how and when He will reward His saints, and it seems advisable not to tamper with that program.

A partial-rapture implies a partial resurrection. In considering the merits of the partial-rapture viewpoint, some attention must be given to the many generations of Christians whose bodies sleep in death. According to the Bible, at the rapture the dead in Christ rise first; living believers are then translated and together they meet the Lord in the air. (I Thess. 4:16, 17). But, if the rapture experience is selective for those who live, it would seem that justice and equity must demand that the resurrection of believers from the dead be selective also. Not all of these were, in life, counted among the overcomers, nor did they all cultivate the upward look. If the lives of the living are to be surveyed to determine who shall be purged by fiery Tribulation and who shall enter with joy into the presence of the Lord, then there must be among the dead some selection made to determine who shall merit prior resurrection.

Such, however, is not the case, for Paul writes plainly that "we shall *all* be changed," when "the dead shall be raised incorruptible" (I Cor. 15:51, 52). *All* those which "sleep in Jesus" will God bring with Him (I Thess. 4:14). The only qualification for these who are to rise first is that they be "in Christ" (I Thess. 4:16). Since, then, it is futile to argue that only a choice group from among the Christian dead will be in the rapture, is it any the less futile to argue that the contrasting group of living believers who will be caught up will be a small, select company chosen on the basis of their works? God does not deal capriciously with His people. The only designation for either group is that they be "in Christ."

There are other problems involved. As it has been seen, the partial-rapture theory teaches that many of God's people must pass through the fires of the Great Tribulation to purge their dross and make them fit for the presence of Christ. This is exactly the same, in principle, as the Roman doctrine of purgatory, except that this "protestant purgatory" would be on earth, and before death. Allis comments on this point:

> The doctrine of a partial rapture practically necessitates the acceptance of the Romish doctrine of purgatory. For it must be admitted that many Christians have died, to all appearances, in the imperfect state which we are told will characterize those who at the rapture are left on earth to be purified by the great tribulation. So, unless it is to be held that in the very article of death they have or will have endured purifying or chastening sufferings equivalent to those which will be endured by those who are left behind at the time of the rapture, the argument that these latter need to pass through the tribulation falls to the ground, unless the doctrine of purgatory is accepted. There is no warrant for such teachings. The dying thief was in all probability a very imperfect and a very ignorant believer. But the Lord said to him, "Today thou shalt be with me in paradise."[10]

Since "watching" is said to be one of the main requirements for early rapture, what then of the many Christians who have never been taught to look for Christ's appearing? As Waugh remarks:

> There have been long periods when the Maranatha watchword was scarcely ever mentioned in the churches. There are multitudes of Christians in the world today who have never been taught on the subject, and who know next to nothing about it. Others have only heard it ridiculed or caricatured by ignorance, and the idea of this being the true hope of the Church has never once occurred to them. Will their loving Lord punish their ignorance, and any unwatchful or worldly spirit to which it may lead, in such a special manner as this? Is *this* the *only* inconsistency that will exclude Christians from the blessedness of the Rapture, and expose them to the awful perils of "the great tribulation" that will follow it? I have not so learned Christ or His word.[11]

The partial-rapture theory is contrary to I Thessalonians 4:13-18, the primary passage on the rapture of the Church, in a number of particulars. Paul does not say that those who are to be caught up will be "we who are watching," or "we who are overcomers," but "we which are alive and remain" — clearly designating the whole body of living believers. So also, it is not the "dead who watched" that arise first, but the entire body of "dead

[10] Oswald T. Allis, *Prophecy and the Church*, pp. 221, 222.
[11] T. Waugh, *When Jesus Comes*, pp. 108, 109.

in Christ." Nor do the living saints, even those of "spiritual maturity," have any precedence over the dead in Christ. Even more important, this is a message of encouragement and comfort (v. 18), whereas, if the majority of the Church were in dread danger of entering the Tribulation, the apostle might better have written, "Wherefore *warn* one another with these words." Indeed, rather than being a message of comfort, the news of Christ's return would be to the majority of the Church a message of *alarm*. Far better to be dead at His coming and enter immediately into the presence of the Lord, unless it be admitted that the resurrection of the dead is partial also. But such a view, as it has been seen, cannot be tolerated.

A partial rapture discredits the vital Pauline doctrine of the unity of the body of Christ. Since the Scriptures are so explicit at this point (Eph. 2:14-3:6; 4:1-6, 12-16; Col. 3:11, 15, etc.), here is an objection of no mean proportions. Yet it is true that if only certain believers are caught up, while some go through part of the Tribulation and others are not raised until the end, or even until the Great White Throne, the important truth of the body of Christ as an organic unity is set aside. It is said that Pember was forced by the very logic of his position to claim that the body of Christ was not the whole Church at all, but just those who were surrendered to God.

The Scriptures set forth the vital relationships which the true Church sustains to the Lord Jesus Christ in seven metaphors, or comparisions, which illustrate the dependence of believers upon their Saviour and their vital union with Him.[12]

(1) Christ is the Shepherd, and we are the sheep of His pasture (John 10:1-18).

(2) Christ is the Vine; we are the branches, joined to the vine and expected to bear fruit (John 15:1-8).

(3) We are stones in the building of God, of which Christ is the Chief Cornerstone (Matt. 16:18; Eph. 2:19-22; I Pet. 2:5; Heb. 3:6).

(4) Christ is our High Priest, and we are a kingdom of priests engaged in the services of sacrifice (Rom. 12:1), worship (Heb.

[12] L. S. Chafer, *Systematic Theology*, IV, 54-143, gives a complete and heart-warming analysis of these relationships.

13:15), and intercession (I Tim. 2:1; Heb. 10:19-22; I Pet. 2:5-9).

(5) Christ is the Last Adam, and we are the new creation (I Cor. 15:22, 45; II Cor. 5:17; Eph. 2:10, 15).

(6) Christ is the Bridegroom, and we are His bride (Rom. 7:4; II Cor. 11:2; Eph. 5:25-33; Rev. 19:7, 8).

(7) Christ is the Head, and we are the members of the "body of Christ" (I Cor. 12:13; 12:27; Eph. 5:30; Col. 1:18).

These relationships (it hardly needs to be added) are true of every believer in Christ, and are theirs, not by virtue of good works, but solely because of the infinite goodness and the sovereign grace of God. Any theory which discredits one or more of these relationships finds itself in the position of disputing the Word of God.

According to John 14:1-3, Christ has gone to prepare a place for us, for it is His will that "where I am, there ye may be also." When these words were first spoken, Christ had just finished rebuking Peter, foretelling his defection (John 13:36-38), yet there was no hint given that Peter might be excluded from the rapture privilege. According to I Corinthians 12:12, 13, *all* Christians are members of one body through the baptism of the Holy Spirit. According to Ephesians 5:25-27, Christ shall present to Himself a glorious Church, without spot or wrinkle or blemish. He sanctifies and cleanses it by the washing of the water of the Word, not by fiery trial and Tribulation. From Ephesians 2:4-7, it is seen that, positionally, the Church is already sitting together in heavenly places in Christ Jesus with a standing before God as perfect as though its members had never sinned. These key verses all indicate that there will be no rending of the body of Christ when He comes for His own. Revelation 19:7-9 and 21:9 reveal the bride of Christ, the Lamb's wife, arrayed in the fine linen of God's righteousness, joined to Christ at the marriage supper of the Lamb.

A partial rapture can hardly be made to fit the joy and the dignity of that glad day, but comes perilously close to offering to the Lord Jesus Christ a dismembered body and a partial bride. Surely the bride of Christ, born of the Spirit, washed in precious blood, made perfect by His righteousness, and espoused to Christ as a pure virgin, needs not to be plunged into earth's worst hour as the preliminary of her wedding feast and hour of greatest glory! None, in themselves, are worthy of salvation, or rapture, or a place in the body and bride of Christ, but in Him, all who believe have been made worthy. Even as we are caught up, "we shall all be changed," all earthly dross being purged away as we behold His face in righteousness. Weak and sinful in this life, but in the ages to come, put on display before all the universe as a trophy of "the exceeding riches of his grace in his kindness toward us through Christ Jesus" (Eph. 2:7).

Partial-rapturists accommodate Scriptures to suit their theory. Although the sincerity of their Scripture interpretations is not questioned, many of the verses appealed to must be unnaturally forced before they can be made to support their viewpoint.

Matthew 24:42 gives the command: "Watch therefore: for ye know not what hour your Lord doth come." Similar is the exhortation of Luke 21:36: "Watch ye therefore, and pray always, that ye may be accounted worthy to escape all these things that shall come to pass." Comparable is the parable of Mark 13:34-37. But the primary reference in these passages is not to the Church at all, but to Israel in the Tribulation (Matt. 24:29, 30). Christian watchfulness is based on verses such as I Thessalonians 5:6 and Titus 2:13, and these say nothing about being accounted worthy to escape.

I Corinthians 15:23 — "Every man in his own order"— has been used to bolster their position. However, although τάγμα, "order," means *a band*, as of soldiers, and implies that there will be a certain "order of succession"[13] in the resurrection of all the righteous dead since Adam, there is no hint here that the Church will form more than one of those "bands." The resurrection of the Church will be one of the successive stages which make up the total resurrection of the righteous (see pp. 240-41). The resurrection of Christ secures that of His people, even as the "firstfruits" are the guarantee of the completed harvest, but this does not intimate that the Church herself will be divided.

Hebrew 9:28: ". . . unto *them that look for him* shall he

[13] Charles Hodge, *An Exposition of the First Epistle to the Corinthians,* p. 326.

appear the second time without sin unto salvation," has also been made to condition rapture upon "looking for Christ." The writer is speaking of three appearings of Christ on behalf of the saints. In this instance, instead of using the term "believer," or "church," he utilizes a descriptive phrase for the whole body of Christ which reflects the normal, natural attitude of God's people, distinguishing them from those who have not appropriated the benefits of the first coming. There is no thought here of a second group of believers, those who "do not look for Him." It is true that many will be ashamed at His coming (I John 2:28) and will lose the crown of righteousness, but being "ashamed" does not mean that they will be left behind when the others are caught up. Likewise, no one is bidden, in Philippians 3:20, to look for the Saviour. It is said that Christians *do look*, for such an attitude is the normal sequel to conversion, in spite of the fact that many do not attain unto it.

Philippians 3:11: "If by any means I might attain unto the resurrection of the dead," has been made to imply that even Paul expressed some doubts as to his right to a place in the rapture. The answer to this proposal lies in the context. Paul had been reviewing his past life as Saul, the enemy of the early church and persecutor of Jesus Christ. Now he states his highest spiritual aspirations as the servant of Christ, but in words which reflect true humility in the light of his former unworthiness, and also the urgent need of self-watchfulness lest he stumble and be disapproved (I Cor. 9:27). Again, it needs to be asked, "If Paul was not sure of his place in the resurrection, who then can be?" Yet Pember writes of this heavenly calling:

> Paul unmistakably affirms that these high privileges are a prize and not a gift, and are accessible only by the gate of the First Resurrection — a gate through which, after all his sacrifices and labours and sufferings for Christ, he was not yet absolutely sure that he would be permitted to pass.[14]

Though some may sincerely believe that the rapture will be selective, and that the Great Tribulation is to be "the purifying, fitting fires for those who, though believing in Christ, remain carnal and babes,"[15] the vast majority of God's people will see

---

[14] Pember, *op. cit.*, pp. 211, 212.
[15] Hubbard, *op. cit.*, p. 37.

clearly that when the body of Christ is finally complete, then Christ will come for His own. That coming will unite the body with its resurrected Head, and will be a time of union rather than a time of rending within the body. They will remember the words: "He that hath this *hope* in him purifieth himself, even as he is pure" (I John 3:3) and will not permit the words to be distorted to read: "He that remembereth this *threat*." In spite of their many imperfections and their utter failure to love His appearing as they should, they will retain their confidence that the blessed hope is *their hope*. With joy, and without fear, they will join in the expectation of Denham Smith, who wrote:

> And this I shall find, for such is His mind,
> He'll not be in glory and leave me behind.

CHAPTER NINE

THE MIDTRIBULATION RAPTURE THEORY

Less objectionable than the posttribulation rapture theory, although still with very little to commend it, is the view which claims the Church will endure the first half of the Tribulation period, to be raptured at some midpoint, generally associated with the sounding of the seventh trumpet of Revelation 11. According to this view, the Church not only is promised Tribulation, the ease and worldliness of its members demand that she shall be purged and purified. Passages which indicate that believers shall be exempt from this hour of trial are not recognized, although it is seen that the Church shall be spared anything characterized as wrath. Rapture at Revelation 4 is denied; the event is placed rather in Revelation 11, symbolized by the resurrection of the two witnesses. The cloud of Revelation 11:12 is said to be a reference to the presence (*parousia*) of Christ, and the seventh trumpet is identified with the "last trump" of I Corinthians 15.

In common with the pretribulational position, midtribulationalists generally identify the restrainer of II Thessalonians 2 as the Holy Spirit, and insist on the removal of the Church before the revelation of the Antichrist.

In common with posttribulationalism, they deny the imminent return of Christ, insist that the Church is seen on earth after Revelation 4:1, and affirm that the Church needs at least part of the Tribulation's purifying fires.

In a real sense, midtribulationalism is a compromise view between the other two alternate positions and lacks the strength of either, meanwhile being involved in additional problems peculiar to its own prophetic system. The slender number of its advocates and the dearth of convincing midtribulational literature both put a large question mark over the validity of the viewpoint. Nevertheless, its major claims demand some investigation and the more important difficulties involved must be observed.

I. THE CHURCH AND THE TRIBULATION

A. *The Church Is Promised Tribulation*

Midtribulationalists press this argument in the support of their views, making an erroneous assumption that, since persecution is the lot of the believer in this age, Tribulation must be his portion in the period to come.

> Persecution, whether during the reign of Antichrist or in the present time, is (speaking generally) the allotted portion of those who will live Godly, and such suffering during the time of tribulation is therefore quite in harmony with the character and calling of the Church of Christ, and the teaching of the New Testament.[1]

This same writer expresses the viewpoint of his school when he asks: "What is the difference in character between persecution now, and the probably more intense persecution yet to come, since *both* are for the testimony of Jesus?"[2] Since this question is sufficiently answered in the second chapter of this investigation, it need not prolong the discussion at this point, save to reiterate the fact that the Tribulation to come differs from even the most intense persecution of this age in source, in degree, and in the basic purpose for which it is sent. Moreover, the Church has been expressly promised deliverance, as demonstrated earlier from many Scriptures, even though this author makes the amazing assertion: "We search in vain for *one single text* containing a promise either expressed or implied that the Church will be taken away prior to the Tribulation"![3] To keep the record straight, here are several: Romans 5:9; I Thessalonians 1:10; 4:17,18; 5:4,9; II Thessalonians 1:6-9; II Peter 2:5-9; and Revelation 3:10,11.

B. *The Church Needs to be Developed and Purged*

The imperfections of the Church are readily admitted, but tribulationalists have erred in maintaining that the wrath to come includes sanctifying values:

---

[1] H. W. H., *The Church and the Great Tribulation*, p. 24. Here is a midtribulationalist writer who places the rapture in Revelation 7, following the sixth seal.

[2] *Ibid.*, p. 41.

[3] *Ibid.*, p. 19.

Thus the Great Tribulation will be a true mercy to the Lord's people by fully developing and sanctifying them for their heavenly destiny and glory.[4]

Pretribulationalists believe that conviction of sin and progress toward godliness is available through the work of the Spirit (John 16:8) and the application of the Word of God (John 15:3). There is no Tribulation in view, nor is it needed, in the vital truth of Ephesians 5:25-27:

Husbands, love your wives, even as Christ also loved the church, and gave himself for it; that he might sanctify and cleanse it with the washing of water by the word, that he might present it to himself a glorious church, not having spot, or wrinkle, or any such thing; but that it should be holy and without blemish.

The untruthfulness of the statement hardly needs comment, when it is maintained that pretribulationalism "involves that the utmost measure of unfaithfulness or carnality in a believer puts him in no peril of forfeiting the supreme honour of rapture or of having to endure the dread End Days."[5]

Pretribulationalists believe, rather, that the last living generation of believers has no more need of purging than other generations which, through death have gone immediately into the presence of the Lord. A Church, cleansed by the blood of Christ and made both perfect and complete in Him, needs no "Protestant purgatory" to fit it for heaven (Rom. 8:1). Chapters 2 and 7 more fully develop this important theme.

C. *The Church Will Be Removed Before Wrath Is Poured Out*

With this statement, all three groups would largely agree. The difficulty comes in determining the *time* when wrath is poured out. Posttribulationalists are forced to say that there is no *wrath* until the catching up of the saints on the day of the appearing of Christ, that is, not until Revelation 19:15. Midtribulationalists insist that nothing before the outpouring of the vials can be called *wrath*, as indicated in Revelation 16:1. The following illustrates that view:

I do not believe that the Church will go through any part of that period which the Scripture specifically designates as the wrath of God, but I do believe that the abomination of desolation will be a specific signal for a hasty flight followed by a very brief

---

[4] G. H. Lang, *Firstfruits and Harvest*, p. 44.
[5] *Ibid.*, p. 37.

but a very terrible persecution, and that followed very quickly by the rapture of the Church *preceding* the outpouring of the vials of the wrath of God.[6]

Pretribulationalists insist that the entire period covered by Revelation 6:1-19:15 is primarily a period of divine wrath (as demonstrated in chapter 2), and believe that since *wrath* is found as early as 6:17 and since it is impossible to get entirely away from the chronological succession of these judgments, the weight of Scripture evidence is on their side. All one must do is read the content of the seven seals and the first six trumpets in order to determine whether or not anything before the seventh trumpet should be recognized as wrath.

D. *The Tribulation Lasts Three and One Half Years, Not Seven*

Such a conclusion is not only necessary to the midtribulationalist view, it is insisted upon as a vital truth. Speaking of the divided nature of Daniel's seventieth week, Harrison declares:

> This should forever save us from the common mistake of speaking of the Tribulation as a seven year period. The Bible never so refers to it; rather, it begins in the middle of the seven. It is the latter three and a half years. All that leads up to it Jesus refers to as merely "the beginning of sorrows."[7]

Again, in a more recent publication:

> It is of great significance that a 7-year period is never mentioned in The Revelation; always a 3½-year period. It has no concern with Daniel's Seventieth Week, as such, but with the stirring events connected with and following the mid-week revealing of the Anti-Christ.[8]

By thus making the Tribulation a three and one half year period, instead of a seven, and by placing this time of "great tribulation" *after* the seventh trumpet, Harrison affirms that the Church will be taken out before wrath is poured out, and even calls his position pretribulational.

> "Wrath" is a word reserved for the Great Tribulation — see "wrath of God" in 14:10, 19; 15:7; 16:1, etc.[9]

[6] J. Oliver Buswell, Jr., an extract from a letter published under the title: "Let the Prophets Speak . . ." *Our Hope*, LVI (June, 1950), 720.

[7] Norman B. Harrison, *The End: Re-thinking the Revelation*, p. 229. In this chapter, Dr. Harrison's commentary on the book of Revelation will receive considerable attention because it is probably the outstanding recent publication to endorse at length the midtribulational view.

[8] Harrison, *His Coming*, p. 50.

[9] *Ibid., The End*, p. 91.

The Day of Wrath has *only now come* (11:18). This means that nothing that precedes in the Seals and Trumpets can rightfully be regarded as wrath. He has restrained it until this time. . . . We do not find warrant in Scripture, in any form of its teaching, for the thought that the Church will go through the Tribulation.

. . . .

Let us get clearly in mind the *nature of the Tribulation,* that it is divine "wrath" (11:18; 14:8, 10, 19; 15:1, 7; 16:1, 19) and divine "judgment" (14:7; 15:4; 16:7; 17:1; 18:10; 19:2).[10]

This rewarding is unquestionably at His pre-Tribulational coming.[11]

The Church is in heaven during the Tribulation, not merely to escape the judgments of God but to share in their administration.[12]

To Harrison, Revelation 5-11 is descriptive of the closing scenes of the Church Age, and as was seen at the close of chapter 7, he pictures this first half of the week as a "sweet anticipation to John," "sweet as honey," during which the saints will be "sitting pretty." The seals are not judgments, but "man's folly," neither are the first six trumpets "judgments."[13]

He holds that the first three and one half years of Daniel's seventieth week belong to the end of the Church age,[14] and in order to give a precedent to such a view, insists that after the death of Christ, "the Church paralleled for 40 years the Jewish Age, till the latter closed with the destruction of Jerusalem in 70 A. D. This argues for a similar overlapping at the close of the Church Age."[15]

Such views, although no doubt held with the greatest sincerity, are most questionable and open to severe criticism. Several of these affirmations will now be considered briefly, still remembering that in any such investigation, censure is directed against *ideas* rather than against men.

(1) Harrision's position is clearly midtribulational; he has left normal pretribulationalism, even though he chooses to retain its name.

[10] *Ibid.,* pp. 119, 120.
[11] *Ibid.,* p. 118.
[12] *Ibid.,* p. 152.
[13] *Ibid.,* pp. 111, 112, 94, 105.
[14] *Ibid.,* p. 50. *Cf., His Coming,* p. 51.
[15] *Ibid., The End,* p. 50.

(2) It is contrary to the clear testimony of the book of Revelation to say that nothing before the seventh trumpet is *wrath*, or *judgment*. We may call the seven seals "man's folly," but God calls them "wrath." Revelation 6:16, 17 twice calls the first six seals "wrath": "Hide us from the face of him that sitteth on the throne, and from the wrath of the Lamb: For the great day of his wrath is come; and who shall be able to stand?" It is remarkable that Harrison twice lists the verses in Revelation where *wrath* is found, once in great detail, and in both instances he completely overlooks Revelation 6:16, 17. Certainly, these verses do not forward his argument!

(3) The Great Tribulation is rightly identified with the time of God's wrath, but to support his thesis, our author must force it entirely into the period following the seventh trumpet. Revelation 7:14 refutes this. Since this is the only verse in the book which uses the term "great tribulation," it is significant that it is found before the opening of the seventh seal and before the sounding of any of the trumpets. The writer, "H. W. H.," noted previously, foresaw this and with greater consistency acknowledged the fifth and sixth seal as part of the Great Tribulation.[16] Indeed, he actually makes the *first half of the week* the Great Tribulation, and the latter half the Day of the Lord. He argues that, according to Matthew 24:29, the Great Tribulation *precedes* the signs in the sun, moon, and stars, and that according to Acts 2:20, these signs shall mark the coming of the great and notable Day of the Lord. Since these heavenly signs are found in the time of the sixth seal (Rev. 6:12, 13), he argues that the Great Tribulation is found in the first six seals.

Although not agreeing with him that the Great Tribulation differs from the Day of the Lord, it is interesting to note that here is a midtribulationalist whose arguments effectively cancel out Harrison's view that the Tribulation is limited to the time following the seventh trumpet.

(4) In Revelation 11:18, ἦλθεν can hardly be rendered "only now come," as though this conclusively sets the commencement of the day of wrath. The aorist may carry the force of completed and final action, and this would seem better suited to the con-

---

[16] H. W. H., *op. cit.,* pp. 9-10.

text here. If this verse anticipates (from the viewpoint of heaven — 11:15) the end of the Tribulation, it may refer to the *consummation* of wrath rather than its commencement, for it has been seen that wrath starts at Revelation 6:16. Also, if it be argued that the Greek verb in 11:18 means "only now come," what then of 6:17 where ἦλθεν is likewise used in connection with God's wrath?

(5) The literal fulfillment of Daniel's seventieth week calls for a future period of seven years, and Daniel 9:25-27 clearly identifies this "week" with the Tribulation period and the rule of Antichrist. The "prince that shall come" confirms the covenant for one week, not for half of that time. It is impossible to get away from a literal seven year Tribulation period without making one of two concessions: First, if the entire last "week" is to be fulfilled in three and one half years, the important chronology of the rest of Daniel's prophecy of seventy weeks is destroyed. Second, if only the last half of a seven year "week" falls in the Tribulation period, then the first half must overlap the Church age. Harrison chooses the latter course, which is no less precarious than the former.

As it has been seen from Matthew 24 and Revelation 6-19, the Tribulation is highly Jewish in content, and during this period the Church is never seen. To cast even half of such a period back into the Church age would result in the greatest of confusion. For instance, how could God seal 144,000 for service from the twelve tribes of Israel in an age when His witnessing body is the Church, when converted Jews enter into the Church, into the unity of the body of Christ, and lose their former identity as Israelites? Such a view would also necessitate a secret beginning of the seventieth week and a highly secret first three and one half years, an absolute impossibility in the light of the predicted events which must precede the seventh trumpet. Posttribulationalists scoff at any idea of a *secret rapture;* think of the sport they could have with the concept of a *secret Tribulation!*

An outstanding feature of Daniel's seventieth week seems to be that each part of the week is set off by some striking event. The first sixty-nine weeks commence with the commandment to restore Jerusalem; they end in notable fashion with the cutting off of Messiah. The seventieth week is to end with the visible splendor of the second advent, and it would be most singular indeed if the commencement of the entire week should be on a day, unmarked and unnamed, belonging to a previous age.

Such, however, is not the case, for the beginning of the seventieth week is to be marked by the making of a public covenant, confirmed by Antichrist with the nation Israel according to Daniel 9:27. The covenant must be public, for it will involve the befriending of Israel and the restoration of their ancient worship. Yet the midtribulationalist view necessitates that this be a *secret covenant* made between Israel and the Beast, an utter impossibility for so important an event involving a whole nation. Some smart reporter would get hold of the thing and broadcast it to the world! Yet, if any of the tremendous events of the first half of the week would leak out, it would ruin the doctrine of imminency and enable Bible students to set with reasonable accuracy the time of the rapture, another impossibility in the light of Mark 13:32, 33 and kindred Scriptures. The events of Revelation 5-11 may be thought of, by some, as the "beginning of sorrows," but if these events are thrust into the Church age just before the advent of Christ, they certainly become the "beginning of troubles" for any sane exegesis of God's holy Word.

Harrison's idea of an overlapping of the Jewish age over the first forty years of the Church age only makes the difficulty worse. God does not take up a new work until He has laid down the old one, at least in respect to His dispensational economies. Daniel's first sixty-nine weeks ended with the cutting off of Messiah. The age of law ended *at the cross*, when Christ redeemed men from the curse of the law (Gal. 3:13). Christ fulfilled Daniel's prophecy. *Christ* ended the dispensation of Moses (John 1:17, etc.) — not the Roman *Titus* in 70 A. D. The empty sacrifices and rituals of Judaism are observed, in some quarters, until this day, and did not have their cessation when the nation was scattered and the city destroyed. Yet the theory being propounded involves itself in error at the beginning of the age to justify and set the precedent for other errors which have been attached to its close.

(6) The midtribulational position rejects an imminent return of Christ, while fostering an unscriptural emphasis upon date-setting. Either the first three and one half years are yet future, in which case the truth of an imminent return of Christ is denied, or the seventieth week may already have been entered unwittingly, in which case current events might be expected to synchronize with the seals and trumpets of Revelation 5-11. Harrison wavers between the two positions. In *The End*, he uses typical posttribulational arguments against imminency:

> For *Peter* there was no possibility of such an experience, our Lord having told him that he would live to old age and die a martyr's death. . . . All Peter preached and penned was with the prospect of death. . . . For *Paul* his Lord's commission . . . left him facing a long preaching career that precluded, for much of his lifetime, any momentary return of Christ. He warns that the apostasy must come first . . . and "that in the last days perilous times shall come."[17]

> We see from the Scriptures that Christ could not have returned in the lifetime of Peter nor yet in the days of the Apostles; nor yet before the Reformation; nor yet before the missionary program is completed; nor yet before the apostasy has overtaken us; nor yet before the last days in which we seem to be living.[18]

In *His Coming*, an attempt is made to salvage an imminent return,[19] but the only way the author finds to avoid abandoning the truth that Christ may come at any time is to say that the Church is already in the time of the trumpets, which, of course, leads to date-setting.

In both of these books by Harrison, the date-setting trend induced by the midtribulational position is abundantly illustrated. It is held, for example, that the "time of the end" began with the World War of 1914-18, that the trumpets of the Revelation began their sounding in World War II, and that the space of about half an hour in Revelation 8:1 measures the time between these conflicts! Such novelty is the natural outcome of the theory that the Church may already have entered the secret first half of the Tribulation period.

(7) Even if the rapture were placed in the eleventh chapter

---

[17] *Ibid.,* pp. 231, 232.

[18] *Ibid.,* p. 233. These are essentially Cameron's arguments, and have been answered in Chapter Six.

[19] Harrison, *His Coming,* pp. 10-13.

of the Revelation, it would be an easy matter to prove that Tribulation conditions exist long before that point, even throughout the first half of the week. An examination of Revelation 6-11 readily reveals if that which precedes the seventh trumpet is called "wrath," or if it is called "great tribulation," or if it includes the Tribulation martyrs. Pretribulationalists and posttribulationalists alike agree that the seals and the trumpets are clearly a part of the Tribulation, and most probably take place during the more severe latter half of this period. Midtribulationalist H. W. H. himself concedes that everything after the sixth seal falls within the Great Tribulation.

However, even on pretribulational grounds, it can be demonstrated that definite Tribulation conditions will prevail during the less severe first half of these seven years. The Holy Spirit as an abiding Presence in this world will be gone; His ministry as restrainer will be terminated. The preservative influence and testimony of the Church will be past, for she will be with her Lord in heaven. Satan will be cast down into the earth (Rev. 12:7-13), and this *before* the woman, Israel, flees to the wilderness for the last three and one half years. During this early period, Antichrist and the false prophet will be in control, though veiled as to their true identity, for they make a covenant with Israel. Even in veiled form, the Antichrist will know his purpose and program, and with Satan as master will not be merely "a peace-loving, well-intentioned statesman"![20]

This first half of the week differs from the present Church age, moreover, because God's primary emphasis is upon the godless nations, and upon Israel, with her temple and covenant and sacrifices (Dan. 9:27). Converts from the Tribulation period will already be subject to persecution and martyrdom. The persecution of Israel obviously starts somewhere in the first half of the week, for she is driven into the wilderness for the last three and one half years (Rev. 12:14). Likewise, the two witnesses begin their prophecy, with accompanying plagues and judgments, during the first half of the week. This seems obvious, for the period of their prophecy is set at one thousand two hundred and threescore days (Rev. 11:3), a full three and one half years, yet

[20] *Ibid.*, p. 50.

they ascend into heaven in the same hour as the second woe
(Rev. 11:12-14). The third woe trumpet, incorporating all seven
vials of God's wrath, follows their death. If the vials comprise the
latter half of the week, then the testimony of the witnesses falls
within the first half. If the vials occupy only a portion of the
last half of the week, then the prophecy of the witnesses over-
laps both halves. In either case, they begin their ministry during
the first three and one half years, and the very nature of their
judgments speaks of Tribulation conditions (Rev. 11:5,6,10).

Whether one places the rapture in the fourth chapter or as
late as the eleventh chapter of Revelation, it is exceedingly difficult to escape the conclusion that the prime characteristic of
the entire seven years is that of awful *Tribulation*.

II. Is the Rapture in Revelation Eleven?

Several reasons have been introduced for placing the rapture of
the Church in the eleventh chapter of the Revelation. These
deserve at least brief comment, before passing on to the central
issue, the identifying of the seventh trumpet of Revelation 11:15
with the last trump of I Corinthians 15:52 and I Thessalonians
4:16. Again, Harrision's clear commitment to the midtribulational
position warrants his views taken as the norm for those who place
the rapture in the middle of Daniel's seventieth week.

(1) The rapture of the Church is seen symbolized in the resurrection and ascension of the two witnesses: "Now, if the two
witnesses are symbolic of 'a larger company of witnesses,' then
their resurrection and ascension must be symbolic of the resurrection and rapture of that larger company."[21] But the two
witnesses are not symbols. The normal, literal interpretation of
the passage, including as it does the details of their dress, their
prophecy, and their plagues, indicates that they are individual
men. They are spoken of as "two prophets," and when they are
killed, their dead bodies lie a definite period of time in a literal
city which is identified as Jerusalem. It would not make good
sense to say that symbolic bodies were killed, only to lie on literal
streets, any more than to deny them literal burial in symbolic
graves. The narrative of the two witnesses is evidently meant to
be taken literally.

[21] Harrison, *The End*, p. 117.

(2) It is claimed that these two witnesses symbolize the two classes at the rapture — the "Dead" and the "Alive."[22] This idea breaks down when it is remembered that both witnesses die and must be raised. Nor is it by any means certain, as averred, that these are Moses and Elijah (others say Enoch and Elijah), even though they witness with power equal to those Old Testament prophets.

(3) The "cloud" of Revelation 11:12 is identified with that of I Thessalonians 4:17, "a definite reference to the Lord's presence — *parousia*."[23] Here again, any identification of the two is exceedingly precarious. Many times in Scripture the presence of God is indicated by a cloud, but that is no indication that two such references in two distinct books by different authors necessarily speak of the same appearing of the Lord, yet alone the *parousia* of Christ.

(4) Nor is the "great voice" which bids the witnesses to "Come up hither" of any necessity even remotely connected with the "shout," or even with the "voice of the archangel" of the Pauline passage. It is not unimportant that at the rapture "the Lord himself shall descend from heaven," while here in Revelation 11, the voice comes *from heaven* and calls them up *thither*.

(5) The mention that "thy wrath is come" after the seventh trumpet sounds is used to show that wrath begins after the Church is caught up, but as noted, the earlier reference to wrath in 6:16, 17 is not cited.

(6) Throughout, it is assumed without any particular proof that the seventh trumpet falls in the middle of the week. However, in 11:17-19, the sounding of the seventh trumpet is clearly associated with the reign of Christ, the judging of the dead, and the rewarding of "thy servants the prophets," all of which occur at the end of the Tribulation with the revelation of Christ and the resurrection of Israel, at which time "The kingdoms of this world are become the kingdoms of our Lord, and of his Christ; and he shall reign for ever and ever" (Rev. 11:15). It is most evident that the seventh trumpet brings the chronology of the book right up toward the time of the end, and makes it exceedingly difficult to identify it with a supposed midtribu-

[22] *Loc. cit.*
[23] *Loc. cit.*

lational rapture. Posttribulationalists are a little more consistent at this point, for they identify the seventh trumpet with the day of Christ's revelation, the last day of the seven year period. Yet even they have difficulty in so doing, for the seven vials of wrath, containing the seven last plagues, all follow the sounding of this seventh trumpet, although evidently in rapid succession as the consummation of the judgments of God. The seventh trumpet is evidently *near* the end of the Tribulation, associated as it is with resurrection, rewarding, and reigning, yet cannot be on the final day because of the seven vial judgments which are to follow. Midtribulationalists must labor to explain why they believe nothing *preceding* the seventh trumpet belongs to the Tribulation, while posttribulationalists are embarrassed by the record of seven vials *following* the trumpet which presumably marks the revelation of Christ and the end of all such judgment.

Both difficulties grow out of a fallacious identifying of the seventh trumpet of John with the "last trump" of Paul, which problem will be dealt with shortly. Pretribulationalists, who make no such assumption, are free to give the seventh trumpet a normal and natural place in the chronology of the Tribulation, evidently well toward the end of the period, yet not on the last day, and certainly not in the middle of the week. A Revelation 11 rapture makes havoc with any attempt of understanding the chronology of what admittedly is a difficult book.

(7) In Revelation 10:7, "In the days of the voice of the seventh angel, when he shall begin to sound, the mystery of God should be finished, as he hath declared to his servants the prophets," — in this verse, midtribulationalists find proof of the completion of the Church, just before her rapture. The text is obscure, as indicated by the fact that Harrison also links it with the "mystery of godliness" (I Tim. 3:16), and with the "mysteries of the kingdom of heaven" (Matt. 13).[24] A better explanation, it would seem, is that which has been offered by Ironside on this "mystery":

> This is the theme of the seven-sealed roll; the vindication of God's holiness in having so long tolerated evil in His universe. What greater mystery confronts and confuses the human mind than the question, Why does God allow unrighteousness so often

[24] *Ibid.*, pp. 107-9.

to triumph? It is what men call the mystery of Providence; but Providence is only another name for God. This is *His* secret. He will disclose it in due time, and all shall be clear as the day. . . . His final triumph over all evil is what is so vividly presented in the rapidly-shifting tableau of the Revelation. . . .[25]

Here, then, is not the mystery of the completion of the Church, but the finishing of the mystery of Satan's sway and of God's long toleration of iniquity, consummated in the binding of Satan when Christ destroys His enemies with the brightness of His appearing. It is the bringing to a climax of the "mystery of iniquity" found in II Thessalonians 2:7.

It seems unnecessary to prolong these comments upon the theory that rapture falls in Revelation 11. To say that "the temple of God was opened in heaven" (v. 19) indicates that the bodies of believers (the temple of the Holy Spirit, I Cor. 3:16) are now in heaven;[26] to say that the two witnesses symbolize the dead and the living at Christ's coming; to say that the "mystery" and the "cloud" are those found in I Thessalonians 4 — this is an attempt to prove a doctrine upon surface similarities. These are the husks, and not the wheat of true exegesis. True, some interesting parallels between the experience of the witnesses and the experience of the Church may be demonstrated, but this can be done with the translation of Elijah or the ascension of Christ, for parallels and similarities abound through Scripture. The actual identification of one event with another must rest upon more definite and more Biblical similarities than these. As Newell (tersely) writes concerning Revelation 11 and the two witnesses:

> Where are the churches? Brethren, they are not there! The people are occupied with *something entirely different.* "And they that dwell upon the earth shall rejoice over them, and make merry, and shall send gifts one to another; because these two prophets tormented them that dwelt on the earth." The whole earth was in their hands for judging and tormenting. Where is the ministry of *reconciliation* in that day? Where are the ambassadors that were formerly pleading in Christ's stead to be reconciled to God? That day is gone! People with discernment see that. God is doing something else then; judgment is on. And Israel and the nations are involved in it — not the Church![27]

[25] H. A. Ironside, *The Mysteries of God,* pp. 95, 96.
[26] Harrison, *The End, op. cit.,* p. 119.
[27] William R. Newell, *The Church and the Great Tribulation,* p. 20.

III. THE SEVENTH TRUMPET AND THE "LAST TRUMP"

The identification of the *seventh trumpet* of Revelation 11:15 with the *last trump* of I Corinthians 15:52 and I Thessalonians 4:16 is probably the most important key to the midtribulation rapture theory. The entire structure of this view stands or falls with the ability of its adherents to prove three related propositions: first, that the seventh trumpet falls in the middle of the week; second, nothing before this trumpet is Tribulation; and third, that the seventh trumpet is identical with the "last trump." The obvious weaknesses of the first two propositions have been demonstrated, and the fallacy of the third will be even more transparent.

(1) Any identification of these two trumpets is, at best, based on the surface similarity that one is designated "last," while the other completes a series of seven. In rather a naive way, both midtribulationalists and posttribulationalists assume that this is sufficient evidence to prove that they are identical.

> Then the same mighty angel lifts his hand to heaven and swears that the End-Time has come, declaring that during the days in which the seventh angel sounds his trumpet, the mystery of God would be finished. It will be remembered, that the rapture is to take place, according to First Corinthians, fifteen, fifty-two, at the sounding of the seventh trumpet, and that the Church is spoken of as a mystery. Apparently the Church ascends as the seventh angel sounds his trumpet.[28]

The same assumption is made even more emphatically:

> St. Paul, by inspiration of the Spirit, definitely places the Resurrection and the Rapture of the saints through the coming of Christ *"at the last trumpet"* (I Cor. 15:51, 52). This is a specific locating of the event. Unquestionably the Holy Spirit revealed the fact and inspired the recording of it. How dare any one locate it otherwise? . . . *Can we postulate the Rapture at any other place than that given by and through the Apostle Paul and claim to maintain the integrity of God's Word?* . . . When, however, we reach the last Trumpet in The Revelation, last in the series, we shall find much satisfying evidence that the event is actually taking place.[29]

This identification of the two trumpets is not new. Hermann Olshausen, in his *Biblical Commentary on the New Testament*,

---

[28] Oswald J. Smith, *The Book of Revelation,* p. 37.
[29] Harrison, *The End, op. cit.,* pp. 74, 75. Italics in the original.

had made the same claim almost one hundred years before, although adding: "The expression [last trump] is of course to be understood figuratively of some stupendous spiritual influence, which arouses mankind for some mighty purpose."[30] However, we are more inclined to agree with Ellicott, who says:

> There are no sufficient grounds for supposing that there is here [in I Cor. 15:52] any reference to the seventh Apocalyptic trumpet (Rev. 11:15). . . . This σαλπιγξ [trumpet] the Apostle here terms εσχατη [last], not with reference to any preceding series . . . but as connected with the close of this αιων [age] and the last scene of this world's history.[31]

We believe that the "last trump" will close the Church age, but that it will sound several years prior to the seven judgment trumpets of Revelation.

(2) There are many references to trumpets in the Word of God. Unless there is clear and concrete evidence, it is most precarious to identify trumpets found in different parts of the Bible. Paul's "last trump" need not be the same as John's "seventh trumpet," and particularly so, since different subjects are in view. Then too, trumpets serve for various purposes. In Leviticus 23:24, there was "a memorial of blowing of trumpets, an holy convocation" (cf. Num. 29:1-6). From Numbers 10:1-10 it is apparent that the same trumpets were used for vastly different purposes: "the calling of the assembly," "the journeying of the camps," the gathering together of the "princes . . . of Israel," to "blow an alarm," and to "blow with the trumpets over your burnt-offerings, and over the sacrifices."

The actual blowing of the trumpets was not the central issue: "But when the congregation is to be gathered together, ye shall blow, but ye shall not sound an alarm" (v. 7). The important question is, "What tune did the trumpets play?" Even though two trumpets may be clearly identified as the same, that in itself does not suffice to prove that each trumpet blast commands the same action. Nor did the trumpets of Israel serve to call the heathen, or any other nation outside the camp. It is most arbitrary to claim: "The Trumpets, in their religious aspect, serve

---

[30] Hermann Olshausen, *Biblical Commentary on the New Testament*, IV, 398.
[31] Charles J. Ellicott, *St. Paul's First Epistle to the Corinthians*, p. 325.

to assemble God's earthly people in their land and His heavenly people in heaven."[32]

(3) Now, dealing more directly with the matter of the identification of the two trumpets, it is asked: "How can a trumpet sound for the Church before seven other trumpets, and still be called the 'last trump'?" This is a fair question, but the simple answer is that the "last trump" and the seventh trumpet are each last in their own sphere. The "last trump" is last in respect to the Church, and if mention of it must be found in the book of Revelation, then let it be identified with the trumpet voice of 4:1 which said, "Come up hither," and not with the last of a series of trumpet judgments which pertain, not to the Church, but to Israel and the nations in the Tribulation. The "seventh trumpet" of Revelation 11 is "last" only in respect to the other six of the series. It certainly is not the last trumpet to sound in time and eternity, or even in respect to the Tribulation and the return of the Lord. The trumpet of Matthew 24:31, which serves to gather together the elect of God, is "after the tribulation of those days" (v. 29), and so follows (in point of time) the sounding of the seventh trumpet. Harrison admits this,[33] but Lang is in error when he states: "The last trump of Scripture is recorded in Rev. 11:15-18."[34] The very fact that another trumpet must blow after the Tribulation, which is obviously after the seventh trump, gives one to believe that the sounding of a trumpet will have a prominent place in the experience of Israel during the Millennium — this, a very normal expectation if one is to judge from Israel's history. It would be very abnormal to dogmatize that no trumpet will sound its voice throughout eternity, simply on the basis that the closing signal of the Church age is designated as the "last trump."

(4) Again, one may inquire: "How can a trumpet blown for the Church at a pretribulational rapture be rightfully called 'last,' when no trumpet precedes, and seven trumpets follow?" As it has been seen, the fact of subsequent trumpets is no problem. Even a schoolboy knows that the sounding of "the last bell" in the morning does not mean that the bell will not ring at regular

[32] Harrison, *op. cit.*, p. 99.
[33] *Ibid.*, p. 75.
[34] Lang, *op. cit.*, p. 33.

intervals during the day. As to the objection that a single trumpet cannot properly be called "last," the explanation of Silver in this respect is very plausible: "It is not improbable that there are two blasts sounded in quick succession. The 'trump of God' sounds and the dead arise: almost instantly it sounds again and the living are translated."[35] If such is the case, since the dead are to rise first, the trumpet of I Thessalonians 4:16 will awaken the dead in Christ, and the trumpet of I Corinthians 15:52 (the "last trump") will summon those who have been raised and those who are alive and believe in Christ, into the Lord's presence.[36]

Nor is it improbable that there will be additional trumpet signals in the last days other than those indicated by Scripture. While the merits of pretribulationism do not depend on details such as these, there is certainly nothing to overthrow or weaken the position in the alleged identification of Paul's "trump" with the "seventh trumpet" of John.

(5) Moreover, there are distinct points of dissimilarity between these trumpets. The contexts in question are vastly different. The trumpets of Revelation introduce judgments of God; they bring into being a time of unparalleled suffering, and comprehend the godless nations of the earth. The trumpet of I Corinthians 15 and I Thessalonians 4 is distinctly for the Church, implies nothing of judgment or anything else connected with the godless, and introduces for the believer in Christ a time of unprecedented glory and privilege, even the joy of His presence. In the trumpet portion of the Revelation, there is no hint of translation, but a rushing onward toward the climax of God's fearful wrath and certain judgment. There are indications that the blasts of the seven trumpets extend over the respective period of judgment each introduces, even as in Exodus 19:19, "the voice of the trumpet sounded long, and waxed louder and louder," and in Joshua 6:5, 13, at the conquest of Jericho, "the priests went on continually, and blew with the trumpets." So, Revelation 10:7 speaks of "the *days* of the voice of the seventh angel, when he shall begin to sound." There is no parallel here to a trumpet

[35] Jesse Forrest Silver, *The Lord's Return*, p. 235.
[36] Henry C. Thiesson, *Lectures in Systematic Theology*, p. 485.

signal for the hosts of the redeemed to ascend, characterized as it must be: "in a moment, in the twinkling of an eye, at the last trump." All this speaks of brevity, of speed, of an instantaneous translation, and certainly not of a prolonged trumpet blast and a period of days or weeks during which are poured out the seven last judgments of God.

In addition, the very terminology which describes the trumpets differs. The seventh trumpet is said to be blown by an angel, but the "last trump" is clearly designated as "the trump of God." While it is not contended that each angelic trumpet may not be *a* trump of God, inasmuch as angels are commissioned to do God's bidding, it does not follow automatically that the last of these seven is *the* trump of God. Strombeck comments:

> In the search for "the last trump" one must, then, be guided by the fact that it is God's own trumpet, sounded by the Lord Himself. In view of this one would hardly be willing to contend that the last trumpet of God is the last of a series of trumpets blown by the priests of the Aaronic priesthood. These were not in a class with the trumpet of God. Remembering that the angels are only a little higher than man, it is just as contrary to the laws of logic to say that "the last trump," which is God's own trumpet, is the last of a series of trumpets blown by angels. Both men and angels are creatures of God. They cannot sound the trumpet of the Creator.[37]

When midtribulationalists identify the rapture of the Church with the ascension of the two witnesses in Revelation 11:12, they seem to overlook completely the fact that the seventh trumpet is not blown until 11:15, with the great earthquake of the "second woe" intervening. Thus, in Revelation 11, the resurrection (if such is typified) *precedes* the seventh trumpet and is found in the time of the sixth, while in I Corinthians 15, resurrection is "at [ἐν] the last trump," and in I Thessalonians 4, the Lord descends "with the trump." The supposed identification of these trumpets strains the Scriptures at every point of investigation, yet this is the core of the midtribulational argument. Instead of a positive identification of the two trumpets in question, the best midtribulationalism can offer is a shallow, surface similarity — a similarity which breaks down wherever and whenever it is examined in the light of relevant Scriptures.

[37] J. F. Strombeck, *First the Rapture*, p. 109.

(6) By the very nature of their position, midtribulationalists must go to the eleventh chapter of the Revelation, with its account of the resurrection of the two witnesses and the sounding of the seventh trumpet, to find anything which even vaguely resembles a rapture of the saints in the midst of the week. From the viewpoint of those who endeavor to find therein some tangible support for this theory, the chapter must be most disappointing. In view is the ancient city of Jerusalem, with its temple, its court and its altar—hardly the setting in which to find vital Church doctrine. The witnesses and their ministry give every evidence of being literal and cannot be relegated to the position of symbols, particularly of the dead and the living believers in Christ. The chronology of the entire scheme is in error, for the witnesses are raised in the time of the sixth trumpet rather than the seventh, while this seventh trumpet is identified with events at the close of the week rather than with its midpoint. If anything prior to the sounding of the seventh trump falls within the dispensation of grace, then grace is no longer grace, or else the seals and the trumpets must be made sweet and desirable, in which case language fails to have any significant meaning. Nothing less than the most flagrant spiritualization can deny that Tribulation commences with Revelation 6 and "great tribulation" at least by 7:14. As demonstrated, the barest surface similarity links the trumpet of Revelation 11:15 with the "last trump" which sounds at the rapture of the Church; beyond this, all else is contrast. Harrison presents "sixfold evidence linking World War II with the Trumpets of Revelation 8,"[38] but since error is so evident in the chronology of the first six trumpets, making their blowing in the neighborhood of 1941, it is hardly to be expected that the chronology of the seventh should be any the less in error. Concerning the eleventh chapter of the Revelation, Ottman says: "Interpreters of the Revelation exhibit more confusion in the exposition of this chapter than elsewhere," and cites the words of Dean Alford that this chapter is "undoubtedly one of the most difficult in the whole Apocalypse."[39] It is upon this chapter that midtribulationalists lean most heavily to demonstrate their thesis, but instead of substantiating it as

[38] Harrison, *His Coming, op. cit.*, p. 46.
[39] Ford C. Ottman, *The Unfolding of the Ages*, pp. 260, 261.

true, the chapter exposes its error and breaks the theory into pieces.

IV. REVELATION 4 AND THE TWENTY-FOUR ELDERS

There is one remaining midtribulational line of argumentation which demands some recognition. Stated simply, it is the negative proposition that there is no indication of the rapture in Revelation 4, not even symbolically when John responds to the summons, "Come up hither." Harrison proposes seven reasons why rapture cannot occur at this point in the book and for the sake of a complete hearing, these will have brief consideration — although there is little to be gained by such a denial if the place of the rapture cannot be established later on in the Revelation.

A. *What Happens at Revelation 4:1?*

(1) "After these things I saw . . . I heard . . . I was" merely records the personal experience of the seer. It is just a change of viewpoint, it is argued, for John has seen and recorded "these things" and now turns to record "other things." But there is more to the verse than this! Change of time and place are involved, for with the words "come up hither," the scene moves into the future and shifts from earth to heaven. Jesus is no longer seen as a mediatorial Priest "walking in the midst of the lampstands," but comes into view in an entirely different character, and for the execution of other purposes.[40] To see the rapture at this point in the Revelation corresponds perfectly with 1:19, which is the almost undisputed chronological key to the book. The present Church age corresponds to "the things which are," and "the things which shall be hereafter" ($\mu\epsilon\tau\grave{\alpha}$ $\tau\alpha\hat{\upsilon}\tau\alpha$) refers evidently to events which shall transpire after the Church age has been completed. This being the case, it becomes apparent that 4:1 commences the futuristic section of the Revelation, identified as it is by the double use of the expression $\mu\epsilon\tau\grave{\alpha}$ $\tau\alpha\hat{\upsilon}\tau\alpha$. John has been speaking of things which pertain to the churches, but now he is about to unfold his vision of conditions upon earth and events in heaven after God's program for the churches is finished.

(2) It is said further that "these things" refer to the visible

[40] *Ibid.,* p. 103.

churches which go on into the Tribulation, and (3) that a rapture at this point is inconsistent with the structural plan of the book: the Church, once mentioned, is left to play its part even though it is not again mentioned. It is difficult to find any weight to support these two arguments, for they so largely assume that which the author has undertaken to prove, namely, that the Church continues beyond this point in the book.

(4) It is argued that the revealed order of harvesting, "first the tares" (Matt. 13:30), indicates that the seals and trumpets must harvest the tares before the Lord of the Harvest gathers the "wheat" into His barn. But this is hardly conclusive, for in Matthew 13, the *angels* do the reaping, not the Beast, nor Satan. The time of reaping is set by God and starts with Revelation 14:15, not in chapter 6 with the opening of the first seal. It is most peculiar that our author argues that seals and trumpets harvest the tares, for according to his view, these fall in the *sweet* half of the seven years and are not part of the Tribulation at all, but are rather in the closing scenes of the Church age.

(5) There fails to appear any redeemed company in glory. The position and description of the twenty-four elders fail to suggest any company of people such as would have to be present after the rapture. Since both midtribulationalists and post-tribulationalists argue strenuously that the elders cannot represent the Church, the identification of this interesting company will receive a more detailed treatment very shortly.

(6) None of the revealed accompaniments of the coming of Christ are here in this passage. But this is not true, for translation is suggested in the words "come up hither," and there is a voice as of a trumpet, an open door in heaven, and a redeemed company with their crowns. All of this, however, is not directly to the point. There is no need that all the accompaniments of the rapture be restated at every mention of the event. Nor is it necessary to pretribulationalism to find the rapture at all in this experience of John.

Chronologically, the rapture most probably occurs between the third and fourth chapters. The Tribulation section of the Revelation presumes that rapture is past, and neither *rapture* nor *Church* find mention at all in it. Judgment is in view and the persons involved are those who dwell on the earth. From this point on, the redeemed are seen in glory, and when Christ returns to the earth, He brings His saints with Him.

(7) The last of these reasons, said to be conclusive, is that Paul places the rapture at the "last trumpet," identified with the seventh trumpet of Revelation 11. Some of the difficulties of this view have already been demonstrated. From these seven reasons, it is safe to conclude that, although John's experience *need not* typify the rapture, it has not been proved that it *could not,* and more important, nor has it been disproved that rapture occurs at this point in the chronology of the book. Pretribulationalists believe that from the viewpoint of Revelation 4:1, John looks down upon a world torn by Tribulation judgments, from which the Church and the restraint of the Holy Spirit have already been removed. As for the company John beheld in heaven, although it is not essential to pretribulationalism to prove that the elders do indeed represent the Church in glory, if such an identity can be demonstrated, the case becomes that much more unassailable.

B. *Who Are the Twenty-four Elders?*

The first momentous sight to greet the eyes of the Apostle John when he was caught up into heaven to behold "things which shall be hereafter," was a throne set in heaven, and One sitting upon the throne surrounded by twenty-four elders, each of which was upon a throne, wearing golden crowns and white raiment. Who are these glorious and privileged individuals, seated in such a place of prominence about the glorified Christ? Is there any way of determining their real identity? They are mentioned twelve times in the Revelation, and only in that portion where the Church is no longer seen on the earth (Rev. 4:4, 10; 5:5, 6, 8, 11, 14; 7:11, 13; 11:16; 14:3; 19:4). Do they, as so widely believed, represent and picture the glorified Church? There are a number of factors involved in finding an answer to these questions.

They are not a symbolic group. It is most difficult to conceive of John holding conversation with one-twenty-fourth part of a symbolic host (Rev. 5:5). These elders are individuals, although their title and their actions indicate that they function in a representative sense (Rev. 5:8). It will be remembered that when Moses was commanded to give God's message to the children of Israel, he did so through the elders of the people (Ex. 19:3-8). Likewise in the New Testament eldership is a representative office (Acts 15:2; 20:17), so although the elders of the Revelation cannot *symbolize* the Church in glory, they can be *representative* of the Church, and thus still indicate the presence of that glorified body in heaven before Tribulation judgment. To recognize these elders as representative of the Church overcomes the objection: "If so great a company of redeemed were present, their failure to appear and join in the New Song is utterly inexplicable."[41]

> But it must be remembered that the rapture will only add a relatively small number to the multitude of saints already "with Christ." Even if Dr. Harrison were right, there still ought to be a great number of saints in heaven. In private conversation, Dr. Harrison has recognized this fact, but stated that these believers must be in some other part of heaven; for it is vast enough that they do not appear in the scene described by Revelation 4-5. If this be so, why could not the raptured saints also be there in that remote part of heaven? It is easier to believe that the twenty-four elders do represent the Church.[42]

Harrison says that "there is no suggestion that those whom they represent are there with them. Quite the opposite: they always appear and act in their individual capacity."[43] If this were true, after the rapture which Harrison places in Revelation 11:12, their number should materially increase, which, however, is not the case (Rev. 11:16). Twenty-four may well be the very number of representation, as was the case in the number of courses of the Levitical priesthood (I Chron. 24:1-19).

To further the identification of the elders, they are not angels (Rev. 5:11; 7:11), for the angels are grouped around the elders; nor are they the same as the four living creatures. Every time the elders are mentioned, they are clearly distinguished from celestial beings. Scripture never speaks of the angels being crowned or seated on thrones; they are never designated elders, neither are they said to sing. Nor could angels ever join with the song of

41 Harrison, *The End*, p. 83.
42 Miner B. Stearns, book review: *The End: Re-thinking the Revelation*, *Bibliotheca Sacra*, 10 (January-March, 1942), 125.
43 Harrison, *op. cit.*, p. 78.

the redeemed, for no redemption was provided for angels who left their first estate, while angels who did not fall need no redemption. However, all of these privileges from which angels are excluded are open to the Church (Matt. 19:28; I Pet. 5:4; II Tim. 4:8).

> These 24 elders are not *angels* . . . as is shown . . . by their white robes and crowns, the rewards of *endurance* . . . but *representatives of the Church,* as generally understood.[44]

There are five characteristics which seem adequate to identify the elders as representatives of the glorified Church: their *position,* their *worship,* their *raiment,* their *crowns,* and their *song.*

Their *position,* in proximity to a throne which evidently is that of Christ, and the fact that they themselves occupy thrones, indicates that the Church is in view. They are found in the place of honor, with a royal association between their own thrones and the one central throne. To the Church alone is co-enthronement with Christ promised (Rev. 3:21; Matt. 19:28), as also the authority to judge angels (I Cor. 6:2, 3). Neither the twenty-four elders, nor their thrones, ever appear after Revelation 19: 7-9. From that point, the Church is seen as the bride of Christ, and evidently sits together with God's Son upon His throne.

The identification of the elders with the Church is furthered by considering their *worship.* The initial act recorded of these elders is that they worship Him who sits upon the throne. In fact, throughout the book, whenever the elders are found in the presence of Christ they are prostrate in worship before Him.

> The four and twenty elders fall down before him that sat on the throne, and worship him that liveth for ever and ever, and cast their crowns before the throne, saying, Thou art worthy, O Lord, to receive glory and honour and power: for thou hast created all things, and for thy pleasure they are and were created (Rev. 4:10, 11).

> And the four beasts said, Amen. And the four and twenty elders fell down and worshipped him that liveth for ever and ever (Rev. 5:14).

> And the four and twenty elders, which sat before God on their seats, fell upon their faces, and worshipped God (Rev. 11:16).

> And the four and twenty elders and the four beasts fell down and worshipped God that sat on the throne, saying, Amen; Alleluia (Rev. 19:4).

[44] Henry Alford, *The Greek Testament,* IV, 596.

This attitude of worship, coupled with their intimate knowledge of God and His doings (John 15:15; Rev. 5:5; 7:13-17), is what would be expected of saints so recently caught up into the presence of their Lord.

The identification is made more certain by their *raiment*, for they are clothed in white (Rev. 4:4), everywhere typical of the righteousness of saints (Rev. 3:4, 5, 18; 7:9, 13, 14; *cf.* Isa. 61:10). It was an express promise to the overcomers at Sardis that they should be clothed in white raiment, even to walk with the Lord in white. Coupled with this raiment is the fact that the elders wear *crowns*, mindful of the promise made with those at Smyrna (Rev. 2:10) and the warning to those at Philadelphia (Rev. 3:11). They do not wear the monarch's crown, or diadem (διάδημα), but the victor's crown, won in conflict (στέφανος; *cf.* II Tim. 4:8; James 1:12; I Pet. 5:4). The fact that these representative elders are crowned also indicates that resurrection is past, for disembodied spirits wear no crowns. As Seiss comments: "The coronation time is the resurrection time; and no one can be crowned until he is either resurrected if dead or translated if living."[45]

Thus the saints, represented by the elders, have been translated and have received their resurrection bodies. They have been rewarded, as the Lord has promised (I Cor. 3:12-14; 9:25; I Thess. 2:19; II Tim. 2:12), and are now wearing their crowns. The clear indication is that resurrection and rapture are past. In fact, it is rather obvious that they have just received their crowns, for why should angelic beings who have worshiped and adored Christ from eternity past wait so long and for this particular moment to cast their crowns at His feet? Is it not more logical to conclude that the rapture and the rewarding of Church saints have just taken place — that the Church, fresh from scenes of earthly conflict, in gratitude and humility cast their every reward before the feet of the Saviour, joining the four living creatures in ascribing to Him all glory and honor and power? (Rev. 4:9-11).

A fifth identifying mark that these elders do represent the Church is found in the *song* they sing and the important claims that are made therein:

45 Joseph A. Seiss, *Lectures on the Apocalypse*, I, 250.

And they sung a new song, saying, Thou art worthy to take the book, and to open the seals thereof: for thou wast slain, and hast redeemed us to God by thy blood out of every kindred, and tongue, and people, and nation; and hast made us unto our God kings and priests: and we shall reign on the earth (Rev. 5:9, 10).

At this point both midtribulationalists and posttribulationalists introduce their primary argument against identifying the elders with the Church, or with representatives of the Church, or with redeemed people at all. There is a textual problem involved with the pronoun "us," as found in the song of the elders. The important Codex Alexandrinus, of the fifth century, omits the word completely in verse 9, and a variety of manuscripts support the third person, "them" and "they," in verse 10. From this, it is argued most strenuously that the elders do not sing their own redemption song, but rather, they sing of *others* from every tribe and nation who have been redeemed. While admitting that this is the reading favored by most of the revisers, it needs to be pointed out that the evidence is in no wise overwhelming.

"Thou hast redeemed us . . ." (v. 9). This text is supported by the Textus Receptus, Codex Sinaiticus (4th century), Codex Basilianus (8th century), Codex St. Petersburg (apparently 8th century), Minuscule 1 (of uncertain date), and several other minuscules of late date, the Coptic, Latin, and Armenian (5th century) versions, and quoted by Cyprian, Bishop of Carthage (248 A.D.), and by Primasius (6th century).

"And hast made us . . ." (v. 10). This is supported by the Textus Receptus, Codex Fuldensis (6th century Latin version), Codex Coislinianus (10th century), and quoted by Arethas, Bishop of Caesarea in Cappadocia (10th century).

"and WE shall reign on the earth . . ." (v. 10). This text is supported by the Textus Receptus, MSS. Demidovianus (12th century), MSS. Lipsienses (14th and 15th centuries), and quoted by Arethas (10th century), Primasius (6th century), Julius Firmicus (345 A.D.), Idacius (the name under which Vigilius of Thapsis, 484 A.D. published his work).[46]

Also on this matter of manuscript evidence for maintaining the wording of the Authorized Version, Seiss writes:

Ηγορασας ημας hast redeemed us. Some critics and expositors have rejected this ημας, for the reason that it is omitted in the Codex Alexandrinus, and in the Ethiopic version; though the latter is not much more than a loose paraphrase. The Codex Sinaiticus,

---

[46] R. Ludwigson, *Simplified Classroom Notes on Prophecy*, pp. 111, 112.

however, which was discovered in 1860, and which is of equal antiquity and authority with the Codex Alexandrinus, contains it. The Codex Basilianus, in the Vatican, contains it. The Latin, Coptic or Memphitic, and Armenian, which are of great value, contain it. And so do *all other MSS. and versions*. And to discredit it, simply and only because it does not appear in that one single Codex of Alexandria, is most unreasonable and unjust to the weight of authority for its retention. Dr. Tregelles, on full examination, was firmly convinced of its right to a place in the text, *before* the Codex Sinaiticus appeared; and the presence of this ημας in that MS., ought to settle the question of its genuineness forever. The evidences from the context, also argue powerfully for a construction which necessarily embraces it, whether expressed or not. We regard it as indubitably genuine.[47]

Lang has further noted:

It is said that Alford, upon Dr. Tregelles assuring him that Codex Sinaiticus has the word, stated that he would re-insert it in his text. But this was not done, on account, we are told, of his death.[48]

Since there is such textual support for the reading of the Authorized Version, advocates of the new reading can hardly be said to have won a sweeping victory. It would seem, to the contrary, that there is much in favor of retaining the old reading. Yet, even if the "us" were omitted and these verses thrown into the third person, still, there would be no adequate grounds for insisting that the elders were singing of the redemption of others. The song of the redeemed, sung by Moses and the children of Israel, as recorded in Exodus 15:13, 17, is obviously sung about themselves, but it was sung objectively *in the third person*.

Thou in thy mercy hast led forth the people which thou hast redeemed: thou hast guided *them* in thy strength unto thy holy habitation. . . . Thou shalt bring *them* in, and plant *them* in the mountain of thine inheritance, in the place, O Lord, which thou hast made for thee to dwell in. [Italics added.]

There are other cases in the New Testament where the third person is used in the place of the first person, no doubt for the sake of modesty. Paul evidently speaks of himself when he said: "I knew a man in Christ . . ." (II Cor. 12:2). Similarly, John referred to himself as "the disciple whom Jesus loved" (John

---

[47] Seiss, *op. cit.*, III, 249.
[48] G. H. Lang, *The Revelation of Jesus Christ*, p. 126.

21:20). Even though textual evidence be massed against the older reading of Revelation 5:9, 10, which to date has not been achieved, still it would not prove that the elders were referring to others as the redeemed of God. Of verse 10, Bengel writes: "The *Hebrew* construction of the third person for the first, has a graphic relation to *the redeemed,* and also has a more modest sound than *us, priests.*"[49]

In the light of such evidence, it seems valid to conclude that the elders' song is not sung by some unknown celestial beings, but by those who have experienced for themselves the cleansing power of the blood of Christ. That which they sing of themselves can be true only of the Church of Jesus Christ, of which they are a part, for the Church has been "redeemed" (I Pet. 1:18); its members are "priests" (I Pet. 2:5, 9; Rev. 1:6); they have been gathered "out of every kindred, and tongue, and people, and nation" (Acts 1:8); and certainly they "shall reign" with Christ on the earth (II Tim. 2:12). Israel, too, is to have a "new song" (Rev. 14:3, *cf.* 15:3) and will sing it themselves before the throne and the living creatures and the elders. It is, therefore, not strange that the *"new song"* of the Church will be sung by those to whom it rightfully belongs. How could glorified saints stand by in mute silence while others sing redemption's story and not join in the refrain?

Considering the textual support for the song of the elders, and in view of the many other striking marks of identification, it is most surprising how lightly some of the brethren pass over all of this and insist that the elders are not redeemed, in fact, are not even human at all. It has been said that prejudice "squints when it looks," and possibly that is the reason why the elders have fared so badly. Commentators, who have mustered all their arguments to prove that the elders cannot represent the Church, have given only the most vague ideas as to what or whom they think the elders *do* represent. Lang calls them "the senior executive officers of the Most High," and "the noblest princes of heaven"[50] while Reese is satisfied to designate them as "angelic lords."[51]

---

[49] J. A. Bengel, cited by Jamieson, Fausset and Brown, *Commentary on the Whole Bible,* p. 566.

[50] Lang, *op. cit.,* p. 188.

[51] Alexander Reese, *The Approaching Advent of Christ,* p. 94.

Most, however, will prefer to use the names the elders themselves suggest, namely, "redeemed from every nation," and "kings
and priests unto God." They will see in them the Church of
Jesus Christ, caught up to God, rewarded and glorified, preserved from Tribulation fires, and ascribing all glory and praise
to the Saviour they love with a pure heart fervently.

It is important that these elders are never seen in heaven
prior to the fourth chapter of the Revelation. In a vision, Isaiah
saw the Lord and the heavenly seraphim, but saw no elders
(Isa. 6:2,3); Ezekiel looked up into glory and saw the four
living creatures, but not the twenty-four thrones with their
elders. With good reason, English inquires:

> Why did Isaiah, who viewed other wonders of heaven, who
> looked upon the seraphim, fail to see the elders? Why did Ezekiel,
> who beheld other marvels — the precious, colorful stones, the rain-
> bow, the glories; who viewed the four living creatures, miss the
> four and twenty elders seated upon thrones? Why did not John,
> in his former vision, take note of their presence in heaven? These
> servants of God did not see or describe the four and twenty
> thrones, and the four and twenty elders seated upon them, be-
> cause the elders were not yet in heaven. It was when John was
> caught up into heaven in an experience quite similar to the com-
> ing translation of the Church — as a spectator, however, and not
> as a participant — that the four and twenty elders are first seen
> enthroned about the throne of the Lord. Here is a new body in
> heaven, at the end of the Church age and prior to the tribula-
> tion. They are not angels. They are not the seraphim. They
> are not the cherubim. They are not the four living creatures.
> They are evidently human beings, redeemed saints, as further
> examination of the passage will confirm.[52]

In this present chapter, the leading arguments for midtribulationalism have been discussed, including the two main passages
involved, the fourth and the eleventh chapters of the Revelation, and the key problems of the trumpets and the elders. Now,
it must be left for the reader to judge whether or not the midtribulational theory has been disproved, and that from the passages most commonly cited in favor of the position. Returning
once more to the elders, the following analysis by Armerding will
be of interest to many, and will form a suitable conclusion to
this phase of the investigation.

[52] E. Schuyler English, "Re-Thinking the Rapture," *Our Hope*, LVII (September, 1950), 149.

Again we see them, together with the four living creatures, listening to the new song of the 144,000 who stand on Mount Sion with the Lamb (Rev. 14:3). And the last thing that is said of them is that they fall down, in company with the four living creatures, and worship Him who sits on the throne, saying, "Amen, Alleluia" (Rev. 19:4). This last act of theirs is characteristic of them. Indeed, there are three things which seem to characterize them all through: (1) their intimate knowledge of Christ, (2) their nearness to Him, and (3) the worship they give Him. And we recall that our Lord, when praying for His own, asked that they might know Him, that they might be with Him, and that they might behold His glory (John 17:3, 24). And they were none other than the men which the Father had given Him out of the world.[53]

[53] Carl Armerding, *The Four and Twenty Elders*, p. 10.

Chapter Ten

THE POSTTRIBULATION RAPTURE THEORY

It is never a pleasant task to refute favored beliefs held by those who are brethren in Christ, particularly men of like precious faith not only respecting the person and work of Christ but also concerning the fact and certainty of His premillennial return. While it is possible to fill a book with differences of opinion over the relation of the rapture to the Tribulation, it would not be difficult to fill many such with points of agreement as to the importance, certainty, and blessing of Christ's return, the anticipation of rewarding and reigning, the task of the Church prior to the rapture, and the many other important features of our mutual premillennial faith.

The points of disagreement are small indeed when compared with the widely divergent views of amillennialism, and premillennialists would do well to remember the basic unity which exists in spite of their differences. Nevertheless, it must also be remembered that the Bible does not teach two different systems of prophecy, nor three, nor four, and with vital issues at stake such as the hope and comfort of the Church, the intelligent believer will seek to learn "what saith the Lord" on these issues. The interpretation of an amazingly large segment of Scripture depends directly upon whether one accepts or rejects pretribulationalism.

Much of the first seven chapters has been given over to the defense of that viewpoint, or to the analysis of problems kindred to both the midtribulational and the posttribulational positions. In this chapter, several of the claims and problems peculiar to posttribulationalism will be discussed, with particular attention given to the viewpoint of its leading advocate.

I. POSTTRIBULATIONAL ATTITUDES AND METHODS

A. *Offensive Attitudes*

In any investigation where there is a sharp cleavage of opinion, there are always those who resort to unwise and intemperate language. Such has been the case with the issue at hand. However, anyone who reads widely in the literature of the four viewpoints involved will be forced to conclude that much of the harsh language and offensive attitudes stem from the posttribulational camp. Some of those who argue so strenuously that they must go through the Tribulation reflect in their writings an attitude of bravado, mingled with contempt for those who, either from ignorance or cowardice, do not share that conviction. Fromow, for instance, puts it this way: "We would lovingly ask, is there not a strain of weak-kneed, invertebrate, spineless sentiment in this idea of escaping tribulation?"[1] To Reese, pretribulationalists are "Darbyites," who follow "the Rapture craze, fathered by theorists," and whose views are held to be "supreme rubbish."[2] Scruby, in his writings, seems not to give even the common courtesies of debate, but speaks (all on one page) of carrying "the war into the enemy's country (Beard the lion in his den, so to speak) . . . bring my guns to bear . . . on these deceptive doctrines . . . rank absurdities . . . helpful in the fight against this latter-day delusion."[3] Certainly, this is not the way to convince the brethren of their love, and fortunately, all posttribulationalists are not as picric.

The book which has come to the fore as the most outspoken attack upon the pretribulational position is a large volume by Alexander Reese entitled *The Approaching Advent of Christ*. The title is somewhat misleading, for instead of giving a well-ordered, helpful analysis of the doctrine of the second advent, it is a sharp and unveiled attack upon the writings of Darby and the dispensational school, concerning itself primarily with the supposed merits of posttribulationalism over pretribulationalism. Lest the convictions of the present writer be thought to dominate

---

[1] George H. Fromow, *Will the Church Pass Through the Tribulation?* p. 4.
[2] Alexander Reese, *The Approaching Advent of Christ*, pp. 142, 207.
[3] John J. Scruby, *The Great Tribulation: The Church's Supreme Test*, p. 19.

at this point, here is part of the analysis of Hogg and Vine, conservative British commentators:

> The book, issued by Marshall, Morgan & Scott, London, 1937, owes its bulk not to the variety or abundance of its matter, nor to the necessities of its argument. If its attacks upon the character and competence of teachers, all of them God-fearing men, who sought to live honestly and to write sincerely, and many of whom were at least as competent and as well furnished as Mr. Reese himself, were eliminated, the size of the volume would have been considerably reduced and its general atmosphere sweetened. Erudite-seeming, lengthy, and irrelevant quotations could have been omitted with the same advantage. . . . He gives large space to modern translations of the New Testament. . . . The paraphrasists become not translators but interpreters of Scripture. Their readers should always bear this in mind. Wade, for example, p. 128, paraphrases Tit. 2:13 thus: "Looking forward to the hope (so fraught with happiness) of witnessing the Manifestation." Mr. Reese calls this a "translation," which it assuredly is not. It may be "idiomatic," but it is not what Paul said. The Christian does not look forward to being a spectator of "the appearing of the glory," but to being a sharer in it, according to Rom. 8:19, 29 and Col. 3:3, 4.[4]

This introduces something of the type of argument used in the book, but of the objectionable attitude which prevails throughout, Hogg and Vine continue:

> I have just been reading, in a secular Review, of "the courtesies of debate" observed in the world, but these have escaped the notice of Mr. Reese. . . . Mr. Reese does not seem to have made up his mind whether those whom he attacks so trenchantly are fools, or only knaves; his language, indeed, frequently suggests that they are both! Here are some things he says about them, taken at random as the pages are turned: They are guilty of "aggressive sophistry and fantastic exegesis," and of "paltry reasoning." They prefer "any rubbish to the true and obvious explanation" of a passage, and they "wrest the Scriptures." Their preference for the line of teaching they favor is "no longer a question of exegesis. . . . It is simply a question of ethics. . . . Have we the right moral disposition toward the truth, or will we still cling to error . . . shall we act against the truth or for the truth?" (This, on p. 244, causes the balance to dip rather toward the knave theory!) They are not God-fearing readers of the Bible, but "theorists," "showing little acquaintance with great exegesis." Their teaching is "consistent and ludicrous" in its "absurdity." Its

[4] Hogg and Vine, *The Church and the Tribulation*, pp. 9, 10.

> effect is to blight "Bible study and Christian fellowship all over the world." "It has cursed the (Brethren) movement from the beginning." "They wrote their errors on their broad phylacteries." (For the significance of this grave judgment reference must be made to Matt. 23:5 and its context.) They "are misguided and misleading teachers." . . . The list is not exhausted, but let this suffice.[5]

Reese follows the objectionable practice of attacking, not ideas, nor conclusions, but individuals, characterizing the men of God with whom he cannot agree as Sadducees and Darbyists! In one section, he says:

> I must leave to another place William Kelly's contortions of exegesis on the nature of the Great Tribulation, put forth with studied offensiveness in his two books on the Second Coming. His statement, as miserable as it is inexact. . . .[6]
>
> But, even if the Apostle had mentioned a Rapture at 2 Thess. i. 7, Darbyists would arrange three shifts to get rid of it. This is not cruel or churlish, but the plain fact.[7]

The reader will have to judge if these statements are "cruel or churlish," or if Reese, in his denunciations, manifests the fruit of the Spirit which is (to quote Reese's favorite translator, Moffatt) "good temper, kindliness, generosity" (Gal. 5:22). Indeed, if in dealing with his fellow brethren, a man fails to manifest such fruit of the Spirit, including as it does *love, longsuffering, gentleness,* and *self-control,* is he to be trusted as one who is Spirit-taught in the understanding of things to come? (John 16:13). It is one thing to rebuke false doctrine. It is entirely another to whip the brethren.

B. *Questionable Methods*

Many undesirable methods could be mentioned, but three or four will suffice. One of these is to imply that those who expect a pretribulation rapture are unqualified to judge, are of inferior intellect, and are unacquainted with the truly great literature in the field. Those of posttribulational persuasion, however, are among the greatest of exegetes! Reese expresses an attitude of mock humility when he says: "I have refrained from giving a bibliography; a long list of learned works is apt to convey the impression that the author is a scholar or a theologian; as I am

[5] *Ibid.,* pp. 10, 11.
[6] Reese, *op. cit.,* p. 222.
[7] *Ibid.,* p. 211.

neither I have omitted it."[8] He then goes on to spoil all this by speaking with all the dogmatism of a pope, and by concluding the book with page after page of authors and publications either referred to or quoted.[9] Some of the authors examined reveal that for them, posttribulationalism became a lifetime hobby, conducted along the line of a proselyting campaign — making converts, and always insisting that leading pretribulationalists saw the light just before they died. Scruby obviously spent the better part of his time making converts for posttribulationalism. Reese speaks in his Preface of a friend who maintained an interest in the venture of his own book for over twenty years prior to publication. Of Cameron, Newell writes:

> Robert Cameron, of *Watchword* and *Truth*, whose later life was largely a proselyting campaign for post-tribulationalism, used to claim that Dr. Brookes, of St. Louis, had given up this hope "before he died, in an interview with him!" But both the last books and the later associates of Dr. Brookes deny this. Others claimed that Prof. W. G. Moorehead gave it up, etc., etc. Someone told me that R. A. Torrey weakened. *I challenged him.* He could produce no proof whatever! Mrs. Torrey, when told that a Canadian magazine had claimed that her husband had given up the hope of Christ's coming for the *whole* Church, was much distressed, and wrote the editor to publish her denial of such a false report.[10]

> Much capital has been made of the fact that the revered George Muller of Bristol, misled by the mistranslation above alluded to ["day of Christ" in 2 Thess. 2:2, instead of "day of the Lord"] declared his belief that the Church would go through the Great Tribulation. He is quoted by Mr. Scruby as one of his witnesses [as also by Reese, Cameron, Fraser, et al.]. What was the result of this unfortunate mistake of beloved George Muller? I speak now from personal knowledge. The truth of the coming of the Lord was tabooed at Bethesda, where I was brought up, and was for many years a member and most regular attendant at the services. But I never once heard Mr. Muller or any other preacher say that they believed the Church would

[8] *Ibid.*, p. xlv.

[9] McPherson, a close follower of Reese, speaks of himself in like manner as "making no profession of being either a scholar or theologian," although he shows considerably better spirit but no bibliography. Norman S. McPherson, *Triumph Through Tribulation*, p. 4.

[10] William R. Newell, *The Book of the Revelation*, p. 399.

go through the Great Tribulation. And what is more, long after I had left Bristol Mr. Muller at the last conference at which he spoke said plainly that he believed the Lord might come at any moment. . . . Mr. Muller evidently changed his opinion a second time, which he would do, for he "could do nothing knowingly against the Truth."

C. H. Spurgeon is another of Mr. Scruby's [and Reese's, etc.] supposed supporters. That mighty man of valor was not ashamed to confess publicly that he once believed the Lord would not return till the world was converted, but that he came to see that this could not be done in "an eternity and a half." Mr. Spurgeon did not then believe the Lord would come before the Tribulation, but I heard Mr. Spurgeon at the Tabernacle not long before he died. It was at a conference on the coming of the Lord. Other speakers were Dr. Alexander Maclaren and Dr. John McNeill, and the impression left on my mind in the absence of any statement to the contrary was that all the speakers believed in the imminent coming of the Lord without any premonitary signs or the revelation of Antichrist. These facts show how futile it is to rest our faith on what great men may have believed. The greater the man the more ready he will be to revise his conclusions if he receives fresh light from the Word of God.[11]

This latter quotation comes from the pen of F. W. Pitt, who indicates that he was taught the posttribulation rapture position "from my youth up," but who said, after carefully examining the Scriptures for himself: "When I saw these things I did not have to give up 'Post-Tribulation Rapturism,' it melted away."[12] Yet posttribulationalists often argue that those who believe the pretribulational doctrine do so only because they are taught it, and that most of the "great men" finally see the light.

More objectionable than this is the method resorted to of bending facts to suit the posttribulational fancy. Miles writes of Reese's book:

I . . . opened the book in a spirit of expectancy. The first hundred pages or so filled me with astonishment. It is almost incredible that any considerable number of Christians could believe in the fantastic and grotesque theories dealt with. They seemed to me to be so many 'Aunt Sallies' set up to be skittled down. . . .

The writer is so thorough that it comes as a shock to find him confusing things that differ and bending things to suit his case

[11] F. W. Pitt, "The Great Tribulation," *Our Hope*, XLI (October, 1934), pp. 240, 241.
[12] *Ibid.*, p. 238.

while engaged in criticising others for doing the same, which certainly many have done.[13]

Pollock, who gives this citation, goes on to say: "We think it is a pity to have raked up so many silly fantastic opinions of this writer and that. It appears to us very like the trick of the lawyer with a bad case, who, to make up his deficiency, resorts to abusing the other side."[14]

Such inconsistencies abound in the book. Everywhere, pretribulationalism is criticized as something *new* and *novel*, but when it comes to the pretribulational view on the twenty-four elders, "The *old* interpretation is abandoned, except by those who need it as a prop to an edifice reared on insecure foundations."[15] Extreme positions are set up, then attacked. Normal pretribulational positions are dismissed, and preference is given to Darby, with his own peculiar views, on the one hand, or to Bullinger, who muddies the waters with hyper-dispensationalism and "two church" theories, on the other. Yet when exigencies arise, both Darby and Bullinger (attacked so vigorously on other issues) may be appealed to when they can be used to prove a point.

On page 71, Reese writes of "the wild dispensational theories of Dr. Bullinger," yet, when it comes to the elders: "Bullinger, also, I believe, gives the true interpretation . . . from his commentary on the Apocalypse."[16] On page 123, "happily, it is only an odd expositor like Bullinger who deprives Christians of the Epistle to the Hebrews," yet on pages 59, 295, etc., Bullinger again becomes the authority, or else the views of Moffatt, who is a liberal. Dalman, also, who sees Christ on earth as "merely a man,"[17] is cited with approval. Of this business of attacking extreme views and citing "off brand" authors, Pitt writes in the *Advent Witness*:

> We find that Mr. Reese not only sets one side against the other but chooses the authors who shall engage in the controversy, and selects from their writings such passages as suits his purpose. Torn thus from their context the Darbyists are made to say what Mr.

---

[13] F. J. Miles, *The Friend of Russia*, cited by A. J. Pollock, *Will the Church Go Through the Great Tribulation*, p. 7.
[14] Pollock, *loc. cit.*
[15] Reese, *op. cit.*, p. 94.
[16] *Ibid.*, p. 94.
[17] *Ibid.*, p. 253.

Reese wants them to say and no more or less, while the anti-Darbyists without regard to the subject in question are called upon to express their views on the different side issues which shore up the main proposition.

This is like playing a game of chess with yourself. If you are white you move black into positions where you know you can beat him.[18]

Certainly the large number of authorities that Mr. Reese quotes is astonishing. One would rather that he had expounded Scripture in such a clear way as to carry conviction of the truth. To come to an understanding of what Scripture says by depending on what others say is rather a weak way of arriving at the truth, and certainly beset with peril.[19]

One more objectionable method should be noted before passing on to more constructive matters. Reese makes the statement: "Darbyist advocates . . . smooth over a thousand difficulties in their programme of the prophetic future by judiciously keeping silent on inconvenient texts, and hoping for the best."[20] Reese rather notoriously falls into the same condemnation, picking and choosing what is convenient and letting the rest go by. For example, he admits that John 14:3 is one of the three leading texts on the rapture, but where in his voluminous treatment of other matters does he give the verse anything more than a passing mention? Certainly, the fact that when Christ comes He will take His own to be with Himself, where many mansions are being prepared, does not forward the argument of those who say that the rapture is only an incident in the downward sweep of a returning and wrathful King.

Similar is the tendency to attack the non-representative positions, all the while dismissing main issues. An illustration of this is the adoption of Darby's position on the *coming* and the *appearing* and on the Day of the Lord as the norm for pretribulationalism, while completely dismissing the more acceptable interpretation of other Brethren leaders, Hogg and Vine, whose position on these matters completely avoids both the attack and the conclusions drawn by Reese.[21]

For one who would study Reese's volume, it is important

[18] F. W. Pitt, *Advent Witness*, cited by Pollock, *op. cit.*, p. 6.
[19] Pollock, *loc. cit.*
[20] Reese, *op. cit.*, p. 72.
[21] *Ibid.*, pp. 28, 183.

that these methods be kept in mind, for to do so goes a long way toward answering his arguments and takes the sting out of many of his rebukes. To note the approach and method a man uses is particularly important when his work is voluminous, for it is manifestly impossible to answer all arguments point for point and line for line without making the rebuttal as lengthy as the original document.

II. THE HISTORICAL PROBLEM

Chief among posttribulational arguments is the contention that anything else is new and novel, and that pretribulationalism in particular did not come into existence until about the year 1830. Although embodying the doubtful value of an "argument from silence," the charge is thought to be an unanswerable one and is pressed to the limit. Pretribulationalism has been variously attributed to the writings of Edward Irving, to the utterances of a woman-prophet in a trance, to the writings of Darby and his associates, to a godly clergyman named Tweedy, and ultimately to the Devil himself! The following quotations illustrate the general tenor of posttribulational claims:

These views, which began to be propagated a little over one hundred years ago in the separatist movements of Edward Irving and J. N. Darby, have spread to the remotest corners of the earth.[22]

About 1830, however, a new school arose within the fold of Pre-millennialism that sought to overthrow what, since the Apostolic Age, have been considered by all pre-millennialists as established results, and to institute in their place a series of doctrines that had never been heard of before. The school I refer to is that of "The Brethren" or "Plymouth Brethren," founded by J. N. Darby.[23]

Darby, the *author* of a new programme of the End — a secret, pre-tribulation Parousia, followed by the rise of Antichrist. . . .[24]

Darby . . . *sponsored* a doctrine of a secret, pre-tribulation Rapture, brought from the West Indies by a godly clergyman. [Mr. Reese has difficulty making up his mind who authored the doctrine, and in which hemisphere!][25]

I am not aware that there was any definite teaching that there would be a secret rapture of the Church at a secret coming, until

22 *Ibid.*, p. 41.
23 *Ibid.*, p. 19.
24 *Ibid.*, p. 60.
25 *Ibid.*, p. 316, identified on p. 174 as Mr. Tweedy.

this was given forth as an "utterance" in Mr. Irving's Church.[26]

The theory that "the great tribulation comes after the rapture," is not taught in the Bible. It is traceable to the Irvingites and the Plymouth Brethren, with whom it is quite definitely shown to have originated about the year 1830. It is said to have been first suggested by Margaret McDonald, an Irvingite woman, supposed to be speaking in an "unknown tongue," which was interpreted that: "The Church will not go through the tribulation."[27]

It remained for a nineteenth-century "Irvingite" woman to introduce the flesh-pleasing doctrine, and that at a time when Irvingism admittedly had begun to corrupt. And the "weak" "flesh" causes the vast majority of Pre-Millennialists to hold that doctrine today, although they reject almost all else that the Irvingites taught.[28]

Indeed, *no one, in all Christian History from the Apostles to Edward Irving*, ever heard any other view (i.e. than that the true Church has no hope of the Lord's Coming at any moment, but must remain on earth during the time of the Great Tribulation). *Such a thing is not even hinted at as a possibility until the women-prophets* of Irving's assembly gave it out in those awful *days of demoniac delusion*. [Italics in the original citation.][29]

Here then is the alleged origin of pretribulationalism: either Darby, or Irving, or Tweedy, or Margaret McDonald, or Satan. It originated in both Great Britain and the West Indies. It was produced because of craven cowardice, to please the flesh, and ultimately, because of demonic delusion. Reese concludes that "the secret, pre-tribulation Rapture is a Gentile conceit of the nineteenth century,"[30] but even he is outdone by another who speaks extravagantly of "the Scripture wresting, God insulting, Christ dishonoring, saint-deceiving doctrine of Pre-Tribulation Rapturism."[31] Nor is this the worst example of posttribulational bitterness, but let it suffice. The point is that pretribulationalism is looked upon as a new and novel doctrine,

[26] S. P. Tregelles, *The Hope of Christ's Second Coming*, p. 35. On the same page, an interesting concession is made: "But when the theory of a secret coming of Christ was first brought forward (about the year 1832), it was adopted with eagerness; it suited *certain preconceived opinions*."

[27] George L. Rose, *Tribulation Till Translation*, p. 245.

[28] Scruby, *op. cit.*, p. 78.

[29] Citation by A. C. Gaebelein, "The Attempted Revival of an Unscriptural Theory," *Our Hope*, XLI (July, 1934), 19.

[30] Reese, *op. cit.*, p. 174.

[31] Cited by Gaebelein, *op. cit.*, p. 24. In this article, Gaebelein examines the writings of Irving, and finds that "the prophetic teachings of Irving are rather hazy," but without reference to women prophets who invented an imminent return of Christ, or the other teachings attributed to him.

with "no hint of such a belief . . . from Polycarp down . . . never taught by a Father or Doctor of the Church in the past . . . without a friend, even . . . amongst the orthodox teachers or the heretical sects of Christendom — such a fatherless and motherless doctrine . . ."[32] What, then, is there to say in answer to such claims?

(1) At the very best, all of this is an argument from silence, the absence of a record never proving the absence of a belief. There have been times in history when even the most cardinal doctrines of Christianity have been obscured by ignorance or ecclesiasticism. Were the great reformation doctrines recovered by Luther and Calvin, such as justification by faith alone, "new and novel" just because they had for centuries been in obscurity?

(2) As it has been demonstrated in chapter 6, the early church lived in expectation of the imminent return of Christ. They viewed his coming as a momentary possibility — so much so that some had left their work, and all had to be exhorted to patience. They were disturbed by the false report that the Day of the Lord had already come, hardly the attitude of men who view the Tribulation as the prelude to Christ's coming. In a word, the soon coming of Christ was the hope and expectation of the early church, which would never have been the case if they first expected the Tribulation and Antichrist, if not the certainty of a martyr's death. In this connection, Anderson writes:

> It is a fact of great significance that the Coming of the Lord is never mentioned in the Epistles of the New Testament save in an incidental manner — never once as a doctrine that needed to be expounded, but only and always as a truth with which every Christian was supposed to be familiar. . . . The fact is clear then, that in Apostolic times the converts were taught to expect the Lord's return.[33]

(3) It can likewise be demonstrated that, although the advanced details of a pretribulational theology are not found in the ancient church Fathers, belief in an imminent return was widely held, and if imminent, then pretribulational. Belief in the soon coming of the Lord Jesus Christ was standard doctrine

---

[32] Robert Cameron, *Scriptural Truth About the Lord's Return*, pp. 72, 73.
[33] Sir Robert Anderson, *Forgotten Truths*, pp. 68, 69.

in the Church throughout the first three centuries. Almost any church historian will grant that "the early Fathers lived in expectation of our Lord's speedy return,"[34] although there is not too much clear reference in the writing of the Fathers to the Tribulation itself.

> According to Moffatt [*Expositor's Greek Testament*, on Rev. 3:10], "Rabbinic piety . . . expected exemption from the tribulation of the latter days only for those who were absorbed in good works and in sacred studies." Thus there was a Jewish background for the expectation that some men would not pass through the Tribulation. When we come to the early Fathers we find an almost total silence as to the Tribulation period. They abundantly testify to the fact of tribulations, but they say little about the future period called by preeminence The Tribulation. This fact should cause us no perplexity. These writers lived during the second and third centuries, and we all know that those were the centuries of the great Roman persecutions. The Church was passing through sore trials, and it did not much concern itself with the question of the Tribulation yet to come. . . . Silver says concerning the Apostolic Fathers, that "they expected the return of the Lord in their day. . . . By tradition they knew the faith of the Apostles. They taught the doctrine of the imminent and premillennial return of the Lord."[35]

It is not necessary to enter into a detailed analysis of the belief of the early church Fathers pertaining to the coming of Christ. There is an abundant literature to prove that they were almost without exception premillennial, down to the end of the third century. There is also sufficient evidence to prove that many of them held the coming of Christ to be an imminent event, as seen in the following quotations.

Clement of Rome, undoubtedly a fellow-laborer with Paul as indicated by Philippians 4:3, wrote in his *First Epistle to the Corinthians* (about 95 A. D.):

> Ye see how in a little while the fruit of the trees come to maturity. Of a truth, soon and suddenly shall His will be accomplished, as the Scriptures also bear witness, saying, "Speedily will He come, and will not tarry"; and "The Lord shall suddenly come to His temple, even the Holy One, for whom ye look."[36]

[34] T. G. Crippen, *History of Doctrine*, p. 231.

[35] Henry C. Thiessen, "Will the Church Pass Through the Tribulation?" *Bibliotheca Sacra*, XCII (April-June, 1935), pp. 189-90. This article has an excellent digest of the expectation of the Ante-Nicene Fathers.

[36] Alexander Roberts and James Donaldson, *The Ante-Nicene Fathers*, I, 11.

Again, in his *Second Epistle*:

> If therefore we shall do what is just in the sight of God, we shall enter into His kingdom, and shall receive the promises, which neither eye hath seen, nor ear heard, nor have entered into the heart of man. Wherefore, let us every hour expect the kingdom of God in love and righteousness, because we know not the day of the Lord's appearing.[37]

We read in the *Didache,* dated about 100 A. D.:

> Watch for your life's sake. Let not your lamps be quenched, nor your loins unloosed; but be ye ready, for ye know not the hour in which our Lord cometh.[38] [The post-communion prayer in the *Didache* ends with "Maranatha — The Lord Cometh."]

Of special interest is a passage taken from *The Shepherd of Hermas,* written about 100-120 A. D., and thought by many to be the person mentioned by Paul in Romans 16:14. In a vision, Hermas was told:

> You have escaped from the great tribulation on account of your faith, and because you did not doubt in the presence of the beast. . . . Go, therefore, and tell the elect of the Lord His mighty deeds, and say to them that this beast is a type of the great tribulation that is coming. If ye then prepare yourselves, and repent with all your heart, and turn to the Lord, it will be possible for you to escape it, if your heart be pure and spotless, and ye spend the rest of your lives serving the Lord blamelessly.[39]

Lest it be asserted that all the passage teaches is the hope of preservation *in* Tribulation, let it be noted that according to the dialogue only the "double-minded" enter the Tribulation that they might be purified. Hermas, who "opened (his) heart to the Lord, believing that salvation can be found through nothing save through the great and glorious name," completely escaped the beast and "passed it by." The Greek word used throughout (*ekphugo,* to escape) is very explicit, as a careful comparison with its New Testament usage will confirm. It does not speak of patient endurance in tribulation, but of complete exemption from the judgment of God (Luke 21:36; Rom. 2:3; Heb. 2:3; I Thess. 5:3). Moreover, the maiden of the vision herself typifies the Church, as expressly stated. She is "adorned as if

[37] Cited by Silver, *The Lord's Return,* p. 59.
[38] Roberts and Donaldson, *op. cit.,* VII, 382.
[39] *Ibid.,* II, 18.

coming forth from the bridal chamber," hardly the description
of one locked in dread encounter with the beast!

While pretribulationalists get their doctrine directly from the
Bible and not from early Christian writers such as Hermas, this
passage direct from the turn of the first century completely voids
the argument that the concept of escaping the Tribulation is
something "new and novel," originating with Darby and Tweedy,
etc.

Cyprian, Bishop of Carthage, who flourished as a writer
220-250 A. D., declared:

> It were a self-contradictory and incompatible thing for us, who
> pray that the kingdom of God may quickly come, to be looking
> for a long life here below. . . . Let us ever in anxiety and
> cautiousness be waiting the second coming of the Lord, for as
> those things which were foretold are come to pass, so those things
> will follow which are yet promised; the Lord Himself giving as-
> surance and saying, "When you see all these things come to
> pass, know that the kingdom of God is nigh at hand." [40]

Similar passages might readily be cited from other writers
of this period. Although the Fathers were not always consistent
in their views, it is apparent that not a few of them looked
upon the return of Christ as imminent, expressing a definite
conviction that the Church may escape the Great Tribulation.
As for the testimony of the apostles themselves, their belief
in the imminency of Christ's coming shines forth from nearly
every book of the New Testament. To reiterate, a belief in
imminency implies a belief that the rapture will precede the
Tribulation; this fact is further attested by the bitter attack
which posttribulationalism has launched upon the very idea
of an imminent return. In the light of such evidence from
the early church and from representative Apostolic and Ante-
Nicene Fathers, it can hardly be sustained that pretribulational
beliefs "are new and novel, and have never been heard of in
the whole history of the Christian Church since the Apostolic
Age."[41]

(4) Cameron himself suggests a logical solution why the
doctrine of a pretribulational return *apparently* started about
the year 1830. While he claims that no mention of this doctrine

[40] Cited by Silver, *op. cit.*, pp. 67, 68.
[41] Reese, *op. cit.*, p. 29.

is found "from the first century until A. D. 1830,"[42] he notes a little later that "the doctrine of the Lord's Coming was *recovered* about ninety years ago."[43] Now, ninety years before the publication of Cameron's book in 1922 takes us right back to the date he sets for the first mention of pretribulationalism. In other words, up until the first quarter of the nineteenth century, the *entire doctrine* of the Lord's return had been obscure, if not almost lost to the Church. The Brethren and other godly men of that period were used of the Lord to restore to the Church the whole truth of the second coming of Christ, and *when that truth was restored it was pretribulational!* For centuries, prophetic study had been in disrepute. During the time of Roman ascendancy even justification by faith was almost lost and had to be recovered. The Reformers, occupied as they were with the cardinal issues of the gospel, largely carried over a Romish amillennial eschatology, and when the doctrine of the second coming was finally restored, pretribulational distinctions shared in the restoration.

(5) One more important fact must be noted, for it helps to explain the resurgence of interest in prophecy which has marked the course of the last century. Early centuries were occupied primarily with Bibliology and Theology Proper: the problems of inspiration and canonicity, the deity of Christ and the relationship of His two natures, and kindred problems. Later centuries debated Angelology. At the time of the Reformation, the primary issue was Soteriology. Then followed the rise of the great denominations, the chief issues of which fell largely in the area of Ecclesiology.

During these past nineteen centuries, there has been a progressive refinement of the details of Christian theology, but not until the last one hundred years has Eschatology come to the front to receive the major attention and scrutiny of foremost Bible scholars. It is not that the doctrine of Christ's coming, or any of its special features, is new or novel, but that the doctrine has finally come into the place of prominence it rightfully deserves. With that prominence there has come a greater

---

[42] Cameron, *op. cit.*, p. 138.
[43] *Ibid.*, p. 150. Italics added.

discernment of prophetic detail. A distant mountain range, upon closer inspection, may turn out to be two distinct ranges with a great valley lying between. Even so, a general view of the second coming may reveal one united event, but upon closer scrutiny, two separate aspects may be seen. This progressive attention to and refinement of Christian doctrine satisfactorily explains the lack of emphasis prior to the nineteenth century upon anything but the most obvious outline of prophecy. James Orr, in his *Progress of Dogma*, may well be quoted to sustain this thesis:

> Has it ever struck you . . . what a singular *parallel* there is between the historical course of dogma, on the one hand, and the scientific order of the text-books on systematic theology on the other? The history of dogma, as you speedily discover is simply the system of theology spread out through the centuries — theology as Plato would say, "writ large" — and this not only as regards its general subject-matter, but even as respects the definite succession of its parts. . . . If now, planting yourself at the close of the Apostolic Age, you cast your eye down the course of the succeeding centuries, you find, taking as an easy guide the great historical controversies of the Church, that what you have is simply the projection of this logical system on a vast temporal screen. . . . One thing, I think, it shows unmistakably, viz., that neither arrangement is arbitrary — that there is law and reason underlying it; and another thing which forces itself upon us is, that the law of these two developments — the logical and the historical — is the same.

> . . . Using, then, the controversies which impelled the Church in the formation of its creed as a guiding clue, mark, in a rapid survey, the exactitude of the parallel. The second century in the history of the Church — what was that? The age of *Apologetics* and of the vindication of *the fundamental ideas of all religion* — of the *Christian* especially — in conflict with Paganism and with the Gnostics.

> . . . We pass to the next stage in the development, and what do we find there? Just what comes next in the theological system — *Theology Proper* — the Christian doctrine of God, and specially the doctrine of the Trinity. This period is covered by the *Monarchian, Arian,* and *Macedonian* controversies of the third and fourth centuries.

> . . . What comes next? As in the logical system theology is succeeded by *Anthropology,* so in the history of dogma the controversies I have named are followed in the beginning of the fifth century by the *Augustinian* and *Pelagian* controversies, in

which . . . the centre of interest shifts from God to man.

. . . From the time of Augustine's death we see the Church entering on that long and distracting series of controversies known as Christological — *Nestorian, Eutychian, Monophysite, Monothelite* — which kept it in continual ferment, and rent it with the most un-Christlike passions during the fifth and sixth, on even till near the end of the seventh, centuries.

. . . Theology, Anthropology, Christology had each had its day— in the order of the theological system, which the history still carefully follows, it was now the turn of *Soteriology* . . . the next step, that taken by the Reformers in the development of the doctrine of the *Application of Redemption.* This, as we saw, is the next great division in the theological system. . . .

What now shall I say of the remaining branch of the theological system, the *Eschatological?* An Eschatology, indeed, there was in the early Church, but it was not theologically conceived; and a Mythical Eschatology there was in the Mediaeval Church — an Eschatology of Heaven, Hell, and Purgatory . . . but the Reformation swept this away, and, with its sharply contrasted states of bliss and woe, can hardly be said [note] to have put anything in its place, or even to have faced very distinctly the difficulties of the problem. . . . Probably I am not mistaken in thinking that, besides the necessary revision of the theological system as a whole, which could not properly be undertaken till the historical development I have sketched had run its course, the modern mind has given itself with special earnestness to eschatological questions, moved thereto, perhaps, by the solemn impression that on it the ends of the world have come, and that some great crisis in the history of human affairs is approaching.

. . . I am very far from disputing that there is still room for fresh developments in theology. . . . I do not question, therefore, that there are still sides and aspects of divine truth to which full justice has not yet been accorded. . . . All I am contending for is, that such a development shall be a development *within* Christianity and not *away* from it.[44]

Posttribulationalists should have seen this progress in doctrinal study as the logical solution to the problem they have raised, even though they missed the concept of imminency in the early church and in the writings of the Fathers. Even Reese admits: "Darby had his place in causing fresh light to break forth from God's Word. . . . And the great work goes on:

---

[44] James Orr, *The Progress of Dogma*, pp. 21-31. Italics in the original.

fresh light always breaking from God's Word, in all sections of the Church."[45]

If God used Darby and his associates to restore to the Church doctrines long obscure and neglected, his name should be remembered with gratitude and not profaned as the originator of a twentieth century heresy. In this whole matter concerning the history of the imminent, pretribulational return of Jesus Christ, there is little by way of factual support or by way of attitudes taken to commend the writers from the posttribulational school.

III. THE RESURRECTION OF THE SAINTS

The argument against a pretribulation rapture based on texts pertaining to the resurrection of the dead receives little attention from most posttribulationalist writers, and is evidently thought of little consequence. In the hands of Reese, however, the issue is blown up to giant proportions and made the number one argument, both from emphasis and from position given to it in his treatment. Of this argument, a disciple of Reese says in summary:

> The argument based on the time of the first resurrection throws much light on this theory of the double coming of Christ. Alexander Reese in his study, *The Approaching Advent of Christ*, has devoted sixty pages to elaborating this argument which seems well-nigh unanswerable. He presents evidence from the Old Testament, the Gospels, the Pauline epistles, and the Apocalypse. The argument in brief is this.

> Clearly the resurrection of the holy dead takes place at the Rapture of the Church (I Thess. 4:16). Therefore, "wheresoever the resurrection is, there will the Rapture be also." Upon examining passages that speak of the resurrection of the holy dead, which is the first resurrection (Rev. 20:5-6), we find that this first resurrection is associated with the coming of the Lord (Isa. 26:19), the conversion of Israel (Rom. 11:15), the inauguration of the Kingdom (Luke 14:14-15; Rev. 20:4-6), the giving of rewards (Rev. 11:15-18), the Great Tribulation coming before it (Dan. 12:1-3).[46]

Here, the main line of argument is suggested, together with the more important Scriptures used by Reese in his lengthy treatment—all of which is labeled "well-nigh unanswerable."

[45] Reese, *op. cit.*, p. 316.
[46] McPherson, *op. cit.*, p. 41.

It is not the purpose here to engage in a point by point analysis and refutation of the argument (although the writer is confident that this could be done), but to expose the erroneous premises upon which the argument is built, leaving the application of the same to the reader who pursues these pages and those of Reese. When David arose against Goliath of Gath, he chose five smooth stones out of the brook, any one of which was sufficient to fell the giant. Even so will lengthy argumentation fall, without examination of all its detail, by the proper application of a few well-placed, fundamental truths from Scripture and from logic.

In his examination of "The resurrection of the saints in the Old Testament," Reese's argument takes on the form of a syllogism, the major premise being (1) that the Old Testament Scriptures prove that the resurrection of Old Testament saints is at the revelation of Christ, just prior to the millennial kingdom; the minor premise being (2) that all Darbyists agree that the resurrection of the Church synchronizes with the resurrection of Israel; hence, the conclusion is drawn that (3) the resurrection of the Church sets the time of the rapture as posttribulational. To put the argument in the words of our author:

> But a blind man can see that the exact contrary is the truth. The resurrection *follows* the tribulation. The angel tells Daniel that at that time Israel would be delivered — that is, delivered from the time of trouble just mentioned [Dan. 12:2]. Then it is that the sleepers in the dust awake to inherit eternal life and the glory of the resurrection. . . .
>
> Now the termination of the week is characterized by two events, among others — first, the destruction of Antichrist, and, secondly, the deliverance of Daniel's people. . . . Nothing can be surer than that here we are at the close of the tribulation. What happens then? The resurrection of the saints. . . .[47]

The minor premise is expressed in several different ways:

> Darbyist writers themselves assert that if we can fix the epoch of this resurrection, we can know the time of the resurrection of the Church, since the two synchronize.[48]
>
> I must again remind the reader that we are not looking for the resurrection of the Church in this passage. We are concerned only with the question whether the text teaches the resurrection

[47] Reese, *op. cit.*, pp. 44, 45, 46.
[48] *Ibid.*, p. 34.

> of the holy dead of Daniel's people, the Jews. . . . It will be
> sufficient if we can prove that the righteous dead in Israel are
> raised, for it is these writers [Darby, Kelly, etc.] who tell us that
> the Church will be raised at the same time.[49]

Putting together these premises, Reese concludes that the
resurrection of the Church, and hence, the rapture, is posttribulational:

> These conclusions are fatal to the new theories of the Second
> Advent, because it is a fundamental point in those theories that
> the sleeping saints of Israel will rise some years before the de-
> struction of Antichrist, the deliverance of Israel, and the Coming
> of Jehovah and His Kingdom.[50]

In this chapter, Reese insists upon the literal interpretation
of the Old Testament resurrection passages, which is highly
commendable. But as for his main line of reasoning, he incorporates a false premise and of necessity arrives at a false conclusion.
Darby and his associates, to whom we owe so much, were not
always right. When they insisted that the resurrection of Israel's
dead occurs at the beginning of the Tribulation, that is, at the
same time as that of Church saints, they were very probably in
error, Reese adducing material proof from the Scripture that
Israel's resurrection follows the Tribulation. The syllogism should
more correctly follow this order: (1) The Old Testament saints
are raised after the Tribulation; (2) Darby says that Israel's resurrection occurs before the Tribulation with the resurrection of
Church saints; (3) therefore, Darby was wrong in respect to the
time of Israel's resurrection. Such a conclusion is all that this chapter by Reese warrants, yet it suits his theory to adopt an erroneous
premise in order to arrive at the conclusion posttribulationalism
demands.

A similar cycle of argumentation is found in Reese's discussion of "The resurrection of the saints in the Gospels." His
first premise is that the Day of the Lord is a definite point in
time, the last day of this age and immediately prior to the
Millennium. This has been stated in several different ways:

> In addition to this we were able to locate with relative exact-
> ness the time of that resurrection. It is to take place at the Day
> of the Lord, when Antichrist is destroyed, Israel converted, and

[49] Ibid., p. 42.
[50] Ibid., p. 49.

the Messianic Age introduced by the Coming of the Lord. . . .
The "resurrection of the just" . . . in every case . . . takes
place "at the last day." Here is a very definite point of time. . . .
And having regard to His [Christ's] fundamental ideas on Eschatology there can be no doubt that "the last day" is the
closing day of the Age that precedes the Messianic Kingdom of
glory.[51]

Proof cited to identify "the last day" in the Gospels with the
day preceding the Messianic Kingdom follows along the line
that it was a fundamental idea of Hebrew eschatology that
time falls into two ages, "the Messianic Age," and that which
preceded it; and it was adopted by our Lord and His Apostles.
. . . The Apostle Paul, like Christ, continues to employ the
usual expressions of Hebrew eschatology — "this age" and "the
age to come."[52]

At this point, it might be well to ask: When did the ideas
of Hebrew eschatology ever become the norm for determining
the eschatology of the Church, particularly since the Church
is an entirely separate body from Israel, differing from Israel in
a score of ways, and nowhere seen in the prophecy of the
Old Testament? Pretribulationalists believe that when the expression "last days" is used, and the Church is in view, that
these are the last days for the Church, and that when Israel
is in view, that these are the last days for Israel. This is the
normal, unstrained interpretation of the phrase. To further
substantiate his point, Reese cites Bullinger — of whom he says
in the following chapter: "Into the wild dispensational theories
of Dr. Bullinger it is not my intention to enter; one must draw
the line somewhere in investigating the labyrinth of prophetic
fads and theories."[53] But that is in chapter 4; here in chapter
3, Bullinger is the authority as Reese records:

> The true sense of the phrase "the last day" is also given by
> Bullinger in his Apocalypse: "Martha expressed her belief in the
> resurrection 'at the last day' (John xi. 24); i.e., the last day, at
> the end of the present age, and immediately before the introduc-
> tion of the new age of the thousand years."[54]

The second premise of the argument is quickly drawn, that

51 *Ibid.*, pp. 52-54.
52 *Ibid.*, pp. 53, 55.
53 *Ibid.*, p. 71.
54 *Ibid.*, p. 53.

"all Darbyists agree" that the resurrection of Church saints will
be "years or decades" before the Day of the Lord:

> In other words, does it indicate that the resurrection of the
> saints is to occur several years or decades before the Day of
> the Lord, as Darbyists insist? . . . On his theory the resurrection
> belongs in time to "this present age," a decade or a generation
> *before* the Day of the Lord begins.[55]

Therefore, it is concluded, "Darbyists" are in error when they
speak of a resurrection of Church saints prior to the Day of
the Lord.

> If we adhere to the simple terminology of our Lord and Paul
> about "the last day," "the present Age," and "the coming Age,"
> all will be plain, and we shall be saved at the very outset from
> the danger of getting lost in a labyrinth of dispensational tradi-
> tions, which lose nothing by comparison with the refinements of
> the Rabbis.[56]

Once again, a fallacy is introduced into the argument by
taking all the views of Darby and the earlier Brethren as
the absolute norm for pretribulationalism. It has been demonstrated in chapter 4 of this investigation that the Day of the
Lord is not the final day of the age, but a period which incorporates the Tribulation and, very probably, the Millennial age
also. Reese has seen this, for he says:

> Some may object that the expression "last day" refers not to
> a literal day, but to the last period of God's dealings with men
> in time; that is, to the age of the kingdom, which follows this
> present age, and will extend to the Last Judgment, when the rest
> of the dead are raised. Something might be said in favour of
> this, for Peter has a saying that one day with the Lord is as a
> thousand years; and the Day of the Lord in the O. and N. Testa-
> ments sometimes refers, not only to the day when Messiah comes
> in glory, but also to the period of His Reign. But even this ad-
> mission does not help the objector, for on his theory the resur-
> rection belongs in time to "this present age," a decade or a gen-
> eration *before* the Day of the Lord begins.[57]

So he dismisses the Day of the Lord as a period of time
solely on the grounds of Darby's position, that the Day of the
Lord is the day of the revelation of Christ. But the Day of the
Lord, seen as *a period including the Tribulation*, makes un-

[55] *Ibid.*, p. 71.
[56] *Ibid.*, p. 56.
[57] *Ibid.*, p. 55.

warranted the claim that a decade comes between it and the rapture.

As in the previous argument, the second premise is taken for granted, just because Reese and Darby happen to agree at that point. The logical conclusion of the argument is not that there is no prior resurrection of the Church, but merely that Darby—like Reese—was wrong in making the Day of the Lord a single day, thus necessitating an interval between it and the rapture. In fact, in this particular argument, Reese's major and minor premises are both in error, making the chance of drawing any accurate and acceptable conclusions very slim indeed.

Before proceeding further with Reese's argument on the resurrection, some wise words from the conclusion of his own book may be considered with profit:

> Careless readers and others who believe what pleases their fancy, are misled by specious reasoning, since they do not stop to examine it and test its validity. In one of the greatest controversial masterpieces of our language . . . a great theologian and mathematician expresses himself thus on the art of presenting a bad case:
> "It is a common rhetorical artifice with a man who has to command a false conclusion deduced from a syllogism of which one premise is true, and the other false, to spend an immensity of time in proving the premise which nobody denies. If he devotes a sufficient amount of argument and declamation to this topic, the chances are that his hearers will never ask for proof of the other premise" [Provost Salmon, *Infallibility of the Church*, p. 63].
> . . . By brilliant argument and declamation the major premise, which no one disputed, was easily demonstrated; the minor premise was dismissed with a wave of the hand and a casual remark that its truth was "self-evident"; the conclusion was then pressed home with easy success, for most people are easily persuaded into believing what they want to believe.[58]

All of this, Reese goes on to apply to pretribulational argument, particularly as it concerns escaping the Tribulation:

> But, even at the risk of seeming irksome or slow-witted, we wish to remind them of something that has escaped their notice. Why not give some attention to the minor premise, and prove to us that the Great Tribulation is the wrath of God? This, however, is the last thing that Darbyists can be brought to do. Scores

[58] *Ibid.,* p. 283. Italics added.

of tracts pass it by. And naturally; because that part of their syllogism which they adroitly hurry over is completely false. It is a blunder that the Great Tribulation consists in God's wrath; their conclusion, therefore, that the Church will escape the Great Tribulation, is false, since *if falsity attaches to one of the premises, it attaches to the conclusion.*[59]

Reese may well have pondered this truth of his own writing!

It is most doubtful if pretribulationalists so studiously avoid proving that the Great Tribulation consists of God's wrath. The Scriptures are all on their side, as has been demonstrated in some detail in chapter 2. Nevertheless, false reasoning is an error into which any author may slip, particularly one overly zealous to prove his case, and Reese is no exception. He assumes that the Day of the Lord is a point in time. He assumes that it is equivalent to the day of Christ's revealing. He assumes that the Old Testament saints are raised with the Church, particularly since Darby said so. And "if falsity attaches to one of the premises, it attaches to the conclusion." With this we agree.

Readers of Reese will be stimulated to make a fresh study of the Scriptures, particularly if they have accepted pretribulational positions solely on the basis of the research of others rather than from their own labors. Such a study and re-evaluation can be immensely profitable. However, this word of caution must be added for those who may unwittingly channel their thoughts after the pattern of Reese's argument. Watch for false premises! Often they appear on the very first page or two of a chapter, and if lightly accepted, the reader runs the risk of being led whithersoever the author will.

After arguing from "the last day" of John 6, Reese turns his attention to three other passages, all from the synoptics and all largely Jewish in content. For instance, the context of Luke 14:14, 15 finds Jesus answering Jewish lawyers and Pharisees, and the subject under discussion is that of healing on the Sabbath, and that in its relationship to Mosaic law. Hardly the setting for Church truth, unless the assumption is granted that Israel and the Church are identical and are raised on the same day! As to Matthew 13:43, it is sufficient to note

[59] *Ibid.,* p. 283. Italics added.

that the kingdom in its mystery form is that which it takes during the absence of the King. It goes on through the Tribulation and includes, but is not coextensive with, this present age of the Church.

Passing on to Reese's discussion of "The resurrection of the saints in St Paul's epistles," the argument is pressed from four chief Scriptures: Romans 11:15; I Corinthians 15:50-54; I Thessalonians 4:13-18; and I Corinthians 15:21-26. Since the second and third of these passages are cardinal, and also receive the most attention by Reese, the discussion will be limited to these. The gist of the argument from the Corinthian passage is as follows:

> Paul not only describes the resurrection and transfiguration of the saints: he emphatically indicates the time for the fulfillment of these wonderful events. Here are his words: "So WHEN this corruptible shall have put on incorruption, and this mortal shall have put on immortality, THEN shall be brought to pass the saying that is written, 'Death is swallowed up in victory'" (v. 54).
>
> Nothing could be clearer than the Apostle's argument here. The resurrection and transfiguration of the faithful dead will take place in fulfillment of an O. T. prophecy. This occurs in Isaiah xxv. 8. . . . The resurrection of the saints, and the victory over death, *synchronise with the inauguration of the Theocratic Kingdom, the Coming of Jehovah, and the conversion of living Israel.*[60]

Paul is obviously writing of the Church in I Corinthians 15; he then cites an Old Testament passage to emphasize that resurrection brings victory over the enemy, Death; this passage in Isaiah has for its context entrance into the kingdom age. To Reese, it is transparently clear that Paul "emphatically indicates the time for the fulfillment of these wonderful events." However, there are weak links in this chain of thought. So much is made to depend on the demonstrative adverb *then* (τότε). Primarily an adverb of time, it may also be used in the sense of the Hebrew *waw* consecutive, thus simply continuing the narrative. Even when used in the temporal sense, it does not necessarily mean "at that moment," or "without intervening events," as in John 8:28, "When ye have lifted up the Son of man, *then* shall ye know that I am he." Rather than the apostle's using this Old Testament quotation to set the time of

60 *Ibid.*, p. 63. Italics in the original.

the resurrection in its relationship to the kingdom, it would seem that he is merely setting forth the simple and obvious relationship between the future resurrection and the present reign of Death. Since the victory of Christ over death at His resurrection, Death has been a defeated enemy, although still having a sting until that time when the Christian puts on his resurrection body. *Then,* when this occurs and *not before,* Death will lose its sting. The relationship of this event to the *time* of the kingdom is hardly in view. If it were, and if it is as obvious as Reese seems to think, the fact that so many of the finest commentators overlooked the entire matter is surely a cause for wonder.

It is always precarious in prophetic Scriptures to assume that two events, seen side by side, of necessity occur together. If Isaiah 25:8 proves from its context that resurrection is associated with the bringing in of the kingdom, then on the same basis, and much more clearly, is it possible to prove that the resurrection of Isaiah 26:19-21 *precedes the Tribulation,* for after saying to Israel: "Thy dead shall live," the prophet continues: "Hide thyself . . . until the indignation be overpast, For, behold, the Lord cometh out of his place to punish the inhabitants of the earth for their iniquity." All of these difficulties argue against Reese's conclusion, but there are yet three others:

(1) Revelation 21:4 cites the same Old Testament prophecy, but the setting now is *past* the kingdom age, entering into the eternal state after the creation of a new heaven and a new earth. If there is any temporal significance to the allusion to resurrection in Isaiah 25:8, at what time does the resurrection occur in the light of Revelation 21:4?

(2) It is manifestly impossible to date Church events by Old Testament Scripture. Final victory over death may be seen, but the Church herself, as also the manner of her resurrection and rapture, are mysteries not revealed until the New Testament.

(3) It is highly disputed if I Corinthians 15:54 alludes to Isaiah 25:8 at all; most commentators find this to be an allusion to Hosea 13:14, which is a closer parallel — and where the difficulty raised by Reese is avoided. Yet Reese chooses to make the teaching of these two passages in question a "grave dis-

crepancy" with "the new scheme of the End," continuing: "So far as I am aware, no Darbyist writer has ever honestly faced the question."[61] Perhaps it was not that the argument was considered unanswerable, but that it was not considered necessary to answer an argument that reveals so many obvious difficulties.

The second main argument from the Pauline Epistles concerns the familiar passage, I Thessalonians 4:13-18. Reese says that the passage furnishes no evidence for the time of the rapture, although, having made so much of the order of events in the context of Isaiah 25:8, he should have noted that the context here in I Thessalonians 4 is "study to be quiet" (v. 11) before the passage (hardly a Tribulational setting) and "the day of the Lord so cometh as a thief" *after* the passage — a perfect pretribulational order of events. But hear our author's reason for introducing this passage:

> Darbyists themselves furnish us with reasons that smash their central position. They all admit, in the first place, that this resurrection in I Thess. iv. includes the resurrection of all the righteous dead since Abel; this is a fundamental point in the scheme.[62]

Here is the false premise, the same in substance with that previously introduced in the study of the resurrection in the Old Testament. Pretribulationalists do not particularly relish being called so constantly "Darbyists" (elsewhere, Darbyists and Sadducees), but in good humor may overlook the intended stigma. But they will not, for the most part, "admit" that all of the righteous dead since Abel are raised at the rapture. Far be this from being a fundamental point of pretribulationalism; it is considered by many to be inconsistent with the Scriptures and is therefore rejected.

Daniel 12:1, 2 is outstanding among Old Testament passages on the subject of resurrection, and here the unprecedented time of Tribulation sorrow *precedes* the awakening and resurrection of Israel's dead from the dust of the earth. Similarly, in verse thirteen of Daniel 12, the prophet's own resurrection is identified with the end days of the Tribulation following the unmasking of Antichrist and the abomination of his rule. In Isaiah

[61] *Ibid.*, p. 65.
[62] *Ibid.*, p. 68.

25:8, when death will be swallowed up in victory, then the Lord God will wipe away tears from off all faces. The implication seems plain that Israel's resurrection is associated with the glory and comfort of Christ's appearing, for it would hardly follow that all tears shall be wiped away *before* "the time of Jacob's trouble" (Jer. 30:7). Rather than synchronize the resurrection of Israel's righteous dead with the rapture of the Church, an entirely different group with a separate eschatology, it would seem far more in keeping with the prophetic Word to synchronize it with the sound of the trumpet which shall gather the elect of God from the four winds and from one end of heaven to the other (Matt. 24:31), and this occurs "after the tribulation of those days."

Again, Revelation 11:18 and its immediate context is best explained if it is seen that "the time of the dead" when saints and prophets shall be judged and rewarded refers to Israel's resurrection at the end of the Tribulation and not to some small and unidentified remnant of the end time. It is not without reason that many pretribulationalists must part company with Darby on this particular point of the time of Israel's resurrection, and it is most foolish for one to make Darby's view not only the norm, but also the touchstone for all pretribulationalism. However, Reese builds his entire case at this point upon Darby's view:

> Very well then, this means that I Thess. iv. synchronises with the resurrection in Isaiah xxv. 8, xxvi. 19, Dan. xii. 1-3, 12-13 [etc.]. And we have already proved that these passages clearly locate the resurrection of the saints in Israel at the commencement of the Messianic Kingdom, when Antichrist is destroyed, and Israel is converted by the appearing of Jehovah.[63]

Nor is this second premise without its difficulties, but we press on to the conclusion of the argument:

> The whole Darbyist case collapses, therefore, before their admission that I Thess. iv. includes the raising of the O.T. saints.[64]

Once more a false conclusion has arisen from a false premise. The true conclusion should be that Darby was wrong in respect to the time of Israel's resurrection — that, and nothing more. Yet Darby was right about so many other things, even his case

[63] *Loc. cit.*
[64] *Loc. cit.*

does not collapse over one or two inconsistencies, and even though it did, normal pretribulationalism which makes no such concession is not weakened in the least. By the failure of the pretribulationalist to agree with Darby at this particular point, it is the argument of the opposition which undergoes collapse.

Reese concludes his sixty page argument concerning the time of the resurrection with a discussion of "The resurrection of the saints in the Apocalypse," the discussion revolving around the two disputed and difficult chapters, the eleventh and the twentieth.

The first passage considered is Revelation 11:15-18, bringing up the familiar matter of the seventh trumpet. Immediately, there is an uncertain premise:

> And here in Rev. xi. 15, we have these very events under the seventh or last trumpet, which also blows at the Day of the Lord. The conclusion is inevitable, therefore, that the Last Trumpet of John are one and the same. We are right, therefore, in inferring the resurrection from Rev. xi. 15-18.[65]

Reese attempts to bolster his argument a little, but avoids the fact that the seventh trumpet cannot fall on what he calls the Day of the Lord because it is followed by yet seven vials of wrath upon the earth before the Tribulation period is terminated. There is great difficulty resident in any view which lumps together in one day the Day of the Lord, the Day of Christ, the revelation of the Son of God, and other events which Scripture takes pains to separate. Yet the seventh trumpet "finishes the mystery of God, and heralds the introduction of the Kingdom of Christ and of God, the resurrection, judgment, and rewarding of the saints, and the Coming of the Lord."[66] Included also is the marriage of the Lamb and the Marriage Supper, and all on one day! Other difficulties with identifying the seventh trumpet and the "last trump" have been discussed in the last chapter (where with equal determination, it was argued that the seventh trumpet marks the exact midpoint of the week) and so need not detain us here.

Next follows Reese's attack upon the view that the Church is represented in Revelation 4 by the twenty-four elders. This

[65] *Ibid.*, pp. 73, 74. So also, p. 78.
[66] *Ibid.*, p. 75.

also has been discussed under the consideration of the mid-tribulation rapture view. Reese does point out the inconsistency of Kelly and others, who held that the elders represent the Old Testament saints as well as the Church, but such a difficulty is obviated when it is seen that the elders represent the Church alone. Were the Old Testament saints to be raised together with the Church, then the elders might represent both, but it is here contended that Israel is raised at the end of the Tribulation, thus avoiding their inclusion with the elders and also explaining the rewarding of certain saints in Revelation 11:18. The terminology, "thy servants the prophets," is likewise more suitable for Israel than for the Church, for the Church is seen at the time of these events as the glorious bride of Christ. Reese states: "Inasmuch, therefore, as Rev. xi. 18 depicts the giving of rewards to the whole company of the redeemed, we may be sure that this also is the time of the resurrection of the just."[67] Were he speaking of Israel alone, we would agree, but as he includes the Church, we can not. There is no contradiction in Revelation 11 to the view which sees the Church raptured and rewarded before the Tribulation and Old Testament saints raised and rewarded at its close. Both here and elsewhere, difficulties occur only when Israel and her prophetic program is confused with the Church and her own distinct eschatology.

A more pressing problem arises with the consideration of Revelation 20:4-6. Reese wisely limits the discussion, accepting two literal resurrections according to the normal premillennial pattern, and counting it unnecessary to enter into the millenarian controversy which has raged over the passage. He sets the stage for the present disputation in the following manner.

What conclusion can we draw from the vision in Rev. xx. 1-6? Just this, that here we have the clearest refutation possible of the Darbyist system; for, according to those theories, the first resurrection is to take place at least seven years before the Day of the Lord and the millennium: some time even before the *rise* of Antichrist: according to this vision of the Apocalypse, the first resurrection takes place in immediate association with the *destruction* of Antichrist, and the establishment of the Messianic King-

[67] *Ibid.*, p. 77.

dom. Thus we have exactly the same teaching as in all the earlier Scriptures.[68]

It is the position of pretribulationalism that the resurrection of the saints occurs at a point earlier than the vision here recorded in Revelation 20. To this, Reese has two objections, namely, that John records no earlier resurrection, nor could there be a resurrection prior to that which is called the first. In his own language:

> Not a word is said by John in the whole of the Revelation of any such resurrection. Nothing can be found of an earlier one, either here or in any other part of the Word of God. If such a prior resurrection was known to John — as the theory presupposes — then how is it conceivable that he would call this resurrection the *first?* . . . But that he wrote *first* resurrection will be proof to all candid readers that he knew of none before it.[69]

Since this is the heart of Reese's argument, and since he makes this "the clearest refutation possible of the Darbyist system," it should suffice to answer him on these two points. The first objection, that John records no earlier resurrection, is easy to refute. Reese is depending upon the familiar and untrustworthy argument from silence. Unless there is something with which to back up an argument drawn from silence, it is better to argue from what the text does say rather than from what it fails to say. The most extended and complete passage in all the gospels on the subject of the Tribulation and the return of Christ to earth is that of Matthew 24. Yet, in his consideration of the resurrection of the saints in the gospels, Reese chooses to allude to other passages. Can the reason be that Matthew 24 maintains silence as to any resurrection, and that Reese insists that where the resurrection is, there will the rapture be? If the argument from silence is valid, this absence of resurrection in Matthew 24 is most striking. As to John's failure to mention the resurrection of the dead in Christ, such mention is hardly to be expected in a book which foresees the Church in glory and deals with God's judgment upon the earth, and not primarily with His mercy toward saints already in heaven. As to the notion that "not a word is said by John" of any prior resurrection, what then of the resurrection of the

[68] *Ibid.,* p. 81.
[69] Reese, *loc. cit.*

two witnesses in 11:11,12, and what of the great multitude from all nations, clothed in white and standing before the throne, in 7:9-17? These are resurrected saints and are identified as "they which have come out of great tribulation." Pretribulationalists believe that the rapture occurs, chronologically, before the opening of the fourth chapter of Revelation, or else in 4:1. What then of the twenty-four elders, representative of the Church and seen in glory far in advance of Revelation 20? Are not these suggestive of a prior resurrection?

This, however, anticipates the answer to Reese's second objection, that there can be no prior resurrection because that of Revelation 20:5 is termed "the first." Is an earlier resurrection as impossible as Reese presumes?

All premillenarians are agreed that there are two resurrections, the first being the resurrection of the righteous dead before the millennial kingdom, and the second being the resurrection of the wicked dead one thousand years later at the great white throne judgment (Rev. 20:11-15). The first resurrection is that of the just; the second is that of the unjust. All who have part in the first resurrection are *saved;* all who are raised to stand before the great white throne are *lost.* Two resurrections are in view — and two classes of men.

This alone indicates that the important distinguishing feature between the two is the *kind* of resurrection, rather than the *time* of resurrection. Pretribulationalists believe that the term "first resurrection" indicates that those raised are the *first in kind,* and that such a distinction is far more important than the time factor involved. They believe that the first resurrection speaks, not necessarily of an event, but rather of *an order of resurrection.* It may occur in several successive stages, but all the saved are in the resurrection designated *first* in distinction from those in the *second,* who are lost. Nor is this concept without Scriptural warrant:

> For as in Adam all die, even so in Christ shall all be made alive. But every man in his own order: Christ the firstfruits; afterward they that are Christ's at his coming (I Cor. 15:22, 23).

Even as the gathering of the firstfruits becomes the token and assurance of the completed harvest, so Christ was first raised and forms the pattern for the resurrection of those who believe in Him. As He lives, so shall we live in His presence; as His body was raised incorruptible, so shall we also be raised incorruptible. "As we have borne the image of the earthy, we shall also bear the image of the heavenly" (I Cor. 15:49). The resurrection of Christ is the seal and the assurance of the resurrection of those that are His.

> But if there be no resurrection of the dead, then is Christ not risen: And if Christ be not risen, then is our preaching vain, and your faith is also vain . . . ye are yet in your sins. Then they also which are fallen asleep in Christ are perished. If in this life only we have hope in Christ, we are of all men most miserable (I Cor. 15:13-19).

Here, then, is an order of harvest: Christ the firstfruits, and after Him, "every man in his own order." Christ had part in the "first resurrection," and indicates that other "orders" are to make up the completed harvest. What may some of these other orders be?

> And, behold, the veil of the temple was rent in twain from the top to the bottom; and the earth did quake, and the rocks rent; And the graves were opened; and many bodies of the saints which slept arose, And came out of the graves after his resurrection, and went into the holy city, and appeared unto many (Matt. 27:51-53).

> For the Lord himself shall descend from heaven with a shout, with the voice of the archangel, and with the trump of God: and the dead in Christ shall rise first (I Thess. 4:16).

> After this I beheld, and lo, a great multitude, which no man could number, of all nations, and kindreds, and people, and tongues, stood before the throne, and before the Lamb, clothed with white robes, and palms in their hands. . . . And he said to me, These are they which came out of great tribulation, and have washed their robes, and made them white in the blood of the Lamb (Rev. 7:9, 14).

> And they of the people and kindreds and tongues and nations shall see their dead bodies three days and an half, and shall not suffer their dead bodies to be put in graves. . . . And after three days and an half the spirit of life from God entered into them, and they stood upon their feet; and great fear fell upon them which saw them. And they heard a great voice from heaven saying unto them, Come up hither. And they ascended up to heaven in a cloud; and their enemies beheld them (Rev. 11:9, 11, 12).

> There shall be a time of trouble, such as never was since

there was a nation even to that same time: and at that time thy
people shall be delivered, every one that shall be found written
in the book. And many of them that sleep in the dust of the
earth shall awake, some to everlasting life. . . . (Dan. 12:1, 2).

It is most apparent that here are different orders of harvest:
Christ, the firstfruits; the saints who were raised after His resurrection, probably taken to heaven when Christ ascended to His
Father; the dead in Christ at the rapture, before the Tribulation;
the martyred saints of the Tribulation period; the two witnesses;
and the Old Testament saints at the close of the Tribulation.
None of these are in the resurrection of the unjust; therefore,
all of them must have part in the resurrection of the righteous,
which is termed "the first resurrection." Each is raised, but in
his own order. The word translated "order" is a military term
meaning a band, brigade, or division of an army. Christ catches
home the army of the redeemed of all ages, but they arrive
in different bands. Yet all are in the one resurrection of the
redeemed. There is no difficulty here, except for those who
gloss over every indication of resurrection prior to Revelation
20 in order to protect the theory that there can be no rapture
prior to the Tribulation.

Admittedly, there is no clear indication of various stages of
resurrection in the words, "This is the first resurrection," but
a doctrine is never built upon one verse of Scripture when there
are others on the same subject which call for consideration.
It is also quite characteristic of prophetic Scriptures that the time
element involved is not always clearly stated. In some cases,
events placed side by side in prophecy actually find their fulfillment hundreds of years apart. A familiar example is found
in Isaiah 61:1, 2, in which both advents of Christ are seen
side by side. When the Lord read these verses in the synagogue
at Nazareth, He "closed the book" in the middle of the second
verse of Isaiah 61, saying: "This day is this scripture fulfilled in
your ears" (Luke 4:16-21). The rest of the verse, concerning
"the day of vengeance of our God," will not reach its fulfillment until the second advent, yet Isaiah sees both advents in
one view and records them side by side in a single verse. John
5:28, 29 may be cited as another illustration of the same principle:

> Marvel not at this: for the hour is coming, in the which all that are in the graves shall hear his voice, And shall come forth; they that have done good, unto the resurrection of life; and they that have done evil, unto the resurrection of damnation.

In this passage, there is not the slightest hint that the resurrection of life will differ in point of time from the resurrection of damnation. Other Scriptures make it obvious that the entire kingdom age of one thousand years intervenes between the two, but the passage in John deals with the *fact* of these resurrections and not with the *time* element involved. Who could foresee, without searching other Scriptures, that "the hour" of which John speaks actually includes an interval of one thousand years? Fallacy arises when it is assumed that two events mentioned side by side must of necessity fall together. On that basis, one might gather that Christmas falls on December 31 from statements linking Christmas and New Year together, or connecting both with the end of the year.

Moreover, in Revelation 20:14 is recorded: "And death and hell were cast into the lake of fire. This is the second death," but in Revelation 19:20, speaking of Antichrist and his false prophet, John records: "These both were cast alive into a lake of fire. . . ." Yet, the former is after the millennium, the latter, preceding it. If the "second death" embraces two judgments separated by a thousand years, who can rightfully deny successive stages in the "first resurrection"? The terminology of 20:14 is exactly the same as that of 20:5: "*This is* the second death," "*This is* the first resurrection."

Reese remarks that on pretribulational grounds "John ought to have written: 'this is the *second* resurrection: blessed and holy is he that hath part in the second resurrection.'"[70] With the same line of reasoning, John should have written: "This is the *third* death," but of course he did not. McPherson writes that having a "first" before a "first" is a riddle, and that to include earlier resurrections in the first resurrection is a "mathematical nightmare."[71] However, the "riddle" is readily answered when it is seen that "first" is an *order of resurrection* referring to all the redeemed, and this in harmony with other

---

[70] *Ibid.*, p. 81.
[71] McPherson, *op. cit.*, p. 40.

Scriptures where the fact, and not the time, of an event is being stressed. Posttribulationalists have yet to explain the fact of previous resurrections, if Revelation 20:5 *were* actually first in point of time.

Reese's further arguments from the resurrection of the saints in the Apocalypse are of little consequence and need not detain us long. He touches upon the seventh trumpet, and goes into some detail as to whom the twenty-four elders are *not,* but these matters have been adequately discussed in the previous chapter. He argues that the twenty-four thrones of Revelation 4 were empty, on the basis of 20:4, where it says: "I saw thrones, and they sat upon them." To Reese, this proves that John sees them as "a company *in the very act of sitting down on their thrones,*"[72] but this is slender evidence upon which to build a doctrine. He asks: "If the Twenty-four Elders represent the raptured saints in heaven before the Seventieth Week, why do we not see the saints themselves instead of twenty-four symbols?"[73] Aside from the fact that the elders are individuals rather than symbols, it is just as reasonable to ask why Christ is seen throughout as a Lamb. It is argued: "If no mention is made in the Apocalypse of the Rapture, surely it is the part of a careful student to enquire whether the Christian hope is not portrayed under different imagery and expressions."[74] That being an acceptable principle, there is everything to favor the Church being seen in heaven prior to the Tribulation under the imagery of the elders. Yet Reese fails to deal with the principle evidence which determines the identity of the elders, seems to be unaware of the textual support for the old reading for the song of the elders, calls them "angelic lords" despite the fact that they are always differentiated from angels, and takes comfort in the fact that Bullinger agrees with him as to their identity!

The chapter presents no ordered principle for interpreting the book of Revelation, and mere criticism of the views of others is an empty shell without something genuine and conclusive to offer in their place. The problem of the resurrection is Reese's

---

[72] *Ibid.,* p. 83.
[73] *Ibid.,* p. 87.
[74] *Ibid.,* p. 89.

main emphasis and argument, and one leaves it with an awareness that he has not substantiated his position, that he has left much unsaid, and that much of what has been said by way of ridicule was entirely unnecessary.

IV. ADDITIONAL POSTTRIBULATIONAL ARGUMENTS

Since every chapter previous to this (with the possible exception of chapter 8) contributes one or more answers to some phase of the posttribulational argument, it is not necessary here to give additional space to the same consideration. In the words of another: "One must draw the line somewhere in investigating the labyrinth of prophetic fads and theories." Yet, lest it be said that many posttribulational arguments were omitted in a chapter given over to an examination of that theory, other leading points of posttribulationalism should at least be stated and the chapters mentioned where a fuller discussion may be found.

A. *The Wheat and the Tares*

The argument is that the parables of Matthew 13 describe the mystery form of the kingdom of God, setting forth the course of this present age. Just as the wheat and the tares grow side by side until the harvest, so Christians and unbelievers exist together until the "end time," identified by Matthew 24:3ff. as at the revelation of Christ. Therefore, Christians are on earth until the final judgment, and the rapture is said to be posttribulational.

In answer, the chapter describes the mystery form of the kingdom of heaven—the form the kingdom is to assume during the absence of the King—which period includes both the Church Age and the Tribulation. The opposing argument is beside the point since Matthew 13 and the Church Age are not entirely co-extensive; the mystery form continues after the Church is removed. The parable of the wheat and the tares simply illustrates the presence of the righteous and the unrighteous, side by side upon the earth. God is patient in His dealings with unregenerate men, but nevertheless, the tares are steadily ripening for the harvest and certain judgment. To make the parable a proof for posttribulationalism is unwarranted, for, even according to this view, at the revelation of Christ, He will first take out His Church — while the parable insists "first the tares." Nor do angels gather the Church at the rapture, but Christ Himself. Nor is it entirely certain that the parable has the Church in view at all, for in Matthew 8:1-13, it is Israel that is called "children of the kingdom." Moreover, there is no resurrection in the parable. Instead of straining to find therein proof for the time of the rapture, is it not reasonable to limit its teaching to that which is more obvious, even God's present patience with the unrighteous and their certain ripening toward judgment?

B. *The Parousia of Christ*

It is the position of Reese that the *parousia* of Christ (discussed in chapter 1) "far from being a prolonged period, is a single crisis breaking with the utmost suddenness."[75] He insists that the proper translation of the word is "arrival," rather than "presence," and speaks of it as a "kingly word." Thus, he seeks to make *parousia* a technical word for a kingly visit, characterized as a sudden crisis, for in so doing, his theory of the rapture is strengthened. However, *parousia* is quite an ordinary word for coming, used for instance of the coming of Stephanas (I Cor. 16:17; cf. II Cor. 7:6) and in a very unkingly sense in II Corinthians 10:10: "his bodily *presence* is weak, and his speech contemptible." This last verse, together with Philippians 1:26, 2:12, and many others, illustrates the use of *parousia* in the sense of *presence*. In II Corinthians 7:6, 7, it was not merely the arrival of Titus which comforted Paul, but rather his *continued presence* with him subsequent to that arrival. Even so, the importance of Christ's *parousia* lies not so much in the sudden splendor of His appearing as it does in the fact that the Christian shall be with Him where He is.

There is an excellent summary of the verses where *parousia* is used, together with the doctrinal implications thereof, in *The Church and the Tribulation*, by Hogg and Vine. C. F. Hogg has concluded his discussion by saying:

> But enough of the word, which, as Mr. Reese recognises, is a key to the understanding of the end times. Let that be my apology for devoting so much space to it. I think it may be claimed that his witnesses, under cross-examination, fail to sup-

[75] *Ibid.*, p. 152.

port him in his contention that "the humblest in the first century knew that the word meant the triumphant arrival of Messiah to put down all authority, and then to reign." And Mr. Reese himself makes no better showing. He seeks to impress his uncritical readers with a mass of undigested quotations, many of them from doubtful sources, calculated to confuse the mind of those who are not in a position to estimate the true value of the formidable array of "authorities" who, for the most part, have only opinions to offer, not facts.[76]

C. *The Church Promised Tribulation*

Through much tribulation, believers must enter into the kingdom of God. To shirk suffering for Christ is a sign of degeneracy in the Christian life. Pretribulationalists accept their doctrine through cowardice, or an excessive desire for worldly ease — these are the postulates of posttribulationalism. The true nature of Christian suffering, the distinction between persecution and wrath, the nature and source of the Tribulation to come, the fact that Revelation 6-19 is all characterized as *wrath*, and some of the express promises of the Word that the Church will be spared the wrath to come — these, and kindred themes, are found in chapter 2 of this investigation.

D. *Do Christ and Paul Agree?*

Matthew 24:29 places the coming of Christ "after the tribulation of those days." It is argued that if the rapture of I Thessalonians 4 is before the Tribulation, then Paul is made to disagree with Christ. But this is to assume that there is no rapture separate from the appearing, which is the fallacy of arguing in a circle. Chapter 3 sets forth some of the basic distinctions between Christianity and Judaism and proves that posttribulationalism is largely founded upon Scriptures given directly to Israel. A comparison of Matthew 24 with I Thessalonians 4 reveals some similarities, but primarily it yields striking and convincing contrasts.

E. *The Day of the Lord*

According to Reese, "that day," "the Day of the Lord," and "the Day of Christ" are all synonymous expressions for the day

[76] C. F. Hogg and W. E. Vine, *The Church and the Tribulation* (a review of the book entitled *The Approaching Advent of Christ*), pp. 27, 28.

of the *parousia,* which closes the present age and ushers in the age to come. Posttribulationalists make some headway showing the inconsistencies of Darby's position on the Day of the Lord, but when this Day is seen as a period including the Tribulation, as demonstrated in chapter 4, their argument falls to pieces.

F. *The Restrainer of II Thessalonians 2*

Reese identifies the restrainer as the Roman Empire, a magnificent system of law and justice, surviving in the Papacy, "the ghost of the deceased Roman Empire"! Other posttribulationalists are divided in their opinion, one accepting the identification of the Holy Spirit, another identifying the restrainer with Satan. While pretribulationalism does not hinge upon identifying the restrainer as the Spirit, chapter 5 presents reasons why this is thought to be the most reasonable and acceptable view. If this thesis can be sustained, it gives a devastating blow to the posttribulation rapture theory.

G. *The Doctrine of Imminency*

Posttribulationalists are the violent opponents of the doctrine of the imminent return of Christ, for they deny that the Christian attitude is to be that of momentarily expecting God's Son from heaven. Their argument is drawn from certain New Testament predictions as they are applied to the first century Church, which objections are answered in chapter 6. Early Christians were obviously looking for the return of the Saviour and were encouraged to do so, and the normal Christian attitude has ever been to watch and to wait for His coming. Posttribulationalism robs the Church of a doctrine which has long been a primary source of blessing and comfort, as well as one of her chief incentives to holiness and service. Newell writes:

> Who have been the teachers and preachers of Christ's imminent coming? We have such men as John Darby, who was probably the greatest interpreter of Scripture since Paul, with such early Brethren as C. H. Mackintosh, J. G. Bellett, Wm. Kelly, and the rest, a marvelous coterie. Then you have C. H. Spurgeon. It is idle to . claim that he was not *looking* for Christ's coming. He split no hairs such as the post-tribulationalists do, but boldly and constantly proclaimed the second coming of Christ as *an actual and a daily possibility.* D. L. Moody was a wonderful witness to any truth God revealed to him; and his sermon on "The Second

Coming of Christ" is a classic. He was looking for the Lord's coming. George C. Needham, beloved Irishman; Wm. E. Blackstone, whose life has been to *look for* his Lord; James H. Brookes, a mighty warrior, now with the Lord; A. B. Simpson, of whom Moody said, "Everything he says reaches my heart." All these were looking for Christ's appearing. It was the *hope of their lives*. H. M. Parsons, of Toronto, and Dr. Weston . . . faithful witnesses alike. Grand old I. M. Haldeman, of New York, as well as J. Wilbur Chapman, now with Christ. A. T. Pierson, of wonderful penetration in the meaning of Scripture; A. J. Gordon; George E. Guille . . . devoted, gentle, sane, yet a *contender* for Christ's *imminent coming*; our Brother Ironside, whose praise is among the real churches of Christ; Lewis Sperry Chafer at Dallas; A. C. Gaebelein, of New York, Editor of *Our Hope*, perhaps the most persistent, faithful witness for over fifty years to the imminent return of our Lord . . . James M. Gray, late President of the Moody Bible Institute of Chicago . . . a host of faithful witnesses to Christ's *imminent* coming, in Great Britain, Scandinavia, the mission fields, and Australia.[77]

H. *The Rapture and the Revelation*

Posttribulationalists argue that "to meet the Lord in the air" means to meet the Lord and quickly return with Him to the earth, all in a single crisis. They claim further that the rapture cannot be separated in point of time from the revelation of Christ and that the rapture is but an insignificant detail in the downward sweep of the Lord to earth at His glorious appearing. For all of these contentions there is clear proof to the contrary. Some of this evidence has already been given, while the following chapter will take up in particular the distinctions between the rapture of the Church and the revelation of the Lord to the earth. It hardly needs to be said, that if rapture and revelation can be distinguished the one from the other, on that ground alone the posttribulational argument is lost.

V. A Word in Conclusion

It is never a welcome responsibility to oppose the views of men who are brethren in Christ, particularly concerning issues over which even premillennial men are divided. While there is wisdom in the words of Bishop Butler: "A truth being established, objections are nothing; the one is founded upon our knowledge,

77 William R. Newell, *The Book of the Revelation*, pp. 400, 401.

the other upon our ignorance,"[78] yet the establishment of a doctrine is not complete until at least basic tenets of the opposing views have been dealt with. Particularly is this true when one of the opponents argues as voluminously and as vociferously as does Reese — such a voice cannot be ignored. In the words of another, who writes of Reese's book: "If there were a little more good will, less argument, and more chastened enquiry, how much we might learn together!"[79]

It is the belief of this investigator that by the close of the following chapter the main views and the chief objections of the posttribulational system will have been fully and fairly met. To touch upon all the details would be to prolong the analysis to a tedious length, for it is more or less irksome to be overly persuaded on points concerning which there is very little doubt in the first place.

Posttribulationalism has been met and answered on its own ground, particularly on the three issues which are often called unanswerable: the argument that pretribulationalism is new and novel, the argument as to the time of the resurrection, and the argument against the possibility of Christ's return being imminent. Among the leading weaknesses of posttribulationalism, aside from the intolerant attitude of many of its advocates, is the tendency to depart from the fundamental principle of literal interpretation, the failure to comprehend that the Tribulation is essentially a time of divine retribution, the tendency to take ordinary words of Scripture and force them into the mold of technical usage, the refusal to recognize the truth and appreciate the value of an imminent return, a steadfast refusal to accept Paul as the primary revelator to the Church of God, and a lingering legalism combined with a failure to grasp the real character and scope of divine grace.

[78] Cited by Reese, *op. cit.*, p. 225.
[79] Hogg and Vine, *op cit.*, p. 15.

CHAPTER ELEVEN

THE RAPTURE: INCIDENTAL OR FUNDAMENTAL?

In addition to the many themes touched upon in the preceding chapters, it yet remains to clarify the major differences between the rapture of the Church and the revelation of Christ to earth. If the posttribulational view is correct, the center of Christian thought and expectation should rightly be the revelation of Christ, the rapture becoming an incidental part of His return to earth from glory. If, however, the rapture stands by itself as an individual crisis and if it is the next major event upon the program of God, it becomes the one issue of fundamental importance to all who look with hope to the end of the age.

Christians must read the Word of God with discernment. No matter how earnest the Bible student, his interpretations will go astray if he fails to distinguish between things that differ. While it is a mathematical axiom that "things equal to the same thing are equal to each other," it does not always follow that Biblical events which bear some similarity are therefore identical. Particularly is this true of eschatology. All judgments are not the same judgment, nor are all resurrections the same resurrection, no matter how hard some may try to press them into a single mold.

A typical example of prophetic generalization may be noted from the Westminster Confession:

1. At the last day shall be a general resurrection of the dead both of the just and of the unjust.
2. All found alive shall be immediately changed.
3. Immediately after the resurrection shall follow the general and final judgment of all angels and men, good and bad.[1]

With clear evidence to the contrary, such "lumping together"

1.Cited by A. A. Hodge, *Outlines of Theology*, p. 576.

of prophetic events can only confuse the student and discredit the Sacred Text. While the author does not advocate making complex the things of God, the tendency of many to over-simplify God's prophetic program is nevertheless an error of the first magnitude.

I. THE POSTTRIBULATIONAL CONCEPT OF THE RAPTURE

When posttribulationalists refuse to distinguish between the rapture and the revelation of Christ, blending them together into a single event which occurs "in the twinkling of an eye, at the last trump," they fall into the same reductive error. The outcome is to make the rapture an insignificant and meaning-less detail. In the words of Reese, it is "a mere incident of the appearing,"[2] spoken of only to show that the living will have no advantage over the dead in Christ at His appearing. According to this view, "both the rapture of the saints, with the change of living believers, and the visible appearance of our Lord in glory and in judgment will occur at one and the same time."[3] It is the purpose of this chapter to show that such a theory is in conflict with the Scriptures at every point of investigation. Two facts in particular will be outstanding: first, the rapture of the saints and the revelation of Christ to earth are separate in point of time, and second, these events differ the one from the other in many of their leading characteristics.

Now it is rather obvious that one will search in vain if he looks for a crystalized statement such as "The rapture will precede the revelation by seven years." If any such declaration existed there would be no argument whatsoever. But similarly, nor does the Bible say in just so many words that "God is a trinity," yet an abundance of Scripture attests this fact. The absence of a word or a definition is of little consequence if the doctrine is woven into the very fabric of Scripture. The solu-tions to all Bible problems do not lie on the immediate surface, but must be settled by inference, by comparing Scripture with Scripture, by reverent Spirit-taught exegesis. Such is the case with the question at hand, and the lack of a clear, concrete

---

[2] Alexander Reese, *The Approaching Advent of Christ*, p. 266.
[3] Alexander Fraser, *Is There But One Return of Christ?* pp. 9, 10.

statement is more than replaced by a wealth of relevant verses — sufficient, it would seem, to afford a clear and satisfying answer.

II. IS THE RAPTURE SIMULTANEOUS WITH THE REVELATION OF CHRIST?

In making the rapture of Church saints a secondary part of the same crisis with the revelation of Christ to earth, posttribulationalists stand alone. All others, pretribulationalists and midtribulationalists, as well as partial-rapturists, unite in viewing the rapture as a phase of the second advent, distinct from the return to earth. Fraser, a posttribulational author, recognizes that the rapture and the revelation are "two phases of our Lord's Second Coming," but it is representative of his school of thought when he adds: "they occur together at the full end of the age." The thought is that the saints will meet the Lord in the air "and will return with Him at once."[4] In answer to the query: "If Christ comes *for* His saints on the Day of the Lord, how are we to reconcile this with the statement of Scripture that He then comes *with* His saints?" Reese responds:

> There is no need to reconcile them; Christ comes for His saints and with them at the same crisis. When He comes according to I Thess. iv. 13-17 and Matt. xxiv. 31, He is on His way to earth to establish the Messianic Kingdom. But before the blow falls upon the ungodly, the Elect are gathered from one end of heaven to the other to meet the approaching Lord. They meet the Lord in the air and follow in His train.[5]

As the authority for this view, there is cited the meaning of the Greek verb in I Thessalonians 4:17, where it is recorded: "Then we which are alive and remain shall be caught up together with them in the clouds, *to meet* the Lord in the air; and so shall we ever be with the Lord." In the opinion of Cameron:

> A very definite truth is settled, however, by the word translated "to meet," which has a distinct and definite meaning. It is only used three times in the New Testament, and in every case it means to *meet and to return* with the person met. Therefore, those caught up, meet the Lord and return with Him.[6]

Actually the noun ἀπάντησις, meaning a *meeting* or an *encounter*, is found four times in the Greek New Testament (Matt.

[4] *Ibid.*, p. 14.
[5] Reese, *op. cit.*, p. 237.
[6] Robert Cameron, *Scriptural Truth About the Lord's Return*, p. 116.

25:1,6; Acts 28:15; I Thess. 4:17). Reese has drawn the post-tribulational interpretation of these verses a little more sharply than Cameron, as follows:

> There are only three other places in the New Testament, where the phrase here translated "to meet" occurs; and in all of them (Matt. xxv. 1, 6; Acts xxviii. 15) *the party met continues after the meeting to advance still in the direction in which He was moving previously.*[7]

By concluding that the Church saints who are caught up to meet Christ continue in the direction of the Saviour, the post-tribulationalists find evidence that the rapture and the revelation are joined together in a single crisis.

However, this is slender evidence indeed to warrant robbing the Church of its pretribulational hope. While Acts 28:15 *may* indicate that the brethren from Rome returned with Paul to that city, it is far less clear (in both Matthew 25:1 and 25:6) what direction the bridegroom takes after he has been met by the virgins. How can one be sure when the destination is not given? But in I Thessalonians 4:17, the destination of the bridegroom after He meets His bride in the air is not open to question. According to John 14:2,3, His coming again to receive His own unto Himself is for the express purpose of taking His bride to the heavenly mansions now being prepared for them. Here is clear Biblical evidence that the party met by Christ *does not* continue "after the meeting to advance still in the direction in which He was moving previously." For posttribulationalists to attack the hope of Christ's pretribulational coming on the strength of what presumably happened when Paul was met by brethren from Rome is precarious indeed. Of the two passages cited by Reese, Thiessen writes:

> In neither of these Scriptures is it clear that they returned *immediately* after meeting. Paul undoubtedly had a time of fellowship with the brethren that came to meet him, before they started for Rome. The Greek word here used means simply a *meeting*, and the cognate Greek verb, *to go to meet, to meet.* Thayer, *op. cit., s. v.* Indeed, in the Textus Receptus reading of Luke 14:31, and in the LXX text of I Sam. 22:17; 2 Sam. 1:15; I Macc. 11:15, 68, and in other Greek writers, the thought of a return is

---

[7] Reese, *op. cit.,* p. 238, citing John Lillie, *Lectures on the Epistles to the Thessalonians,* pp. 267, 268. Italics in the original.

impossible. Therefore we affirm that although Christ will return with His own, the language nowhere implies that He will return *immediately.*[8]

The evidence against the posttribulational contention is even more devastating from a study of the Greek verb which bears the same stem and meaning as the noun in question. The cognate verb ἀπαντάω, *to meet,* which Reese fails to mention, occurs seven times in the New Testament. Anyone who can read for himself the simple narrative of the passages involved will immediately discover that the interpretation suggested by Reese is arbitrary and misleading. In Matthew 28:9, 10, the women who met Christ did not continue with Him but were sent on ahead into the city. In Mark 5:2, a man with an unclean spirit comes out of the tombs to meet Jesus. Rather than continuing together in the same direction, Christ commands him to go home to his friends telling what great things were done for him (v. 19).

Again in Mark 14:13, the idea of Reese and Cameron proves to be in error. Christ instructs His disciples to go into the city, there to meet a man bearing a pitcher of water. The fact that Christ then adds the command, "follow him" shows clearly that the verb itself does not convey the meaning that they were to continue together. To say otherwise is to accuse the Lord Himself of redundancy.

Equally as striking is the account of Luke 14:31, which involves kings at war. Thayer's *Lexicon* points out that the verb "to meet" is used here "in a military sense of hostile meeting," which hardly implies going along in the same direction. Liddell and Scott, in their *Greek-English Lexicon* also bear out the fact that the verb is *often* used in Greek literature in a "hostile sense, *to meet* in battle." In Luke 17:12, ten lepers meet Christ and are cleansed of their dread disease. Although the same verb, "to meet" is used, it is significant that none continue with Christ and only one returns long enough to glorify God and give thanks. Even this one whose faith has made him whole is sent on his way by the Lord.

[8] Henry C. Thiessen, *Lectures in Systematic Theology,* p. 483. Also, Thiessen, "Will the Church Pass Through the Tribulation," *Bibliotheca Sacra,* XCII (July-September, 1935), 303.

Of the seven references where the verb ἀπαντάω is used, John 4:51 alone implies that those who meet continued on their way together — but this is gathered, not from the meaning of the verb, but rather from the fact that they were members of the same household. In the final reference, Acts 16:16, the damsel with the spirit of divination which met Paul and Silas hardly travelled on with these disciples, for they were almost immediately put on trial and thrown into the Philippian prison. Nor can it be presumed that the evil spirit cast out from the damsel cared to journey further in the same direction with these men of God.

It is therefore entirely in order to conclude that the post-tribulational position in regard to the rapture, that the saints will meet the Lord in the air and return with Him to the earth in one simultaneous action, is hopelessly in error both theologically and linguistically. Such a view can only confuse and mislead the members of Christ's Church. There is no Scriptural warrant or lexicographical precedent to require an immediate return of the saints to earth, save the demands of the post-tribulational scheme.[9]

III. RAPTURE AND REVELATION DIFFER IN POINT OF TIME

A. *A New Testament Pattern*

In addition to I Thessalonians 4:17 and these other verses which prove an immediate return of the Church with Christ highly improbable, the analogy of other New Testament Scriptures suggests that an interval between the rapture and the revelation is necessary. Brookes has indicated how other dealings of Christ with His people favor a twofold aspect of the second coming:

> Christ at His first coming was revealed only to His own who waited for the consolation of Israel, and, then after an interval He was publicly manifested to the world on the banks of the Jordan. . . . We are justified before God by faith alone; we are justified before men by works. We are sanctified now in Christ Jesus, and we are sanctified progressively also as we go through the world. The Lord has private dealings with his own before there is any public exhibition of himself or of them; and it is

[9] A helpful analysis of this entire problem, particularly in respect to the Greek, is found in G. H. Lang, *The Revelation of Jesus Christ*, pp. 262-65.

easy to believe that he will not make their reception into His presence and His revelation in judgment a simultaneous act.[10]

The prior rapture of the Church is in complete harmony with the angelic testimony recorded in Acts 1:11. The ascension sets the pattern for His coming, for Christ shall return "in like manner." Christ left the earth in the presence of His disciples, not seen by His enemies as are the two witnesses of Revelation 11:12. Is it not implied that the return of Christ will first be for His friends before He is manifested in the sight of all men? This same truth is illustrated by the parable of the pounds in Luke 19. When the nobleman returned, he first called together his servants and had a reckoning with them concerning service rendered during his departure, *after which* he dealt with his enemies.

Many times during this investigation, it has been indicated how the overall pattern of New Testament doctrine is in accord with the presence of an interval between the rapture and the revelation. The Pauline Epistles deal extensively with the walk of the Christian while on earth, yet there is no instruction for the behavior of the Church during the trials of the Tribulation period and the conflict with the Beast. This is not an oversight, or a subject thought unnecessary to expound, for Israel is certainly so instructed (Matt. 24:15-26), with the reminder "Behold, I have told you before."

Nor is the Church mentioned in the fourteen chapters of the Revelation given over to the detailed description of the Tribulation and its actors. In chapters two and three, during which John writes of "the things which are," the *ekklesia* of God is mentioned no less than nineteen times; but when the vision turns to "the things which shall be hereafter," that is, during the Tribulation, the Church is no longer an actor upon the world stage. Nor is she seen again until Revelation 19:8, 14, at which time she is found returning with the armies of heaven to rule and to reign with Christ. During the Tribulation, Israel is protected from the anger of the Beast (Rev. 12:13-17), but no place of protection is recorded for the Church, implying that it is not needed.

10 James H. Brookes, "Kept Out of the Hour," *Our Hope*, VI (November, 1899), 156.

It is important to recognize this basic harmony between the pretribulational view and the other themes of the New Testament. The hope of a prior rapture for the Church is not something foreign to the Sacred Text. Indeed, it is an integral part of the total pattern.

B. The Jewish Remnant

Although it is good premillennial doctrine that God will yet revive His ancient people, Israel, and send them out as witnesses to His saving grace in the end time, posttribulationalists find it convenient to ridicule those of Israel who are redeemed during the Tribulation. Reese pours out his scorn upon this "half-converted, half-Christian Jewish Remnant (unconverted, un-Christian would fit the facts better) . . ."[11] but does not seem to recognize that his defense of a theory has thrown him into conflict with the Word of God. By divine inspiration, John calls them "servants of our God," "they which follow the Lamb," "redeemed from among men," "firstfruits unto God," and "without fault before the throne of God." Testimony such as this should be clear enough to satisfy anyone.

The point, however, is that these redeemed ones are seen *as Jews*. They are listed according to their genealogy from the twelve tribes of Israel (Rev. 7:4-8; 14:1-5), yet they belong to Christ for they bear His testimony (Rev. 12:17). Here is proof indeed that the Church is not on earth during the Tribulation. Probably the most distinguishing characteristic of the Christian Church is that both Jews and Gentiles have been placed into the body of Christ by the baptizing ministry of the Holy Spirit (I Cor. 12:12, 13).

Contrary to anything previously known, the Jew and the Gentile has been reconciled to God in one body by the cross; the middle wall of partition has been broken down; both now constitute "one new man" in Christ so making peace (Eph. 2:11-18). Now if the Church were still on earth during the Tribulation, making that period merely the awful climax of the present Church Age, the redeemed of the Tribulation would automatically become members of the Church and would never

[11] Reese, *op. cit.*, p. 208.

be classified as members of a distinct Jewish group. To force the Church into the Tribulation is to necessitate the simultaneous presence on earth of two separate, redeemed, witnessing groups, each retaining their separate identities — but to do so is to deny the vital Pauline doctrine of the unity of the body of Christ. The only other alternative is to deny that there is any redeemed Jewish remnant at all during the Tribulation. As demonstrated, such is the expediency of the posttribulationalist. It is self-evident that the Scriptures do not sustain his thesis.

While it is evident that Israel's national conversion will not be complete until the revelation of Christ, when they shall look upon Him whom they have pierced (Zech. 12:10; Rom. 11:26, 27), nevertheless a remnant from among Israel shall be redeemed and become God's primary witnessing body during the Tribulation. The Church, her witness complete, will be already with the Lord. Thus, the presence of redeemed Jews on earth during the time of Jacob's sorrow necessitates a period of time after the rapture and before the revelation during which they will be converted and go forth to witness.

C. *Important Events Separate Rapture from Revelation*

According to the posttribulational view of the rapture, the Church is caught up to meet Christ in His triumphal sweep toward the earth, both rapture and revelation occurring almost simultaneously "in the twinkling of an eye," or at the most in a matter of moments. Alexander Fraser, an ardent posttribulationalist, has quoted with approval the view of James R. Graham, Jr.:

> On the same "day" and probably only a few moments apart, He comes for His saints, and with His saints (I Thessalonians 4:16, 17). The dead and living go up to meet Him as He descends, join His train and accompany Him back as He stands on the Mount of Olives and destroys Antichrist and his armies.[12]

Reese is of the same mind when he says that the rapture is a mere incident of the Appearing and that the coming *for* and the coming *with* the saints belong to the same crisis.[13] Cameron

---

[12] James R. Graham, Jr. (editor), *Life in the Spirit*, p. 55. Cited by Alexander Fraser, *The "Any Moment" Return of Christ: A Critique*, p. 21.

[13] Reese, *op. cit.*, pp. 237, 266.

affirms that these events are "synchronous, and cannot be separated."[14] Unfortunately, however, this is an unsustained opinion. While posttribulationalists are forced by clear revelation to admit two distinct phases of the second advent, it is believed that they do not face squarely the evidence of two additional predicted events which necessitates an interval between rapture and revelation.

The first such event, which cannot occur until the rapture has passed, is the judgment seat of Christ (generally called the Bema seat, from $\beta\hat{\eta}\mu\alpha$, Gr. *tribunal*). Mentioned primarily in the writings of Paul, it constitutes a warning that each believer shall give God account of his stewardship, and an incentive for faithfulness in the Christian life and fruitfulness in Christian service.

> For we must all appear before the judgment seat of Christ; that every one may receive the things done in his body, according to that he hath done, whether it be good or bad (II Cor. 5:10).
>
> Now if any man build upon this foundation gold, silver, precious stones, wood, hay, stubble; Every man's work shall be made manifest: for the day shall declare it, because it shall be revealed by fire; and the fire shall try every man's work of what sort it is. If any man's work abide which he hath built thereupon, he shall receive a reward. If any man's work shall be burned, he shall suffer loss: but he himself shall be saved; yet so as by fire (I Cor. 3:12-15).

This is not the Great White Throne (Rev. 20:11); salvation is not in view, but Christian works; none who stand before the Bema seat of Christ are lost, but some will come there almost empty handed having gathered little fruit in God's harvest field (Ps. 126:6; John 15:8). Paul speaks of a crown of righteousness "which the Lord, the righteous judge, shall give me at that day" (II Tim. 4:8). Again, he mentions the prospect of a crown of rejoicing at the coming of the Lord Jesus Christ (I Thess. 2:19). Peter encouraged believers with the hope that "When the chief Shepherd shall appear, ye shall receive a crown of glory that fadeth not away" (I Pet. 5:4; cf. Rom. 14:10; I Cor. 9:24-27; John 5:22).

This judgment of the believer's works is clearly associated

---

[14] Cameron, *op. cit.*, p. 92.

with the return of the Lord Jesus Christ for His own. It is after the rapture but before the marriage supper, for it is inconceivable that the church should be judged and her works tried by fire *after* she is joined to Christ as His bride. This viewpoint is in complete harmony with the twenty-four elders, who represent the raptured church in heaven and are seen as crowned before God's wrath falls upon the world.

The second major event to occur after the rapture but prior to the revelation is the marriage of the bride of Christ and the marriage supper of the Lamb:

> Let us be glad and rejoice, and give honour to him: for the marriage of the Lamb is come, and his wife hath made herself ready. And to her was granted that she should be arrayed in fine linen, clean and white; for the fine linen is the righteousness of saints. And he saith unto me, Write, Blessed are they which are called unto the marriage supper of the Lamb (Rev. 19:7-9).

This is the time for the Church to be presented "as a chaste virgin to Christ" (II Cor. 11:2), "a glorious church, not having spot, or wrinkle . . . but . . . holy and without blemish" (Eph. 5:27). From John's record it is rather obvious that the presentation of the bride and the marriage of the Lamb occur in heaven (Rev. 19:1, 4, 11). The call to the marriage and the whole wonderful union (which Paul calls a "great mystery" in Eph. 5:32) takes place *before* heaven opens and the Son of God descends to the earth in power and great glory. If there is any chronology at all to the Revelation account, and if any harmony at all to the prophetic Word, the call to the marriage, the presentation of the bride, and the marriage of the Lamb occur in heaven before the revelation of Christ upon earth. In context the event is associated with heavenly worship, the presence of the twenty-four elders and the four living creatures, a voice "out of the throne," and the mighty voice of the heavenly multitude (Rev. 19:1-6). Without doubt, the whole wonderful scene takes place in heaven. The saints have all been raptured (for there will be no partial bride!), but as yet the revelation has not taken place.

Here, then, are two notable events—the Bema seat of Christ and the marriage of the Lamb—both of which must occur in heaven *after* the rapture but *before* the return to earth.[15] Now, these events have long been anticipated; they have been looked for with much rejoicing (Rev. 19:7) and will not be hurried. The bride has time to make herself ready (19:7). There is worship and praise involving all of the hosts of heaven (19:6). The Hallelujah Chorus of the redeemed must be sung, and with all eternity ahead it will not be limited to "the first and the last stanza"! Before the marriage and the supper will be the presentation of the bride. This is the most glorious, crowning experience in all the long history of the Church, and will be a time of greatest joy for the Christ who redeemed her. When all the saints go marching in, "He shall see of the travail of his soul, and shall be satisfied" (Isa. 53:11).

The Bema seat, and now the presentation of the bride and the marriage supper — these are literal events, not symbolical fancies. They cannot and will not be fulfilled all in one fleeting moment. The lives of the saints must be reviewed, their works must be tested, the rewards will be administered, the bride will prepare herself and be presented to Christ, the marriage must be performed and the marriage feast celebrated and enjoyed. Yet for the sake of a theory, which by sheer necessity unites the rapture and the revelation and all which intervenes into one solitary climax, some would have us believe that all these blessed experiences occur in an instant, in the twinkling of an eye, as part of the downward sweep of the Lord to earth, with no preview of heaven, and with no glimpse of the "many mansions" prepared by a loving Saviour for the Bride whom He will receive unto Himself when He comes again (John 14:2,3).

There is one posttribulationalist who sees the grave inconsistency of such a program. He, at least, faces the inescapable fact that a time interval is required between the ascension of the saints to meet Christ and their return with Him to reign. Rose makes the following interesting and notable confession:

> There is no direct statement in the Bible concerning the length

[15] Some see four events: (1) the Church judged (II Cor. 5:10), (2) the Church rewarded (I Cor. 3:14), (3) the Church presented (Eph. 5:27; Heb. 2:13; Jude 24), and (4) the Church married (Rev. 19:7-9).

of time between the going up to meet the Lord in the air and the returning with Him. However, "forty days" is a significant period of time in Holy Writ. The flood rains descended in destruction of the wicked for "forty days and nights." Moses was on the Mount with God "forty days and nights." Christ showed Himself alive to His disciples for "forty days" after His passion before He ascended to His throne in heaven (Acts 1:3). If this is the pattern which the resurrected and translated saints will follow, the "forty days" will provide space for "the marriage supper of the Lamb," before returning to the earth to reign with Christ upon His throne. There is no definitely stated length of time which the saints will be away from the earth. It may be a full year, or they may return the same day. The main thing is to be ready for His coming, and to escape the deluge of outpoured WRATH.[16]

Here, then, is the conclusion of a thorough-going posttribulational author, quoted from his book: *Tribulation Till Translation*. He acknowledges the absolute necessity for an interval of time between the catching up of the saints and the return with Christ. He suggests that forty days may be an adequate interval for intervening events, but admits that the length of time may be longer. "It may be a full year." One is reminded of the words of Reese: "Such is the admission of a friendly writer; and if such a damaging concession is made from within the camp, what must be the sober truth from without?"[17] The idea of even one event, intervening between rapture and revelation, is fatal to the posttribulationalist scheme. We have indicated from two to four such events. How then can the rapture and the revelation be synchronous? How then a single crisis?

Once a time element is admitted between the rapture and the revelation, as it is here by Rose, and as it is further conceded by other posttribulationalists who maintain a judicious silence at this point, there remain but a few short steps to a position which is clearly pretribulational. From Rose's admission and in the light of the findings of preceding chapters, let the reader reason back to the place the rapture must occupy in God's prophetic program. It will obviously take place before the marriage of the Lamb, for this is in heaven. Consistent thinkers will grant

16 George L. Rose, *Tribulation Till Translation*, p. 261.
17 Reese, *op. cit.*, p. 90.

that it must transpire before the Bema seat of Christ, for the time when Church saints are judged and rewarded will not precede their translation into His presence. Furthermore, II Thessalonians 2:3-10 establishes that the removal of the Church will be before the manifestation of the Man of Sin, a fact which places the rapture before Revelation 13 and probably as far back in the chronology of that book as 6:1, before the opening of the first seal and the rider upon the white horse. From this point, a quick review of the nature of the Church and the character of the Tribulation, of promises which exempt the Church from any wrath poured out by God, of the shift in viewpoint from earth to heaven at Revelation 4:1, revealing crowned and glorified elders who worship Christ and sing the song of the redeemed — such a review should convince any candid mind that the place of the rapture in the chronology of the Revelation and in the order of prophetic events is clearly pretribulational. On the other hand, since intervening events require a marked interval between the rapture and the revelation, the whole posttribulational idea that these two phases of our Lord's return are only moments apart, if not simultaneous, is demonstrated to be utterly untenable.

IV. RAPTURE AND REVELATION DIFFER AS TO THEIR LEADING CHARACTERISTICS

A time interval being established between the rapture of the saints and Christ's return at His glorious appearing, it now remains to indicate briefly that these two phases of Christ's coming also differ widely as to their leading characteristics. Since both involve actions on the part of the Lord and of His Church, one rightly would expect to find some similarity between the two, but there are striking contrasts as well. The discussion which follows purposes to tabulate many of these contrasts — some of which are obvious enough to constitute additional proof that two separate events are in view, others providing examples of further differences once the primary distinction has been demonstrated.

A. *Differences, as They Apply to the Redeemed*

There will be a marked contrast in the *spiritual fervor* of God's earthly testimony. At the rapture, the Church for the most part will be in a state of Laodicean lukewarmness (Rev. 3:14-19), while prior to the revelation, Tribulation saints will be on fire with zeal toward God (Rev. 12:11; 14:4,5; cf. Isa. 27:6). The apostasy at the end of the Church Age is a subject of clear prediction (II Tim. 3:1-5; II Pet. 3:3,4), but this is in direct contrast with the testimony of persecuted Tribulation saints which will be at a white heat. History records that severe persecution produces a church that is either hot or cold, with believers who seal their testimony with their blood or capitulate weakly to the enemy. The former will characterize the Tribulation saints, but the Church prior to the rapture will be nauseatingly tepid.

The two phases of the Lord's return differ widely as to their *manner*, Christ coming first for the saints (I Thess. 4:16), then returning later with the saints (I Thess. 3:13). A difference in the matter of *location* is also apparent, the scene of the rapture being in the air, but that of the revelation being upon earth. *Destination* provides a further point of distinction, for after the rapture the Church will be associated with Christ in heavenly mansions (John 14:1-3), but after the revelation she will reign with Him upon the millennial earth (Rev. 20:6).

Again, these two events differ as to their immediate *prospect*. At the rapture the prospect for the Church will be that of the Bema seat judgment and the marriage of the Lamb, while at the revelation these events will be in retrospect, the prospect being the culmination of God's judgment and wrath upon His enemies. At the rapture, the Church is judged in view of rewards (II Cor. 5:10); at the revelation, Israel and the Gentile nations are judged in respect to their treatment of Christ and their entrance into the kingdom (Matt. 25:31-46). At the rapture, it will be a blessing to be taken, but at the revelation it will be a blessing to be left upon earth to enter Christ's kingdom, the wicked being taken away in judgment. At the rapture, the marriage supper of the Lamb is in view; at the revelation the judgment "supper of the great God" is in view (Rev. 19:17; Ezek. 39:17-20). All of these are clear distinctions and necessitate two entirely separate events. To disregard such contrasts as these by blending everything into one single action or crisis can only lead to confusion of mind as to the future program of God.

B. *Differences, as They Apply to Christ*

At the rapture, Christ appears as the Bridegroom, Lord, and Head of the Church. At the revelation, He comes as King, Immanuel, and Messiah of Israel (Rev. 19:16; Ps. 2:2; Isa. 7:14; Zech. 12:10; 13:6; 14:4-11). Before the Tribulation, Christ appears as the "bright and morning star" (Rev. 2:28; 22:16), but after the Tribulation His appearance to the remnant is as "the Sun of righteousness with healing in his wings" (Mal. 4:2). These are apt symbols of the two phases of Christ's coming, for the morning star is seen by comparatively few and rises in the heavens before the sun appears. At the revelation, Christ shall rule the nations with a "rod of iron" (Rev. 19:15), but at the rapture (to use the language of Song of Solomon 2:4) His banner over us is love.

C. *Differences, as They Apply to the Events Themselves*

In several important factors, the coming of Christ for the Church differs from His return to earth with the Church. When Christ appears from glory to subdue His enemies and set up an earthly kingdom, the whole order of life as it is now will be changed and improved. Creation will be liberated from its bondage (Rom. 8:19-23) and "the desert shall rejoice, and blossom as a rose" (Isa. 35:1ff.). Zoological behavior will be radically altered, for the lion shall lie down with the lamb, and at that time "the earth shall be full of the knowledge of the Lord" (Isa. 11:6-9; Ezek. 34:25; Hos. 2:18). Governments shall be altered and wars abolished (Isa. 2:2-4); sickness and death shall be diminished (Rev. 21:4), and all the earth shall know experimentally that it is God's Son who reigns upon the throne of David. These and other vast changes will occur when Christ returns to set up His glorious millennial reign upon earth, yet none of these take place at the snatching away of the Church. At the rapture, the sin of the world remains unjudged and the creature continues subject to bondage. However, at the revelation not only will sin be judged, but Satan himself will be bound (Rev. 20:1-3) and the curse of sin largely lifted from the earth.

At the former, Israel's covenants remain unfulfilled, while at the latter, Israel enters into her heritage. At the rapture, the dead in Christ are raised and caught up to heaven; at the revelation, Old Testament saints are raised and Israel shall stand in judgment before her King in respect to entrance into an earthly kingdom.

The very fact that the rapture of the saints is declared a mystery (I Cor. 15:51), a truth "hid from the ages and from generations, but now . . . made manifest to his saints" (Col. 1:26), makes it impossible to merge it with the revelation of Christ to earth. This fact alone serves to confirm the many contrasts already discussed. A Pauline mystery is a truth which previously had not been revealed, but now has been plainly declared. It is a truth, previously unforeseen in the Old Testament, but now clearly revealed in the New Testament. The translation of the saints, "in a moment, in the twinkling of an eye, at the last trump," is such a mystery (I Cor. 15:51, 52).

This "mystery" character of the coming of Christ for His Church sets it distinctly apart from the return of Christ to earth prior to His kingdom reign. The revelation of the Son of Man is nowhere a mystery, but is the subject of plain Old Testament prophecy (Deut. 30:3; Isa. 11:11; 61:2; Zech. 14: 4, etc.). Jude 14 records: "And Enoch also, the seventh from Adam, prophesied of these, saying, Behold, the Lord cometh with ten thousands of his saints, to execute judgment upon all. . . ." How then can the rapture of the saints be a Pauline mystery if it is not comprehended as a separate event from the revelation of Christ? Also, the coming of Christ to earth, as viewed by Old Testament prophets, is associated with signs and predicted events which first must be fulfilled. The rapture, however, is viewed in the New Testament as imminent; it is not subject to prior events, nor is it a topic of Old Testament prophecy.

It is a decided inconvenience to the posttribulation rapture theory that the saints are raptured at all, but even they have to admit that the Bible teaches it. And having so admitted, they have yet to explain what benefit is derived for the Church by a round-trip into the clouds and back to earth, all of which is instantaneous, or at best, in a matter of moments. They have yet to harmonize the many obvious distinctions by which the rapture is set apart from the revelation, and also have yet to offer an orderly interpretation of prophetic events — one that will include an acceptable view of the Bema seat and the marriage supper, with all their attendant details. The posttribulational view would lose absolutely nothing if the saints were not raptured at all, yet they cannot deny that when Christ returns to earth the second time, His own are seen coming from heaven with Him. Their view is out of harmony with almost every detail of I Thessalonians 4:13-18, with its comforting hope; it cannot reconcile the mystery character of the rapture in I Corinthians 15:51, 52; it has very little to say about the promise of heavenly mansions in John 14:1-3. Yet even they acknowledge that these are the three absolutely cardinal Scriptures as touching the rapture of the saints. If only men would let the Scriptures speak for themselves! How clear is its testimony that rapture and revelation deal with separate issues. *We* shall not all sleep, but *we* shall be caught up to meet the Lord in the air — but when *they* say, Peace and safety, sudden destruction cometh upon *them*. The contrast is clear. One has but to compare I Thessalonians 4:16-18 with II Thessalonians 1:7-10 to see immediately that something different is in view.

IV. WHO SHALL POPULATE THE MILLENNIAL EARTH?

The Scriptures which describe the end time make it rather obvious that there shall be righteous men living upon the earth when Christ returns in the glory of His revelation. Both Testaments indicate that a believing remnant of Israelites shall be preserved from the Tribulation to welcome the return of their Messiah (Isa. 11:11; Jer. 23:3; Zech. 13:8, 9; 14:4, 5; Rev. 12:17). The tribes of Israel certainly will be upon earth when the Son of Man comes in the clouds of heaven and His elect are gathered together from the four winds (Matt. 13:30, 31). Matthew 25:31-33 gives not the slightest indication that the "sheep" who stand at Christ's right hand have ever been caught up from the earth in translation experience. When the Son of Man comes in the blaze of His glory, both the "sheep" and the "goats" are gathered together unto Him. Furthermore, the two redeemed companies of Revelation 7 bear witness that men are washed white in the blood of the Lamb right up to the time of the revelation.

It is important to consider this phenomena, that there are righteous ones on earth who meet the Lord when He descends with ten thousands of His saints. These form an important group to enter the millennial kingdom of Christ. Few seem to have noticed that their presence at the turn of the age has a vital bearing on the position of the rapture in the schedule of end time events.

If, as the posttribulational brethren maintain, all the saints yet alive when Antichrist has done his worst and Tribulation is past are caught up to meet Christ and return in triumph in His train, how then is one to account for this presence of righteous men on earth when Christ descends to establish the millennial kingdom? Is one to believe that some were overlooked, that there was a divided bride and a partial rapture? Or is one simply to understand that there must be a period of time between the rapture and the revelation during which they were brought to a knowledge of salvation? Of the two alternatives, this latter is the obvious conclusion, logical and uncomplicated. But such a conclusion is fatal to posttribulationalism.

Now look at the same issue from a slightly different angle. Who shall populate the millennial earth after the return of Jesus Christ? Certainly not the saints who have been raptured, for I Corinthians 15:51-54 testifies that the dead and the living in Christ "will be changed," receiving at the rapture their glorified, resurrection bodies. Before the kingdom reign of Christ even begins upon earth, they will have "put on immortality." Nor shall the unrighteous populate the millennial earth, for those not killed by Tribulation judgments shall be destroyed by the brightness of His appearing (Rev. 19:15; II Thess. 2:8-12).

There are many indications that the unrighteous shall in no wise inherit the kingdom of Christ. God shall purge from among Israel all of the rebel Jews (Ezek. 20:38). The tares shall be rooted out from among the wheat and burned with fire, and this before "the righteous shine forth as the sun in the kingdom of their father" (Matt. 13:30, 40-42). Christ, in the Olivet discourse, constantly warns that none but the righteous shall enter His kingdom. Who then shall populate the millennium? Can immortal beings be married and beget children? "In the resurrection they neither marry, nor are given in marriage, but are as the angels of God in heaven" (Mat. 22:30). Will men who have put on immortality own property, plowing their fields and cultivating each his own vineyard? (Micah 4:3, 4). What disorder is wrought by the posttribulational theory that all the saints are raptured and changed just prior to the kingdom!

Where do unbelievers in the millennium come from if all who enter in are saints who have put on immortality? "When the thousand years are expired, Satan shall be loosed out of his prison, and shall go out to deceive the nations which are in the four quarters of the earth . . . the number of whom is as the sand of the sea" (Rev. 20:7, 8). These who succumb to this final Satanic delusion are not redeemed men, and certainly have never been caught up to meet the Lord in the air.

Practically all that is known about the millennial age is thrown into hopeless confusion by the notion that rapture and revelation occur almost simultaneously on the day which ends Tribulation and ushers in the kingdom reign of Christ. Harmony of the prophetic Word is achieved only when a period of time is recognized *after* the rapture but *before* Christ's revelation in glory. Seven years of Tribulation intervene between the two during which God speaks in wrath, yet not so loudly that He cannot in grace call sinners to Himself. Multitudes are saved during the Tribulation. Many shall be martyred, but those who endure to the end shall in the flesh enter the kingdom. The redeemed of the Tribulation period are the ones who populate the millennial earth.

CHAPTER TWELVE

HIS COMING—OUR HOPE

A major obstacle in the way of greater unanimity on eschatological subjects is the fact that the prophetic field is so vast, the Scriptures involved are so numerous and the issues become so complex. The problem of the time of the rapture in its relationship to the Tribulation period is no exception. In fact, it is but part of the larger doctrine of the premillennial faith, yet it is in itself an important and determinative issue. Let those who consider it a mere detail of eschatology ponder the fact that the Christian's hope, incentive for purity of life and zeal for service, all are involved. What is decided in respect to the time of the rapture will affect an amazingly large part of the prophetic Scriptures, for prophecy is a strangely interwoven tapestry.

A further obstacle to greater unity in the area of prophetic study is the tendency of some to avoid discussion of subjects thought to be controversial. The comment of Chafer in respect to an entirely different problem is just as applicable at this point:

> It is not easy to disagree with good and great men. However, as they appear on each side of this question, it is impossible to entertain a conviction and not oppose those who are of a contrary mind. The disagreement now under discussion is not between orthodox and heterdox men; it is within the fellowship of those who have most in common and who need the support and encouragement of each other's confidence.[1]

Others avoid private investigation of subjects considered not readily understandable. The experience of James H. Brookes, noted Bible student of a past generation, is a case in point:

> It was Dr. Brookes' habit to read the Bible through in course, but he stopped habitually at the end of Jude and turned back to Genesis, accounting that The Revelation was not understand-

---

[1] Lewis Sperry Chafer, *Systematic Theology*, III, 183, 184.

able and hence not worth reading. One day he was convicted that he was not dealing fairly with the Bible since The Revelation is an integral part of it. He read on into it and through it. That reading changed the whole course of his life. Dr. Brookes found himself possessed of a key to Bible truth; using it he became known as one of our greatest Bible scholars and expositors. More: he became surpassingly helpful to others.[2]

Even more, through his study he became an ardent believer in the hope of the imminent, pretribulational return of our Lord Jesus Christ. Too few thus search the Scriptures for themselves. The demands made upon our overly busy lives make it easy, rather, to follow the sometimes undigested opinions of a favorite teacher or author. While the thinking of men may be a valued guide, if accompanied by a sincere scholarship and godly understanding, final authority must ultimately rest in the Word of God. May we all be more like the Bereans, who "searched the scriptures daily, whether those things were so" (Acts 17:10, 11).

After all of the facts are in, there may yet be some disagreement as to the time and manner of the rapture — but this should not be permitted to deter evangelical unity on the reality of that blessed hope. Believers need more emphasis upon their common faith in the great verities of Christianity, that they may be of one mind before an unbelieving world. Nevertheless, any Bible problem which involves issues as important as the unity of the body of Christ, the doctrine of imminency, and the hope of the believer, has a right to a thorough hearing. In the very nature of the case, three of the four viewpoints involved cannot be in accord with Bible truth. While all discussions which shed light on the problem are highly in order, through it all the Bible sustains but one program of prophecy.

It is the firm conclusion of this present investigation that pretribulationalism is highly defensible and has far more to commend it than any of the three alternate viewpoints. Even Cameron must admit that "it would be a blessed thing *if* this view could be substantiated,"[3] and Reese himself recognizes that a pretribulational hope is a "brighter and more comforting view" and that if the Scriptures were with it, the case would

---

[2].Norman B. Harrison, *The End: Re-Thinking the Revelation*, p. 27.
[3] Robert Cameron, *Scriptural Truth About the Lord's Return*, p. 168.

be convincing.[4] The writer earnestly believes that his thesis has herein been substantiated, and that it has been clearly demonstrated from the Scriptures that the Church will enter no part of the Tribulation. All of the major arguments, objections, and Scriptures used by opposing views have been dealt with, together with not a little by way of detail. The writer is aware of the fact that there are additional Scriptures, some less significant objections, and even some arguments in favor of pretribulationalism which have not been included in this study, but a halt must be called somewhere. It is believed that any additional inquiry into the details involved will only serve to substantiate further the conclusion of this present investigation that the rapture of the Church is truly imminent and will be pretribulational.

Pastors and teachers, and others in positions of authority over the visible church of Jesus Christ, are in particular exhorted to study these issues for themselves and, being persuaded, to stand upon this ground. The imminent return of Christ, preached — not argumentatively, but from a heart which loves His appearing — will provoke within the flock of God a quickening interest in spiritual things, a new enthusiasm, a desire to live and serve so as to be unashamed at His coming.

It is not possible to give an adequate summary of all the evidence presented in favor of pretribulationalism in the preceding chapters. It has been demonstrated that the Tribulation period differs in its fundamental nature from any trials and tribulations which may now be a normal ingredient of Christian experience. The Church is expressly promised deliverance from the wrath of God and from the hour of trial which shall fall upon the dwellers of the earth. Proof was offered that the Church is not Israel, and that her eschatology cannot be built upon that which is clearly predicated of Israel in the end time. Moreover, it was seen that two different redeemed and witnessing bodies in the Tribulation at the same time would involve God in a serious dilemma and make void the cardinal doctrine of the unity of the body of Christ. It was seen that the Day of the Lord, viewed as a period rather than as a single day, strengthens more than

[4] Alexander Reese, *The Approaching Advent of Christ*, p. 225.

it weakens the pretribulational position. Evidence was presented to prove that the restrainer of II Thessalonians 2 is none other than the Holy Spirit, to be removed with the Church prior to the manifestation of the Man of Sin. Arguments against the doctrine of imminency were dealt with, and the doctrine substantiated by the Scriptures, the hope of the Early Church, and the attestation of the Church Fathers.

Other lines of evidence included an identification of the twenty-four elders, and analyses of the seventh and the last trumpets and of the time of the resurrection. The rapture was distinguished from the revelation of Christ by the presence of intervening events and by a score or more of their leading characteristics. The ideas and claims of some of the most prominent contenders for the three alternate positions were discussed and objections noted. Thus pretribulationalism has been defended and substantiated by the cumulative force of positive argument, by analysis of the Scriptures involved, and by a portrayal of the weaknesses of all opposing systems.

It is sincerely hoped that many who read these pages will be confirmed in the truth of the imminent return of Jesus Christ. There is abundant evidence that the last generation of believers shall be *kept from the hour* of trouble, not in response to human merit but because of the limitless grace of God. While Christians stand fast in this assurance, may others who know not this hope come to share the joyful expectation of those at Thessalonica, of whom Paul wrote:

> For others are telling of their own accord, concerning me, how gladly you received me, and how you forsook your idols, and turning to the service of God, the living and the true; and that now you wait with eager longing for the return of His Son from the heavens, even Jesus, whom He raised from the dead, our deliverer from the coming vengeance.[5] (I Thess. 1:9, 10).

There is practical value to such a hope. If Christ may momentarily appear, how pointed John's exhortation to godly living:

> Abide in him; that, when he shall appear, we may have confidence, and not be ashamed before him at his coming (I John 2:28).

Our citizenship is in heaven, and since Christ's coming may

[5] Translation of W. J. Conybeare and J. S. Howson, *The Life and Epistles of St. Paul,* I, 392.

be soon, how vital it is to "look for the Saviour, the Lord Jesus Christ" (Phil. 3:20). Yet this looking, this waiting for the Redeemer, does not consist of idly "gazing up into heaven" (Acts 1:11). God would not have us so detached from the world that we lose our vision for service. The second coming is not the sum total of theology. There must be balance. Therefore, Christ prayed not only that we might be with Him and behold His glory (John 17:24), but that while in the world we should be kept from evil, and go forth into the world that through our words men might believe on Him (John 17:15, 18, 20).

To this end have believers been commissioned "ambassadors for Christ." Our opportunity and privilege is to acquaint the lost with the good news of His salvation, for it is little gain for an unsaved man to hear of the second advent before he has understood and appropriated the blessings of the first advent. As ambassadors, we beseech men in Christ's stead to be reconciled to God (II Cor. 5:20). May we keep before us the solemn responsibility of this task, knowing full well that it may not be long before Christ begins His work of judging the living and the dead. For believers, there is the bright pospect of rapture experience before the day of Tribulation wrath. *Ambassadors are called home before war is declared.* Even so shall we be called into His glorious presence.

The promise of Christ is, "Surely, I come quickly." May each heart respond fervently, "Even so, come, Lord Jesus." In this dark night, let us look toward the morning. His coming is our hope. Let us be among the number who "love his appearing" (II Tim. 4:8).

> Lift up your heads, Pilgrims aweary,
> See day's approach, now crimson the sky.
> Night shadows flee, and your Beloved,
> Awaited with longing, at last draweth nigh.
>
> Dark was the night, sin warred against us;
> Heavy the load of sorrow we bore;
> But now we see signs of His coming;
> Our hearts glow within us, joy's cup runneth o'er.
>
> O blessed hope! O blissful promise!
> Filling our hearts with rapture divine;
> O day of days! Hail Thy appearing!
> Thy transcendent glory, forever shall shine.

Section II

LITERAL INTERPRETATION, FIGURATIVE LANGUAGE AND PROPHECY

No other book of human history has been criticized and attacked as much as the Bible. Enemies from without have attempted to tear its pages to shreds with the barbed darts of satire and stinging ridicule, while enemies from within — posing as scholars and exegetes — have attacked more insidiously by emptying its contents of any real or significant meaning. Liberal churchmen, having abandoned the cardinal doctrine of inspiration, making the Bible a book *about* God rather than a book *from* God, have now set about to determine if possible "the spiritual contribution of the Bible to this modern age." Any doctrine not considered "modern" they have relegated in the process to their theological trash pile.

Men who are prone to drift in their Biblical interpretations from the sure anchorage of the literal method would do well to consider the theological company in which they have chosen to travel, and the strange destinations arrived at by some who have unwittingly charted their course by the allegorizing method of Origen. A completely liberal theology is the natural and ultimate terminal of all who approach the Scriptures unencumbered with convictions about verbal inspiration and grammatical, literal interpretation. That the shameful position of liberalism today is the logical result of the denial of the literal method is evinced by Roehr, a higher critic. In describing Jesus as just another man, the product of his age and nation, Roehr exclaims: "Those who deny this are stupid, servile, and *literal*."[1]

Speaking of the allegorizing school, Farrar concludes:

Origen borrows from heathen Platonists and from Jewish phil-

[1] Cited by W. A. Criswell in the published sermon, "The Curse of Modernism," Dallas: First Baptist Church, 1949.

osophers a method which converts the whole of Scripture, alike the New and the Old Testament, into a series of clumsy, varying, and incredible enigmas. Allegory helped him to get rid of Chiliasm and superstitious literalism and the "antitheses" of the Gnostics, but *it opened the door for deadlier evils.*[2]

Origen, though not wantonly liberal, could not avoid liberal conclusions once he affirmed the allegorizing method. "No man, not altogether unsound and hypocritical, ever injured the Church more than Origen did," is the conclusion of Milner, the great English historian of the past century.[3] The allegorizing method fosters modernism. It is well known that many of the leading Protestant denominations, avowedly amillennial, are now engaged in a death struggle with liberalism. On the other hand, it is practically impossible to find a liberal premillenarian.

A second major departure from the literal school of interpretation is the amillennial view of eschatology. This view, which spiritualizes the reign of Christ and makes the millennial promises to be fulfilled, if at all, in this present age, is found among three distinct groups: (1) It is the eschatology of liberalism. Among the doctrines herein denied are those of literal resurrection and literal judgment. (2) It is the eschatology of the Roman Catholic system. Significantly, *The Catholic Encyclopedia,* an authority on the amillennialism of Rome, describes amillennial interpretations as "allegorical."[4] (3) It is the eschatology of a considerable body of men of conservative Reformed faith, who as a whole accept the literal method but feel that the rule is not valid for the interpretation of prophetic portions, particularly the kingdom passages.

No one defends or employs the allegorizing method of exegesis. Calvin and the other great Bible students of the Reformation saw clearly that the method was wrong and taught the now generally accepted "grammatical-historical" literal interpretation, so far as the Scriptures in general are concerned. That they retain the spiritualizing method in expounding many of the prophecies was

[2] F. W. Farrar, *History of Interpretation* (London: Macmillan and Co., 1886), p. 196. Italics added.
[3] Charles Feinberg, *Premillennialism or Amillennialism?* (Grand Rapids: Zondervan Publishing House, 1936), p. 51, citing Milner.
[4] J. P. Kirsch, "Millennium," *The Catholic Encyclopedia,* X, 307-9.

because they found themselves forced to do so in order to be faithful to the New Testament.[5]

The difference, then, between a premillennialist and a *conservative* amillennialist is not, simply, that one is a literalist and the other is an allegorizer. The conservative amillennialist uses *two* systems of interpretation: the literal for most areas of Biblical study, but the allegorical for all passages which, if taken literally, would lead to a premillennial conclusion. Both groups are theologically harmonious wherever the literal method is followed. It should be noted that the basic doctrinal agreement among premillennialists, even in respect to the main outline of prophecy, argues strongly in favor of their interpretive method. Conversely, the wide and basic diversity of amillennial belief reveals the weak foundation of that structure. Any system which at the same time fosters liberalism, Roman Catholic eschatology, and a measure of conservatism, is open to serious question.

It has been demonstrated in chapter 7 that midtribulationalists and posttribulationalists resort to the spiritualization of much of the Tribulation period to sustain their respective theses. It now remains to answer the amillennial contention that the presence of figurative and symbolic language in Scripture is inharmonious with the literal method and justifies a departure from it.

I. Three Cardinal Rules of Bible Interpretation

It is not the purpose here to enumerate and discuss the many varied laws of Bible interpretation,[6] save to suggest, in brief, three of the most important. The last of these will lead directly to the major problems at hand.

A. *Interpret According to Context*

In the words of Myles Coverdale:

>It shall greatly helpe ye to understande Scripture,
>If thou mark not only what is spoken or wrytten,
>But of whom, and to who,

---

[5] Albertus Pieters, "Darbyism vs. The Historic Christian Faith," *Calvin Forum*, II (May, 1936), 225-28.

[6] These can be obtained from any good source book. Bernard Ramm, *Protestant Biblical Interpretation*, (Boston: W. A. Wilde Co., 1950), pp. 78-96, is recommended.

> With what words, at what time,
> Where, to what intent, with what circumstances,
> Considering what goeth before and what followeth.[7]

There is nothing better, in the interpretation of a difficult passage, than to have the author explain himself. This explanation must take precedence over any other interpretation. Frequently, the author's purpose may be discerned by careful attention to "what goeth before, and what followeth" after. The general purpose and spirit of the book — indeed, of the entire Bible — must also be taken into account, for that which is a problem in one setting may well be restated and clarified elsewhere. Particularly should one guard against snatching a phrase out of context and making it say something far removed from the author's original purpose.

> Bishop Wilberforce once attended morning worship and heard a discourse on "Hear the Church" (Matt. 18:17). The following day the preacher asked the Bishop what he thought of the sermon which had been along the lines: if in doubt, hear the Church; if in darkness, hear the Church, etc. The Bishop admitted that the matter, method, and delivery were all good, and concluded his comment with the statement, "But, you know, my friend, I should have as much right to preach on 'Hang all the law and the prophets.' It is imperative that we should consider 'what goeth before' and 'what followeth after.'"[8]

B. *Interpret After Comparison With Other Scriptures*

The Bible is not a collection of good texts put together without any relation the one to the other. Rarely does a doctrine stand upon a single isolated text; the pattern is usually woven into the entire warp and woof of the fabric of Scripture. It is therefore important to heed the old rule of comparing Scripture with Scripture, rather than grasping at an isolated text which may seem to support some preconceived opinion. "A doctrine clearly supported by the Analogy of Faith, can not be contradicted by a contrary and obscure passage."[9]

> As in an organism no member or part, however minute, can be fully understood aside from its relation to the whole, so in Scripture every paragraph and sentence is part of its totality and must

---

[7] Cited by F. J. Miles, *Understandest Thou?* (London: Marshall, Morgan & Scott, 1946), p. xi.

[8] *Ibid.*, p. 25.

[9] Charles Ellicott and W. J. Harsha, *Biblical Hermeneutics* (New York: Anson D. F. Randolph & Co., 1881), p. 181.

be studied in relation to all the rest. The text will be illuminated by the context, or scripture immediately preceding and following. Every occurrence and utterance should be studied in its surroundings. How, why, when, a word was spoken or an act done, helps to explain it, is its local coloring.[10]

C. Interpret the Bible Literally

The Bible should be interpreted, wherever possible, according to the usual, ordinary meaning of the words of the text. Grammatical and historical rules should be strictly observed, including the use of lexicons to solve problems of translation and other helps to determine the influence of local custom and historical setting. As Neil has said: "A passage is to be taken literally provided it is not limited by age conditions or local church customs."[11] According to Farrar "Scripture must be interpreted in accordance with the ordinary rules of human language."[12] Verbal inspiration demands literal interpretation, and basic to both is correct grammatical study from these sources: the text itself, the context, parallel texts, and other pertinent materials, though foreign to the text.[13] Cellerier presents this fundamental rule as follows:

> The interpreter should begin his work by studying the grammatical sense of the text, with the aid of Sacred Philology. As in all other writings, the grammatical sense must be made the starting-point. The meaning of the words must be determined according to the linguistic usage and the connection.[14]

Granting that the literal interpretation of the Bible includes within its scope the right use of figurative language, for even types and figures were given to convey some literal truth, what then is the rule for determining that which is clearly literal? Allis cites H. Bonar, "literal wherever possible," and Govett, "literal unless absurd," but cannot accept these statements, lamenting "This literalistic emphasis has shown itself most plainly in their insistence that Israel means Israel. . . ."[15] Clinton

---

[10] Arthur T. Pierson, cited by James H. Todd, *Principles of Interpretation* (Chicago: Bible Institute Colportage Association, 1923), p. 21.

[11] James Neil, *Strange Figures: or the Figurative Language of the Bible* (London: Simpkin, Marshall & Co., 1895), p. 56.

[12] Farrar, *op. cit.*, p. 475.

[13] Ellicott and Harsha, *op. cit.*, p. 78.

[14] *Ibid.*, p. 73.

[15] Oswald T. Allis, *Prophecy and the Church* (Philadelphia: Presbyterian Reformed Publishing Co., 1945), p. 19.

Lockhart states the issue more helpfully:

> Look carefully for a literal meaning before accepting one that is figurative. . . . The literal or most usual meaning of a word, if consistent, should be preferred to a figurative or less usual signification.[16]
>
> By literal interpretation is meant that which should be interpreted word for word in its primitive or most fundamental current sense.[17]

Lockhart gives two tests for literal interpretation: *sense,* and *usage,* explaining that "If the literal meaning of any word or expression makes good sense in its connections, it is literal; but if the literal meaning does not make good sense, it is figurative."[18] Pascal expresses it this way: "Whoever wishes to give the sense of Scripture, and does not take it from the Scriptures, is the enemy of Scripture."[19] Further, "If plain sense makes good sense, do not seek any other sense or you will find nonsense."[20] Cooper sums up the matter quite adequately:

> Take every word at its primary, ordinary, usual . . . meaning unless the facts of the immediate context, studied in the light of related passages and axiomatic and fundamental truths, indicate clearly otherwise.[21]

"There are many definitely and directly stated truths," Rogers writes, "by which God says clearly what He means, and in which He means what He says, and which allow for no tampering or spiritualizing."[22] This is clearly evident, but it would seem that an exaggeration of this truth has been stated by Owen: "If the Scripture has more than one meaning, it has no meaning at all."[23]

Literal interpretation need not be this restrictive: it incorporates the recognition of figurative language, and allows for a spiritual application of that which first has been literally interpreted. Within limits, it recognizes the *double sense* of certain passages, but this in no wise permits an allegorized interpretation

---

[16] Clinton Lockhart, *Principles of Interpretation* (Fort Worth: S. B. Taylor, 1915), pp. 159, 160.

[17] *Ibid.,* p. 49.

[18] *Loc. cit.*

[19] Pascal, cited by Wm. H. Rogers, *Things That Differ* (New York: Loizeaux Bros., 1940), p. 17.

[20] *Loc. cit.*

[21] David L. Cooper, *The World's Greatest Library Graphically Illustrated* (Los Angeles: Biblical Research Society, 1942), p. 17.

[22] Rogers, *op. cit.,* p. 3.

[23] Owen, cited by Lockhart, *op. cit.,* p. 24.

to enter and rob the words of their literal meaning. For example, one may sing "O, Zion, haste, thy mission high fulfilling," and recognize that "Zion" is used of the Church in a figurative sense, but this does not cancel out the fact that Zion is a literal geographic location in Jerusalem, the capital city and spiritual center of the nation Israel.[24]

Although there may be problems attached to the right use of the literal method, it yet remains that literal interpretation (rightly understood) is one of the golden rules of Biblical hermeneutics. It permits God to say what He means without straining it to fit some pre-conceived notion, and holds in check the "spiritualization" of those passages which should merely be classified as figurative. The interpretation of Biblical types and figures has long been an exegetical stumbling stone, and deserves more detailed analysis.

II. THE PROBLEM OF INTERPRETING FIGURATIVE LANGUAGE

Every language used by man abounds in figures of speech, and the original languages of the Bible are no exception. When a word, which has been appropriated by usage to designate one thing, is transferred to a new and different meaning, it is said to be used *figuratively*. When a word is used in its primitive, natural, or usual sense, it is said to be used *literally*. Figurative language, then, is a departure or deflection from the usual, primary meaning of a word. We speak of "stony ground": this is literal. We speak of a "stony heart": this is figurative. Christ in particular was accustomed to clothe His thoughts in the figurative and popular language of the day: "I am the vine," "living water," "destroy this temple," "this is my body which is given for you," to mention a few instances.

The fact that such figures are in the Bible is a good indication that they were meant to be understood, but the part must

---

[24] *Cf.* Homer Payne, *Amillennial Theology as a System* (unpublished doctor's dissertation, Dallas Theological Seminary, 1948), pp. 102-25. Payne tests the usage of three specific terms: *Zion, Kingdom, and Israel.* It is claimed by representative amillennial theologians that these terms are spiritualized outright in the New Testament to mean the *Church,* making this age the fulfillment of the promised Israelitish kingdom. Payne offers convincing evidence that these terms cannot legitimately be said to be spiritualized in the New Testament, but are to be taken literally in keeping with the premillennial view.

be in harmony with the whole, and interpretation must not be allowed to give way to license.

A. Ten Practical Suggestions

The following suggestions may not be exhaustive, but it is believed that they will materially aid in the interpretation of Biblical figures:

(1) When is language figurative? In the greater number of cases, the fact that language is figurative appears in the very nature of the language itself, or from the connection in which it stands. Christ is the door to heaven, but not a literal door. Christians are the sheep of His pasture, and the salt of the earth, but not literally sheep, nor salt.

A figure is called a *trope*, from the Greek word στρέφω, "I turn." It is the turning of a word from its common, ordinary meaning, as in the expression "so many head of cattle," generally on the principle of resemblance. If that which is said, when taken according to the letter, cannot harmonize with the essential nature of the subject spoken of, the language must be regarded as *tropical*. Or conversely, if the language when taken literally would imply something incongruous, or morally improper, the figurative sense is presumably the right one. If the literal proves to be absurd, or inconsistent with that which is being discussed, one may conclude with at least tolerable certainty that the language is figurative.

(2) The use and interpretation of figurative language does not compromise literal interpretation, nor is it contrary to verbal inspiration. The interpreter should not limit himself to the literal meaning of individual words comprising the figure, but seek the literal sense intended and illustrated by the figure as a whole. This is no concession to the spiritualizing or allegorizing method, for it enables the figure to yield its full and obviously intended meaning.

Spiritualizing also attacks the non-figurative portions of Scripture. It seeks to water down the text and robs it of any true and significant meaning. It is not bound by rules of speech or of reason, but solely by the fancy of the interpreter. Paul says: "Let not the sun go down upon your wrath" (Eph. 4:26), meaning, not that anger is permissible for a time, but that *should* wrath arise, it should not be continually harbored in the mind, but one should subdue it before the end of the day. But see how fantastically Thomas Fuller draws out the passage, making it the carrying of news to another world of one's revengeful nature, and saying that if understood literally, "men in Greenland, where day lasts above a quarter of a year, have plentiful scope of revenge."[25]

The Premillenarian insists that spiritualization is an element foreign to Scripture, to rhetoric, and to logic, since it is a direct and immediate substitution of one idea for another, arbitrary in its method and often violent in its use.[26]

The most dangerous form of "second-sense" interpretation is that in which the interpreter supplies the proposed connections from his own imagination. Over this there is no control. Double-sense interpretation is not an evil itself; but as a method it is fraught with difficulties and dangers. Therefore, to state that the principal meaning of the Bible is a second-sense meaning, and that the principal method of interpreting is "spiritualizing," is to open the door to almost uncontrolled speculation and imagination. For this reason we have insisted that the *control* in interpretation is the literal method.[27]

Therefore the "literal" meaning of a word is the *basic, customary, social designation of that word. The spiritual, or mystical meaning of a word or expression is one that arises after the literal designation and is dependent upon it for its existence.*[28]

(3) The literal meaning is preferred first. Since the literal is the customary usage of a word, this sense occurs much more frequently than the figurative. Therefore the term will be regarded as literal until there is a good and sufficient reason for regarding it otherwise.

(4) Where there is doubt as to whether the language is literal or figurative, the interpreter should endeavor to dissolve the doubt by reference to the parallel passages (if there are any) which may treat the same subject in more explicit terms.

(5) There is a vital difference between interpretation and application. The former shows the one and only true meaning

[25] Patrick Fairbairn, *Hermeneutical Manual*, (Edinburgh: T. & T. Clark, 1858), pp. 148, 149.
[26] Gerrit H. Hospers, *The Principle of Spiritualization in Hermeneutics* (East Williamson, New York: Author, 1935), p. 10.
[27] Ramm, *op. cit.*, p. 65.
[28] *Ibid.*, pp. 64, 65. Italics in the original.

according to the laws of hermeneutics. The latter permits a greater degree of freedom in applying it to the varied spiritual needs of men. Some may overwork this freedom, but if so, it is an error of *degree* and not of *kind*.

(6) Care should be taken to give the figure of speech, as much as possible, a fair and natural meaning, in preference to a far-fetched or fanciful interpretation. The Bible was given to point men to God and to direct their steps on their earthly sojourn. It was not given to satisfy the curiosity or to foster fanciful imaginations. This rule can be applied to all Biblical interpretation, and those who are prone to seek theological novelties, particularly in the field of prophecy, would do well to heed it.

(7) In connection with figurative language that refers to the eternal order of things, to God, and to His Son, Jesus Christ, it must be remembered that figures offer but a very inadequate expression of the perfect reality. God is called Light, a Rock, a Fortress, a Tower, a Sun and a Shield. Christ is the Door, the Vine, the Good Shepherd, the Lamb of God. It takes far more than one figure to express the nature of God; therefore, such expressions should not be overly pressed, but understood in the light of all other such figurative descriptions.

(8) If in doubt as to the meaning of a figure, one can test his insight into its meaning by attempting to express his interpretation in literal language.

(9) Discover the principle idea of the figure, without placing too much importance on the attendant details. In figures of similitude or of analogy, very few points of comparison are normally to be expected. When extended figures based on similitude are being analyzed, the major points should be interpreted first, from which the minor points should be worked out reservedly. Any indications of the interpretation suggested by the author should be carefully followed. Doctrines must not be based on details; in fact, the figure is to be interpreted by the doctrine, rather than the doctrine by the figure. Parables in particular emphasize one truth, or point out one principle. When Christ's coming is likened unto that of a thief, it is obvious that the figure must not be pressed beyond its intended purpose.

(10) Since the figurative use of words is founded essentially on resemblance or similarity, every effort should be made to have a clear conception of the things on which the figure is based. Details must not be supplied from the imagination, but from a historical study of the times and a geographical study of the places. This is important, for Biblical figures are so often drawn from the physical features of the Holy Land, the religious institutions of Israel, the history of the Jews, and the daily life and customs of the various people who occupy so prominent a place in the Bible.

It is sincerely hoped that the ten principles set forth above will be sufficiently comprehensive to aid the Bible student in his interpretation of Biblical figures. May they help him to select meanings which will open the Scriptures, and prevent him from shutting them by idle speculation.

B. Recognizing Figures of Speech

In order to aid in the recognition of Bible figures, it may be helpful to give the general classifications into which most of them will fall, together with (in briefest form) an illustration of each:

Figures of speech are divided into two great classes: figures of words, and figures of thought. "The distinction is an easy one in that a figure of words is one in which the image or resemblance is confined to a single word, whereas a figure of thought may require for its expression a great many words and sentences."[29] Figures of words include *metaphor* and *metonymy*, in which the comparison is reduced to a single expression (as in Luke 13:32, "Go ye, and tell that fox"). Figures of thought are seen in *similes*, *allegories*, and *parables*, where no single word will convey the comparison intended.

(1) A *simile* is a figure in which a comparison is distinctly stated, marked by the words "like" or "as." "His countenance was like lightning" (Matt. 28:3). "Is not my word like as a fire? saith the Lord; and like a hammer that breaketh the rock in pieces?" (Jer. 23:29; cf. Matt. 7:24; Ps. 2:9; 59:6; Prov. 10:26. Isaiah 55:10, 11 is a beautiful example of a simile).

[29] Milton S. Terry, *Biblical Hermeneutics* (New York: The Methodist Book Concern, 1883), p. 160.

(2) A *metaphor* is a direct comparison much like the simile, but it is not set off by the words "like" or "as." Often more brief and more forceful than the simile, one object is likened to another by the simple expedient of asserting or implying that it is the other. "Judah is a lion's whelp" (Gen. 49:9). "All flesh is grass" (Isa. 40:6). "Ye are the salt of the earth" (Matt. 5:13). "I am the vine, ye are the branches" (John 15:5). What sorrow and bloodshed could have been averted by a right understanding of Matthew 26:26, 28. "This is [represents] my body. . . . This is [represents] my blood."

> If to take a statement of this kind, which occurs in Scriptures, literally would involve an absurdity, be contrary to the evidence of our senses, contrary to reason, and contrary to other plain statements of Revelation, then we both may and must conclude that it is a metaphor.[30]

(3) A *metonymy* (from the Greek μετά, denoting *change*, and ὄνομα, a *name*) is a figure of speech where there is a change of name, one name being used for the other, or one noun for another, in order to make an impression not otherwise attainable. "At the mouth [word, testimony] of two witnesses" (Deut. 17:6). So also, when the part is used for the whole: ". . . then shall ye bring down my gray hairs with sorrow to the grave" (Gen. 42:38). It is also metonymy when an object is used to represent something intimately connected with it, as in Isaiah 51:3: "For the Lord shall comfort Zion," and in Matthew 10:13: "And if the house be worthy, let your peace come upon it." "Zion" is used for the people that dwell there, and "house" speaks figuratively of its inhabitants (*cf.* Luke 16:29; Isa. 22:22).

(4) A *synecdoche* is quite similar to a metonymy, except that it stresses a physical rather than a mental resemblance. It is generally found when a part is used for the whole, or the whole used for a part. In Luke 2:1, "all the world" is used for the Roman Empire in its greatest extent. In Acts 27:37, "two hundred threescore and sixteen souls" speaks, of course, of two hundred seventy-six persons.

(5) *Personification,* often found in Scripture, occurs whenever objects of nature, inanimate things, or even abstract ideas, are

[30] Neil, *op. cit.,* p. 25.

spoken of as if they were living creatures, or as if they were indued with the characteristics of life. Both Numbers 16:32: "the earth opened her mouth, and swallowed them up," and Matthew 6:34: "Take therefore no thought for the morrow: for the morrow shall take thought for the things of itself," illustrate this particular figure.

(6) *Apostrophe* occurs when a speaker turns from his immediate hearers to address some absent person, either living or dead. David does this when he laments the death of his son, crying as if the departed soul were present to hear: "O my son Absalom, my son, my son Absalom! would God I had died for thee, O Absalom, my son, my son!" (II Sam. 18:33). If an inanimate object is addressed, the figures of apostrophe and personification combine in the one passage. This is well illustrated by Psalm 114:5-7: "What ailed thee, O thou sea, that thou fleddest? thou Jordan, that thou wast driven back? . . . Tremble, thou earth, at the presence of the Lord, at the presence of the God of Jacob."

(7) *Hyperbole* is a rhetorical figure which consists in the exaggeration or the magnification of an object beyond true reality. "Oh that my head were waters, and mine eyes a fountain of tears, and I might weep day and night for the slain of the daughter of my people" (Jer. 9:1; *cf.* Gen. 49:11; Psa. 6:6; John 21:25).

(8) *Irony* is a figure of speech in which the speaker says for effect the very opposite from that which is intended. The words of Elijah to the prophets of Baal: "Cry aloud: for he is a god . . ." (I Kings 18:27) is an example of irony. Words of scorn and derision, like the mockery of the soldiers in Matthew 27:29: "Hail, King of the Jews!" might better be considered as examples of sarcasm, rather than irony.

Passing now to the less common figures of speech found in the Bible, one finds *fables, riddles, enigmas, allegories, parables, proverbs, types,* and *symbols,*[31] only two or three of which need to be mentioned here.

(9) An *allegory* is generally defined as an extended metaphor,

_____

[31] Terry, *op. cit.,* has devoted several chapters to Biblical figures of speech, and has given them complete and generally satisfactory treatment. Some of the above definitions are drawn from this section.

bearing the same relation to the *parable* as the metaphor does to the simile. The important thing in the interpretation of an allegory is to seize the main truth which it intends to set forth, interpreting the lesser details in harmony with that truth. Psalm 80:8-15 is an example of an allegory, but the most famous is that of Paul in Galatians 4:21-31.

It is constantly claimed by those who seek to take liberties with the theology of the Bible that the presence of allegories in Scripture is a confirmation of their allegorizing method of interpretation. Nothing could be further from the truth! To interpret correctly a plain allegorical figure of speech according to the laws of figurative language offers not the most vague comparison to that method which takes plain, non-figurative statements, wrests from them their obvious meaning, and substitutes something entirely different, even opposite, in its place. Legitimate interpretation seeks to determine the purpose of the author in giving the allegory, while allegorizers seek to change the plain intent of the author.[32] Returning to Paul's allegory in Galatians, the spiritual meaning is solidly based on a literal foundation, for the geographic locations and the characters involved are all literal. Lightfoot has expressed it well:

> With St. Paul, on the other hand, Hagar's career is an allegory because it is history. The symbol and the thing symbolized are the same in kind. This simple passage in patriarchal life represents in miniature the workings of God's providence hereafter to be exhibited in grander proportions in the history of the Christian Church. With Philo the allegory is the whole substance of his teaching; with St. Paul it is but an accessory. He uses it rather as an illustration than an argument.[33]

It seems evident that the occasional use of allegories, along with other legitimate figures of speech, in no wise constitutes a departure from the basic method of literal interpretation.

(10) A *parable* has been called "a short earthly story with a heavenly meaning." The name is derived from the Greek verb παραβάλλω, "to throw" or "place by the side of," and car-

[32] R. T. Chafer, *The Science of Biblical Hermeneutics* (Dallas: Bibliotheca Sacra, 1939), p. 80, comments: "The defenders of the postmillennial and amillennial systems openly espouse the allegorizing of plain Scriptures to meet the needs of their systems of interpretation, a fair example being Wyngarden's rather recent work, *The Future of the Kingdom and Fulfillment.*"

[33] Lightfoot, cited by Hospers, *op. cit.*, pp. 21, 22.

ries the idea of placing one thing by the side of another for the purpose of comparison. It is, in a sense, an extended simile, but unlike the simile, its imagery never departs from that which is real and factual. Terry says: "It moves in an element of sober earnestness, never transgressing in its imagery the limits of probability, or of what might be actual fact."[34]

> The general design of parables, as of all other kinds of figurative language, is to embellish and set forth ideas and moral truths in atractive and impressive forms. Many a moral lesson, if spoken in naked, literal style, is soon forgotten; but clothed in parabolic dress, it arouses attention, and fastens itself in the memory. Many rebukes and pungent warnings may be couched in a parable, and thereby give less offense, and yet work better effects than open plainness of speech could do. Nathan's parable (in 2 Sam. xii, 1-4) prepared the heart of David to receive with profit the keen reproof he was about to administer.[35]

Some of the Lord's most pointed rebukes against the Jews were clothed in parables. According to Matthew 13:10-17, a parable has a two-fold use: to reveal divine truth to those who are ready to receive it, and to conceal this same truth from those who would meet plain precepts with derision. Thus, Christ instructed his followers by means of the same instrument that He used at other times to reprove those who had rejected His words.

C. *The Typology of Scripture*

While *types* and *symbols*, strictly speaking, are not figures of speech, since their presence in the Scriptures also has been used to excuse the spiritualizing method, they deserve brief consideration at this point.

Type, from the Greek τύπος, denotes the mark of a blow, an impression made by a die, or an example or pattern. "Types are the emblems which are designed by God to represent and prefigure some great and good things to come."[36] Many New Testament verses sanction typology (Luke 24:27; I Cor. 10:11; Matt. 12:40). It has truthfully been said: "The typology of the

---

[34] Terry, *op. cit.*, p. 189.

[35] *Loc. cit.*

[36] Joseph Samuel Frey, *Frey's Scripture Types* (Philadelphia: American Baptist Publishing Society, 1841), p. 13.

Old Testament is the very alphabet or the language in which the doctrine of the New Testament is written."[37]

Types have three main characteristics: (1) There must be a notable real point of resemblance between the type and its antitype. (2) The type must be designed by divine appointment to bear a likeness to the antitype, although not necessarily so designated in the New Testament. (3) A type always prefigures something future, differing only in form from predictive prophecy.[38]

Five classes of types have been distinguished: (1) *persons*: Adam, Abraham, Elijah, David, etc., (2) *institutions*: Levitical rites, the sabbath, the passover, etc.; (3) *offices*: the prophetic office, the high priest, Melchizedec, etc., (4) *events*: the exodus, the smitten rock, the brazen serpent, etc.; (5) *actions*: the ministry of the high priest on the day of atonement, etc.[39]

The following rules should be observed in the interpretation of types: (1) That which is evil cannot typify that which is good. There must be congruity. (2) Old Testament types were also symbols of spiritual truth to their own day. (3) The type can be fully understood only in the light of its New Testament antitype. (4) Types are not of a complex nature, but have one radical meaning. (5) The antitype must be on a higher spiritual plane.[40] Rome loses sight of this when she finds the antitype of Old Testament sacrifice in the mass, Old Testament priesthood as the type of apostolic succession of priests and bishops, and the high priest as a type of the pope. (6) The historical, literal meaning must be taken first, then the typical. In this way, the interpretation of Biblical types falls within the framework of the literal method and in no wise constitutes a departure from it.

It may be concluded, therefore, that the stress of the premillennial fundamentalist upon the literal method of Bible interpretation is a valid one, even in those areas which are most

---

[37] Sir Robert Anderson, cited by Ada R. Habershon, *The Study of the Types* (London: Pickering and Englis, n.d.), pp. 10, 11.

[38] Suggested by Louis Berkhof, *Principles of Biblical Interpretation* (Grand Rapids: Baker Book House, 1950), p. 145.

[39] Suggested by George H. Schodde, *Outlines of Biblical Hermeneutics* (Columbus: Lutheran Book Concern, 1917), pp. 219, 220.

[40] Rules 1 to 5 suggested by Berkhof, *op. cit.*, pp. 146-48.

hotly contested, namely, typology and figurative language. The literalist does not disparage the presence of types and figures in the language of the Bible, for they have formulated orderly principles and definitions to aid the interpreter both to recognize them and to determine their contribution to the passage as a whole. Figures of speech are a normal ingredient in any language, but even a figure must be framed out of basic literal elements; moreover, it would not be in the Sacred Text at all unless given to convey or illustrate a literal thought.

III. SPECIAL RULES FOR THE INTERPRETATION OF PROPHECY

In these days of world unrest and confusion, with nations in upheaval, with Israel unwittingly fulfilling ancient prophecy, with voices in increasing number crying "Lo, here," or "lo, there" (Matt. 24:23), Bible students have felt constrained to turn with a renewed interest to the examination of the prophetic Scriptures. Unfortunately, conclusions reached have differed so extensively that the Church has appeared before the world as a trumpet of "uncertain sound" (I Cor. 14:8), unable to unite its testimony or utter persuasively its warnings. Since prophecy, like other Scripture, is inspired of God and is profitable, and since God Himself is not the Author of confusion, it is quite evident that most wrong interpretations stem from incorrect principles and faulty exegesis.

Premillennialists are convinced that the basic rule of literal interpretation still holds good for prophecy, even though its peculiar problems may call for additional rules to govern interpretation. Amillennialists deny this, claiming that prophecy calls for the forsaking of the literal principle and the adoption of a new hermeneutical principle at least in this area. Terry says: "It is principally those portions of the prophetic Scriptures which forecast the future that call for special hermeneutics."[41] Hamilton claims that a departure from the literal sense is justified if that sense creates an apparent contradiction:

A good working rule to follow is that the literal interpretation of the prophecy is to be accepted unless (a) the passages contain obviously figurative language, or (b) unless the New Testament gives authority for interpreting them in other than a literal sense, or (c) unless a literal interpretation would produce a con-

[41] Terry, *op. cit.*, p. 315.

tradiction with truths, principles, or factual statements contained in the non-symbolic books of the New Testament.[42]

This might be well, were it not for the fact that the amillennialist heavily favors his own system when he chooses that which is "obviously figurative" or that which would "produce a contradiction" with other New Testament truth. Hamilton himself says: "Now we must frankly admit that a literal interpretation of the Old Testament gives us just such a picture of an earthly reign of the Messiah as the premillennialist pictures."[43] But rather than give up a favored theory, he gives up his basic hermeneutical rule, and is illustrative of the fact that conservative amillennialists reject literal interpretation, not only in the area of eschatology, but wherever the Scriptures touch upon the millennial issue.

> While considerable difference of opinion exists among amillenarians regarding the best method of disposing of the mass of Old Testament prophecies which seem to indicate a future earthly kingdom for Israel, they agree in the main principle, that is, that these promises will not be fulfilled to Israel in a kingdom age to follow the present dispensation. Whether cancelled because of rejection of Christ as Messiah or spiritualized according to Calvin's formula, amillennialism with one voice condemns any literal fulfillment of these promises.[44]

That such rejection of the literal principle is considered unwarranted even by some amillennialists is seen by the statement of Case:

> Premillennialists are thoroughly justified in their protest against those opponents who allegorize or spiritualize pertinent Biblical passages, thus retaining scriptural phrases while utterly perverting their original significance.[45]

Yet an allegorizing of millennial passages is the only alternative open to men who reject a literal earthly kingdom. It is a return to allegory — a return to a method theologically unsound and historically discredited — that is demanded by amillennialism. Literal for all else, but allegory when it comes to the covenanted kingdom. To do otherwise would be to concede the premillen-

[42] Floyd Hamilton, *The Basis of Millennial Faith* (Grand Rapids: Wm. B. Eerdmans Publishing Co., 1942), p. 53.

[43] *Ibid.*, p. 38.

[44] John F. Walvoord, "Amillennial Ecclesiology," *Bibliotheca Sacra*, CVII (October, 1950), 428.

[45] Shirley Jackson Case, *The Millennial Hope* (Chicago: The University of Chicago Press, 1918), p. 216.

nial view. This fact already has been seen in the admission of
Pieters that the Reformers could not defend the allegorizing
method of exegesis so far as the Scriptures in general were concerned, but that *they retained the spiritualizing method in expounding many of the prophecies.*[46]

One must not lose sight of the fact that a great number of
prophecies contained in the Bible already have been fulfilled,
and that in every case the fulfillment was literal rather than
otherwise. Feinberg illustrates this point by recalling the five-
fold promise of the angel to Mary, as recorded in Luke 1:31, 32:

> All the prophecies of the suffering Messiah were literally ful-
> filled in the first advent of Christ. We have no reason to believe
> that the predictions of a glorified and reigning Messiah will be
> brought to pass in any other manner. Take, for example, the
> words of Gabriel in the first chapter of Luke where he foretells
> of the birth of Christ. According to the angel's words Mary
> literally conceived in her womb; literally brought forth a son; His
> name was literally called Jesus; He was literally great; and He
> was literally called the Son of the Highest. Will it not be as
> literally fulfilled that God will yet give to Christ the throne of
> His father David, that He will reign over the house of Jacob
> forever, and that of His glorious kingdom there shall be no end?[47]

In the words of Todd: "If any prophecy which is clearly known
to have been fulfilled is examined, it will be found that the
fulfillment was literal."[48] The basic harmony of the Scriptures
would require, one might judge, that all future fulfillment must
follow the same pattern.

One must also remember that although strict literalism may
not have led to harmony of opinion on every detail of prophecy,
yet the over-all pattern arrived at is harmonious, and all the
Scriptures involved have been treated. Those who depart from
literal procedures rarely attempt to treat all the Scriptures, and
have yet to produce a system which is basically harmonious.

When it comes to the actual rules for the interpretation of
unfulfilled prophecy, many and varied have been the suggestions
made. Ramm gives a digest of the interpretative principles of
a number of leading authorities: Oehler, Von Orelli, Meyrick,
R. T. Chafer, Terry, Angus and Green, and Davidson. Since

[46] See footnote 5.
[47] Feinberg, *op cit.*, p. 39.
[48] Todd, *op. cit.*, p. 44.

this summary is readily available,[49] there is little point in repeating the various rules here. Ramm himself has suggested the following principles:

(1) Determine the historical background of the prophet and the prophecy.

(2) Determine the full meaning and significance of all proper names, events, geographical references, references to customs or material culture, and references to flora and fauna.

(3) Determine if the passage is predictive or didactic.

(4) If predictive determine if fulfilled, unfulfilled, or conditional.

(5) Determine if the same theme or concept is also treated elsewhere.

(6) As a reminder, keep vividly in mind the flow of the passage, i.e., pay attention to context.

(7) Notice that element of the prophecy that is purely local or temporal.

(8) Take the literal interpretation of prophecy as the limiting guide in prophetic interpretation.[50]

It has been seen that in the interpretation of prophecy not yet fulfilled, those prophecies which have been fulfilled provide the pattern. The literal fulfillment of scores of Old Testament predictions concerning the first advent of Christ is a familiar matter. W. E. Blackstone, *Jesus Is Coming*, lists some three dozen plain prophecies about many different aspects of the second advent, and the presumption is that these will be fulfilled after the same manner, that is, literally. It should not go unnoticed that it would have been easy for the Old Testament Jew to spiritualize very many of the details which were minutely fulfilled by Christ, such as the virgin of Isaiah 7:14; Bethlehem, of Micah 5:2, that tiny village which was called in derision "a mere weed-patch by a Roman highway," and so on throughout the life of the Suffering Servant to the shame of the cross.

Perhaps it is not going too far to say that if present amillennialists were transported back to the time when these predictions were first uttered, they would have insisted on spirit-

[49] Ramm, *op. cit.,* pp. 157-62.
[50] *Ibid.,* pp. 162-73.

ualizing them away as "obviously figurative." Yet the fulfillment was consistently literal, and as Walvoord tersely remarks:
"A method that has worked with such success in the past is
certainly worthy of projection into the future." [51]

The above rules for the interpretation of prophecy are not
exhaustive. Stress has been given to the law of fulfillment,
that in the interpretation of unfulfilled prophecy, the pattern
of those which have been fulfilled should be followed. There
is also the law of time relationship, that two events placed
side by side in a prophecy will not necessarily be fulfilled
simultaneously, or even in immediate succession. There is the
law of double reference, that both an immediate and a future
fulfillment of the same prediction may be found. There is
the principle that the prophets often took in great periods of
time in a single glance, called by Delitzsch "the foreshortening
of the prophet's horizon." There is the principle that even
when the language contains symbols, the language is not
necessarily symbolic throughout.

> When Joel speaks of locusts, he means those creatures. When
> he speaks of the sun, moon and stars, he means these bodies.
> When he says, "How do the beasts groan?" he means the beasts,
> and not as Hengstenberg thinks, "the uncovenanted nations of
> the heathen world." [52]

These are, in the main, the principles which govern the
right interpretation of prophecy. When coupled with the rules
for the recognition and interpretation of Biblical figures, they
should enable the careful interpreter *to steer his course through
the difficulties of predictive prophecy without sacrificing or
compromising the basic tenet of literal interpretation.* To study
the Book, and to face its interpretative problems according to
established rules and accepted methods — this is the orderly,
the God-honoring way of rightly interpreting the Word of
Truth. To read the Bible loosely, spiritualizing whatever appears to be difficult or contrary to preconceived theology — this
is the way fraught with danger, the way which opens the door

[51] Walvoord, "The Theological Context of Premillennialism," *Bibliotheca
Sacra*, CVIII, 274.
[52] Davidson, *Old Testament Prophecy* (Edinburgh: T. & T. Clark, 1903),
p. 171.

for liberalism to spiritualize the essential doctrines rather than the secondary details of the Christian faith.

Special laws for the interpretation of prophecy do not destroy literalism as the basic principle, but merely become a part of its outworking. Payne has summarized the situation adequately:

> If there is to be a departure from the generally accepted literal sense of language it must be positively justified. Then a new rule must be laid down to insure uniformity and that rule in turn must be substantiated by evidence as to its correctness. This is the only true and scholarly approach to the problem of spiritualizing interpretation.[53]

This is the crux of the prophetic problem, and a conclusion which might well be heeded by all who apply to Scripture two different and opposing principles of interpretation, whether they be Tribulationalists or Amillennialists. To delete the literal principle from the interpretation of prophecy is to admit the spiritualizing method. Once admitted, spiritualizing becomes exceedingly difficult to regulate, for it tends automatically to spread to other areas of Christian doctrine. When it does, it may destroy the very Book it once set out to interpret!

IV. THE SYMBOLISM OF THE BOOK OF REVELATION

To some, the Revelation is an obscure book, full of deep mysteries and dark sayings, and so loaded with prophetic symbolism that the possibility of a clear understanding of its meaning is most doubtful. To the contrary, the very title of the book reveals its true nature. "It is not an obscuration but a revelation; it reveals, not conceals. Its symbols are not to hide the meaning but to illuminate it. Symbols form part of its method of instruction, but they teach, not confuse."[54] It is an unsealed book meant to be read and understood, for it carries a promise of blessing for those who keep the sayings of its prophecy (Rev. 22:7).

There have been a great many attempts made to allegorize the Revelation in order to make its events appear as fulfilled during some particular era of history. Those who have so

[53] Payne, *op. cit.*, p. 90.
[54] G. H. Lang, *The Revelation of Jesus Christ* (London: Oliphant's, Ltd., 1944), p. 70.

labored are called Preterists, time alone serving to reveal the
utter bankruptcy of their interpretive methods. In this connection, Walvoord remarks:

> There are literally scores of interpretations of the book of
> Revelation by the amillennarians who have attempted to interpret
> this book by the historical setting which was contemporary to
> them. The history of interpretation is strewed with the wreckage
> of multiplied schemes of interpretation which are every one con-
> tradictory to all the others. The writer has personally examined
> some fifty historical interpretations of Revelation all of which
> would be rejected by any intelligent person today. The literal
> method which regards the bulk of Revelation as future is the
> only consistent approach possible. The spiritualizing method of
> interpretation is a blight upon the understanding of the Scriptures
> and constitutes an important hindrance to Bible study.[55]

Interpreters who believe the prophecies of Revelation (particularly from the fourth chapter) are to be fulfilled at some
future date are designated simply as Futurists. Even among
these there is considerable division of opinion over the extent
to which the literal method may be applied. It is not our purpose here to attempt a solution of this phase of the problem
but rather to demonstrate that the book of Revelation, although
known for its symbols, is not without a heavy literal content,
and that even in this book there is no need for departures from
the basic method of literal interpretation.

Some expositors have given so much emphasis to apocalyptic
symbolism that one wonders if they have not overlooked just
how much of a literal nature the book of Revelation contains.
The chief personages involved are all literal: God the Father,
Christ, the Holy Spirit, Michael the archangel, Satan, Antichrist, angels, men, and so forth. So also are the places literal:
heaven, earth, the abyss, mountains, islands, seas, Jerusalem,
Babylon, and the seven cities of Asia Minor, to name a few.
Revelation 11:8 speaks of "the great city, which spiritually is
called Sodom and Egypt," and in so doing employs a metaphor,
but the city is none the less literal, clearly identified as that
"where also our Lord was crucified." The twenty-four thrones
and twenty-four elders of chapter four are literal rather than

---

[55] Walvoord, "Amillennialism as a System of Theology," *Bibliotheca Sacra*,
CVII, 156, 157.

symbolic, as many opponents of pretribulationalism insist, for John records that one of the elders conversed with him (Rev. 7:13). It is far more sensible to understand the elder to be a literal individual than it is to maintain that one-twenty-fourth part of a symbolic group held conversation with the apostle. Similarly, the two witnesses of Revelation 11:3-12 evidently are literal. They do not symbolize the Church, as the details of their ministry, death, and resurrection indicate (although Lenski ignores such details and makes them the principle of "competent legal testimony," [56] whatever that may mean during torturous Tribulation days). Following the death of the witnesses there is to be a great earthquake. The tenth part of Jerusalem shall fall and seven thousand sinners will perish. Those who refused burial to God's two prophets now lie buried beneath the rubble of their own buildings. Of this incident, Lang has written: "Attempts to 'spiritualize' such details are hopeless; their plain sense is simple." [57] So also must the forty-two months be literal rather than symbolic, for they comprise half the seven year period of Daniel's "seventieth week," measured also in days and by the formula "a time, and times, and half a time" (Rev. 11:3; 12:14). A non-literal interpretation of such specific periods and events would introduce much confusion, if not bring the entire book to chaos.

However, it is the twentieth chapter of the Revelation, when interpreted literally, which comes in for the lion's share of scorn and criticism. Charles R. Erdman, speaking of this chapter and of the Millennium, writes:

> This obscure and difficult passage of Scripture contains a highly figurative description of a limited time during which Satan is bound, and the nations are at rest, and risen martyrs reign with Christ: but after this "Thousand Years" Satan is loosed and leads the nations of the earth against "the camp of the saints," and "the beloved city"; but his hosts are destroyed by fire from heaven and he is "cast into the lake of fire and brimstone." All this is full of mystery. These symbols cannot be interpreted with certainty or with confidence. No prediction of such a limited period of peace and blessedness is found elsewhere in the Bible. [58]

[56] R. C. H. Lenski, *The Interpretation of St. John's Revelation* (Columbus: Lutheran Book Concern, 1935), p. 332.

[57] Lang, *op. cit.*, p. 186.

[58] Charles R. Erdman, "Parousia," *International Standard Bible Encyclopedia*, IV, 2251-F.

The Scriptures challenge all such trembling uncertainty. The Old Testament prophets are full of predictions of Israel's golden age, and whole handfuls of Scripture can be cited to substantiate the kingdom reign of Christ of which Revelation 20 speaks. Note from a random selection the promise of the land and of an everlasting seed (Gen. 26:2-4; 28:13-15; Ezek. 37:24, 25); the final and permanent restoration to the land and the extent of its boundaries (Amos 9:15; Hos. 3:4, 5; Gen. 15:18-21); the perpetuity of the nation in spite of disobedience (Jer. 31:35-37; II Sam. 7:14, 15; Ps. 89:30-37); the time of Israel's fullness and national conversion (Jer. 31:33, 34; Rom. 11:12, 23); the everlasting throne and kingdom (Isa. 9:7; II Sam. 7:12, 13; Luke 1:31-33); the period of safety under the Davidic King (Jer. 33:14-17, 20, 21); its peace and its blessedness (Jer. 23:5, 6; 30:8, 9) with the curse largely removed from nature (Isa. 11:6-9). Other portions of the Revelation harmonize with its twentieth chapter, as in Revelation 5:10, which records that the saints shall reign on the earth, and as in Revelation 12:12, which intimates the binding of Satan by saying that he knows his time is short.

This is the time of rest and peace upon earth of which Revelation 20 specifically speaks. In language which is neither obscure nor highly figurative, the length of the period is set by a six-fold reference to a duration of one thousand years. It is both interesting and pathetic to behold how allegorizers dismiss the plain force of these Scriptures in their effort to exchange what God has spoken for a meaning more in accord with their own ideas. Auberlen gives the following significant bit of "exegesis":

> *Thousand* symbolizes the world is perfectly pervaded by the divine: since *thousand* is *ten*, the number of the world, raised to the *third* power, the number of God.[59]

Another would make the thousand years symbolize "potentiated

[59] Cited by Jamieson, Fausset and Brown, *Critical and Experimental Commentary*, VI, 720.

ecumenicity"! In view of such trifling,[60] it might be well to ask: "Suppose God actually meant one thousand years, how else would He, or how else could He write it? This one chapter of the Revelation repeats the figure six different times in as many verses."

The binding of Satan, in this same chapter, has become another center of confusion at the hands of those seeking an allegorized interpretation of the event. Lenski says: "The binding of Satan means that he shall not prevent this heralding of the Gospel to all the nations."[61] Warfield, however, provides a more outstanding example of how sane and sensible men can be led astray by parting company with the principle of literal interpretation. Concerning the binding and the loosing of Satan, Warfield writes:

> . . . The element of time and chronological succession belongs to the symbol, not to the thing symbolized. The "binding of Satan" is, therefore, in reality, not for a season, but with reference to a sphere; and his "loosing" again is not after a period but in another sphere; it is not subsequence but exteriority that is suggested. There is, indeed, *no literal "binding of Satan" to be thought of at all:* what happens, happens not to Satan but *to the saints,* and is only represented as happening to Satan for the purpose of the symbolical picture. What actually happens is that the saints described are removed from the sphere of Satan's assaults. The saints described are free from all access of Satan — he is bound with respect to them: *outside of their charmed circle his horrid work goes on.*[62]

All of which serves to demonstrate that the plain meaning of Scripture can be reversed completely by the application of an allegorizing principle. No wonder havoc is made of the faith when this vicious method is applied to more cardinal points of Christian doctrine. Peter has stated plainly: "Be sober, be vigilant because your adversary the devil, as a roaring lion, walketh

[60] "What can happen when men cut loose from literality may be seen in Gregory the Great's exposition of the book of Job, where we learn that the patriarch's three friends denote the heretics; his seven sons are the twelve apostles; his seven thousand sheep are God's faithful people; and his three thousand hump-backed camels are the depraved Gentiles!" Alva J. McClain, "The Greatness of the Kingdom," *Bibliotheca Sacra,* 446: 111, 112.

[61] Lenski, *op. cit.,* p. 580.

[62] B. B. Warfield, *Biblical Doctrines* (New York: Oxford University Press, 1929), p. 651. Italics added.

about, seeking whom he may devour" (I Pet. 5:8; cf. I Cor. 7:5; II Cor. 4:3, 4; II Thess. 2:9; I Tim. 1:20; I John 3:8). Yet fundamentally, the modern amillennial view still embraces this unscriptural Augustinian concept that Satan was bound at the first advent of Christ. Judging by present day Satanic activity, he must be tethered on a long chain!

The statement by Warfield is most significant, for it illustrates the power of the spiritualizing method, even in the hands of an outstanding conservative theologian, to alter if not to reverse the plain teaching of the Word of God. Also, it shows how allegorizing may invade and enter other areas of theology (here, angelology) in addition to eschatology.

As to the actual treatment of the symbols contained in the book of Revelation, the writer makes the following five suggestions:

(1) Revelation is a message to the Church directly from the throne of God. Since it is evidently meant to be understood, seek the interpretation of the book by careful study and prayerful meditation. The deep things of God are open only to those walking in full fellowship with God. Revelation is the great watershed of all Biblical doctrine; therefore, a grasp of the teaching of the entire Bible is essential, particularly the book of Daniel, the Olivet discourse, and other major prophetic passages. Prophecy must be studied with great dependence upon the teaching power of the Spirit of God, who has come not only to guide His own into all truth but also to show them "things to come" (John 16:13).

(2) Not all of the word-pictures of the Revelation are symbols. Many are plain, everyday figures of speech, and should be identified and interpreted by the special rules for figurative language — just as one would go about interpreting a figure in the non-prophetical portions of the Word of God. For example, Revelation 1:12 introduces a metonymy: "the voice that spake with me." The book simply abounds with simile: "his hairs were white like wool . . . his eyes were as a flame of fire"; "the moon became as blood"; "the stars of heaven fell . . . as a fig tree casteth her untimely figs, when she is shaken of a mighty wind"; "the heaven departed as a scroll when it is rolled

together"; "the nations of the earth . . . the number of whom is as the sand of the sea" (Rev. 1:14; 6:12, 13; 20:8). Revelation 20:9 uses the figure of personification: "fire came down from God out of heaven, and devoured them." Examples of figurative language in the book might be extended almost indefinitely, but since every legitimate figure is incorporated within the scope of the literal method of interpretation, there is certainly no need for superimposing the many figures of the Revelation over that which actually is symbolic.

(3) In the study of the apocalyptic visions of John, do not fail to distinguish between "things seen and heard" in a vision and the facts evidently given John directly by God or by His angel apart from the vision. For instance, John might see an angel or elder, a heavenly city or a shaft to the abyss, but even when transported to heaven he could not *see* "a thousand years." It is evident that the duration of Satan's binding and the length of the reign of the saints must have been given to John by direct revelation. As such, the thousand year figure cannot be treated to the hazards of "symbolic interpretation."

(4) When a symbol or sign does appear in the Revelation, it is often plainly designated as such in the immediate context, together with what the symbol represents. Lange gives this rule:

> Nothing should be symbolically interpreted which is not proved to be symbolical in the Apocalypse itself or by Old Testament visions. Nothing should be apprehended literally which is demonstrated to be a symbol.[63]

In Revelation 12:3 "there appeared another wonder in heaven; and behold a great red dragon . . ." who is clearly identified in verse nine as "the great dragon . . . called the Devil, and Satan." Another example is Revelation 17:18, where the woman sitting upon a scarlet colored beast is identified: "And the woman which thou sawest is that great city, which reigneth over the kings of the earth." It is religious Babylon wherein are seven mountains (verse nine), the place of ecclesiastical scarlet and the blood of martyrs, evidently the city of Rome.

(5) It must be remembered that the book of the Revelation

---

[63] John Peter Lange, *The Revelation of John* (New York: Scribner, Armstrong & Co., 1874), p. 77.

is not independent of previous prophecy. There are in the book some three hundred allusions to some other part of the Bible, and the main roots of the book are in Daniel. Some themes are carried through the entire Scriptures, the book of the Revelation being the final terminal. It is to be expected, therefore, that much of the imagery of the Revelation is to be found, and to some extent explained, in some of the earlier books of the Bible. Such is indeed the case. As Ironside explains:

> This book is a book of symbols. But the careful student of the Word need not exercise his own ingenuity in order to think out the meaning of the symbols. It may be laid down as a principle of first importance that every symbol used in Revelation is explained or alluded to somewhere else in the Bible.[64]

Thus, the sharp sword of Revelation 19:15 may well speak of judgment through the application of the Word of God, according to Hebrews 4:12. The star which fell from heaven unto the earth, in Revelation 9:1, is identified in its own context as a person (verse two, "he opened"), but may well be an angel or heavenly ruler, according to parallel passages such as Numbers 24:12, Isaiah 14:13, and Revelation 12:4. Light is shed on the nature of the four "living creatures" of Revelation 4:6-8 by a comparison with the four "living creatures" of Ezekiel 1:5-14. Likewise must the "four and twenty elders" be interpreted in the light of those called "elders" elsewhere in the Bible.

Especially is the vision of Christ in the first chapter of the Revelation highly symbolic, but here also the key is in the Scriptures. Daniel 7:9 speaks of one called the Ancient of Days, with "the hair of his head like the pure wool." Isaiah 11:5 notes that "righteousness shall be the girdle of his loins." His voice "as the sound of many waters" is part of the imagery of the twenty-ninth Psalm. John fell at His feet as dead, but so did Isaiah, Moses, Job, and others, when they beheld His glory. Because the pattern is plain, the conclusion is obvious. The interpreter must be one who searches the rest of the Sacred Text rather than his imagination for the interpretation of prophetic symbols. As it has so often been said, all of the

[64] H. A. Ironside, *Lectures on the Book of Revelation* (New York: Loizeaux Bros., 1919), p. 13.

Scriptures are self-explanatory, and although the Revelation is not the easiest book to understand, many of its basic problems yield to earnest, Spirit-led Bible study.

These conclusions and suggestions, although a bare introduction to the vast field of prophetic study, should be of value to the student of prophecy because they are all in harmony with the principle of literal interpretation. This method, when applied to the book of the Revelation, alone yields consistent answers to its interpretive problems, unfolding a prophetic program in complete harmony with the rest of Scripture.

Literal interpretation, whether examined historically or in the laboratory of actual exegesis, is the foundation principle of conservative Protestant theology. It needs not to be bolstered, or confounded, or modified, by allegorizing or anything which resembles it. Literal interpretation, returning to the wise words of Bonar, is "the only maxim that will carry you right through the Word of God from Genesis to Revelation."

SECTION III

THE LITERATURE OF THE RAPTURE DEBATE

A mounting wave of interest has swept across America and the United Kingdom on the subject of the return of Christ. Near the crest of the wave is the turbulent question, being asked with ever increasing intensity: "Will Christ return before the Tribulation, or must the Church pass through that dread hour?"

Through the many years since the first publication of this volume, among evangelical Christians there has been a sustained interest in this frequently debated question. Perhaps the increasing social violence and governmental upheavals of the present era have encouraged such concern. Whatever the cause, much new material has been written as the Rapture debate enthusiastically continues. The time of the Rapture and its relationship to the coming Tribulation has become one of the burning issues of Biblical study and Christian theology.

Kept from the Hour was first written as a doctoral dissertation, completed in 1952 and published by the Zondervan Publishing House in 1956, followed by Marshall, Morgan and Scott (London) in 1958 while the author was professor of Systematic Theology at Talbot Theological Seminary, Los Angeles. While this volume makes no claim at being exhaustive, it does present the four main positions on the time of the Rapture and most of the primary issues and Scriptures involved. Subsequent volumes by many other writers have developed these themes and filled in a host of exegetical details.

Already in the early 1950's there was considerable interest in the time of the Rapture, stirred up no doubt by a blistering attack upon the prevailing pretribulational view by the publication of *The Approaching Advent of Christ*, authored by a Presbyterian missionary to Brazil, **Alexander Reese**. Persuasive and "embarrassingly bombastic" (Gundry), Reese's book became the standard posttribulational polemic and later writers have borrowed extensively from his attitudes and arguments.

Although the Rapture debate has four main viewpoints, in the intervening years the discussion has largely narrowed to an increasingly detailed and technical debate between the advocates of pretribulationism and the advocates of posttribulationism. Some of the best theological minds of our day have been attracted to each side of the issue and a considerable literature has been generated.

With all due respect for each author, it is our purpose here to review the books which, in the opinion of the writer, have the most to contribute or which take positions worthy of consideration.

THE BLESSED HOPE

In 1956, almost simultaneously with the publication of *Kept from the Hour*, there appeared a major posttribulational defense entitled *The Blessed Hope*, written by **George E. Ladd**, former professor of history and theology at Fuller Theological Seminary. Dr. Ladd sets forth and defends the proposition that "the Blessed Hope is the second coming of Christ and not a pretribulation rapture." Ladd is a Premillennialist who believes in an infallible, authoritative Scripture, but who now marshals the primary arguments in support of a posttribulational Rapture.

Unlike Reese, he is generally courteous, although he falls away from this high ground when he joins with Oswald J. Smith in labeling the Pretrib view "a dangerous heresy," because it (in Ladd's words) "sacrifices one of the main motives for world-wide missions, viz., hastening the attainment of the Blessed Hope" (146, 150). This simply is not true, for Pretrib missionaries and overseas professors have gone worldwide preaching and teaching Jesus Christ and His "so great salvation," possibly in far greater numbers than their Posttrib brethren.

The Blessed Hope is promoted on its front cover as "A Biblical Study of The Second Advent and The Rapture." It is therefore quite surprising to discover how little attention is given to the acknowledged three primary Scriptures on the Rapture, namely **I Thessalonians 4:13-18, I Corinthians 15:51-54** and **John 14:1-3.** Nor is it difficult to discover why they are neglected. They simply do not teach posttribulationism! They give no suggestion of Tribulation preceding the Rapture, or of an earthly reign of Christ immediately following. They set forth the Rapture as a comforting hope, and it would be of small comfort to tell suffering saints that far worse things might be in store. They distinguish the Rapture from the Revelation by calling the Rapture a "mystery," a truth heretofore unrevealed (Col. 2:6), and not like the Second Coming which is clearly taught in the Old Testament (Zech. 14:4, 9, etc.). They promise that translated saints will be taken directly to the Father's house, clearly a reference to heaven. Small wonder that Ladd and others almost ignore these vital Rapture passages.

Rather, he writes a whole chapter disputing dispensationalism and two long chapters, almost a third of the book, on the historical argument for posttribulationism. He erroneously defines dispensationalism as "the method of deciding in advance which Scriptures have to do with Israel," (130) and falsely argues that pretribulationists make the Tribulation entirely Jewish. In his book, *The Rapture Question*, Walvoord comments that Ladd has set up "a straw man" to knock down, for pretribulationists agree that the Tribulation finalizes the "times of the Gentiles," and is a period when God brings judgment upon rebellious nations. Ladd then makes matters worse by suggesting that the 144,000 from the twelve tribes of Israel (Rev. 7:2-8) may represent the "true Israel of God," by which he means the Church. But then he fails to explain why the Church originates from twelve tribes – are these the major denominations? Significantly, he can find no clear reference to the Church in any of the Tribulation passages.

Concerning the history of the Pretrib doctrine, Ladd asserts: "Pretribulationism was an unknown teaching until the rise of the Plymouth Brethren among whom the doctrine originated" (162). He names as Darby's source an eloquent but erratic early charismatic preacher by the name of Edward Irving, about the year 1830. Many will resent the statement: ". . . that supposed revelation . . . came not from Holy Scripture, but from that which falsely pretended to be the Spirit of God" (41). This ugly implication that pretribulationism came from a Satanic source is a quotation from Tregelles, but Ladd includes it as if it were true. He also minimizes the fact that a host of God's people are convinced that the idea of escaping Tribulation sprang from the words of Christ, John and Paul, and is rooted in the Apostolic hope of Christ's imminent return.

Ladd gives no real evidence that Irving was pretribulational beyond the fact that he proclaimed "the imminence of Christ's coming." If this is sufficient evidence of pretribulationism, then on Ladd's own admission the early Church must have been pretribulational. While most will agree that the early Church fathers were not entirely clear on the details of their eschatology, "many posttribulationists, such as J. Barton Payne, concede that the early church fathers believed in imminency and that this is the historic position" (Walvoord 1976, 47).

It is becoming increasingly evident that *many* Bible students in the general era of Irving believed and actively taught that the Church would not go through the coming Great Tribulation. This came about by a return to Biblical studies and the rise of futurism in the interpretation of prophetic Scripture. After centuries of neglect the *whole doctrine* of Christ's return was being rediscovered, including a Pretrib Rapture, and it was attended with spiritual power and great blessing wherever it was proclaimed.

Although Ladd effectively presents the Posttrib position, there are many chinks in his theological armor. As authorities he prefers to choose and quote authors who agree with him, even those who may appear immature or Amillennial in their eschatology. He attacks the concept of a "secret Rapture," and thinks that by refuting "secrecy" he has disposed of a Pretrib resurrection and translation of the saints. He spends a full chapter discussing the Greek vocabulary for the Blessed Hope and in so doing attacks a non-representative position. While it is true that an early writer endeavored to make *parousia* a technical word for the Rapture, it is now broadly recognized that the three distinctive Greek words associated with the return of Christ are non-technical and apply equally to the Rapture and the Second Coming (cf. Pentecost 156-8; Stanton 20-22; Walvoord 1957, 155-58). The term "secret" and a technical use of *parousia* are no longer valid issues in the Rapture debate.

Ladd declares that we cannot accept a view which is not "explicitly taught" in Scripture, but later he makes the damaging admission: "With the exception of one passage, the author will grant that the Scripture nowhere explicitly states that the Church will go through the Great Tribulation" (5). That one exception is in Revelation 20, where "the Resurrection is placed at the return of Christ in glory." But such an argument merely assumes what it sets out to prove. It ignores the obvious fact that the "first resurrection" is first in *quality* and not in *time*. For the first resurrection has many stages (I Cor. 15:23), and prior to the Revelation 20 resurrection there are others, such as the resurrection of Christ, the raising of certain Old Testament saints (Matt. 27:51-53), the resurrection of God's two faithful witnesses (Rev. 11:11-12), and the raising of the dead in Christ at the Rapture (I Thess. 4:16). These are all included in the "first resurrection" because all are righteous.

In discussing the nature of the coming Tribulation, Ladd correctly states: "It is inconceivable that the Church will suffer the wrath of God" (122). But then he goes on to speak of unparalled bodily suffering and widespread martyrdom of the saints during the Tribulation, making this period "the most fearful the world has ever seen." "Martyrdom has ever been a mark of faithfulness to Christ. . . . Why should it be any different at the end?" (129).

He fails to explain how the saints will be protected from divine judgments which are *worldwide*, such as the sun scorching men with fire, the pollution of all fountains and waters, devastating earthquakes and possible nuclear holocaust. "There is no way to escape it," says Blackstone, "but to be taken out of the world by the Rapture, in as much as the Great Tribulation covers the whole habitable earth" (Biederwolf, 550).

In addition, Ladd waters down the command to "watch" for the return of Christ, saying this does not mean "looking for" the event but merely a "spiritual and moral wakefulness." He hardly considers the removal of the Restrainer with its strong pretribulational implications. He makes Revelation 3:10 teach "a promise of preservation and deliverance in and through" the hour rather than physical removal from the hour itself, and fails to note that martyred saints have not been preserved or delivered (Rev. 13:7).

In arguing against an interval between Rapture and Revelation, he ridicules the idea that seven years would give God enough time to reward the saints at the Judgment Seat of Christ, as though God were limited by human chronology! He then is forced to merge the Marriage Supper of the Lamb with the coming of Christ to wage war and judgment.

Also unanswered is the important Pretrib argument, that if every living saint is raptured at the Second Coming and none of the wicked are allowed to enter the Kingdom, this would make unnecessary the separation of the sheep and the goats in Matthew 25, and would leave none on earth in their natural physical bodies to populate the Millennial Kingdom.

Dr. Ladd is to be commended for his generally gracious attitude and his appeal to hold God's truth in love and the unity of the Spirit. Certainly those who "love His appearing" should close ranks and stand together on the great fundamentals of the Word of God. But his presentation leaves much of the evidence for a pretribulational Rapture relatively untouched and fails to convince this reviewer that the Blessed Hope implies the prospect of martyrdom in the Tribulation rather than the daily hope of meeting Christ face to face.

IS THE RAPTURE NEXT?

A rather simple but effective presentation of the Pretrib viewpoint was published by **Leon Wood** in 1956, under the title *Is* *the Rapture Next*? It represents the result of a faculty study group of the Grand Rapids Baptist Theological Seminary and Bible Institute, who "entered the consideration with open minds to determine what the Scriptures had to say."

Avoiding all personalities and lesser theological disputes, the procedure was to examine and attempt to harmonize two groups of Scripture: (1) Those which supply the stronger reasons for saying "*Yes*, the Rapture will precede the Tribulation," and (2) "those which normally are thought to say *No!*, the Church will not be delivered from that time." The final conclusion was reached that the latter group of verses do not say *No* at all, but "properly interpreted, are very much in keeping with the *Yes* answers" (9).

The following are among the contributing conclusions drawn: (1) The coming Tribulation is in a class by itself, designed with the purpose of punishment rather than purification. "The Church, whose punishment has been borne by Christ, logically should be expected to escape such a time." (2) While "no definite Scripture passages indicate that the Church will then be on earth," other passages such as Revelation 3:10 say clearly that it will not be here. (3) The Tribulation "has a Jewish character which is hard to reconcile with the Church's presence." (4) The Scriptures which urge an attitude of watchfulness for, or else joyful anticipation of, Christ's coming "clearly imply that there will be no warning signal for last-minute preparation." (5) The expression "end of the age" does not connote cessation of time "but rather completion of program by means of consummating events." (6) When, in the Olivet Discourse, Christ answered the questions of His disciples relative to *signs* and *time*, He limited His answers to the Jewish aspect of last things because "the nature of the disciples' thinking" still related to the predicted Kingdom rather than to the future Church. (7) The Posttrib argument from the "first resurrection" in Revelation 20:4-6 is clearly answered when it is recognized that "the word *first* is not intended to be taken in the sense of *initial*, but rather a reference to a type of resurrection, namely that of the righteous as contrasted with that of the wicked" (117-20).

The author concludes that our personal decision concerning

the Rapture debate is significant because it results in "quite a different outlook" as we watch for Christ's coming.

THE RAPTURE QUESTION

A major contribution to pretribulational literature was made in 1957 with the publication of *The Rapture Question* by **John F. Walvoord,** former President and now the Chancellor of the Dallas Theological Seminary. From a lifetime of studying and graduate level teaching of Biblical eschatology, Walvoord discusses in depth all of the primary issues and gives detailed exegesis of the relevant Biblical passages.

Walvoord sets forth the importance of the Rapture question, which is "one of the main areas of dispute in conservative eschatology" (8). He continues with an extensive study of the meaning of the Church, significant in the Rapture debate because Posttribs normally and without proof assume "that the word *church* is synonymous with the terms *elect* and *saints,*" and hold that "saints of all past, present, and future ages are included in the church." While all agree that there are some of God's "elect" present in the Tribulation (according to Pretribs they turn to Christ after the Rapture), if these are to be uncritically classified as members of the Church "it leads inevitably to the conclusion that the church will go through the tribulation."

So widespread is this false assumption that Walvoord declares: "It is therefore not too much to say that the rapture question is determined more by ecclesiology than eschatology" (16). It might be added that if the word "elect" belongs exclusively to the Church, then the Church must include the "elect angels" and indeed all the saints since Adam!

Walvoord continues his discussion with the historical argument, the central feature of which is the doctrine of imminency. He gives important quotations from as early as the second century to demonstrate that the early Church lived in constant expectation of the coming of the Lord. And if the Rapture is truly imminent, it follows that it must be pretribulational.

Under the "hermeneutical argument," he warns that many posttribulationists tend to depart from normal literal interpretation, which is the hallmark of Premillennialism, toward a spiritualization of the key Tribulation passages. He goes on to show the "complete lack of evidence for the presence of the Church in the Tribulation," distinguishing clearly between "tribulation" as a general condition of suffering or persecution and "Tribulation" which refers to the specific period of the outpoured wrath of God. "It has been shown that the purpose of the Tribulation is to purge and judge Israel and to punish and destroy Gentile power. In neither aspect is the church the object of the events of the period" (72).

Dr. Walvoord discusses the work of the Holy Spirit in the present age and the significance of the removal of the Restrainer. He presents the Judgment Seat of Christ in heaven and the judgment of both Israel and the Gentiles upon earth as necessary intervening events between Rapture and Revelation, and finds Ladd's view that seven years would not be sufficient to review the lives of Church saints bordering on the ridiculous. He counters the charge of Oswald T. Allis that the Pretrib view is "singularly calculated . . . " to appeal to those selfish and unworthy impulses from which no Christian is wholly immune" by declaring: "Unless martyrdom is something to be earnestly desired and cheerfully sought, it is difficult to see why it is so contrary to Christian principles to desire to avoid these contingencies" (133).

The last four chapters of the book take up a detailed examination of the three alternate Tribulation positions, closing with a most significant summary chapter entitled "Fifty arguments for Pretribulationism." Coming as they do from a trusted scholar whom many consider the dean of conservative, Biblical theologians for the past three decades, those who differ would do well to evaluate carefully these 50 arguments.

THINGS TO COME

In 1958 there was first published an excellent and extensive (633 pages) overview of Biblical Eschatology called *Things To Come*, written by J. Dwight Pentecost, who since 1955 and until recently has served on the faculty of Dallas Theological Seminary. While his volume covers the entire scope of Bible prophecy, it is important to the Rapture debate because of its detailed examination of the four main positions and other related matters, such as the identity of the Restrainer, the position of Israel and the Gentiles in the Tribulation, and the resurrections and judgments normally associated with the Second Advent of Christ.

Pentecost strongly answers the notion of one general and final resurrection and supports the view that the resurrection of the Church is but one of the *orders (tagma)* found in I Corinthians 15:23.   Therefore the mention of the "first resurrection" in Revelation 20:5-6 does not date the Rapture as posttribulational as the opponents of the Pretrib view constantly proclaim. As previously mentioned, there are many stages in the "first resurrection," for it is "first" in quality rather than in time, distinguishing it from the resurrection of the unrighteous dead, which is the "second resurrection."

Pentecost holds that "Pretribulation rapturism rests essentially on one major premise – the literal method of interpretation of the Scripture" (193). This he sustains by the cumulative evidence of 28 "Essential Arguments of the Pretribulation Rapturist," all expressed convincingly and well supported by Scripture.

These include the scope and purpose of the seventieth week, which is judgmental and "will see the wrath of God poured out upon the whole earth." The concept of the Church as a mystery, "not revealed until after the rejection of Christ by Israel . . . distinct in its inception . . . certainly separate at its conclusion." The distinctions between Israel and the Church show conclusively that these two groups are not to be united as a single entity. The doctrine of imminence "forbids the participation of the church in any part of the seventieth week." The necessity for an interval between Rapture and Revelation to allow time for the Judgment Seat of Christ, the presentation of the Church as the Bride of Christ, and the Marriage Supper of the Lamb. The 24 elders, "representative of the saints of this present age . . . resurrected, in heaven, judged, rewarded, enthroned . . . raptured before the seventieth week begins." The sealed 144,000 from Israel, redeemed but with a "special Jewish relationship," indicating that "the church must no longer be on earth." The chronology of the Book of Revelation, which poses great difficulty for both the Midtrib and the Posttrib Rapture positions (193-218).

The full 28 arguments strongly support a pretribulational conclusion, and demonstrate clearly that the significance of the Rapture debate goes far beyond the mere chronology of our Lord's return. Important also is Pentecost's inclusion of a history of both Premillennialism and Amillennialism, and also a chapter setting forth the essential rules for the interpretation of prophecy.

THE IMMINENT APPEARING OF CHRIST

In 1962 there was published another major defense of the post-tribulation position entitled *The Imminent Appearing of Christ*, by **J. Barton Payne**, at the time an Associate Professor of Old Testament in the Graduate School of Theology of Wheaton College. In keeping with a host of other students of Biblical Eschatology, Payne accepts the Premillennial view of the return of Christ. But in some aspects of his Rapture viewpoint he stands alone, subscribing as he does to the imminency of the return of Christ which Posttribs normally repudiate, yet coupling it with a strong posttribulational conclusion. He defends both of these positions, declaring that they were cardinal views held by the Apostolic Church. However, he should have seen that many early Church fathers were posttribulational simply because they believed they were then living in the Tribulation. Their theology was overly dominated by their strong persecution experience. However since they were in error in equating Roman persecution with the predicted Tribulation, it follows that they were also in error in drawing a posttribulational conclusion.

Payne writes off all Pretribs as "dispensationalists," while most fellow Posttribs are labeled "predominantly negative" because they are simply "reacting post-tribulationists." His own unique position he calls the "classical Christian hope."

The doctrine of imminency, largely based on the hope and comfort of Christ's appearing, coupled with the exhortations to look and watch with expectancy, is normally considered one of the strong supportive arguments for the pretribulational position. How amazing it is that a future event, which will take place on one calendar day of human history, should be so worded that it becomes the hope and joyful expectation of Christians down through the running centuries! There is nothing else comparable to this in the history of the Christian Church. Now while we are glad that Payne acknowledges and supports the truth of imminency, it must be noted that he applies it to the Second Coming of Christ to earth following the Tribulation rather than to the Rapture itself.

How then does he explain the clearly described events of the predicted Tribulation, such as the reign of Antichrist, the defiling of the Temple, and the many judgments of the outpoured wrath of God so clearly revealed in the Book of Revelation? These "alleged antecedents" of the Tribulation, says Payne, do not destroy the imminency of the Second Coming for they are *already past*, fulfilled in early Church history or in the contemporary problems of Christianity!

While Payne argues vigorously, and perhaps to the beginning student convincingly, his conclusions strike this reviewer as inconclusive and strongly opinionated. To preserve the imminency of the return of Christ he is forced to adopt a non-literal interpretation of the entire Tribulation period. Says he: "The great tribulation, as classically defined, is potentially present, and perhaps almost finished" (133). The wrath of God poured out upon those who worship the Beast and upon the cities of the nations and great Babylon (Rev. 14:10; 16:19) "seem to relate to the now historic fall of Rome" (140). The seventieth week of

Daniel, the rebuilt Temple and the abomination of desolation which shall defile it (Ezek. 40-46; Dan. 9:26-27; 11:36-37), declares Payne, "all of which are seen to lie in the portion that has ceased to have prophetic relevance beyond the time of Titus" (153).

In Revelation, Payne continues, "the universal rule (13:7), the emperor worship (v. 8), and the martyring of the saints (v. 7) fit ancient Rome, and ancient Rome only" (155). "The commercial activity that is described in such detail in 18:11-19 is distinctly that of the first century." The fall of Rome and the balance of power found in the ten horns (17:16) "corresponds with such inspired truthfulness to fall of the historic Roman empire, dated in A.D. 476" (155). Pompously, Payne speaks of the "audacity" of those who require "a future reenactment of what had already been completely fulfilled."

But what of the predictive signs signaling the imminent return of Jesus Christ which history cannot satisfy, such as the meteoric rise and career of the Devil's Antichrist, the godless activities of the False Prophet, and the destruction of three of the ten kingdoms which shall arise in the endtime (Dan. 7:8, 24; Rev. 13:1-18; 17:12)? For Antichrist, Payne (at the time of writing) suggests "an unusually apt candidate for the Antichrist is Nikita Khrushchev right today!" (121). For the False Prophet, he suggests "the papacy, or some other anti-Biblical, ecumenical religious development." And for the three unfortunate kingdoms Daniel's "little horn" will destroy, he offers: "If Christ were to come back today, who would they be? The Hungarians . . . constitute a pitiable possibility" (108). All of these appear to be strange and obviously erroneous conclusions.

Large passages of Revelation are made to coincide with the contemporary scene. For example, "the four horsemen of the Apocalypse — aggression, war, famine and death . . . were never more alive than today" (112). The two witnesses of Revelation 11, he suggests, are "a church that witnesses to the law and to the prophets . . . an inevitable torment to the world." Payne continues: "It seems that in many places now, as never before, when

Christians are liquidated 'they that dwell on the earth rejoice over them, and make merry.'" Moreover, "in Latin America, and in other areas of Roman Catholic domination today, the prohibition of burial rights to Evangelicals is far from unknown" (118).

Now while it is sadly true that there are Christians today who have laid down their lives for the cause of Christ, to apply this to the two witnesses of Revelation 11 is an example of flagrant spiritualization of prophetic Scripture.

What then of signs which obviously have not yet been fulfilled? Says Payne, "the signs are brief . . . giving the Christian the opportunity to pull his car over to the side of the road, but perhaps not much more" (92). So brief are the remaining signs before the believer is caught up in the Rapture! And all of these rare pronouncements simply to reconcile the truth of imminency with the theory of posttribulationalism!

The only necessary conclusion to be drawn is that the early Church was correct when it looked for the imminent return of Christ, but very wrong when it identified the Roman persecution with the predicted Tribulation period. If indeed some were posttribulational, it was their suffering and not the prophetic Scriptures which became the essential basis of this persuasion.

Payne's fellow Posttrib, Robert H. Gundry, includes in his book *The Church and the Tribulation* an "Addendum on Imminent Posttribulationalism," which is a severe and detailed refutation of Payne's position. It requires the possibility, says Gundry, "that we have progressed to the very *end* of the tribulation" (193). We cannot suppose that all the great endtime events have passed unnoticed, for "they are *revelatory* signs and must therefore be recognizable upon occurrence." Thus "Payne's potential but uncertain fulfillment falls to the ground" (194).

Continues Gundry, Payne is wrong in denying "the principle of double fulfillment." His view "lacks historical perspective." It fails to provide an adequate fulfillment of the Olivet Discourse, "which describes a complex of events immediately preceding the return of Christ" (200).   There follows much more detail to support Gundry's very critical evaluation of Payne's position.

In addition to the conflicts generated by the attempts to reconcile the imminency of our Lord's return with Payne's so-called "pasttribulational" view, other problems quickly rear their heads. Declares the author, John 14:3 is "irrelevant" to the time of the Rapture because it does not teach being translated to the Father's house. Rather, "the interpretation which seems the more plausible contextually is that *at a believer's death* 'I come and will receive you unto myself' in glory" (74). This makes John 14:3 a funeral promise rather than a blessed expectation of Christ's return!

Payne also claims that Romans 5:9 and I Thessalonians 1:10 and 5:9 are likewise "irrelevant passages," for they "need simply to imply no more than God's certain condemnation of sin. . . . He is *delivering* us from the wrath, right now." Thus, they do not apply to the Rapture question. But such an assertion ignores the fact that the context of I Thessalonians 1:10 is "waiting for God's Son from heaven," and that for 5:9 the prior context is the "day of the Lord," which certainly includes the Tribulation.

His discussion of the primary passage, I Thessalonians 4:13-18, is extremely brief and fails to explain how a Posttrib Rapture could be of comfort to early believers. While agreeing with him that "the chapter division is here an unhappy one," Payne seems not to notice that Paul discusses the Rapture before he discusses the day of the Lord – a perfect pretribulational order.

Rather, he limits his exegesis to the expression "to meet the Lord in the air," explaining that "the ones who do the meeting then turn around and accompany the one who is met for the rest of his journey. . . . The church is to meet Christ in the air and thus join in His triumphant procession down to earth." Since they "advance without pause," the Judgment Seat of Christ "could be instantaneous, in the air" (136). This would hardly comfort Dr. Ladd who argues, as we have seen, that seven years would not be long enough to judge and give reward to all His saints.

The return of Christ for His Church is certainly a wonderful hope, and *The Imminent Appearing of Christ* is an attractive theme and title. But in the writer's opinion, much of the content of this book is a fallacious interpretation of prophetic Scripture. Certainly, it is a sad deteriation from the Bible and theology he was taught by the faculty during his own years at Wheaton College and its Graduate School. As a theologian who has spent a lifetime in the study and teaching of eschatology, it is with great regret that this reviewer judges Payne's central conclusion to be wrong, his objections to pretribulationism answerable, and his attitude toward his Pretrib brethren frequently abrasive.

ENCYCLOPEDIA OF BIBLICAL PROPHECY

A much greater and less controversial work was published by J. Barton Payne in 1973, called the *Encyclopedia of Biblical Prophecy*, and subtitled "The Complete Guide to Scriptural Predictions and Their Fulfillment." Because of its scope and scholarly content it is a volume of considerable value, weakened no doubt by Payne's continued adherence to the viewpoints previously discussed.

Thus, the Rapture is minimized and the Church goes no further than meeting Christ in the air and returning immediately to earth on the Mount of Olives. In the words of Payne, this is "our rapture *to Jerusalem*" (561), which is certainly a peculiar view! The Restrainer is not seen as the Holy Spirit but is identified as "lawful government," Paul using veiled language "as a means for avoiding offence to the Roman power" (565). Revelation 3:10 applies only to the first century church at Philadelphia, for "their devotion will carry them through the storm of Roman persecution" (606). Such an explanation completely ignores the immediate context found in verse 11, which is the return of Christ at the end of the Church age.

The prophecy and blessed promise of John 14:1-3 is skipped without mention. The 144,000 witnesses of Revelation 7 become "a chosen youth group of the church, the Israel of God" (597). And the Rapture is identified with Revelation 14:1-7 where the representative groups of the tribes of Israel are now seen in heaven! Much of this, of course, is one man's opinion and cannot fail to disappoint those who now look for God's Son from heaven.

THE CHURCH AND THE TRIBULATION

Also in 1973 there was published yet another significant book length presentation of the posttribulational view, entitled *The Church and the Tribulation* by **Robert H. Gundry,** Professor of Religious Studies at Westmont College.

While Payne is a preterist, holding that much of the Revelation was fulfilled in the Roman persecution of the early Church, Gundry is a futurist, joining with Pretribs and most of his fellow Posttribs in placing Revelation 4-22 in the eschatological future. Payne strongly believes in the imminency of our Lord's return, while Gundry just as strongly rejects imminency, declaring that those "who find imminence in the Ante-Nicene fathers are grasping at straws" (182). Posttribs typically scorn dispensationalism and its implications, but Gundry upholds this method of Scripture interpretation, especially in its important distinction between Israel and the Church. Unlike Payne, who thinks that John 14:1-3 speaks of the believer's death, Gundry holds it to be a promise of the Rapture. Also unlike most of his fellow Posttribs he does not "ignore the distinctions between tribulation in general and the time of unprecedented tribulation at the end of the age" (49).

Such extreme divergence of opinion within the posttribulational camp even on the primary issues of the Rapture debate makes critical analysis most difficult. It leads one to suspect that the Posttrib conclusion may be based more upon divergent human opinion than upon sound Biblical exegesis. In his book, *The Blessed Hope and the Tribulation*, Walvoord discusses *four* distinct schools of posttribulationism which have emerged in the twentieth century (21ff.), of which Gundry's "entirely new approach" is but one. Since the Bible does not contradict itself, this notable lack of theological unanimity among posttribulationists reflects a fundamental flaw in their interpretive system.

There is considerable complexity to Gundry's arguments. He

agrees of necessity with pretribulationists that the Church will be exempt from the outpoured wrath of God (I Thess. 1:10; 5:9), declaring "the theological necessity that God's wrath not touch a saved person" (46). But then he endeavors to distinguish *different kinds* of distress in the Tribulation period: the wrath of God upon the unregenerate, the ravages of Satanic and demonic forces, violence which stems from man's own wickedness, the persecution of saints by Antichrist, and the final chastisement upon Israel (46). By so doing he relieves the severity of the Tribulation for the saint, making it more a time of Satanic wrath than divine wrath, thus endeavoring to give the Church safe passage through the Tribulation. Revelation 13:7 denies such a possibility.

He rearranges the sequence of judgments in the Revelation so that the seventh seal, the seventh trumpet and all seven bowls of wrath are "clustered at the end" of the period in one great "cataclysmic blast of judgment at Armageddon" (75-77). He argues that the wrath associated with the seal judgments (Rev. 6:15-17) falls only on unbelievers. The passage describing the multitude which "came out of great tribulation" (Rev. 7:9-17) is called an "episodical vision which leaps to the end of the tribulation" (76). From all this, Gundry concludes: "Divine wrath does not blanket the entire seventieth week, probably not even the latter half of it, but concentrates at the close" (63). After this ingenious scheme the Church goes through the entire Tribulation but is spared its primary judgments and the outpoured wrath of God!

Gundry is forced to admit that there is no clear reference in the Bible to a posttribulational Rapture of the Church. But then he holds that with many clear references to the resurrection of Old Testament saints and a gathering of the Tribulation "elect," which is "indisputably located after the tribulation," it is implied that the Rapture will occur there also.

Posttribulationists must then add to all this end-time activity the gathering and judgment of the nations, the conversion of national Israel, the Judgment Seat of Christ, the Marriage Supper of the Lamb, the defeat of invading armies at Armageddon, the destruction of the Beast and the False Prophet, the fulfillment of dire Old Testament prophecies concerning end-time judgments, plus the final catastrophes of the seven seals, seven trumpets and seven vials of wrath. All in close proximity at the Second Advent of Christ! Posttribs thus have a way of lumping together all these future events into an already heavily overloaded "day of the Lord," and they do so without really producing any orderly chronology of these events.

Why not a seven year period of wrath and judgment to give time for all this activity, as the Scriptures seem to indicate? The Church would escape both divine and satanic wrath by being translated with rejoicing prior to that final period of trouble, and there would be adequate time for the many other activities and events normally associated with Christ's appearing.

Among his unique views, Gundry holds that "some of the wicked will survive the tribulation." Hence, the judgment of the nations will be after the millennium. He believes that the 144,000 will be "orthodox (though unconverted) Jews," both men and women, who will resist the Antichrist and go into the Kingdom to "populate and replenish the millennial kingdom of Israel" (82). The redeemed multitude who come out of the great Tribulation "constitute the last generation of the Church" (80).

He escapes the clear Pretrib inference of John 14:1-3 by declaring that the "Father's house" is simply "a metaphor for the place of believers in the Father's domestic domain." So Christ is not promising that He will return and transport believers to heaven, but rather "He is going to prepare for them *spiritual abodes within His own person.* Dwelling in these abiding places they belong to God's household" (154). Such an approach is commonly called "spiritualizing," yielding an odd and novel interpretation to a familiar and blessed promise.

Concerning the Restrainer of II Thessalonians 2, Gundry gives some credence to "the prevalent view in the early Church" that the restraint of iniquity may be that of "divinely ordained human government." He suggests that Paul speaks vaguely for fear that "the letter might fall into wrong hands and . . . be considered a teaching of sedition" (124). But this view fails, for human government is not removed during the Tribulation. Rather it is expressed by the presence of ten kings and then seized and dominated by Antichrist.

Gundry goes on to favor the identification of the Restrainer as the Holy Spirit, for several of the early Church fathers held this view. Further, "it would seem that a person is required to restrain a person." Also, the change of gender from the neuter to the masculine conforms to the same shift in gender when Paul writes concerning the Spirit. Thus far we would agree. However, Gundry then argues that the Greek grammar does not demand removal from the world. Rather, he says, the Spirit merely blocks the entrance of the Antichrist "until the appointed moment when He will step out of the way and allow the man of lawlessness to stride onstage before the admiring eyes of mankind" (127).

He further declares: "His partial withdrawal in a retrogression to the beggarly elements and immature status of the old covenant would amount to an annulment of Christ's exhaltation" (126). How well he argues, and with such eloquent language! But what is he saying, and is his argument reliable? For Satan, cast down to the earth having great wrath (Rev. 12:12), does imply a major removal of restraint during that period. Moreover, to declare that the return of the Spirit to heaven would diminish His "Pentecostal fullness and power" might, by implication, suggest that Christ also has limited His power and ability to save just because He, too, has shifted from earth to heaven. The language of the text clearly implies a removal of the Spirit before the unveiling of Antichrist. He does not merely step to one side; rather, He is "taken out of the way." Then, because the Spirit abides within the Church forever (John 14:16) and since the Church finds no mention in the many passages describing the Tribulation, it is fair to conclude that the removal of the Spirit has set the time of the removal of the Church as pretribulational.

Much more needs to be said in response to Gundry's complex defense of posttribulationism, but it would probably take another book equal to his 200 plus pages – far beyond the scope of this present review. He writes with considerable scholarship and debating skill, and his arguments are stimulating if not entirely convincing. A far more extensive answer to Gundry's position is available in two books by John F. Walvoord, *The Blessed Hope and the Tribulation* and *The Rapture Question: Revised and Enlarged Edition* (to be reviewed later in this series).

Gundry departs from the views of his fellow Posttribs so frequently that Walvoord is forced to conclude: "His arguments, in the main, are new and propound a form of posttribulationism never advanced before." This causes him to "refute most of the posttributationists who have preceded him." Indeed, "in a number of particular judgments, if Gundry is right, every previous expositor of the Bible has been wrong" (1976, 19, 60-62).

Yet another commentary upon *The Church and the Tribulation* may be found in the chapter entitled "The Case for the Pre-tribulation Rapture Position" by Paul D. Feinberg, in the book *The Rapture: Pre-, Mid-, or Post-Tribulational?* However, the most extensive critique of Gundry's book discovered thus far is the 75 page syllabus by John A. Sproule, entitled *A Revised Review of The Church and the Tribulation by Robert H. Gundry*. A scholarly presentation, it is especially helpful in its Greek exegesis of the cardinal Scriptures and in its firm answers to Gundry's attack against the Pretrib concept of imminency. On this issue, Sproule concludes that Gundry assumes his conclusion, so that "his arguments crumble because their foundations are built upon presumptions rather than upon essentially conclusive evidence" (12).

THE INCREDIBLE COVER-UP

In 1973, **Dave MacPherson,** then a newspaperman of Kansas City, Missouri, published a vigorous repudiation of pretrib-ulationism under the title *The Unbelievable Pre-Trib Oriqin*. It was revised and expanded in combination with another booklet by the same author, *The Late Great Pre-Trib Rapture*, and published in 1975 under the title *The Incredible Cover-Up*.

In MacPherson's widely distributed "A Letter to Southern

Christians," yet another title by the same author was promoted, *The Great Rapture Hoax*, "packed with the sort of shocking data that's been known – and covered up – by Pre-Trib leaders for decades." This letter further claims that "the Pre-Trib view wasn't heard of anywhere on earth before the 1800's," that it was "originated by a young lassie in Scotland in the *sprinq of 1830*," and that it was "pirated" and spread by John Darby, a Britisher who "regarded Americans as inferior creatures, worthy of exploitation." Among other nasty declarations, MacPherson goes on to attack the honesty and morality of C. I. Scofield and promises that his book "will turn you inside out!"

It will immediately be apparent that his book titles are provocative, if not abusive. There has been no "cover-up" or "hoax," for Pretrib authors and leaders have arrived at their conclusion from Biblical exegesis rather than from any presumed history of the doctrine, and most certainly with no desire to defraud. Furthermore, to attack the morality and integrity of fellow believers just to further an eschatological opinion is a disgrace to the Name and cause of Christ.

What then is MacPherson's primary thrust throughout these several paperbacks? In his own words, "the two-stage teaching is an early nineteenth century invention which first saw the light of day in Great Britain and does not reflect the teaching of the New Testament" (1975, 6). "The pre-trib rapture theory ascended from the mists of western Scotland in the spring of 1830" (1975, 138). It had a "hidden background," a "bizarre origin" (1975, 90, 101), when a "dangerously sick" young woman by the name of Margaret Macdonald came under the influence of the Scottish revival and had a revelation in which she proclaimed an utterly new view that the Church would escape the coming Tribulation.

Extensive quotations from Robert Norton, at the time of M.M.'s "revelation" a 22 year old medical doctor, indicate that she, her sister and brothers, were members of the Catholic Apostolic Church of Edward Irving and came under early charismatic influence with the "gifts of prophecy" and "speaking in an unknown tongue." Under such influence, Margaret Macdonald

supposedly revealed that the Church would escape the
Tribulation. Some have gone so far as to attribute her declaration
to demonic forces. This "utterance" of M.M., MacPherson states
repeatedly, is the origin of the pretribulational view that the
Church will escape the coming Tribulation.

The true facts of the case prove otherwise. The recorded
declarations of Margaret Macdonald show clearly that she was not
trying to establish the details of the prophetic future, but rather
lamenting the weak and sinful condition of the professing church.
She cries over "the awful state of the land," the "distress of
nations," the need for "purging and purifying of the real members
of the body of Jesus." She prays for "an outpouring of the Spirit"
upon the Church so that believers will be "counted worthy to
stand before the Son of Man." "Those that are alive in him . . . will
be caught up to meet him in the air." But she declares also that the
Church will go through "fiery trial" from the "wicked" one, who
shall be revealed "with all power and signs and lying wonders."
Then, even more clearly, she declares "the trial of the Church is
from Antichrist" – which to say the least is hardly a pretribulational concept!

Those interested in reading the entirety of M.M.'s "revelation"
will find it recorded in the Appendix of at least two of
MacPherson's books, and also in pages 169-72 of *The Rapture* by
Hal Lindsey.

What then are we to conclude from all this emphasis upon
Margaret Macdonald? (1) Its importance has been blown far out
of all proportion by those who seek to discredit pretribulationism.
Alexander Reese traces the Pretrib view to the "separatist
movements of Edward Irving and J. N. Darby." George Ladd,
quoting Tregelles, traces "the idea of a secret rapture" to an
"utterance" in Edward Irving's church, which "came not from Holy
Scripture, but from that which falsely pretended to be the Spirit of
God." J. Barton Payne says that "soon after 1830 a woman, while
speaking in tongues, announced the 'revelation' that the true
church would be caught up (raptured) to heaven before the
tribulation" (156).   Even Robert Gundry declares that

"pretribulationism arose in the mid-nineteenth century. The likelihood is that Edward Irving was the first to suggest the pretribulation rapture" (185).

However, Gundry in all fairness observes that "the origin of an interpretation of Scripture is not the measure of its correctness." He says also of Irving that "tongues and prophetic utterances did not begin to appear in his church until late 1831, i.e., after the appearance of pretribulationism" (187). It remained for MacPherson to try to demonstrate that beyond question the pretribulation view began with an 1830 "utterance" of Margaret Macdonald.

(2) It is cruel to imply that her utterance was purely emotional, or perhaps Satanic. She was a young and humble Christian endeavoring to call a cold and careless church back to the power and control of the Holy Spirit. The writer thoroughly concurs with Hal Lindsey when he says: "Although I don't agree with the authenticity of her vision, records show her to be a beautiful sister in the Lord, filled with love and compassion for others" (1983, 173).

(3) There is nothing in the M.M. quotation to indicate that she was a pretribulationist. She did not distinguish between the Rapture and the Second Coming of Christ, but rather divided the Rapture itself into two or more parts based on spiritual readiness. This is the Partial Rapture position, very different from pretribulationism. MacPherson is forced to admit this: "Margaret saw a series of raptures (and she was actually a partial rapturist, with or without the label)" (1975, 85). Indeed, she seemed to believe that the Church had already entered the Tribulation, a possibility strengthened by a statement published by Irving December 1831 in *The Morning Watch*: "We have, blessed be God, lived to see the commencement of the seventh vial, DURING THE OUT-POURING OF WHICH THE LORD WILL COME!" (Huebner, 23, emphasis his). This is certainly not pretribulationism!

Readers who desire to pursue in detail the alleged origin of the Pretrib view with Margaret Macdonald and Edward Irving will appreciate the scholarly historical sketch by **R. A. Huebner** entitled *The Truth of the Pre-Tribulation Rapture Recovered*. They will also find of interest *The Origin of the Pre- Tribulation Rapture Teaching* by **John L. Bray,** who finds a Pretrib Rapture taught by a Jesuit priest, Lacunza, whose book *The Coming of Messiah in Glory and Majesty* was first published in Spain in 1812 and translated into English and published by Edward Irving in 1827. This yields a possible Pretrib concept at least eighteen years before Margaret Macdonald. We can only conclude that during this general era many were studying the hitherto neglected truth of our Lord's return, with some disagreement concerning the actual time of His coming but with many affirming a pretribulational Rapture.

(4) In his book, *The Rapture Question: Revised and Enlarged Edition* (1979), **John Walvoord** has an extended discussion of the Posttrib's historical argument which includes five criticisms of MacPherson's position (150-57). In brief, he does not prove any "cover up" for the Pretrib view is based on biblical exegesis and not upon the presumed history of the doctrine. The allegations of Tregelles are without support, and he was obviously a prejudiced witness. His quotations from Margaret Macdonald and Edward Irving prove that they were not pretribulational. There is no evidence that Darby derived his views from such a source, but rather from the study of the Bible itself and from his conclusion that the Church is the body of Christ. "Under the circumstance," says Walvoord, "it would seem that common honesty would call for Dave MacPherson to write another book confessing that his entire point of view has no basis in fact as far as MacDonald and Irving are concerned" (155).

Another strong refutation of the Rapture views of Dave MacPherson has recently been published in the theological quarterly, *Bibliotheca Sacra* (April-June 1990). Entitled "Why the Doctrine of the Pretribulational Rapture Did Not Begin with Margaret MacDonald," author **Thomas D. Ice** discusses Mac-Pherson's background, claims and errors, and the response to his claims by a number of Biblical scholars. Important also is the author's discussion of the "Progress of Dogma" and its relationship to the "Development of Eschatology," and the emergence of the doctrine of the Pretribulational Rapture. All of this is highly recommended reading.

It is MacPherson's contention that the Pretrib Rapture view is a relatively modern heresy with a plot on the part of its adherents to hide its dubious background. He makes the awful charge that in China "The Pre-Trib Rapture view has caused the deaths of thousands of persons" because missionaries did not warn the people of coming persecution (1975, 103). His final conclusion seems to be that "the pre-trib rapture view is on its last legs – if it ever had a leg to stand on!"

Why such a tirade from a young newspaperman? Is it possible that we are witnessing a personal vendetta?

Dave learned his posttribulationism at an early age from his father and pastor, Norman Spurgeon MacPherson, a fine gentleman but an enthusiastic follower of Alexander Reese, whose arguments he considered unanswerable and whose viewpoints he actively promoted. He even wrote his own book on the subject: *Triumph Through Tribulation*, dated 1944.

Dave writes openly about the "prophetic narrowmindedness periodically erupting in my father's California pastorate" and its effect upon his mother's health. He recounts his own dismissal from a Bible Institute because he discussed prophetic viewpoints "differing in detail from the school's official position." Two weeks before the end of the semester, he says, "I was dismissed from the premises. . . . My dismissal was possibly the last straw. A few days later my mother died" (1973, 15).

While all of this is most regrettable, one must not respond to personal sorrow by breaking fellowship with fellow believers over prophetic detail, nor by attacking them and impugning their integrity because they support an alternate viewpoint.

THE TRIBULATION PEOPLE

Under the byline, "Before you assume you are not going through the Great Tribulation . . . Read this book!" there was published in 1975 *The Tribulation People* by **Arthur D. Katterjohn,** former chairman of the orchestral instruments department of the Conservatory of Music, Wheaton College.

The son of a Baptist minister, he was taught "to respect the authority of the Word of God, and to love the words of Jesus." Affirming his commitment to "honest debate," he writes his book "for the Christian who wants to take another look at end-times doctrine." Should the Church prepare to endure Antichrist and worldwide persecution, "or make ready for an unprecedented and unannounced return of Christ just before the tribulation period?" (10). His position, clearly declared from the very beginning, is enthusiastically posttribulational. For authority, he leans hard on the writings of Ladd and Gundry — even though these men differ on many essential issues.

Katterjohn writes his book with an easy-going popular style, occasionally unsuited for serious debate. For example, the biblical five foolish virgins who had no oil suddenly become "five flighty women" who "let their oil supply dwindle." Elsewhere, the Christian life should not be "a flighty fixation on bubbly living" when actually it is a "tense and often painful struggle." Perhaps such word pictures are calculated to catch the interest of young people in Sunday School discussion groups. Certainly his study questions at the end of each chapter are designed for that purpose, but unfortunately they are heavily charged with Posttrib innuendo, frequently assuming what he must clearly prove.

While erroneously declaring the millennial question to be a secondary issue, with "little practical difference" between amillennialism and premillennialism, he holds that the time of the Rapture is "the most pressing question of the future" (77, 13). For Antichrist and the Great Tribulation are coming, and we may be the "Tribulation people" who must suffer and endure the ravages of the end-time.

Katterjohn gathers his evidence for a Posttrib Rapture under three main headings: (A) The Gospels and the teaching of Christ; (B) The Epistles and the teaching of Paul; and (C) the Book of Revelation and the teaching of John. This review shall give them a brief consideration in that order.

(A) In the Gospels, the primary focus is placed upon Christ's Olivet Discourse. Katterjohn holds that it was delivered intimately to "the nucleus of the New Testament Church" and "makes no mention of Israel or the Jews." Furthermore, he charges, those who do not agree with him make what Jesus had to say mean nothing for Christians today (17). This is a wild and unworthy charge, for carried to its logical end it would also remove from Christians any instruction and blessing from the Old Testament, which certainly was first given to Israel. "All Scripture is profitable," and it is all *for* us even though it may not always be *about* us.

Most Bible students affirm that the Olivet Discourse, while giving instruction to all concerning the Tribulation yet to come, has at least "a Jewish character," speaking as it does of Judaea, the Sabbath day, the holy place of the Temple, the tribes of the earth, the Jewish marriage custom, and the coming of the King and the Kingdom. This is Israel in the end time, and there is not a shadow of a hint that the Church, the "body of Christ," will be present during that "time of Jacob's trouble" being described by Christ (Jer. 30:7; cf. Dan. 12:1).

There is no legitimate proof for the Posttrib position which makes *parousia* a technical word for the Second Coming, the *elect* a technical word for the Church, or which declares that Pretribs make the "Gospel of the Kingdom" essentially different from the Gospel Christians know and preach today. In the words of the author, Pretribs teach "a different way of salvation for the hard-pressed believers under Antichrist's reign," even teaching "four different Gospels, as pretribulationists do" (19). If Posttribs have to build their case upon such fabricated slander, perhaps it indicates that they have no legitimate case.

Nor is the Matthew 24:40-42 passage, which Katterjohn calls "the sudden snatch," descriptive of a posttribulational Rapture as some suppose, but in context is evidently a removal of some in judgment while others are left on earth to welcome the return of their Lord and enter His Kingdom.

Katterjohn affirms that "the coming of John 14 and the return in Matthew 24 are the same event" (37). But the presence of certain similarities does not prove identity and it would be just as easy to provide a list of differences. He is not sure if the dramatic promise "Where I am, there you may be also" refers to the "thousand-year reign of Christ on earth or the inauguration of His heavenly kingdom." Probably in this context it means neither. However, no matter how plain the promise (which he labels "poetic"), a Rapture to heaven, "my Father's house," must be denied by a Posttrib, for it is entirely contrary to their notion of an immediate return of the Church to earth after her meeting with Christ in the air.

(B) Under Pauline theology, our author declares that the terms elect, brethren, saints and Church are all used interchangeably, for this "unity of all men of faith is one of the cornerstones of Christian doctrine and cannot be jettisoned for the sake of an end-times theory" (41). This contributes to his erroneous view that the term "Church" comprehends the redeemed of all ages, and that the Rapture of I Thessalonians 4 and the posttribulational return of Matthew 24 are one and the same event.

He observes that there is no mention of the Tribulation in the I Thessalonians 4:13-18 passage, (nor should there be), "nor a secret, any-moment coming of the Lord, nor . . . our return to heaven after the rapture" (42). Later, he admits the invalidity of this common "argument from silence" when he observes that even "the term 'second coming,' although a helpful tool for us, does not appear in God's Word" (68).

The "trump of God" in verse 16, he declares, "is not a fickle kazoo beamed at church-age saints to alert them of a secret rapture . . . but a blast, a fearful booming fanfare to the arrival of the King" (44). The reference to a "meeting" in the air changes the direction of the saints, but not of the King as they descend to earth together. Perhaps all of this is a trifle more than Paul intended to say. This and the other major Rapture passages simply do not teach posttribulationism.

His exegesis of I Corinthians 15:51-52 is very thin. Twice he endeavors to define the term "mystery" (57, 91) and in the light of Colossians 1:26 is wrong on both counts. Like other posttribulationists, he identifies the "last trump" with "that final trumpet blast" of Revelation 11:15, implying that it sounds at the Second Coming of Christ. This is a well-worn argument, frequently answered in pretribulational literature. Such an assumption is entirely false because the context is radically different, and because the judgments of the seven vials of God's wrath clearly intervene between the seventh trumpet and the Second Coming of Christ.

Even on the matter of "wrath" Katterjohn is in theological trouble, affirming: "The tribulation, it must be remembered, is not the wrath of God, but the persecution of the faithful, both Jews and Gentiles, by Antichrist" (41). God's "wrath" is understood to be a final flash of divine indignation upon Antichrist's regime. Moreover, "Christians, it must be remembered, will be removed before God's final anger falls" (98). Thus, even an ardent posttribulationist must admit that the only way for the Church to avoid the outpouring of divine wrath is to be removed by a prior Rapture!

Katterjohn finds "no time or place element" for the Judgment Seat of Christ, even though I Corinthians 4:5 seems to locate it at the Rapture (cf. II Tim. 4:8; Rev. 22:12). Concerning the Marriage Supper of the Lamb he declares: "It is after His reign commences that the marriage supper is held" (79). This would place it upon earth after the Second Coming, but perceptive readers of Scripture will find it in heaven before the return of the King (Rev. 19:7-9, 11-16). Indeed, two great events in heaven after the Rapture and before the Revelation give strong evidence that the Rapture is not simultaneous with the Second Coming of Christ.

His view of the important Restrainer passage (II Thess. 2:6-8) also finds itself in difficulty. He admits that "If their connection between 'restrainer' and Holy-Spirit-in-the-Church is correct, pretribulationism also is correct, for the Church certainly cannot live without the Holy Spirit" (49). However, he chooses to identify the Restrainer with "civil government." As for the phrase "taken out of the way," he prefers the meaning "to arise out of the midst." Then without declaring a further opinion on this issue, he refers his readers to the views of George Ladd and Robert Gundry which, incidentally, contradict each other.

(C) Moving on to the Book of Revelation, Katterjohn states that "the Church is not explicitly mentioned in chapters 4-12, neither is the rapture," but he adds "the Church is not mentioned as being in heaven either" (88). Thus he rejects the Pretrib identification of the twenty-four elders, suggesting that they are merely "representatives of the Old and New Covenants." While such a view may be better than Reese's "angelic lords," the elders give small comfort to those who cannot find the Church in heaven during the Tribulation. The Church appears again under a different figure as the Bride of Christ, once more in heaven before the Revelation and reign of the Saviour.

Katterjohn declares that "Revelation 3:10 is a fundamental girder in the superstructure of the modern pretribulation theory" (86). It might be mentioned at this point that while *Kept from the Hour* draws its title from this verse, when Katterjohn lists it among "Books for Further Study," he passes it off as "Arguments for pretribulationism based on Revelation 3:10." This of course is outright fabrication, for a closer look would have revealed that the writer discusses Revelation 3:10 on four pages out of 320, and in the Scripture Index it has a mere two listings among 840. So while the verse is important, it is hardly the sum total of Pretrib evidence as Katterjohn implies.

Our author argues that Revelation 3:10 gives the Church a promise of protection in the Tribulation, but not a removal from that hour. "The promise of protection for God's people is essential to the whole fabric of Scripture" (86). He claims that the verse "is a great promise of protection through tribulation, both historically . . . and as the final persecution under Antichrist finds momentum" (87).

What kind of protection does he offer? Elsewhere he has

written about "the besieged Church . . . headed toward inevitable extinction" (99), when "Antichrist will drive Christians into caves and cloistered shelters" (100). "Resistance to him will be fatal to the flesh" (101). It will be "a horrible persecution" (128) when Antichrist "shall extend his rule over the entire globe and ultimately tread it down and break it in pieces" (129), and when "many will suffer martyrdom" (43).

Is this the nature of our "blessed hope" and our promised protection in the Tribulation? Nothing more hopeless is implied in all of Christian eschatology. Death, and not a Posttrib Rapture, would become our hope! Rather than deep anguish and probable martyrdom in the Tribulation, it would be far better to die and to be immediately and forever with the Lord (II Cor. 5:8).

Katterjohn writes correctly that "the time of the rapture is a vital question, yet it should not be an issue that divides true believers" (115). Yet like many before him, it is not his doctrine but his attitude which divides. He declares that "certain pretribulational distinctives are founded on sandstone" and are "theories which find support only as shadowy inferences from the Biblical text" (101). Those who distinguish between redeemed Israel prior to Pentecost and the New Testament Church, he asserts, are guilty of promoting "caste systems (which) are the invention of selfish leaders who would avoid the humility of shared authority" (102). He states that according to Pretribs, the witness of the 144,000 is "a quasi-gospel preached by a Spirit-less tribulation remnant" (90). It is such inappropriate language, not the doctrine, which divides true believers.

To Katterjohn, pretribulationists are "theorists" and "early removal buffs." Is this what he would have called the writer's former professor, Dr. Henry C. Thiessen, for many years the head of the Bible Department and Chairman of the Faculty of the Graduate School of Wheaton College? Thiessen was a warm and gracious professor, a theological scholar, a recognized Biblical linguist, and also a convinced pretribulationist (*Introductory Lectures in Systematic Theology*, 475-86). For years he sounded out the Word of the Lord to the students of Wheaton College, far more harmoniously it seems than this discordant note later emerging from the music department.

THE BLESSED HOPE AND THE TRIBULATION

Written with a far more commendable spirit than the two previously considered is a book published in 1976 by **John F. Walvoord**, *The Blessed Hope and the Tribulation*, with the subtitle "A Historical and Biblical Study of Posttribulationism." Clearly stated, "It is the purpose of this study to examine the claims of posttribulationists, their exegesis of important passages, and their handling of pretribulational arguments" (8).

In the midst of the "almost complete confusion" which reigns in the current interpretation of prophecy, in the mind of the reviewer this volume by Dr. Walvoord gives the most comprehensive response in print to the various positions and problems of the posttribulational school of thought.

The Rapture debate is not merely a theological argument, for the hope of the Lord's return is a very precious truth, and "it would be difficult to present a greater contrast between the blessed hope of the imminent return of Christ and the prospect of probable suffering and death in the great tribulation" (10). These are dramatically contrasting prospects of the future for the Church of Jesus Christ.

Within the past century, at least four different types of posttribulationism have emerged. Walvoord discusses first the "Classic Posttribulational Interpretation" of J. Barton Payne, whose major contribution to the Posttrib argument is his belief in the imminency of Christ's return. This has previously been discussed under the review of the *Imminent Appearing of Christ.* Relative to this issue, Walvoord concludes that "the early church fathers were obviously wrong in believing that they were already in the great tribulation" (29), and that "Payne stands virtually alone" when he spiritualizes much of the Tribulation and attempts to add the early concept of imminency to a posttribulational conclusion.

A second view is the "Semiclassic Posttribulation Interpretation," best illustrated by Alexander Reese in his book *The Approaching Advent of Christ*. Reese popularized the opinion that the Pretrib position arose about 150 years ago in the separatist movements of Edward Irving and J. N. Darby. He took as a key doctrine the idea that the Church is the true Israel and includes the saints of all ages. He offered evidence that "the resurrection of the Church occurs at the same time as the resurrection of Revelation 20," from all of which he drew a strong Posttrib conclusion.

In this third chapter, Walvoord makes the telling point that "Posttribulationists also have never resolved the pressing question as to why there is a rapture at the second coming. . . . Why would saints meet Christ in the air at the rapture if they are going to return immediately to the earth? Why would it not be preferable for the church to go into the millennium in their natural bodies ... and populate the millennial earth?" (38-39).

The "Futurist Posttribulational Interpretation," as exemplified by George Ladd in *The Blessed Hope*, is the third Posttrib position considered. While accepting a literal, future Tribulation, Ladd makes historical background his major argument, and then "practically ignores the three principal Scriptures revealing the rapture" (50).

In discussing dispensationalism, "Ladd departs from his usual scholarly approach and accuses dispensationalists of holding interpretations that no dispensationalist would support" (56). He finds it difficult to harmonize the "blessed hope" with the idea that "the church must go through the great tribulation and many, if not most, in the church are martyred." Comments Walvoord, far better to live out "a normal life in a period prior to the rapture" and go "to heaven through death rather than living through the great tribulation" (57). Most posttribulational writers do not recognize the force of this problem in their own system.

Walvoord includes under this third Posttrib position the historical views of Dave MacPherson, and brings against him the five criticisms previously discussed in the review of MacPherson's two books.

The fourth distinct Posttrib position is the "Dispensational Posttribulational Interpretation" of Robert H. Gundry. Walvoord comments favorably on Gundry's "maturity of scholarly studies and his skill as a debater" (61), but faults him for using "circular arguments assuming what they are trying to prove," and for presenting "only the evidence that supports his position" (62).

Gundry's pivotal issues include his attack on the doctrine of imminency; his characterization of the Tribulation as primarily a time of Satanic wrath; his beginning of the "day of the Lord" at the end of the Tribulation; his interpretation that the Olivet Discourse discusses the Church and not Israel; his merging of the various judgments of the righteous into one divine judgment at the Second Coming; some novel suggestions regarding who will enter the millennial Kingdom; and his placing of the Rapture just before Armageddon, preceding the Second Coming of Christ (62).

Walvoord concludes that Gundry's approach is different from that of any posttribulationist in the past, and that he abandons literal interpretation whenever it would lead to a contradiction of posttribulationism (68).

In the latter half of his book, Walvoord discusses the post-tribulational denial of imminency and wrath; the contribution of the Gospels, especially of Matthew 24 and John 14; the comforting hope of I Thessalonians 4 and the Day of the Lord in chapter 5; the identification of the Restrainer; and the Rapture in its relationship to end-time events. He closes with two brief but excellent chapters: "Unresolved Problems of Posttribulationism" and "Pretribulationism as the Alternative to Posttribulationism."

From the Pretrib perspective, this book affords a comprehensive and most worthy discussion of the divergent views and unsolved problems of posttribulationism.

THE GREAT TRIBULATION DEBATE

A considerably different presentation of the Posttrib view was published in 1976 and called *The Great Tribulation Debate*, by

Norman F. Douty. Subtitled "Has Christ's Return Two Stages?," it is a revision of an earlier publication dated 1956. Douty claims herein that he was converted to posttribulationism by the "weight of evidence," although he admits he much prefers his former belief, which was that of a pretribulational Rapture (10).

While pointing out some of the dangers of doctrinal controversy, the author affirms that the "Tribulation Debate" is minor rather than major in importance, "a question of detail" (Scofield), requiring "a cool head and a warm heart." Then, having affirmed his love and respect for men like I. M. Haldeman, William L. Pettingill and W. H. Griffith-Thomas, plus Scofield, Barnhouse, Chafer and Thiessen, all pretribulationists with whom he is about to disagree, he writes, "For convenience sake, I have chiefly selected Dr. C. I. Scofield to represent the teaching I herein oppose" (10). This is a very limited objective, for Scofield is not always a representative Pretrib and his notes give a comparatively brief treatment of the subject. Thus from the very beginning, there is introduced an immediate weakness in Douty's evaluation.

A more favorable feature is his constant appeal to the Scripture and to the Greek language in matters of exegesis. But it would take a prime Greek scholar (which Douty does not claim to be) to test the validity of his conclusions. The author is obviously widely read and to support his position quotes a host of other authors and scholars, mostly from a past generation. However, it does become rather tedious to find Dr. So-and-so pitted against Dr. So-and-so almost *ad infinitum*, rather than a warm-hearted and scholarly explanation of what each Scripture actually teaches. Those quoted are no longer with us to explain or defend their views.

Nor is Douty always kind. Pretribs are considered his "opponents," and it would take "divine grace" to bestow on them an open mind, especially when self-interest is involved. "A camel can more easily pass through the eye of a needle than a Pretribulationist, occupying a place of honor, can look into this subject without prejudice" (11).

This reviewer found *The Great Tribulation Debate* a strangely perplexing and exasperating book. It ignores major pretribulational arguments and sometimes attacks non-representative viewpoints. The Pretrib position is frequently misrepresented and wrongly accused. For example, says Douty, "It is to be feared that Pre-tribulationism is producing a generation of soft Christians instead of one composed of those who can endure hardness as good soldiers of Jesus Christ" (130). The Pretrib view of the Gospel of the Kingdom is said to be "not the good news of salvation through the blood of Christ" (14). Pretribs are represented as believing that "what Christ taught during his public ministry was not intended for Christians but for Jews. . . . Thus, by one stroke, the Church of Christ is stripped of a large portion of her spiritual heritage. The Gospels no more belong to you, my brethren, than the Old Testament does" (17-18). Most of those of pretribulational persuasion will find such declarations completely untrue and offensive.

Three entire chapters are spent on the Greek words for Christ's coming, endeavoring to prove that if these words are used of both stages of Christ's advent there is really but one stage, and that posttribulational. As we have seen, a technical use of the Greek *parousia* is not an accepted pretribulational argument. The similarities between the Rapture and the Revelation passages are then catalogued, as though similarity of detail proves identity, making them one and the same event.

The "restraining influence" of II Thessalonians 2 is identified as civil government, for "the Spirit was poured out after Christ's return to the Father for other purposes than to restrain human lawlessness. He did not come to do what was assigned to human government to perform" (98). Furthermore, in Revelation 3:10, "this preservation does not refer to the body, but to the soul. Christ promises, not exemption from physical torture and death, but spiritual keeping, whatever the circumstances" (104-5). To say the least, these are all highly debatable conclusions on the part of our author.

Even worse is his exceedingly limited treatment of the three major Rapture passages. The triple clause of I Thessalonians 4:16 denotes "one and the same thing," so that the "shout" and the "trump of God" are identical with the "voice of the archangel." Then, says our author, if we are "caught up together" we must be "united here upon the earth," so that "Christ is here depicted as escorted to the earth by his saints" (76). To the contrary, the reunion of the saints occurs when we meet together "in the clouds . . . in the air," and not at a posttribulational return to earth.

Douty ties all this together with John 14:1-3, closing with a rare conclusion: "Christ is on his way to the earth to deliver and convert the remnant of Israel, to judge Antichrist and his system, and to introduce his glorious reign – all of which he shall effect with speed. Then to the many mansions of his Father's house will he conduct his glorified ones *and from there carry on his millennial reign*. It is not until the new earth appears after that reign that a glorified Head and Body shall reside below" (76, italics added).

Think of it, the Messianic Kingdom, with an absent King reigning from heaven rather than upon earth! Why so strained a view? Because a Posttrib must do something with John 14:3, for to take it literally leads directly to pretribulationism. As for the important I Corinthians 15:51-52 passage, it is brushed off with the comment that "the last trump" would not precede the seven trumpets of the Revelation. "If not identical with the seventh, it surely must succeed it in order to be the last" (39).

Douty gives major emphasis to the Olivet Discourse which, he declares, "is not essentially Jewish prophecy; it is Christian eschatology. Those addressed in the latter part of chapter 23 are Jews, but those addressed in chapters 24 and 25 are Christians" (36). Forgetting that the disciples did not yet understand either His imminent vicarious death or His subsequent resurrection (Matt. 16:21-23), or that they were primarily occupied with thoughts about the Messianic Kingdom (Matt. 18:1; 20:21; Acts 1:6), Douty holds that they were representatives of the Church and that through them Christ "addresses the prospective Church concerning things to come" (37). Since the coming of Christ in the clouds of heaven with power and great glory is "immediately after the tribulation of those days" (Matt. 25:29-30), Douty assumes this embraces the Rapture of the Church, which would make it clearly posttribulational.

His argument forms an interesting syllogism: The Olivet Discourse sets forth Church eschatology. The return of Christ to earth is clearly "after the Tribulation of those days." Therefore, the Rapture must be postribulational! However, he should not forget the early warning of Alexander Reese concerning a syllogism: If an error is found in either the major or the minor premise, that error also attaches itself to the conclusion. Douty's error is found in his major premise, and this is sufficient to destroy his conclusion.

Douty closes his book with "A Plea For Toleration," the strongest and most extensive this writer has seen in print. "What injury have we done you? True, we have disturbed your complacency, but what sin is there in that?" and so on for four full pages (133-37). In the light of how much we have in common, he pleads for moderation and for understanding. At this point we find ourselves in substantial agreement. Nevertheless, the book itself appears badly outdated in its arguments, making its contribution of doubtful present value. This reviewer is not aware that even his fellow Posttribs acknowledge the book or its arguments as authoritative.

THE LAST THINGS, AN ESCHATOLOGY FOR LAYMEN

In 1978 yet another contribution to the Rapture debate was published by **George E. Ladd,** entitled *The Last Things, An Eschatology for Laymen.* Certainly, it is a worthy endeavor to put theological themes into more simplified concepts and language suitable for the average Christian layman. Better yet, to discuss relevant and encouraging topics such as the predicted course of the present age, the "signs of the times" and world conditions in the end-time, the Rapture as a purifying hope and an incentive for faithful service, the rewards and crowns to be distributed for victorious living at the Judgment Seat of Christ, our position as the Bride of Christ at the Marriage Supper of the Lamb, the power and glory of the coming King, and the prospect of reigning with Him in His millennial Kingdom. If this were the main thrust of Ladd's book, we would all welcome it and applaud the author.

But rather, we find before us a disappointing sequence of problems relating to the time of the Rapture, with a constant and withering attack upon dispensationalism. While we are grateful for certain conclusions we do hold in common with Dr. Ladd, who is a theologically conservative Premillennial scholar, this present volume is hardly an eschatology for laymen. It's subtitle might better be worded: "My latest attack against dispensationalism"!

Actually, Ladd appears to be a modified dispensationalist, for in his own words he recognizes "the eras of promise after Abraham, the law under Moses, of grace under Christ, and of the Kingdom in the future" (9). Most probably he also recognizes the age of innocence before the fall of Adam and the very different situation following his expulsion from the garden. Recognizing six different economies is a fair beginning for an anti-dispensationalist. Years ago, in gracious personal conversation with this writer, Ladd affirmed that he was not a Jew, did not worship on the Sabbath, never prayed that his flight should not be on the Sabbath (Matt. 24:20), nor did he wear "a ribbon of blue" in the fringe of his garments (Num. 15:38). Apparently he does distinguish between Biblical ages and economies and does not always equate Israel with the New Testament Church, clearly forbidden in Revelation 2:9 and 3:9.

It is most unfortunate that such a storm has brewed over the concept of dispensationalism, when the Bible clearly indicates the presence of various ages (Eph. 2:7; 3:5, 21), differing economies (Matt. 16:18; Luke 21:24; John 1:17; Heb. 12:18-24), and even uses the term "dispensation" in the sense of a divinely planned economy (I Cor. 9:17; Eph. 1:10, 3:2; Col. 1:25 AV). While it is true that some have carried the dispensational principle to erroneous and extreme conclusions, not all who use this principle are "speckled birds" as they have been called, nor do any hold to "seven ways of salvation" as others have affirmed. Nor do they downgrade the value of passages obviously addressed to Israel.

What we need to do is to sit down and talk together, discovering what we hold in common as well as areas of disagreement. Then no longer treat dispensationalism as a theological system to be attacked or defended, but rather to restore it to *hermeneutics* (Biblical interpretation) as an extension of the basic question: "To whom, or of whom does this passage speak?" Then most of the bitterness engendered would evaporate.

Erroneously, Ladd makes pretribulationism "the most characteristic doctrine of Dispensationalists" (50). Actually, the more basic disputes fall into the area of ecclesiology. Using a "spiritualizing hermeneutic," he assumes that the Church is "spiritual Israel" because he "finds the New Testament applying to the spiritual church promises which in the Old Testament refer to literal Israel" (24). This is assuming too much, for while it is true that the redeemed of Israel and the redeemed Church do share certain privileges as members of the family of God, it is a fallacy of the first magnitude to equate Israel and the Church on this basis alone.

Israel cannot always be considered as a redeemed community. The Apostle Paul cries out with great agony of heart for the *salvation* of Israel, his kinsmen according to the flesh (Rom. 9:1-3, 10:1). He sets forth the Jews and the Church of God as two entirely separate entities (I Cor. 10:32), so that the time of the resurrection of Israel does not demonstrate or even imply that the resurrection of the Church will be simultaneous. And when we find "immediately after the tribulation" God gathering "his elect" from the "tribes of the earth," the clear inference is that *Israel* has come through the Tribulation, not the Church.

There are other problems. Ladd is not sure that the Suffering Servant of Isaiah 53 can be identified with Messiah, the anointed of God. He calls the Tribulation "a brief but terrible struggle between Satan and the Church . . . a time of fearful martyrdom" (49), hardly a "blessed hope" or a theme so attractive that we can "comfort one another with these words."

Contrary to Ladd, Pretribs do not teach "two Second Comings

of Christ," nor of necessity even two "phases of His coming," although this is merely a matter of definition. Nor do Pretribs need to limit the term *parousia* to the Rapture and *epiphaneia* to the Revelation. While a few have done so, Walvoord and other Pretrib theologians have clearly indicated that the vocabulary of Christ's coming is non-technical, and equally applicable to both Rapture and Revelation.

He finds II Thessalonians 2:6-7 "very difficult" and claims that the "classical interpretation" is quite satisfying, namely that "the hindering power is the principle of law and order embodied in the Roman Empire with the Emperor at its head" (68). To the contrary, rather than being a restraint against evil, it can be demonstrated that the Roman Empire fell under the sheer weight of its own massive iniquity.

Nor can we agree when Ladd declares, "The 144,000 are the church on the threshold of the Great Tribulation," explaining that these are "true spiritual Jews without being literal Jews: in other words, the church" (71). He forgets that in the Church we are no longer seen as Jew or Gentile, but all one in Christ Jesus (Gal. 3:28; Eph. 2:14). He will not recognize a redeemed body of Jews in the Tribulation, clearly identified as being from the tribes of Israel, for this would be tantamount to a confession that the Church is no longer on earth.

In this book, Ladd demonstrates how the Posttrib pattern of thought leads perilously close to the Amillennial position. He departs from normal Premil literal interpretation when he declares: "The number 144,000, like other numbers in the Revelation, is a symbolic number, representing completeness" (71). The measurement of the New Jerusalem in Revelation 21:16 "is obviously a symbolic measurement" (113) and "the Kingdom of God is also a present reality." Christ "is already seated at the right hand of God and reigning as King" (116). In defining Amillennialism, he says, "It must be admitted that there is some Scriptural support for such a view" (111).

He parallels Amillennial theology when he equates Israel and the Church, calling the latter "spiritual Israel." He identifies the judgment of the Gentile nations in Matthew 25 with the Great White Throne of Revelation 20, admitting that if this would be followed literally it would make no room for a millennium and would make him an Amillennialist. He avoids this by claiming the Matthew 25 account to be "a dramatic parable" of welcoming and receiving Christ. In a previous volume he declares: "Many millenarians will not insist that the earthly reign of Christ is to be of exactly 1000 years duration. The 1000 years may well be a symbol for a long period of time, the exact extent of which is unknown" (1952, 147). This type of Premillennialism would make an Amillennialist very happy!

The reviewer refrains from speaking of further problems associated with Ladd's book. It contributes little that is new to the Rapture debate and is hardly "an eschatology for laymen."

CHRISTIANS WILL GO THROUGH THE TRIBULATION

There appeared in 1978 a distinctly different Posttrib book by **James M. McKeever** entitled *Christians Will Go Through The Tribulation: And how to prepare for it*. This is not a serious discussion of Biblical or theological evidence concerning the time and implications of the Rapture. The Posttrib position is strongly assumed, with some Scripture and a few scattered quotations from posttribulational authorities to back up the author's conviction. Rather, its purpose is to give "very practical suggestions on how to prepare for the catastrophes that Christians will be experiencing during the Tribulation," dealing with "physical preparation and the even more important spiritual preparation" (19).

Because of the promises which exempt the Church from divine wrath, Posttrib writers normally picture the Church as thoroughly protected by the sovereign hand of God, passing safely through the Tribulation much like Noah and his family sealed in the ark, placidly riding through the storm and judgment of the mighty Genesis flood. McKeever turns that picture upside down as he portrays the Christian fighting for his life and the welfare of his family in the midst of nuclear tragedy, human brutality and the threat of imminent starvation in a day when no man can buy or sell, save those who capitulate to the Devil's Antichrist and wear the "mark of the beast."

Our author is an ordained minister and Bible teacher, with a background of ten years with IBM and twenty years in the computer business. He gives evidence of being a fine-spirited man, sincere and dedicated. However, the reader will have to judge for himself the validity of certain stated convictions.

McKeever's book is in three main parts, with Part 1 dealing with the "Crucial Questions" of the time of the Rapture and the many Scriptures which, in his opinion, teach that the Church must pass through and endure the entire Tribulation. Ladd and Gundry are his primary authorities on this issue, with a little additional help from Katterjohn.

He discusses evidence that we may be living at the end of the age, and if so, some of the "Catastrophes We Will Face." He reviews the extreme severity of the Tribulation judgments, the seals which are broken, the trumpets of judgment which sound, and the bowls of divine wrath which must be poured out. Plaintively he declares: "I wish that the Rapture were going to occur at the beginning of the Tribulation, and that my fellow believers and I would not have to experience the terrible things that are coming." However, he concludes, "since I believe, as do growing scores of Christians, that the believers *will* go through the Tribulation, my family and I are making both physical and spiritual preparation for it" (56).

Skipping Part 2 for the moment, the third and final part of the book deals with Spiritual Preparation. This includes a "Call to Righteousness" with a challenge from Revelation 2 and 3, plus 12:10-11, to be overcomers of evil and the power of Satan. There follows a presentation of our personal relationship to the Holy Spirit, and the filling of the Spirit which is His control over our lives. Most of this teaching is essential and good, but on the "gifts of the Spirit" many of the Lord's people will decline to follow.

McKeever believes that all the Apostolic gifts are available today and will be increasingly exercised in the coming Tribulation.

He recognizes the dissension caused by "speaking in unknown tongues," but affirms the validity of the gift, including the worship of God with an "angelic language." He also affirms supernatural healing and in Indonesia, supernatural multiplication of food to feed the Christians and "even the dogs." He writes about supernatural control over snakes, scorpions and wild animals, and of Christians having dominion over nature, commanding the rain to stop and a tornado to pass over. Even more, "In the body of believers with whom I fellowshipped in Pasadena, there is a man who was raised from the dead" (269)! Each reader will have to evaluate such unusual claims and read the rest of the book in the light of them. For the Scripture commands: "Prove all things; hold fast that which is good" (I Thess. 5:21).

Part 2 is the natural conclusion of posttribulational theology. Christians must be prepared to survive nuclear war, social chaos, and the menace of Antichrist by constructing and stocking some kind of fallout shelter. "In a home without a basement, you could go in the crawl space beneath the floor and dig a hole . . ." (123). You must be prepared to survive famine. "I would suggest that a family have a three-month supply of wet pack food, and at least a twelve-month supply of air-dried and freeze-dried dehydrated foods" (140). Storage is a problem: "A year's supply of wet pack food for a family of five would take up 60 percent of a two-car garage. . . . You can increase the storage life of canned foods . . . by turning them upside down periodically" (141-42).

You must prepare to survive earthquakes. "Most of the hazards are man-made." Wire your tall pieces of furniture to the wall so they will not topple over, etc. In coastal areas, prepare for tidal waves (167-70). With no ability to buy or sell or even provide electrical or sewer service, you will need to develop a "self-supporting home," with tanks to collect rainwater, a septic tank or other plan to dispose of waste, and a wind-powered generator for electricity. If you cannot move to a farm you must have a garden with small animals and birds for food. A large fish tank for catfish is highly recommended. Plus a food dehydrator, a water purifier, and possibly a composting toilet. Develop a root cellar and a springhouse for large storage; put in a system to collect solar heat, and preferably have most of the house underground to conserve energy. Etc., etc., etc. This is what a consistent posttribulationist must be doing, and how many of their number would qualify? This is Posttrib theology in shoe leather. Wherefore, comfort one another with these words!

WHAT YOU SHOULD KNOW ABOUT THE RAPTURE

A brief but scholarly review of the main issues involved in the Rapture debate was published in 1981 by **Charles C. Ryrie,** under the title *What You Should Know About The Rapture*. Beginners in this subject will appreciate his clear introduction and simple charts of the four main positions, while more mature students will acknowledge that "prophecy is being discussed more than ever on an academic level," as Ryrie debates with Gundry, whom he considers the primary spokesman of the modern Posttrib movement.

Concerning the historic background of pretribulationism, Ryrie deals with the various attempts which have been made to discredit the teaching of Darby by claiming he did not get his views from the Bible, but from a heretic and a mystic. The heretic was Edward Irving, who was deposed in 1833 by the Church of Scotland on the charge that he held the sinfulness of Christ's humanity. The mystic was 15 year old Margaret Macdonald who, as we have seen, has been promoted by MacPherson and others as the first to proclaim a pretribulational Rapture.

Ryrie claims that the Irvingite eschatology was unclear, that there was no connection between Darby's pretribulationism and the Irvingite teaching, and the claim that Pretrib doctrine began in an outburst of tongues in Irving's church is, in the words of E. R. Sandeen, "a groundless and pernicious charge." Furthermore, "As for the very young and chronically ill Margaret Macdonald, we can only truthfully label her as a 'confused rapturist,' with elements of partial rapturism, posttribulationism, perhaps midtribulationism, but never pretribulationism" (72).

Ryrie claims that most Posttribs have concentrated on countering pretribulational arguments rather than putting together an adequate chronology of the future. The Pretrib position is not an "escape mechanism," but an attempt "to proclaim the whole plan of God accurately." While granting that the Greek vocabulary used to describe Christ's coming does not prove either a Pre- or a Posttrib Rapture, he affirms that a careful exegesis of the cardinal Scripture passages does sustain a pretribulational conclusion.

For example, II Thessalonians 1:5-10 emphasizes God's judgment of His enemies, using words such as "righteous judgment," "affliction," "flaming fire" and "retribution," a vocabulary strangely absent from the Rapture passages. This is because the subject of the passage is "vindication," and not as posttribulationists say, a "release of Christians from persecution" (54). Moreover, throughout the most extensive Tribulation passage, Revelation 4-18, the Church is not mentioned nor seen on earth, but is found in heaven symbolized by the 24 elders.

While there will be "saints" in the Tribulation, the term applies equally to the "godly ones" of the Old Testament, the present age, and the Tribulation years yet to come. This term, together with phrases such as those who "die in the Lord," and "those who keep the commandments of God," as well as the word "elect," describe those who shall trust in Christ during the Tribulation. "The chosen ones of the Tribulation days do not have to be the same as the elect of the church simply because the same term is used of both groups" (62).

Ryrie develops the question of populating the Millennial Kingdom. "When the Millennium begins, some people have to be alive in unresurrected bodies, who can beget children and populate that kingdom" (75). The Scriptures seem to teach that all the wicked will be judged prior to the Kingdom, and that all who are raptured will put on immortality. This is a major problem for those who believe in a posttribulational Rapture, for according this view none would be left in normal human bodies to enter and to populate the Kingdom.

For the Posttribs, Robert Gundry presents a twofold answer to this problem: (1) The 144,000 will not be saved during the Tribulation, but shall be "physically preserved" and "converted immediately after the rapture as they see their Messiah descending onto the earth." (2) The Gentile parents will come from the wicked who will somehow escape death and judgment at the end of the Tribulation (Gundry, 83, 137).

Both answers are faulty, for the 144,000 are presented in Revelation 7 and 14 as redeemed witnesses, winning an innumerable multitude to Christ during the Tribulation, evidently dying for their faith and caught up with songs of rejoicing into the presence of the Lamb (Rev. 14:3-5). And Gundry's "partial destruction" of the Gentiles which "would leave the remaining unsaved to populate the millennial earth," plays havoc with the "sheep and the goats judgment" of Matthew 25:31-46, which is both final and soteriological.

Scripture clearly places this judgment at the Second Coming of Christ (Matt. 25:31-32), but Gundry is forced to locate it after the Millennium. Far more simple and Biblical to have a period after the Rapture but before the Revelation, during which many shall be redeemed, some of whom will enter and populate the Millennial Kingdom. This is the view that pretribulationism espouses.

In brief summary, Ryrie counters the Posttrib view that God somehow throws a "mantle of safety" over the Church in the Tribulation. He shows also that the "Day of the Lord" cannot begin with a time of "peace and safety" (I Thess. 5:3) if, as Posttribs proclaim, "it begins with the wrath of God poured out at Armageddon."

Further, "Posttribulationism has a veritable logjam (of endtime events) at the second coming of Christ" (100). It fails to show how the righteous can be protected from the various wraths of the Tribulation period, surviving the wrath of God but subject to the wrath of Satan. Since many shall die, this would be a very "selective protection."

Revelation 3:10 gives a better solution. It is not a selective safe conduct through that hour, but removal from the hour itself. As Ryrie puts it, "The only way to escape worldwide trouble is not to be on the earth" (117). The Rapture is not a threat of near extermination, but a bright and blessed hope which causes us to "love His appearing" (II Tim. 4:8).

THE RAPTURE: TRUTH OR CONSEQUENCES

Widely read and acclaimed are the prophetic books of **Hal Lindsey,** beginning with the popular *The Late Great Planet Earth* (1970) and leading up to *The Rapture: Truth or Consequences,* published simultaneously in the United States and Canada in 1983. The language of these books is generally contemporary rather than theological because he is aiming at another age group and a different culture from the average student of Bible prophecy. Nevertheless, Lindsey deals with some profound Biblical themes as he exercises his "gift of simplicity." His book about the Rapture especially is a serious discussion of the Biblical passages and doctrinal themes which indicate the relationship of the Rapture to the Tribulation, giving us "a blueprint of tomorrow's history."

Readers will appreciate Lindsey's charts of the various Tribulation and Millennial views, and in the Bible exposition passages they will be impressed with his evident scholarship and continual use of the New Testament Greek. Those who enjoy comparing theological systems will find a helpful analysis of midtribulationist Mary Stewart Reife, *When Your Money Fails,* and posttribulationist Robert Gundry, *The Church and the Tribulation.*

Lindsey begins his discussion by clarifying the main issues at stake and stressing the areas of common agreement between the exponents of pre-, mid- and posttribulationalism, many of whom are careful scholars and greatly used of the Lord. He clarifies the true nature of the Church and the importance of dispensational distinctions. He discusses the chronology and judgments found in the Book of Revelation, the important promise of Revelation 3:10, and the "search for the missing Church," by which he means the Rapture. In summary, "the promise of being kept from the hour; the identity of those who dwell in heaven; the Church's absence from earth in chapters 4 through 19; the bride's presence in heaven before the second coming, all fit into the pattern of a pre-Tribulation Rapture scenario" (111).

In discussing the "Restrainer" of II Thessalonians 2, Lindsey presents strong evidence that "he who restrains" is undoubtedly the Holy Spirit. He concludes that "His unique ministries in, through and for the believer will be removed with the Church" (138). In the light of the permanent indwelling of the Spirit within the Church (John 14:16; Rom. 8:9), an even stronger statement might be that the removal of the Spirit before the revelation of Antichrist sets the time of the Rapture as pretribulational.

He argues effectively for various stages in the "first resurrection," showing that the "dead in Christ" rise *before* the translation of living saints at the Rapture while the resurrection of Tribulation martyrs occurs *after* the coming of Christ at His Revelation (Rev. 20:4-6). Lindsey then closes his book with a listing of world events "moving toward a catastrophic end."

Throughout *The Rapture* there is displayed a warm personal and spiritual note, so often lost in the midst of theological argument. Lindsey closes his discussion as follows: "The hope of the Rapture is a very practical force in my life at this point in history. It motivates me to obtain combat knowledge of the Bible in order to be able to face the perilous times that precede the Tribulation." Even more, "It motivates me to win as many to Christ as possible before it's too late. . . . Although I grieve over the lost world that is headed toward catastrophe, the hope of the Rapture keeps me from despair in the midst of ever-worsening world conditions" (176). To which this reviewer adds a hearty "Amen!" – for this is the main thrust of the Blessed Hope!

THE RAPTURE: PRE-, MID-, OR POST-TRIBULATIONAL?

Bridging the considerable gap between the three primary Rapture viewpoints is a "head-to-head" debate entitled *The*

Rapture: Pre-, Mid-, or Post-Tribulational? This 1984 publication is written by four personal friends, three of whom are colleagues on the faculty of Trinity Evangelical Divinity School. Mutually respectful in tone and highly academic in content, their essays provide an important addition to the Rapture literature, especially for those who desire to give careful attention to the use and meaning of the Greek words involved in the exposition of primary New Testament passages. While they are friends, these men do debate vigorously, and each has opportunity to bring his response to the two alternate positions.

Introducing the debate is an excellent essay by **Richard R. Reiter,** "A History of the Development of the Rapture Positions." He traces the history of the Rapture-Tribulation dispute from the Niagara Bible Conference era, 1878-1909, through the period of pretribulational predominance from 1909-1952, to what he calls the "resurgence of posttribulationism" from 1952 to the present. Many will find it fascinating to read the views of great spiritual leaders of the past, such as John N. Darby, D. L. Moody, A. J. Gordon, James H. Brookes, C. I. Scofield, Arthur T. Pierson and Arno C. Gaebelein − all of them staunch pretribulationists − together with the rising challenge of Robert Cameron, Nathaniel West, William G. Moorhead and W. J. Erdman, all of whom espoused a posttribulational eschatology.

The growing harshness of the debate is revealed by "the bitterness of West's tirade" through the "derogatory tone" of Alexander Reese to the abusive comments of Robert Cameron, who speaks of "opposing this Secret Rapture fly-away-from-tribulation theory" which is "only a trick of the Devil to fool God's people so that they will not be on the firing line for God." Such was the vitriolic tirade which began to emerge, primarily from the posttribulational camp.

Refreshingly, the following three authors rise high above such bitter denunciation, calling for "greater humility in regard to detail" and a "unity which allows for diversity and promotes toleration." This is a welcome and timely appeal.

"The Case for the Pretribulational Rapture Position" is

presented by **Paul D. Feinberg,** Associate Professor of Biblical and Systematic Theology. He admits that a surrender of the widely held Pretrib position is not, as some have suggested, "the first step on the proverbial slippery slope that leads one to the rocks of liberalism." Nevertheless, the Rapture question is of the greatest importance because it "touches the extremely important issues of biblical interpretation, the relationship between the church and Israel, and the course of human history" (47).

Feinberg argues for pretribulationism from three main positions: (1) The entire Tribulation period is characterized as the "outpouring of penal, retributive, divine wrath," from which the Church of Jesus Christ is promised exemption – both from the experience of wrath and the time of wrath. He rightly distinguishes between divine wrath and the normal trials and sufferings of the present life, including persecution from evil men. The Christian life is pictured in the Scripture as a battle to be fought and an athletic contest demanding discipline and endurance. However, I Thessalonians 1:10 and 5:9 clearly promise exemption from the coming wrath of God.

He debates the view of Gundry that "divine wrath does not blanket the entire seventieth week, probably not even the latter half of it, but concentrates at the close" by observing that "wrath" occurs in the Revelation as early as the sixth seal, and that it is difficult to see how famine, war and death would fail to touch believers as well as unbelievers. Even Revelation 3:10 indicates that this period of trial falls upon "the whole world," and promises exemption not only from divine wrath but also from the very *time* of wrath. He argues from classical literature, the Septuagint and the New Testament that the Greek preposition *ek* indicates "a position outside its object," and that the combination *tareo ek* promises "a preservation outside of a time period," which demands the removal of the Church prior to the time period called Tribulation (68).

(2) Feinberg then argues for the necessity of an interval between the Rapture of the Church and the Second Coming of Christ, so that some can be saved to go into the coming Kingdom

in nonglorified bodies and thus populate the earth during the millennial reign of Christ. There shall be Gentiles as well as Jews in the coming Kingdom, although Ezekiel 20:37-38 declares that "rebel Jews" shall not enter therein, while Matthew 25:31-46 similarly describes the destruction of wicked Gentiles. Since no wicked shall enter Christ's Kingdom, "there must be a separation of the Rapture from the Second Advent so that people with natural, physical bodies can be saved and populate the millennial Kingdom" (79).

(3) There is a marked difference between Scripture passages describing the Rapture and those which describe the Second Coming of Christ to judge the wicked and to establish His Kingdom of righteousness. While there are no signs to alert the believer that the Rapture is near, very definite signs and events lead up to and signal the return of Christ from glory.

Every passage dealing with the Second Coming is set in the context of Tribulation and judgment, while the Rapture passages make no mention of such distress. The Second Advent texts do not teach the translation of living saints nor the resurrection of those who have died in Christ, but give promise only to martyred Tribulation saints. Also, when the Rapture passages are compared with Second Coming passages, there is a clear inconsistency concerning the time of the Rapture and the destination of those who shall be caught up.

Feinberg closes his section with the plea: "May our differences never becloud the joy and expectation of seeing our Lord at His visible and personal return," and may our disagreements only "serve as a greater impetus to the study and clarity" of the prophetic Scriptures (86).

In the third chapter, **Gleason L. Archer** argues "The Case for the Mid-Seventieth-Week Rapture Position." He prefers this title to "Midtribulationism" because he views the first three and one half years as a "lesser tribulation, not nearly as terrifying or destructive of life as those fearsome plagues that will dominate the last three and one half years" (139). Thus he claims that his view "is really a form of pretribulation Rapture." However, his identification of the "last trump" of the Rapture with the "seventh trumpet" of the Tribulation, and his identification of the raptured Church with the 144,000 of Revelation 14 are much more reminiscent of the Posttrib position.

The final chapter of the book is written by **Douglas J. Moo,** assistant professor of New Testament at Trinity. He is to be commended for writing graciously, for expounding all the primary Scriptures, and for recognizing that "no true believer will experience the wrath of God." However, he harmonizes this statement with the Posttrib position by declaring that "wrath appears to be concentrated in the last part of the Tribulation period." He also uses a theory of selectivity, saying, "God's people can escape divine wrath though present during its outpouring" (174).

Moo counters the obvious fact that many Tribulation judgments fall upon the entire inhabited earth by departing from normal, literal interpretation. He affirms, "No description of the Tribulation indicates that it will involve greater suffering than many believers have already experienced" (176). This weak response is in direct contradiction of Daniel 12:1 and Matthew 24:21, which declare that "the Tribulation, the great one" will be an unprecedented period in the history of suffering humanity.

Unlike many Posttribs, Moo does face up to the implication of John 14:1-3, which strongly implies that those raptured go directly to the Father's house, which is heaven. He responds: "The fact that believers at a posttribulational Rapture would rise to meet the Lord in the air only to return immediately to earth with Him creates no difficulty, for the text does not state that believers will go directly to Heaven . . . only that they will always be with the Lord" (178). Responding to Moo, Archer calls this "a yo-yo procedure of popping up and down," rightfully declaring that if anything, "these upward-bobbing saints will only impede the momentum of His earthward charge as He rushes down to crush the rebellious hosts of the Beast and all his minions. The most that can be said of such a 'Rapture' is that it is a rather secondary sideshow of minimal importance" (215).

To make the Rapture posttribulational, Moo identifies the "last trump" of I Corinthians 15:52 with the trump which gathers the elect of Israel in Matthew 24:31 into the Millennial Kingdom, "an event that is always posttribulational" (179). In discussing the coming "wrath," Moo makes escape from wrath a reward, saying: "Paul exhorts the Thessalonians to live godly lives in order that they might avoid the judgmental aspects of the Day" (186). Here, he sounds more like a Partial Rapturist. However, since his treatment of the main Rapture passages is quite lengthy and involved, it may be best at this point to encourage a careful reading of these pages and then to consider the adequate response of Paul Feinberg found on pages 223-31 of the same book.

Concerning the similarities Moo indicates between the primary Rapture and the primary Second Advent passages, Archer observes that between the two "the differences in atmosphere, mood, and setting are so obvious as to discourage all hope of identifying the two as pointing to the one and same transaction" (217).

We are indebted to these men for bringing us a fair, friendly, and scholarly presentation of the three primary views relative to the time of the Rapture. As already indicated, they have made an excellent contribution to the growing literature of the Rapture question.

THE RAPTURE: A QUESTION OF TIMING

Yet another posttribulational defense was published in 1985 by **William R. Kimball,** entitled *The Rapture: A Question of Timing.* It grants that the Rapture is the "blessed hope" of all true believers, and is "firmly established as a centerpiece in biblical eschatology" (11). In the "Final Appeal" of the book, the author states that he does not wish to cast "a negative reflection upon the integrity, sincerity, or spiritual competency of those believers who may disagree with the prophetic positions I have taken." Furthermore, he declares, "we must always exercise an attitude of tolerance toward those brethren who may disagree with our prophetic positions" (180-81).

This is, of course, the fair and proper attitude in prophetic debate. Differences aside, we are all one in Christ Jesus, and in love we are to honor and respect one another.

However, our author fails tragically to follow his own declared standard, making us wonder if it is more pious talk than true conviction. He calls his fellow Premillennialists with a different view of the Rapture "the pied pipers of pretribulationism." They use "complicated twisting and exegetical gymnastics" and are guilty of "wrenching of scriptures from their context." They hold "novel" and "radical" theories, "prophetic innovations" and "vagaries of . . . ever-changing speculations." Their views are "blatant," "evasive," and "desperate" "maneuvers." They hold a "wistful hope" of a "secret rapture escape," "unheard of prior to 1830," a "secret, silent and mysterious" "split rapture," a "double coming," a "doctrinal quagmire," a "novelty" of "confusion" and "contradiction." The "pretribulationist defense could be likened to the proverbial ostrich who buries his head in the sand." Their "convenient scheme" when dealing with certain passages spells "irretrievable shipwreck to their position." They teach a "mysterious evacuation," a "heavenly elopement of seven years," "a fragmentation of the second coming into two very distinct comings," actually "a third coming." Other men quoted call a Pretrib Rapture "a perversion of Second Coming truth, a delusion of the last days" (121), a "myth" "among the sorriest in the whole history of freak exegesis" (59).

Such comments and namecalling, scattered throughout the book, such verbal abuse, make it difficult to listen to what the author actually has to say. Let us endeavor, however, to bring a brief evaluation of his primary arguments.

Kimball is guilty of broadscale attacks against non-representative positions. It is true that early in the Rapture debate, some used the term "secret Rapture" as a synonym for the pretribulational return of Christ, stressing that the Rapture will occur without warning signs and will find many unprepared. It did not mean "without a sound" or "the world will be unaware," but simply that it would occur suddenly and for many be totally unexpected. However, as used by Tregelles, I. M. Murray and others, it became a term of posttribulational contempt. Like them, Kimball ridicules the term continually, making it "secret, silent and mysterious," and thinks that by disproving "secrecy" he has destroyed the pretribulational Rapture.

The truth is that Pretribs are fully aware of the shout and the trump of God which accompany the Rapture, and agree that the world will recognize that Christians are gone. However, the term "secret" has been so misunderstood and maligned that most modern pretribulationists find no need to continue its use. There is no victory for posttribulationism in attacking the thought of a "secret Rapture." Kimball may prove that it will be "a noisy, open and spectacular event" (59), but he is attacking a position which is no longer relevant.

Kimball opposes the idea that Revelation 4:1 actually makes John's experience "a symbol of the church being raptured" (77). Once again, this is a minority and non-representative view. While the writer respects those who may accept it, he prefers the position that the Rapture falls chronologically between chapters three and four. While the experience of John at 4:1, as well as the resurrection of the two witnesses and the presence of the 144,000 in glory are significant events in themselves, they most probably do not typify the resurrection and Rapture of the Church.

Similarly, E. Schyler English once suggested that the "departure" of II Thessalonians 2:3 might be a reference to the catching up of the Church rather than an end-time apostasy or departure from the faith. His proposal was merely a trial balloon, and Pretribs were the first to shoot it down. It certainly never became representative of pretribulationism, but Kimball labels it "a desperate attempt to defend the any moment rapture theory," and plagiarizing Reese he calls it an "example of freak exegesis."

Posttribs who take minority views and endeavor to make them representative of pretribulational theology because they appear easy to attack are simply tilting at theological windmills, when they should be establishing sound exegesis and end-time chronology.

Concerning the history of the doctrine, Kimball strongly identifies himself with the view of Dave MacPherson, with all of its attendant problems. While correctly recognizing that the Church will not suffer the outpoured wrath of God, he holds that "Christians will weather the opposition and tribulations imposed by men until the second coming of Christ" (76). At this point, he should read Revelation 13:7, then review the warnings and instruction of Jim McKeever.

He holds that the promise of comfort found in I Thessalonians 4:18 is more relevant to the suffering and martyrdom of the first century than it is to their prospect of escaping coming Tribulation. He identifies the "last trump" of the Rapture with the "seventh trumpet" of the Book of Revelation, saying that "the timing of the rapture is restricted to the seventh, or last trumpet" (107). These are common views which have been frequently and convincingly answered. If the Rapture is concurrent with the seventh trumpet, because of the intervening seven vials of wrath it must be considerably *before* the descent of the Son of God from heaven.

Many believe there is a valid distinction between "coming for the saints" and "coming with the saints," drawing from the prophecy found in Jude 14 and many other Scriptures. Kimball is satisfied that this means that Christ will "come again with His holy angels" (127), although it is doubtful if angels may be identified as "saints." Sinless creatures need no sanctification.

Commenting on John 14:1-3, he declares that this does not mean that the Church will return with Christ to heaven, but simply "accompany Him in His final victorious descent to earth" (131). The Church is caught up, briefly "evacuated from the surface of the earth in conjunction with the awesome holocaust which will be suddenly unleashed upon an unregenerate humanity" (132). Thus he agrees that the Church must be raptured to escape the outpouring of divine wrath. But Pretribs find outpoured wrath beginning early in the Tribulation, with Revelation 6:16-17 and not with 19:11 at the glorious coming of the King.

Kimball closes his book correctly by saying: "Our essential

unity and fellowship in Christ should never be severed or undermined because of our differences on prophetic points" (181). In the opinion of the reviewer, he has failed in this high purpose, and has written a book which adds nothing to harmony and little if anything to the posttribulational argument. Rather, the command to "love His appearing" has been completely lost in the midst of the bitterness of yet another posttribulational polemic.

THE RAPTURE QUESTION: REVISED AND ENLARGED EDITION

For the final and most significant defense of the pretribulational position, we have chosen to review the volume by **John F. Walvoord,** *The Rapture Question: Revised and Enlarged Edition.* While the other books herein reviewed have been considered in chronological succession since 1956, including the original edition of *The Rapture Question,* this 1979 re-publication is worthy of special mention. It brings issues and arguments up to date as it answers the more recent challenges to the hope of the imminent return of Christ.

One hundred pages longer than the earlier edition, the book adds a full topical Index, an expanded Bibliography, and attractive boldface subheadings. For Scripture quotations, it has switched from the AV to the NIV, which in some cases yields a more simple and vigorous translation. However, to Bible students raised with the familiar expressions of the King James Version, there are some instances where the NIV terminology will probably come across with a peculiar sound, such as "the parable of the wheat and the weeds," and in John 14, "there are many rooms in my Father's house."

Far more important however is the fact that Dr. Walvoord has added to his earlier edition six new chapters of Biblical exposition. He discusses the Rapture in the Gospels, in First Thessalonians 4 and 5, in Second Thessalonians, in First Corinthians and in the Book of Revelation. Significant also is the fact that his exegesis includes a direct response to the vigorous arguments of Robert H.

Gundry, whose 1973 book *The Church and the Tribulation* was undoubtedly the strongest challenge to pretribulationism since *The Approaching Advent of Christ* by Alexander Reese, dated 1932.

It makes interesting and challenging reading to discover how a mature and skilled theologian like Walvoord answers the clever, spirited, and frequently involved arguments of a scholar like Gundry, both of them maintaining the highest level of Christian courtesy as fellow Premillennialists and brethren in the service of Christ. The fact that two such scholars should disagree at all, serves to illustrate the difficulty and complexity of the debate under consideration.

While the arguments and issues are far too extensive for adequate treatment within this brief evaluation, the main highlights may be pointed out as follows:

THE RAPTURE IN THE GOSPELS

Both Reese and Gundry take the position that explicit references to a Posttrib Rapture are found in the Gospels, especially in Matthew 13 and 24-25 and in John 14. Gundry argues from Matthew 13:30, the wheat and the tares, that the mere professors are gathered for judgment in the same crisis as the transfiguration of the righteous, causing great embarrassment to those who separate the two by several years. This does not logically follow, for the expression "first the tares" disrupts the Posttrib claim that Christ raptures the Church before He deals in judgment with the wicked. Also in the parable of the good and bad fish which immediately follows (vs. 48), the "good fish" are selected first, which is in opposite order from the burning of the tares before the wheat is gathered. On these points, Gundry gives no solid evidence for a Posttrib Rapture. In fact, observes Walvoord, in context Matthew is discussing the judgment of Christ's Revelation, and the Rapture is not in view at all.

In Matthew 24-25, the subject matter concerns the "end of the age," which is not the Church Age as such, but rather the interadvent age previously discussed in chapter 13. The period between the two advents of Christ includes both the Church Age and the coming Tribulation. In the Olivet Discourse, Christ is answering specific questions of the apostles relative to the future of Israel, a fact which Gundry chooses to ignore. While most Premils agree that there will be a gathering of all the "elect," both of Israel and of the Gentiles, at the end of the Tribulation, the "elect" in question refers to Tribulation believers and not Church saints. For the two main features of the Rapture are entirely absent from the passage, namely the translation of the living and the resurrection of the dead in Christ. Our author concludes: "Proof that Matthew's account of this event includes either a translation or a resurrection, however, is lacking" (187).

Furthermore, the Posttrib attempt to find the Rapture in Matthew 24:40-41 is inaccurate, for the context of verse 39 declares that those who are "taken" are the ones who are drowned, and "it would be strange to have a clear illustration like this be completely reversed in the application of verses 40-41" (188). Many will be taken away in judgment and some will be left to enter the millennial Kingdom. The Rapture as such is not under discussion, no matter how similar the language may sound.

Posttribulationism also fails to find the Rapture in Matthew 25:31-46, for the sheep and the goats are intermingled and require separation by a special judgment immediately following the Second Coming of Christ. This would be entirely unnecessary if a Posttrib Rapture had just taken place, for the Rapture "would be the first event and would automatically separate all the saved from the unsaved before Christ's feet ever touched the Mount of Olives and before His kingdom was instituted" (192).

John 14:1-3 is taken by many to be the first clear mention of the Rapture in the New Testament from a chronological point of view. His coming for His own is here quite in contrast with the glorious event of Matthew 24, which is compared with the lightning shining from east to west. "Instead of Christ picturing a coming from heaven to the earth, He describes a coming for His saints to take them to the Father's house" (194). Posttribs labor to eliminate such a Rapture because, as we have seen, it is in direct contradiction to their prophetic system. For example, instead of rapturing the Church to the Father's house, Barton Payne refers John 14:3 to the death of a Christian, while Robert Gundry explains that Christ is going to prepare for them "spiritual abodes within His own Person." And Douty declares that Christ first returns to earth to judge Antichrist and introduce His glorious reign before He returns to heaven to administer it. Such strained interpretations indicate "how posttribulationists, even those given to literal interpretation, will spiritualize when the plain text contradicts their point of view" (195). And in so doing they clearly contradict one another.

THE RAPTURE IN I THESSALONIANS 4

The commentary on I Thessalonians 4 and 5 by both Gundry and Walvoord is quite extensive and should be read carefully by all who seek an understanding of the respective viewpoints. In brief, Dr. Walvoord's discussion includes the following thoughts. I Thessalonians contributes more to the doctrine of the Rapture than any other book of the New Testament, mentioning the Rapture in every chapter. If the Great Tribulation is going to precede the Rapture, this book would be the natural place in which to state it. Instead, the return of Christ for His Church is set before the Christians of Thessalonica as an imminent event for which they should look with hope and expectation. Concerning their Christian dead, they will first be resurrected, and this expectation should bring them comfort in the midst of sorrow.

Now in I Thessalonians 4:13-18, the coming of the Lord at the Rapture will be "with a loud command," and will be joined by the "voice of the archangel, Michael," a shout of triumph and victory from one who has led the holy angels against Satan and his angels throughout the centuries.

The "trumpet call of God" is frequently used in the Old Testament and in the New to signal important events, but the sounding of a trumpet does not identify two events as the same event. The Rapture is herein presented as imminent, with no preceding order of events which must be enacted. "It should also be obvious that if the Thessalonians would have to pass through the Great Tribulation before the Rapture, this would be a matter of greater concern to them than the possible problem of a delayed resurrection of their loved ones in Christ" (203).

In addition, Posttribs have yet to explain why, according to their view, the saints would have to leave the earth at all, since Christ intends them to reign with Him, and since they could so easily become the ones who will populate the millennial Kingdom. To a Posttrib, the Rapture is merely a brief incident of doubtful significance in the sequence of events known as the Second Coming.

Most important, this critical Scripture gives no warning of the Great Tribulation, and to those who think it is implied, "instead of exhorting Christians to comfort, posttribulationists should be preparing Christians for martyrdom" (209).

Walvoord concludes that I Thessalonians 4 is one of the strongest passages for the pretribulational interpretation of Scripture, and offers the least comfort to those who hold the posttribulational position.

THE RAPTURE IN I THESSALONIANS 5

I Thessalonians 5 is a chapter which has generated some heated disagreements, including as it does the difficult problem of the "day of the Lord." Gundry agrees that this expression does not mean a 24 hour day, "but a longer period of time . . . which includes the millennium and the final judgment." Note that he strongly resists any contention that the day of the Lord also includes the Tribulation. Accordingly, Walvoord reminds us that Gundry attempts to re-arrange the Book of Revelation so that the major judgments fall at its close, with "all the catastrophic judgments of the seals, trumpets, and bowls as if they were in some way simultaneous" (223). His motive "is to get the church raptured before major events of the day of the Lord take place." Behind all this is the assumption that if the Tribulation is not a time of divine wrath, then Christians will escape the severity of the period.

Walvoord responds that Gundry is wrong on both counts. Not only do the saints suffer severely but also the Scriptures reveal that the Tribulation is primarily a time of God's wrath. Even if it were only a time of Satanic wrath, Christians could not avoid great suffering and probable death. "The prospect of a church's going triumphantly through the Great Tribulation relatively untouched is not supported in the prophecies of the Book of Revelation, as indicated by the martyrs in chapters 6 and 7" (230).

Actually, chapters 4 and 5 of I Thessalonians are setting forth the broad program of end-time events, with the day of the Lord beginning right after the Rapture. The Church does not enter this period, indicated by (1) the fact that the Rapture is discussed first; (2) by the change of pronouns from "we," "us," and "you" (vs. 1, 2, 4-6, 8-11) to "they" and "others" (vs. 3, 6, 7); (3) by the fact that people will be saying "peace and safety" which implies that the Tribulation has not yet begun; and (4) by the clear statement that Christians are not appointed to suffer wrath but are to obtain deliverance.

In this passage, the pretribulationist has the obvious advantage, for if the Church is raptured before this time of trouble, then all that is said in the passage becomes very clear. "The period of wrath will not overtake the church as a thief because the church will not be there" (221). The Great Tribulation is expressly a time of divine judgment on a world that has rejected Christ. Gundry's posttribulationism forces him into "an extreme and untenable position by trying to bring the church *through* the Great Tribulation without *experiencing* great tribulation" (228).

THE RAPTURE IN I CORINTHIANS

Gundry's position concerning the Restrainer in II Thessalonians 2 has previously been reviewed, so the writer will move on to I Corinthians 15:51-58. This Scripture is important because it is one of the two main passages on the Rapture in the entire

New Testament. Included in the great Pauline resurrection chapter, the Rapture is presented as the major exception to the normal rule of death followed by resurrection. Those who are "alive and remain" at the close of the Church age shall escape death by physical translation into the presence of Christ.

This Scripture is normally given brief treatment by posttribulational writers because, as Walvoord explains, "The passage . . . contributes practically nothing to the posttribulational concept of the Rapture" (247). For the Rapture is a "mystery," not revealed in the Old Testament, and this immediately sets it apart from the Second Coming of Christ, which is revealed. For that matter, "the translation of the church is not mentioned anywhere in the New Testament in a passage that clearly speaks of the coming of Christ after the Great Tribulation" (248).

The main aspect of Gundry's discussion revolves around the phrase "the last trumpet." Posttribs normally associate this "last trumpet" with the seventh judgment trumpet of the angel in Revelation 11:15. Gundry makes the same identification but with a qualifying "perhaps," suggesting also that it might be last "as one sounded at the end of the age, *after* the sounding of the seven apocalyptic trumpets" (Gundry, 148). This appears to be an admission that the seventh trumpet in Revelation 11 actually sounds considerably before the end of the Tribulation, a fact that Posttribs normally do not recognize. But rather than make such an acknowledgement he asks, "how could Paul have had an eye on the seven trumpets when John had not yet written Revelation?"

His final and more restrained explanation is that the trumpet will be the "last in its sphere, i.e., in the Church age, rather than last in a series." This sounds very much like the Pretrib position, except that to Gundry it is a foregone conclusion that the Church age will include the Great Tribulation. He therefore places the trumpet at the very end of that period, which is actually assuming what he is trying to prove. Nor does he solve the significant problem that there are seven bowls of the wrath of God in Revelation 16 following the seventh trumpet but before the Second Coming of Christ.

Walvoord holds that the trumpets of I Corinthians 15, Revelation 11 and Matthew 24:31 are entirely different trumpets, for the one in Matthew deals with the saints of all ages who are assembled at the time of the Second Coming, the ones in Revelation relate to judgment and are blown by angels, while the one in Corinthians relates to the Church and is called the "trump of God." Those who make "last trumpet" a technical term do so based on a prior assumption rather than upon solid Biblical evidence.

Furthermore, the resurrection of I Corinthians 15:52 is absolutely unique, for it is the only case where a resurrection is connected with the translation of the living. Also, in verse 58 there is an exhortation attached to the doctrine of the Rapture, relating it to our present service for Christ, but in no wise warning us that this great event can occur only after the Great Tribulation has run its course.

THE RAPTURE IN THE BOOK OF REVELATION

The last of these distinct chapters relates to the Rapture in the critical Book of Revelation. Declares Walvoord: "The prospect of a church's going triumphantly through the Great Tribulation relatively untouched" is not supported by the prophecies of this great book (230). This is most significant, for in the Revelation specific details are revealed concerning the Tribulation and the coming of Christ nowhere else given in the entire Bible! "If . . . the Rapture is part of the events of the Second Coming, the strange absence of any mention of it certainly is a devastating blow to posttribulationists" (254).

There are, however, several specific passages involved in the Rapture-Tribulation debate. Among the most important is Revelation 3:10-11: "Since you have kept my commandment to endure patiently, I will also keep you from the hour of trial that is going to come upon the whole world to test those who live on the earth. I am coming soon. Hold on to what you have, so that no one will take your crown."

As previously considered, the Greek *tereo ek* and its translation is important to the understanding of the passage. Gundry devotes ten pages to his discussion of Revelation 3:10 and insists that the Greek preposition means "out from within." Walvoord, backed by practically all of the English translations, holds that it has the simple meaning "from." More important, "the purpose of the promise is deliverance from 'the hour of trial,' a period of time, not simply preservation through the trials in that period" (257). The purpose is to keep them from the *time* of persecution, not to keep them through the persecution. This makes "kept from the hour" a valid pretribulational promise.

Revelation 5:8-10 involves the 24 elders in heaven in the presence of Christ, seen by many Pretribs as representative of the Church raptured before the outpouring of divine judgments, and seen by Posttribs as simply angels singing a song of rejoicing over the redeemed. Since the main difference of opinion is based on alternate readings of the Greek text, the matter "remains debatable," although the use of the revised text alone "does not prove that the twenty-four elders are angels" (259).

The fact that they are clothed in white raiment suggests rather that they are redeemed men, and their being described as having golden crowns implies that they have been judged and rewarded, as would be the case if there had been a pretribulational Rapture and a Judgment Seat of Christ following in heaven.

Walvoord reminds us of the main problem related to the Book of Revelation: "There is no clear mention of the rapture of the church from Revelation 4 through Revelation 18," and this gives us a strong implication that it has already taken place (260). Gundry counters this absence by the fact that the book does not mention the Church as being in heaven either. But such an objection hangs on the identification of the elders and forgets that the Church as the Bride of Christ is seen in heaven prior to Christ's Second Coming (Rev. 19:7-9).

Walvoord reminds Gundry that "there is no mention of a local church anywhere in Revelation 4-18," leaving Posttribs to face not only the fact that the universal Church is not mentioned, but also that there is no local church seen on earth (261).

Revelation 7:1-8 and 14:1-5 introduce the calling and spiritual authority of the 144,000. Most Posttribs spiritualize this group and speak of them as representative of the Church on earth during the Tribulation. Gundry departs from this normal Posttrib position by offering an entirely new approach. He suggests that they are orthodox, unconverted Jews, destined to be protected by God during the judgments and then saved at the time of the Rapture. Walvoord counters this idea with the fact that those who go through the Tribulation without Christ must take the mark of the Beast and thus seal their destiny. Also, Gundry's view would allow unsaved men to be called "the servants of God," and later be given a "second chance" to trust in Christ. Furthermore, men clearly designated as saved Israelites cannot be members of the New Testament Church, where we are no longer seen as Jew or Gentile but one new man in Christ Jesus.

Another of the unique views offered by Gundry is that "God's wrath will not stretch through the whole tribulation," but follow Armageddon instead of preceding it. Walvoord calls this "a strange and unnatural exegesis." But when to support his view, Gundry identifies "the first harvest" of the Rapture with the blood-bath of Armageddon in Revelation 14:14-20, Walvoord charges: "Only an expositor desperate to support an insupportable view would appeal to a passage like this" (265).

Finally, Revelation 19 and 20 constitute a major problem for posttribulationists, for they contain no Scriptural proof for a Posttrib Rapture in the very passages which ought to include it. "In the most comprehensive and detailed account to be found anywhere in the Bible of the second coming of Christ, there is no resurrection or translation mentioned as an event occurring in the Second Coming itself." Significantly, "The posttribulational Rapture, which should have been a prominent feature of the Book of Revelation if it were indeed a part of the great climax of the second coming of Christ, is totally missing in the narrative" (268).

Revelation 19 and 20 constitute a major problem for posttribulationists, for there is no proof for a Posttrib Rapture in the very passages that ought to include it. Walvoord concludes that "there is not a single verse in the entire Book of Revelation that teaches a posttribulational Rapture" (268). The Posttrib Rapture is a theory without Scriptural support!

THE PRE-WRATH RAPTURE OF THE CHURCH

Recently there has emerged a strong frontal attack against the pretribulational return of Christ, written by one who claims to have held that view and preached it with conviction for some 35 years. It is entitled **The Pre-Wrath Rapture of the Church** by Marvin J. Rosenthal, former executive director of Friends of Israel Gospel Ministry. His 317 page book is generally well written and is attractively published, with 25 charts to clarify the various millennial and tribulational views, plus his own unique and somewhat complex position on the timing of the Rapture.

Rosenthal is clearly a Bible-believing, conservative and premillennial servant of Jesus Christ. He calls himself a "biblicist" who, although "not a scholar," has invested his life in the preaching of the "whole counsel of God." However, under the prodding of a friend he began to re-examine his view of the Rapture, particularly in its relationship to the coming Tribulation. The view he now espouses is no longer pretribulationism, nor is it midtribulationism or posttribulationism, but one which he calls "pre-wrath rapturism." Although radically different from standard viewpoints, Rosenthal predicts that within five years it will be a "recognized position," and within fifteen years "a major position of the believing church" (293). This reviewer sincerely questions the validity of that ambition or the necessity of adding a fifth position to an already overcrowded Rapture debate.

The primary thrust of the book is that the Church of Jesus Christ will be removed from the earth by Rapture prior to the outpouring of the "wrath of God," and that the correct timing of the Rapture places it just before the fourth quarter of the "seventieth week of Daniel." Speaking of God's "final wrath on an unbelieving world," he declares that "God's children will be delivered from that day. That is the 'blessed hope'" (35). Such a change of emphasis is unfortunate, for it moves the "blessed hope" of the believer away from the expectation and joy of being in the presence of Christ to the more human desire of escaping outpoured wrath in the coming judgment.

Nor does this "pre-wrath" emphasis contribute anything particularly new. Rosenthal freely admits that all Pre- and Mid-tribs expect to be caught up by Rapture before the outpoured wrath of God in the coming Tribulation. He points out that even Gundry's variety of posttribulationism could qualify as "pre-wrath," although Gundry does not use that designation (59). He simply declares "the theological necessity that God's wrath not touch a saved person."[1]

Further research would have revealed a wider agreement among posttribulationists. George Ladd declares: "Everyone must agree that it is inconceivable that the Church will suffer the wrath of God."[2] J. Barton Payne comments: "Posttribulationists unite in affirming that, 'The church will endure the wrath of men . . . but will not suffer the wrath of God.'"[3] Arthur Katterjohn writes: "Christians, it must be remembered, will be removed before God's final anger falls."[4] William Kimball says: "The scriptures clearly teach us that the church will never suffer from the wrath of God.... This point is agreed upon by all.[5] And even so strong a post-tribulationist as Alexander Reese assures us: "The essential fact for us to know is that Jesus by His death, has delivered us from the wrath to come, and that immediately prior to the full

---

[1] Robert H. Gundry, *The Church and the Tribulation* (Grand Rapids: Zondervan Publishing house, 1973), p.46.

[2] George E. Ladd, *The Blessed Hope* (Grand Rapids: Eerdmans Publishing Co., 1956), p. 122.

[3] J. Barton Payne, *The Imminent Appearing of Christ* (Grand Rapids: Eerdmans Publishing Co., 1962), p. 143.

[4] Arthur Katterjohn, *The Tribulation People* (Carol Stream, Ill.: Creation House, 1976), p. 98.

[5] William R. Kimball, *The Rapture: A Question of Timing* (Grand Rapids: Baker Book House, 1985), p. 70.

revelation of divine wrath, He will gather the saints to Himself.[6] So the mere declaration that the Rapture will be "pre-wrath" is hardly a spectacular discovery. It is solidly affirmed by almost all of Pre-, Mid- and Posttribulational persuasion because of the clear declarations of Scripture at this point.

A NEW POSITION FOR THE RAPTURE

It is evident that the *timing* of the Rapture, and not its relationship to divine wrath, is uppermost in the mind of Rosenthal in the writing of this volume. Coming perilously close to advocating a date-setting scheme, he defends with enthusiasm the view that the Rapture will be three-quarters of the way through the seventieth week of Daniel, with divine wrath to be found only in the final quarter. His evidence for such a conclusion is rather lengthy and complicated, based squarely on his personal division of the "seventieth week of Daniel" into three clearly recognizable periods, the "beginning of sorrows," the "great Tribulation," and the frequently predicted "day of the Lord."

The Rapture is then placed immediately between the Great Tribulation and the Day of the Lord, which according to his definitions is after the Tribulation but still "pre-wrath." These viewpoints, Rosenthal proceeds to support by some 200 pages of strong and somewhat overbearing argumentation, with a sharp attack against any response which reminds him of his previous Pretrib position.

His terminology and unique division of the "seventieth week" are central to his argument. He endeavors, with several notable exceptions on his own part, to refrain from using the expression "Tribulation period," saying that it contains a predisposition toward pretribulationism when it is used of the entire seventieth week of Daniel. Rather, he prefers to call the coming seven years of judgment and wrath simply the "seventieth week of Daniel." These seven years he then subdivides as follows: (1) the first

---

6

Alexander Reese, *The Approaching Advent of Christ* (London: Marshall, Morgan & Scott, n.d.), p. 226.

three and one-half years are "the Beginning of Sorrows." (2) The first half of the second three and one-half years (which would be one and three-fourths years or twenty-one months), he calls the "Great Tribulation." (3) The final twenty-one months, the fourth quarter of the seven years, he then designates as the "Day of the Lord," in which is found the "wrath of God." Just prior to the Day of the Lord, at the sounding of the "seventh trumpet," the Rapture occurs. Hence, the Rapture of the Church takes place between the third and fourth quarters of the "seventy weeks of Daniel," just before the outpouring of the wrath of God. Therefore, to Rosenthal, the Rapture takes place at a sharply defined moment of prophecy, and it is posttribulational but pre-wrath.

The thirteen chapters of argumentation in support of these claims are frequently quite tedious and repetitious, with a dogmatism which earns it a unique place in the literature of the Rapture debate. Rosenthal sets forth Walvoord, Pentecost and Ryrie as his former "heroes" in matters of eschatology (25), whose logic in his judgment is now faulty and whose exegesis can no longer be trusted. Rosenthal's own opinions, however, are "indisputable" and "beyond refutation" (105, 109). His facts "cannot be set aside," and for his primary conclusions "there simply is no question" (110). The doctrine of imminence, which he calls "a major pillar of pretribulation rapturism," is "untenable," and that is a "clear, unassailable truth that cannot be dismissed" (150). Differing with Pretribs, he declares that they are locked in an "unsolvable dilemma" (112). Such dogmatism is, to say the least, both unwholesome and irritating, for a great many of his statements clearly warrant further investigation.

Now in spite of all of this, it must be noted in all fairness that there are some excellent sections in the book, especially chapters two, and four through seven. Interestingly, this section is almost wholly irrelevant to the timing of the Rapture. Here much information is given on the history of Israel, together with her customs, feasts and leadership. He discusses the credentials of the King and the certainty of Christ's Second Coming. Other subjects range from the virgin birth of Christ to modern humanism –

themes taken no doubt from the author's Bible lectures. Perhaps the desired impression is that since the author appears to be gracious, godly, and biblical, he would assuredly be a safe and seasoned student of Bible prophecy, bringing trustworthy conclusions concerning the blessed hope of the Church. The latter, however, is not the case.

While it is an unhappy task to bring critical evaluation of a book where on many points there is substantial agreement, as graciously as possible it must be done. Although it should be recognized that when an argument is as lengthy and complex as this, it would take a new volume of equal length to examine every detail. The following are some of the salient points which should be carefully evaluated by all serious readers of this volume.

THE TRIBULATION PERIOD

As previously noted, Rosenthal declares that the designation "the Tribulation period" should be omitted from any honest consideration of the time of the Rapture. It cannot be used as a synonym for the entire "seventy weeks of Daniel," for to do so, he says, predisposes one to pretribulationism, and the expression "Tribulation period" has no biblical justification (103). He believes that Pretribs have coined a technical phrase and superimposed it upon the Scriptures (105). If such is the case, it is fair to ask: "Where is Rosenthal's biblical justification for the new expression, "pre-wrath rapturism"? It is not found in Scripture and comes upon the scene as recently as 1990.

Admittedly, the King James Bible does not use the precise expression "Tribulation period," any more than it uses the term "rapture," "second coming" or "premillennial." But on at least six occasions it does speak of a coming "tribulation," and Rosenthal freely admits that it is a period to be measured in years. Like the other terms, "Tribulation period" is simply a widely used term of convenience, less cumbersome and less in need of explanation than the expression "seventieth week of Daniel," which also does not appear in the Bible. Indeed, on a number of occasions

Rosenthal himself uses the term "Tribulation period" (107, 117, 143) and his own publisher uses it in the promotional material on the back cover of the book! However, his attempt to cancel the expression "Tribulation period" helps to pave the way for his novel three-fold subdivision of the same actual period of seven years.

THE BEGINNING OF SORROWS

Rosenthal calls the first three and one half years of Daniel's "seventieth week" by the name "the beginning of sorrows," borrowed from Matthew 24:8, for he finds a rough parallel between the Matthew passage and the first four seal judgments of Revelation 6. But similarity is not identity, and the likeness is superficial. There is a world of difference between the "many deceivers" of Matthew and the Devil's Antichrist of Revelation; between the "wars and rumors of wars" and battles so powerful they take peace from the whole earth; between the earthquakes of Matthew and the cosmic disturbances of Revelation 6:12-13. Nor does Matthew 24:4-8 even vaguely hint of martyred saints in heaven, nor of an outpouring of God's wrath so severe that a fourth part of earth's population will be slain.

A view that deserves serious consideration is that the "beginning of sorrows" describes the prevailing conditions on earth at the close of the Church age, before the Rapture and the Tribulation. For those who wonder if these descriptions are relevant to our day, for famine, one may note Ethiopia. For pestilence, AIDS is evident. For earthquakes, one need only recall San Francisco and many other unfortunate cities. For nations rising up against nation, two World Wars testify to that reality. Calling the early half of the Tribulation "the beginning of sorrows" in Rosenthal's book is merely a device to minimize this period and shift what he calls the "Great Tribulation" to the third quarter of Daniel's seventieth week.

It is a serious error to claim that "the first three and one-half years are not part of the Tribulation period" because God's wrath does not start until "considerably further" into the seventieth week

(106-7). Rosenthal declares: "The seals are not God's wrath; they are God's promise of eternal protection during man's wrath" (145). Moreover, "the first five seals relate to man's activity under the controlling influence of Satan. God's wrath has not yet begun" (247). But this is not entirely true, for the seals also reflect the judgment of the sovereign God. All seven seals are broken by Christ, and the riders of the first four seals and their accompanying judgments are initiated by four "living creatures" who descend from the very presence of God (Rev. 4:6-8). They are responding to divine holiness when they command these riders, not to "come and see," but simply to "Come!"

The judgments of these four seals include the sword, famine, pestilence and wild beasts, frequently used in Scripture as the expressions of divine wrath. Indeed, they are all included and named when God calls His "four sore judgments upon Jerusalem, the sword and the famine, and the noisome beast, and the pestilence" (Ezek. 14:21). This is likewise true in Leviticus 26:22, 25; Deuteronomy 28:21-25; Jeremiah 15:2-3; 16:4; Ezekiel 5:12, 17, and a host of other passages.[7] It is a denial of Scripture to declare the first four seals are entirely the activity of men and do not include judgment from the Almighty. And a Rapture placed after the first six seals would certainly not be a "pre-wrath Rapture."

THE GREAT TRIBULATION

Rosenthal also has peculiar and erroneous views relating to the "Great Tribulation." Similar to the first four seals, he declares it "the persecution of God's elect by wicked men," namely man's wrath against man, but never God's wrath against man (105). He limits the Great Tribulation by declaring that it will be the third quarter of the seven year period, and that somehow even these

---

[7]Renald E. Showers, Th.D., formerly associated with Marvin Rosenthal at Friends of Israel Gospel Ministry, has written an 88 page "critique and objection" to *The Pre-Wrath Rapture of the Church.* Academic, detailed, and highly Scriptural, at this point he details six pages of Scripture and argument to demonstrate that "the first four seals of Revelation 6:1-8 involve a great outpouring of divine wrath."

days will be "shortened." He fails to relate the Great Tribulation to the detailed descriptions of the book of Revelation. One can only conclude that if the first four seals are the "beginning of sorrows," and the Day of the Lord begins with the opening of the seventh seal (117), then the Great Tribulation which comes between must be limited to the brief compass of the fifth and sixth seal. This is exactly Rosenthal's position, illustrated by a chart on page 161. With such a view he stands alone. It finds no adequate place for the detailed teaching of Christ in Matthew 24:9-26, and makes the Great Tribulation, like the first four seals, simply the activity of Antichrist rather than judgment from God. Then to Rosenthal, the rest of the seven years, the final quarter, starts with Revelation 8:1, and becomes the "day of the Lord" or the final day of the Lord's wrath.

Rosenthal is in serious trouble when he limits the Great Tribulation to the third quarter of the seven year period. For Christ linked the Great Tribulation with the action of Antichrist defiling the Jewish Temple by setting up his image to receive worship, in fulfillment of the "abomination which makes desolate" in Daniel 9:27. This event in the middle of the "week" is the sign for the Jews to flee from the wrath of Satan, from whom they must be protected three and one-half years "from the face of the serpent" (Rev. 12:14). Thus the "time of trouble" for Israel (Dan. 12:1) and the desolation of the "great tribulation" predicted by Christ (Matt. 24:21) must extend at least for a full three and one-half years and not for a period of twenty-one months.

Indeed, the finishing of Israel's "rebellion" and the end of Antichrist's "desolation" are linked with the entirety of the seventy weeks and not with a small portion of it (Dan. 9:24, 27). Even Gabriel testified that Antichrist's "war" with Israel should last until the "end" of the period under consideration, evidently with a "flood" of divine judgment. Antichrist will make war with Israel and all the saints, until he is judged and they possess the Kingdom (Dan. 7:22). He will defile the earth and lead the nations in the final rebellion and war of Armageddon right up to the power and glory of the Second Coming of Christ. In a word, Tribulation conditions cannot be limited to one fourth of that frightful seven year period.

THE FUTURE OF THE CHURCH

From the perspective of Rosenthal's book, how does all this relate to the future of the Church? In brief, he insists that the Church must pass through the first 42 months of the Tribulation period under the pretext that it is only the "beginning of sorrows." The Church must then pass through an additional twenty-one months of Great Tribulation because divine wrath has not yet been poured out. Later, Rosenthal evidently has the Church back on earth during the outpouring of the seven vials of wrath, for "Christ will literally return to assume His kingdom at the seventh trumpet" (146), right at the end of the "seventieth week." The notion that the seven vials will follow the Second Coming is clearly stated on page 146 and charted on pages 147 and 276.

Of the seven-year Tribulation the Church will miss only the small portion of twenty-one months Rosenthal entitles the Day of the Lord. So whereas believers will not experience wrath, they will be on earth during the severe judgment of the seals, according to Rosenthal. They will come under the dominion of the Beast and suffer and die at the hands of the Antichrist (Rev. 13:7), and even be present when the final seven vials of "God's wrath" are poured out. Not much by way of comfort or blessing in an eschatology such as this!

All this can be avoided by recognizing that the "Tribulation," "the great Tribulation," and "Daniel's seventieth week" are all substantially one and the same thing, and share identical features. These terms are simple descriptions of a coming period, not technical names or definitions around which to build a prophetic theory. While granting that the last half of the Tribulation period is more severe than the first, it is all designated "great tribulation" (literally in the Greek, "tribulation, the great one," Rev. 7:14), simply because in the midst of earth's trials there is no other period like it (Jer. 1:7; Dan. 12:1). "Tribulation" and "great tribulation" are spoken of together and clearly equated in Matthew 24:21 and 29. These descriptions have to do with the *content*, not with the *duration* of that period, and certainly do not designate the timing of the Rapture.

THE DAY OF THE LORD

Pretribulationists normally place the beginning of the Day of the Lord right after the Rapture in conjunction with the start of the Tribulation. Rosenthal rather violently opposes such a placement and makes it "perhaps the single greatest error in the debate concerning the timing of the Rapture" (117). To him, the Day of the Lord must commence *after* the Great Tribulation is over. It fills in the final 21 months (half of three and one-half years) of the seven year "Tribulation period," beginning with the opening of the seventh seal (117). But this misses the fact that there can be only *one* completely unprecedented day of sorrow in Israel's future, and Joel 2:1-2 calls it the "day of the Lord," while Daniel 12:1 calls it Israel's "time of trouble," and in Matthew 24:21 Christ identifies it as the "great tribulation." The three are one, not separate periods which follow in sequence.

Rosenthal rightly reviews the frequent use of "day of the Lord" in the Old Testament, but denies that it extends to the "new heavens and a new earth" according to II Peter 3:10-13. He commences it at Revelation 8:1 on the basis of cosmic disturbances under the sixth seal (Joel 2:30-31; Rev. 6:11-12). He argues that the day of the Lord's wrath must begin immediately after the Church is raptured, indeed "on the same day," and cites the commencement of the flood on the same day Noah entered into the ark, and fire and brimstone fell out of heaven the same day Lot went out of Sodom. However, this is weak evidence to help establish a great New Testament doctrine.

A number of Scriptures unite to demonstrate that the Day of the Lord does include the first six seals. While Rosenthal speaks of these seals as the wrath of man, the beasts of the earth and the heavenly bodies of Revelation 6:8 and 12 are not under the dominion of man, but of God. The darkness of Amos 5:18-20 matches the darkness of the sixth seal. The judgment upon the proud and lofty in Isaiah 2:12, 17 finds clear fulfillment in Revelation 6:15, and the announcement of *wrath* in Isaiah 13:6-13 and Zephaniah 1:14-18 finds its counterpoint in Revelation 6:17. Isaiah 2:19 and Revelation 6:15 state that the wicked shall hide in the holes of the rocks and caves of the earth, a fact far too specific to be lightly ignored. Zephaniah 2:3 calls this period the day of the Lord's fierce anger, surely fulfilled in substance at Revelation 6:8 with the destruction of one fourth of the world's population. It is wrong to declare that the Day of the Lord begins with Revelation 8:1 when its predictions find such clear fulfillment in the seal judgments of Revelation six.

How could the Day of the Lord come unexpectedly, "as a thief in the night," if the severe judgments of Revelation six must come first? Why should men be found crying "peace and safety" (1 Thess. 5:2-3) under such horrendous circumstances? Yet it is essential to Rosenthal's prophetic system that the Day of the Lord begins with the opening of the seventh seal (155), which to him signals the end of the Great Tribulation and the moment of the Rapture. It is far better to understand that the Rapture precedes the entire Tribulation period, with the Day of the Lord commencing soon thereafter. This is the order and emphasis of 1 Thessalonians 4 and 5, which happen to be among the prime Scriptures on both prophetic themes.

It has been demonstrated in chapter four of *Kept from the Hour*[8] that the Old Testament predictions of the "day of the Lord" and their fulfillment in the book of Revelation fit together like hand in glove, including the judgments under the first six seals. Placing the Day of the Lord after the Great Tribulation is erroneous and artificial, and denying that it extends to the "new heavens and earth" appears to be in violation of II Peter 3:10-13. For even in the Messianic Kingdom, Christ must rule the nations with a rod of iron and subdue all unrighteousness, and ultimately He must cleanse both the heavens and the earth. Certainly the

[8] *Kept from the Hour,* pp. 70-91.

Day of the Lord, the theme of such extensive prophecy, is of greater significance and extent than twenty-one months or six hundred and thirty days!

Rosenthal's treatment of the three component parts of Daniel's "seventieth week" is entirely unsatisfactory. His view essentially ignores the first three and one-half years and artificially distinguishes between the Great Tribulation and the Day of the Lord, compressing each into a mere one fourth of the Tribulation period. This is a fractured foundation upon which to build any trustworthy conclusions relative to the blessed hope of Christ's return.

SIX EVENTS SET THE TIMING OF THE RAPTURE

It has been demonstrated that Rosenthal dogmatically divides the last half of Daniel's seventieth week into two parts, the Great Tribulation and the Day of the Lord. Between the two he places the Rapture, but that is not all he places at this particular moment of time. So important to Rosenthal is this prophetic juncture of Tribulation activity that he dedicates to it six entire chapters, each with a great prophetic event, all converging at the time of the Rapture and demonstrating that the Day of the Lord relates exclusively to the last quarter of the seven year period. These are (1) Cosmic Disturbances; (2) the Coming of Elijah; (3) the Day of God's Wrath; (4) the Sealing of the 144,000; (5) the Last Trump; and (6) the Apostasy and the Man of Sin. He holds that the convergence of these six events before the seventh seal form an "impregnable" argument supporting a "pre-wrath" Rapture three fourths of the way through the "seventieth week." Such claims demand careful scrutiny. For the vast majority of students of prophecy are still convinced that the Rapture will be unannounced, unheralded by such signs, dateless but imminent. What then of the six signs which Rosenthal thinks will be "the prelude of the Rapture of the church and the Day of the Lord wrath" (153)?

COSMIC DISTURBANCES

(1) There shall be *cosmic disturbances*, according to Joel 2:31, "The sun shall be turned into darkness, and the moon into blood, before the great and terrible day of the Lord come." Rosenthal identifies this with the sixth seal and uses it to date the Rapture and the beginning of the Day of the Lord. But that can hardly be dogmatized, for the predicted Tribulation will not be limited to one display of cosmic power (cf. Rev. 8:10-12; 11:19; 16:8, 21), making Rosenthal's argument uncertain at best. In Matthew 24:27, Christ places yet another great cosmic disturbance after the seventieth week when He shall appear with clouds and great glory and Israel shall mourn as they finally identify Christ as the long awaited Messiah.

Indeed, if there must be a cosmic disturbance before the Day of the Lord can commence, let it be during a brief transitional period after the Rapture but before the announcement of Antichrist. In Scripture, such transitional periods are not hard to find. There was a period of fifty days between Calvary and Pentecost, between "law" and "grace." Rosenthal himself makes much of a transition of seventy-five extra days between the "seventieth week" and the setting up of Christ's Kingdom (273). The whole Church age was thrust between prophecies of the two advents of Christ, as foretold in the Old Testament. Undoubtedly there will be time for the Great White Throne judgment between the Millennial Kingdom and the Eternal Kingdom. Similarly, there is no urgency which demands a tight chronology of events following the Rapture, and so the argument of our author concerning heavenly activity finds a ready answer. Indeed, the immediate context of the prophecy he uses from Joel 2:30-32 seems to relate the heavenly wonders more to the coming of the Messianic Kingdom than to a pre-wrath cosmic disturbance (cf. Matt. 24:29).

ELIJAH MUST COME

(2) Next, Rosenthal teaches that *Elijah must come*, and that if it occurs before a pretribulational Rapture "the doctrine of im-

minence is once again destroyed" (158). He is not sure if the two witnesses are Moses and Elijah or Enoch and Elijah, or whether it is Elijah in the flesh or merely one in the spirit and likeness of Elijah. He supports the view that Elijah will reappear and have a ministry during the last three and one-half years of the Tribulation. Since the witnesses die in the sixth trumpet after a full three and one-half years of witness, this makes it mandatory to place the seven vials of the wrath of God (according to his chronology) *after* the Second Coming of Christ, a radical view which Rosenthal propounds and illustrates on his charts.

He makes much of Malachi 4:5-6, which seems to relate to the Second Coming of Christ when He comes to "smite the earth with a curse," rather than to an earlier manifestation of the Day of the Lord adjacent to the Rapture. It must be noted also that in Matthew 11:14 Christ declared that in a potential sense, Elijah had already come in the person of John the Baptist. But if Malachi is indeed predicting the coming of one of the future two witnesses, the most probable understanding is that the prophecy places their coming relatively early in the prophetic "week" before the Day of the Lord is fully come. There is nothing here to date the Rapture, even if one assumes it should be dated.

THE WRATH OF GOD

(3) Next, Rosenthal uses *the wrath of God* to prove that the pretribulationist has a problem, "larger than big – it is mountainous and unscalable" (164). He makes the expression, "the great day of his wrath is come" (Rev. 6:17) to mean, not a past experience, but a prediction of "an event about to occur" (166-67). This, he declares, is a glaring problem for pretribulation rapturism, for "God's wrath cannot be understood to include the first six seals" (171). "Wrath is impending. It is about to happen; it has not yet occurred" (167).

But the real problem lies at the door of Rosenthal. For he constantly asserts that the outpoured wrath of God does not commence until Revelation 8:1, the seventh seal, which immediately introduces the unprecedented judgments of the seven trumpets. However, his prophetic system is embarrassed, if not refuted, by the obvious fact that one of the strongest references to the wrath of God is recorded in Revelation 6:16-17 in conjunction with the sixth seal. But rather than revising his system, Rosenthal devotes eight pages of argumentation (163-70) endeavoring to prove two main points: (1) that this declaration of outpoured wrath is a prophecy spoken by the prophet John, and not an agonizing cry on the part of the wicked who hide from the face of God in the rocks and the mountains; and (2) that the use of the Greek aorist in the expression "the great day of his wrath is come" demonstrates that it "refers, not to a past event, but to an event about to occur, and that in concert with the opening of the seventh seal" (167).

Even the most casual reading of Revelation 6:12-17 reveals that the cry of verses 16-17 is a scream of terror from the wicked, rebellious human leaders who have endured war and famine, death and destruction, a shattering earthquake and a frightful disruption of heavenly bodies under the earlier seal judgments. Obviously they are responding to past judgments and not judgments yet to come, for wicked men have no ability to speak a prophecy! It is true that the aorist tense normally has no time significance. But the verb *elthen* is in the aorest tense and indicative mood, and when this occurs it refers to a *past action* and not to a future.[9] Hence, the proper translation is "the great day of his wrath *is come*," or as the vast majority of translators put it, "the great day of his wrath *has come*." It is a major error to force the translation to declare, "the great day of his wrath *will come*." One can only conclude that this strong reference to the wrath of God is the direct response of the wicked to their shattering *experience* under the first six seals, and not a veiled prophecy of coming trumpet judgments.

Not only is Rosenthal in error in this matter, he proceeds to make matters worse by making the seals a symbol of ownership

---

[9] H. E. Dana and Julius R. Mantey, *A Manual Grammar of the Greek New Testament*, (New York: Macmillan Co., 1950), p. 178.

and protection, as though that is what God is doing in Revelation 6. While ownership and protection are certainly true for the Church through the sealing ministry of the Holy Spirit (Eph. 4:30), it is not even vaguely related to the Lion of the tribe of Judah loosing the seven seals of the book of Tribulation judgment.

THE SEALED 144,000

(4) The fourth pillar supporting Rosenthal's impregnable argument concerning the time of the Rapture relates to *the sealed 144,000* and the "multitude which no man could number," both found in Revelation chapter seven. He holds that the 144,000 Jews are "sealed for protection" from God's wrath, but not sealed for witness and evangelism. A more normal view is that Israel is beginning to turn back to the Lord, and that these are sealed for service and evangelism to fulfil their destiny as God's witnesses and "a light to the Gentiles" (Isa. 42:6; 43:10, 12; 49:6).

Rosenthal is not sure if they are regenerated, saying that is "a matter of speculation." He flatly rejects the traditional view, as expressed by John Walvoord, that they represent "the godly remnant of Israel on earth in the great tribulation" (183). He at least implies their redemption when he says, "The 144,000 must be sealed for protection to go through the Day of the Lord. . . . God will not leave Himself without a people on earth" (185).

Rosenthal immediately focuses attention on the "*great multitude which no man could number*" and makes this important identification: "This great multitude represents the true church which goes into the seventieth week of Daniel. They are raptured at the end of the Great Tribulation but before the Day of the Lord begins" (185). Here, finally, he reveals the Rapture of the Church, three-fourths of the way through the seventieth week, just before the Day of the Lord, and identifies it with the "innumerable multitude"!

But the seventieth week is a precise period of seven years, each half of which is 42 months or 1,260 days. So mark your calendar! We cannot know the hour, but we can predict the day!

From Antichrist's covenant with Israel it will be 1,260 plus 630 days, a total of 1,890 days. From the commencement of the seventieth week, the date of the Rapture is precisely set! And if Rosenthal is correct that the 144,000 are "God's people," yet distinct from the "innumerable multitude," and they go through the Day of the Lord which is the "wrath of God," then added to all this confusion is a Partial Rapture.

However, the innumerable multitude is not like the Church, which goes to heaven as a group at the Rapture. Rather, they are martyrs who one at a time lay down their lives throughout the seven year period. The Greek present tense in Revelation 7:14 stresses that they "continually come" out of great Tribulation, and obviously do not go to heaven as a single group. It is likewise strange, if they do indeed represent the Church, that John could not recognize them, for John was an Apostle of Christ, a member of the early Church, and part of its essential foundation. Also the Church is composed of all believers since Pentecost, and cannot be limited solely to Tribulation martyrs.

Let it be said as gently as possible: This identification of the Church with the great multitude of the Tribulation is wrong and in fact it is radical eschatology. It teaches that the Rapture is after the Great Tribulation, which is posttribulationism. It implies a divided Church, some of whom are raptured while 144,000 of God's people go through the time of God's wrath. And though Rosenthal does not count up the exact number of days, his dating of the Rapture is so precise that he has fallen into the trap of advocating a date-setting system.

AT THE LAST TRUMP

(5) For his fifth supporting pillar, Rosenthal turns to 1 Corinthians 15:51-52, calling it the clearest text in all the Word of God for determining the timing of the Rapture. The four words, "*at the last trump*," reveal in the clearest possible way the "precise occasion" when the Rapture of the Church will occur (189). He points out correctly that both Midtribs and Posttribs identify their

Rapture position with the "last trump." But pursuing his withering attack on pretribulationism, he declares: "Pretribulation rapturists do not make strong appeals to Paul's statement that the Rapture will occur before the last trump to support their position. . . . If they mention I Corinthians 15 in a Rapture discussion, it is brief and without determinative significance" (189-90). This is a highly prejudiced and erroneous statement.

While he does have a good discussion of the use of a trumpet in the ritual of Judaism, he is content to make an emphatic statement which he supports by italics but not by evidence: "*The last trump will be nothing more, nothing less and nothing different than the final, climactic, eschatological outpouring of the wrath of God*" 193). In his thinking, this makes the "last trump" the equivalent of the entire Day of the Lord. He declares that the "rapture would occur at the last trump" (193), but also that "Christ will literally return to assume His kingdom at the seventh trumpet" (146). This makes the "last trump" a period of twenty-one months, rather than a point of time to signal the Rapture. This confusing position is obviously unacceptable. Rosenthal then returns to his main thesis, that the Rapture must occur at the opening of the seventh seal and immediately before the beginning of God's wrath (194).

There is a more simple and acceptable solution to the problem. The "last trump" is not an Old Testament trumpet of Jewish ritual, nor the same as the seventh trumpet of Tribulation judgment. It is a unique trumpet which sounds for the Church at the Rapture, which is *at* the last trump (and not *before* the last trump, as Rosenthal claims). There are evidently two trumpet blasts, one for the dead and another for the living. Hence, the living are raptured at the second, which is the "last trump." While this view may be too simple for some tastes, it emphasizes that the "trump" is a joyful signal and not a dreaded period of time. It records that the dead in Christ and living believers will be raised in quick succession, to enjoy reunion and recognition together in the presence of Christ. Its purpose is not to reveal the time of the Rapture, a subject which our Lord has chosen not to reveal. It does give assurance that those who have died in the Lord have not missed the Rapture; if anything, they enjoy a slight time advantage because they are caught up just before the living (1 Thess. 4:13-18).

THE APOSTASY AND THE MAN OF SIN

(6) The last of these supporting evidences for Rosenthal's prophetic program is found in chapter 15 of the book, *The Apostasy and the Man of Sin*. This reviewer found it to be a strange co-mingling of truth, speculation, and falsehood. Equally troubling is Rosenthal's stepped-up attack against pretribulationism, assigning it "impossible-to-resolve problems" when it is examined in the light of II Thessalonians 2. It is claimed that these leave "pretribulation rapturism mortally wounded" (196, 210), and in addition he sounds his usual denial of imminency.

In brief, that which is true would include the foreshadowing of Antichrist by the blasphemy and hatred of Israel under the Syrian leader, Antiochus Epiphanes. The speculative is his view of the Antichrist, who "once lived and ruled over a nation, then died, and will be raised to rule over the eighth empire" (209). Also "doubtful" is his claim that all his evidence is "clear and compelling."

Regrettably, that which is false is more plentiful. It involves his declaration that in II Thessalonians 2:3-4, "The apostasy to which Paul referred . . . will involve Israel, not the church" (206). While the normative view of this passage is that the "apostasy" is a widespread departure from true Biblical faith in the end-time, in the light of I Timothy 4:1-3, Rosenthal insists that it is "a specific, definitive, identifiable event" (199), "when many of the Jews will totally abandon the God of their fathers in the *same way* they did in the days of Antiochus Epiphanes" (201). This opinion he primarily supports, not from Scripture, but from various quotations from the Apocrypha.

Moreover, Rosenthal declares, the apostasy has a "very specific and limited meaning," a "total abandonment of Jehovah for a heathen god" (201). Hence, he concludes that the falling away of 2

Thessalonians 2:3 is an identifiable event at a specific point of time, limited to Israel, and associated with Antichrist and his defiling the temple in Jerusalem at the mid-point of the Tribulation. The main thrust of all of this is that the Day of the Lord cannot come until the second half of the Tribulation, "and the Rapture, which occurs at the very outset of the Day of the Lord, cannot possibly be pretribulational." He concludes that this leaves pretribulation rapturism "mortally wounded" (210).

These are highly questionable conclusions. Paul was not discussing a point of time or a final apostasy on the part of Israel, but a spiritual condition among professing Christians. In his previous epistle, he had taught the Thessalonians that the dead in Christ had not missed the Rapture and that living believers would not endure the wrath of the Day of the Lord. Now in his second epistle, he was explaining that they had not entered the Day of the Lord for several reasons. The Restrainer had not yet been removed, the final apostasy had not yet taken place, and the Antichrist with his world dominion had not yet emerged. All of this is a direct refutation of posttribulational thinking, including the view of Marvin Rosenthal.

In addition, almost every point of the summary chart on page 197 is open to question. A comparison with the chart on page 147 reveals that Rosenthal contradicts himself on the extent of God's wrath and the time of the Second Coming of Christ. While his sincerity may be beyond question, many of his definitions appear to be homemade and supporting evidence is completely inadequate. It is part of the teaching ministry of the Holy Spirit to reveal to believers "things to come" (John 16:13), which normally produces within the Church of Christ a certain agreement, a godly consensus even in the interpretation of prophetic truth. While believers do not always agree on the details, it is rare when truth must stand absolutely alone.

It is here contended that Rosenthal is in serious error when he attempts to set the time of the Rapture three-fourths of the way through the seven years of judgment and wrath, some 1,890 days after Antichrist makes his unparalleled covenant with Israel.

Among evangelical Christians from all major Rapture perspectives, Rosenthal walks an isolated path when he asserts that these six notable signs unite in setting the timing of the Rapture. Believers are to wait and watch for Christ's coming and live accordingly, for it is their blessed and purifying hope, evidently next on the prophetic program of God. But the Lord's people should not be confused by vehement argumentation designed to set the day of His appearing, adding yet a fifth and doubtful position to an issue which has already been subjected to more than its share of debate.

THE PRE-WRATH RAPTURE

This closing section of the book consists of five chapters, designed to give final justification for Rosenthal's unique position and a conclusive knockout blow against pretribulationism. In the judgment of this reviewer, who has followed the literature of the Rapture-Tribulation debate closely for nearly forty years, these final arguments as well as many of the former, range somewhere between "curious" and "radical." But those who consider them must exercise considerable caution, for they can be rightly evaluated only by those well established in Biblical theology and well read in the area of eschatology. As always, the Biblical rule is to "examine everything carefully; hold fast to that which is good" (I Thess. 5:21, NASV), with much prayer and with strong dependence upon the illuminating ministry of the Holy Spirit (John 16:13; I Cor. 2:10-12).

Chapter 16 discusses the *primary Greek words* used for the return of Christ, in parallel with much that has already been written on this subject in the Rapture literature. Rosenthal argues that there is only one "coming," with the important feature that it includes not only the Rapture but also a "continuous presence" during which Christ judges the wicked in the Day of the Lord. It also includes His final return in glory (218). To quote the author: *"The Lord's coming . . . is a comprehensive whole.* There is only *one* Second Coming. It includes the Rapture of the church, the outpouring of God's wrath during the Day of the Lord, and Christ's physical return in glory" (221-22, italics his). Furthermore, Rosenthal holds that the "coming of our Lord Jesus Christ with all his saints" (I Thess. 3:13) does not speak of Christ returning to earth with the "dead in Christ" or with raptured living saints, but rather He will come with His "holy ones," namely angelic beings. All this introduces another major problem.

Rosenthal does not explain the destiny of the Church at the Rapture. What happens to all the raptured saints, both dead and living, in the 630 day interval when Christ has a "continuous presence" and is pouring out His wrath upon the wicked? The position of this book demands that the Church is not on earth during the time of outpoured wrath. But they are not raptured to heaven, for to Rosenthal that would imply "two comings." Will the Church triumphant which meets Christ "in the clouds" continue to float about in those clouds for one-fourth of a seven year period while Christ has a "continuous presence" and performs His work of judgment on earth below? It is most significant that Rosenthal rejects the idea of raptured saints going to "the Father's house." Indeed, except for one mention of John 14:1-3 in a quotation of John Sproule, who calls it one of several "debatable Scriptures" (55), Rosenthal does not refer to this important passage at all, for it cannot be brought into harmony with his prophetic scheme. What happens to the Church during Rosenthal's twenty-one month "day of the Lord"? He gives no answer to this. He simply affirms that there will be one "coming," which embraces everything from the Rapture through the last quarter of the seventieth week, right up to the final manifestation of the King.

A further questionable view concerns the "sign" of Christ's coming, requested by the disciples in Matthew 24:3. He writes that this sign will be "the manifestation of the glory of God" at His coming, when "the natural light will be turned off and the super-natural light (God's glory) will be turned on" (221). Most observers would locate this event within the Eternal State following the Millennial Kingdom and the Great White Throne judgment (Rev. 21:23-25), and not with the opening of the sixth seal. Yet Rosenthal argues that this "sign" is sufficiently clear that "the doctrine of imminency is destroyed by the question posed by the disciples" (224).

Chapter 17 introduces the often-debated text of Revelation 3:10 and the disputed phrase, "*kept from the hour.*" Rosenthal states that the dispute among commentators stems from the fact that they "have not generally understood that there are *three* sections to the seventieth week – the beginning birth pangs, the Great Tribulation, and the Day of the Lord" (233). Or, to put it more bluntly, they have not read his book!

This reviewer is disposed to agree with Rosenthal that "each scholar is inclined to interpret this phrase to substantiate his view of the Rapture," as he himself does. Posttribs understand "kept from the hour" as divine protection through the Tribulation, while Pretribs interpret it as exemption from the Tribulation. The latter builds a stronger case, for the verse does not promise protection within the hour but exemption from the hour itself. This point has been well defended in pretribulational literature.

Surprisingly, Rosenthal takes an entirely different approach to the issue, declaring that this watershed Scripture in the Rapture debate "in fact has nothing whatsoever to do with the Rapture." For the promise of Revelation 3:10 "refers to protection from the Great Tribulation, which occurs before the Rapture and the Day of the Lord begins" (234). Since he believes the "hour of temptation" begins in the middle of the seventieth week, some who remain steadfast in the face of adversity "will be kept from that hour . . . by physical removal" (a partial Rapture?), while "others will be kept 'through the hour of temptation' by direct, divine protection" (239). So Rosenthal removes this promise from application to the Rapture, applies both viewpoints to the prior Great Tribulation, and further confuses his readers by declaring that this promise to the church of Philadelphia does not belong to all Christendom. For "it is only the church of Philadelphia which is promised exemption from 'the hour of temptation'" (237), other views interpreting this Scripture "nonliterally." Confusing! At best, he is suggesting that the Scripture promises: I will keep you in one way or another from the last 25 percent of the hour!

In chapter 18 Rosenthal asks the question, "*Are Pretribulation Rapture Arguments Really Unanswerable?*" While admitting that "pretribulationism has more than its share of notables of the faith," he adds that "church history is replete with men of distinction who had blind spots in their theology" (243). Then he gives eleven pretribulational arguments and his rebuttal of each, taking what comfort for his own position he can from each issue.

Space does not permit a further discussion of these arguments, nor a rebuttal of Rosenthal's rebuttals. Suffice it to say that some of the arguments are not entirely representative of normal pretribulational positions, and many valid pretribulational arguments are not introduced at all. Both Walvoord and Pentecost present a substantial summary of pretribulational arguments, and these issues have been abundantly discussed in the literature on the Rapture debate. Moreover, Rosenthal's rebuttals are largely a restatement of positions earlier defended.

However, two hitherto untreated issues are introduced. (1) The twenty-four elders of Revelation 4 are commonly believed to represent the Church in glory before the Tribulation, a position strongly defended by Pentecost and also by the present writer *(Kept from the Hour, pp. 198-208)*. Rosenthal argues that the elders are not the Church at all, but rather "they represented the redeemed of the Old Testament economy," even "redeemed Israel" (252, 254). But Israel is clearly identified in the Revelation and except for 14:1- 5 is always seen on earth and not as a unique group in heaven. However the Church, referred to 19 times in the first three chapters, does not appear on earth at all in chapters 4-18, the critical Tribulation passage. It is more than a coincidence that a new group appears in heaven and is presented in great detail before the opening of the first seal. All the evidence identifies these 24 elders as representing the raptured Church. For they have been redeemed out of many nations and clothed in the righteousness of Christ. They have been crowned at the Judgment Seat of Christ and are now seated in the presence of the Lamb. Everything said in the song of the elders is true of the Church. All the details argue that at this point it is the Church in view rather than Israel.

(2) Also discussed in this chapter is Rosenthal's view of the Restrainer (II Thess. 2:6-8). The normal pretribulational position is that the Restrainer is the Holy Spirit, removed before the open revelation of the Antichrist, and taking the Church with Him back to the Father's house (John 14:2-3, 16). The normal posttribulational position is that the influence which restrains human wickedness is some aspect of human law or government. Rosenthal rejects both of these, declaring that he who restrains until "he be taken out of the way" is actually the angel Michael, who "steps aside" and no longer hinders Antichrist in his persecution of Israel (256-57). This appears to be the very reverse of the teaching of Scripture that Michael will defend and deliver Israel in the coming unprecedented "time of trouble" (Dan. 12:1; cf. Rev. 12:7-16). He will not abandon them in the midst of Israel's worst hour, but will save them from it (Jer. 30:7).

In chapter 19 Rosenthal asks, "*Why This View Now?*" He defends the thesis that his view is neither new nor novel, but only now systematized. His primary defense is from Daniel 12:4, which teaches that Daniel's book would be sealed "to the time of the end," when the knowledge of the book would be greatly increased. He draws the conclusion that it should not be surprising that "a new, more detailed systematic approach to the timing of the Rapture and the events of the seventieth week would be forthcoming" (278).

While it is self-evident that much of Daniel through history has been "sealed," with far greater understanding of his prophecies being achieved as "the time of the end" approaches, this writer takes exception to Rosenthal's idea that this sealing means that "God was guaranteeing its accuracy" (269). Accuracy, not for one, but for every book in the canon of Scripture is guaranteed by the inspiration of the Holy Spirit (II Pet. 1:21) and does not require additional sealing. Nor can Daniel 12:4 be used to justify every new and novel prophetic theory to come along. Nor does it justify Rosenthal's particular view of the timing of the Rapture, for the Rapture is a New Testament "mystery" (I Cor. 15:51), not found at all in the Old Testament, even in so wonderful a book as Daniel. It is self-serving for Rosenthal to claim support for his time of the Rapture theories from Daniel 12:4.

Perhaps there should be mentioned at this point a problem which runs throughout this book. Continually Rosenthal quotes Scripture, which is commendable, but almost invariably in the midst of the quotation he interjects his own definition or explanation, sometimes in brackets and sometimes in parenthesis. The impression is given that the reader cannot understand each Scripture unless he is helped along or prodded by Rosenthal. While separate commentary is legitimate, each Scripture is inspired by the Spirit with the potential of being taught by the Spirit, even the "deep things of God" (I Cor. 2:10-12). This is even true of prophetic material, for "when he, the Spirit of truth is come, he will guide you into all truth . . . and he will show you things to come" (John 16:13).

Rosenthal's last chapter incorporates a final summary of his various positions, and also a final abrasive attack against pre-tribulationism and some of its leaders. The chapter sets forth the "Prewrath Rapture" view as a "catalyst for holy living," without recognizing that much of that catalyst is lost if forty-two months of "sorrows" and another twenty-one months of battle and martyrdom from the Beast must come first.

It is reasonable to inquire about the effect of these new prophetic views upon their author as he prepared them in written form for the Christian public. For this, it is essential to return to the opening chapter, perhaps the most dismal portion of the entire book. Rosenthal testifies that the writing of his book caused him "the most difficult, tension-filled, heart-wrenching two and a half years" of his life (17). He speaks of sleepless nights and excruciating tension, of strained and somber board meetings, of agony of soul and the trauma of lost friendships and a lost job.

While readers respond to this agony with deep regret, it is hardly the mark of being taught and led by the Spirit. One would think that a new clarification of a divisive problem of eschatology which has troubled the Church for more than a hundred years, with the Spirit finally fulfilling the promise of Daniel 12:4 and shedding new light and understanding, would be accompanied by the joy of illumination and the peace of divine guidance. Such was evidently not the case.

Our brother should be commended for his diligence and thanked with appreciation for every insight which bears the clear stamp of truth. He should be the subject of prayer as he searches for further light on the timing of the Rapture. But the considered conclusion of this reviewer is that Rosenthal's published views are a distortion of prophetic truth, sometimes curious, sometimes strange, and frequently false. But taken as a whole they are an unworthy replacement for the blessed hope of Christ's imminent return for the Church in Rapture experience.

NOT A BASIS FOR FELLOWSHIP

To conclude this review of major literature relative to the pre- or posttribulational Rapture of the Church, it should be noted that many of the authors close their arguments with a plea for greater tolerance and warmer fellowship between those who differ so strongly on various points of eschatology. This has been our plea from the very first edition of *Kept from the Hour*, that disagreement as to the time and manner of the Rapture "should not be permitted to deter evangelical unity on the reality of that blessed hope" (272).

It is encouraging to hear others sounding a similar conciliatory note. John Walvoord speaks of the return of the Lord for His Church as "a precious aspect of faith and expectation," and refers to those who have not always agreed as to the chronology of that hope as "learned and devout saints" (1979, 276). In an earlier volume he declares: "Worthy scholars may be found on both sides of this question" (1976, 8).

Barton Payne confirms that "writers of all schools increasingly insist that convictions be expressed with courtesy." One's views should be defended in "a spirit of Christian charity," for the doctrine in question "is not of sufficient importance to cause evangelical cleavage" (1962, 169).

Robert Gundry writes concerning his presentation: "It should (but cannot) go without saying that in matters of disagreement the appearance here of the names of writers on the topic at hand ought not be taken as personal attack, but only as means of documentation." He desires his pages to be written in a manner characterized by "the wisdom from above . . . first pure, then peaceable, gentle, reasonable, full of mercy and good fruits, unwavering, without hypocrisy" (10-11). Such an attitude is most commendable.

George Ladd closes *The Blessed Hope* by declaring: "Neither pretribulationism nor posttribulationism should be made a ground of fellowship, a test of orthodoxy, or a necessary element in Christian doctrine" (167). Douglas Moo concludes: "I cannot, indeed *must* not, allow this conviction to represent any kind of barrier to full relationships with others who hold differing convictions . . ." (211). Even William Kimball hopes that "our essential unity and fellowship in Christ should never be severed or undermined because of our differences on prophetic points" (181). Such mutual respect must be continually encouraged.

While the Rapture debate is far more that a dispute over the time of the Rapture and its relationship to the coming Tribulation, and while widely divergent views cannot be equally true or accurate, the central truth must be reaffirmed that since Christ is our Saviour and Lord, His possible soon coming for the Church is our mutual expectation and our hope! Our love for Him and anticipation of His return is far more important than a disputed point of doctrine or a favored rule of hermeneutics.

All of those engaged in the Rapture debate are Bible-believing, Premillennial brothers in Christ, and whenever He comes, we are going up together to dwell together with Christ for eternity. Meanwhile, as Paul Feinberg has so aptly put it, may our disagreements "serve as a greater impetus to study and clarity," and "may our differences never becloud the joy and expectation of seeing our Lord at His visible and personal return" (86).

Amen, and "even so, come Lord Jesus"!

BIBLIOGRAPHY

A. BOOKS AND PAMPHLETS

Alford, Henry, *The Greek Testament*, 4 vols., Cambridge, England: Deighton, Bell and Co., 1866.

Allis, Oswald T., *Prophecy and the Church*. Philadelphia: Presbyterian and Reformed Publishing Co., 1945.

Anderson, Sir Robert, *Forgotten Truths*. London: James Nisbet and Co., Ltd., 1913.

————, *The Coming Prince*. London: Hodder and Stoughton, 1881.

Archer, Gleason L.; Feinberg, Paul D.; Moo, Douglas J.; Reiter, Richard R., *The Rapture: Pre- Mid- Or Post-Tribulational?* Grand Rapids: Zondervan Publishing House, 1984.

Armerding, Carl, *The Four and Twenty Elders*. New York: Loizeaux Brothers, n.d.

Biederwolf, William E., *The Second Coming Bible*. Grand Rapids: Baker Book House, 1972.

Berkhof, Louis, *Principles of Biblical Interpretation*. Grand Rapids: Baker Book House, 1950.

————*Systematic Theology*. Grand Rapids: Wm. B. Eerdmans Publishing Co., 1941.

Blackstone, W. E., *Jesus Is Coming*. New York: Fleming H. Revell Co., 1908.

Bradbury, John W., ed. and comp., *The Sure Word of Prophecy*. New York: Fleming H. Revell Co., 1943.

Bray, John L., *The Origin of the Pretribulation Rapture Teaching*. Lakeland, Florida: John L. Bray Ministry, Inc., 1982.

Brookes, James H., *Maranatha*. New York: Fleming H. Revell Co., 1889.

————, *Till He Come*. Chicago: Gospel Publishing Co., 1891.

Brooks, Keith L. and others, *The Rapture* (four prophetic papers). Los Angeles: American Prophetic League, Inc., 1940.

Burgon, John W., *Inspiration and Interpretation*. London: Marshall Brothers, 1905.

Burnham, Sylvester, *The Elements of Biblical Hermeneutics*. Hamilton, New York: The Republic Press, 1916.

Cameron, Robert, *Scripture Truth About the Lord's Return*. New York: Revell Co., 1922.

Camping, Harold, *When Is The Rapture?* Oakland, California: Family Stations, Inc., 1978.

————, *The Final Tribulation*. Oakland, California: Family Stations, Inc., 1988.

Case, Shirley Jackson, *The Millennial Hope*. Chicago: The University of Chicago Press, 1918.

Chafer, Lewis Sperry, *Systematic Theology*, 8 vols. Dallas: Dallas Seminary Press, 1948.

Chafer, Rollin T., *The Science of Biblical Hermeneutics*. Dallas: Bibliotheca Sacra, 1939.

Cohn, Joseph H., Will the Church Escape the Tribulation? Findlay, Ohio Fundamental Truth Publishers, *n.d.*

Conybeare, W. J. and J. S. Howson, *The Life and Epistles of St. Paul*. New York: Charles Scribner's Sons, *n.d.*

Cooper, David L., *The World's Greatest Library Graphically Illustrated*. Los Angeles: Biblical Research Society, 1942.

Crippen, T. G., *A Popular Introduction to the History of Christian Doctrine*. Edinburgh: T. & T. Clark, 1883.

Criswell, W. A., *The Curse of Modernism* (published sermon). Dallas: First Baptist Church, 1949.

Davidson, A. B., *Old Testament Prophecy*. Edinburgh: T. & T. Clark, 1903.

Douty, Norman F., *The Great Tribulation Debate*. Harrison, Arkansas: Gibbs Publishing Co., 1956.

Dunham, T. Richard, *The Great Tribulation*, Hoytville, Ohio: Fundamental Truth Publishers, 1933.

Duty, Guy, *Escape From The Coming Tribulation*. Bethany Fellowship, Inc., 1975. Minneapolis: Bethany Fellowship, Inc., 1975.

Ellicott, Charles J., *St. Paul's First Epistle to the Corinthians*. London: Longmans, Green and Co., 1887.

Ellicott, Charles and W. J. Harsha, *Biblical Hermeneutics* (chiefly a translation of *Manuel d'Hermeneuticus Biblicus* by J. N. Cellerier). New York: Anson D. F. Randolph & Co., 1881.

Engelder, Th., *Scripture Cannot Be Broken*. St. Louis, Missouri: Concordia Publishing House, 1944.

English, E. Schuyler, *Re-Thinking the Rapture*. Travelers Rest, South Carolina: Southern Bible Book House, 1954.

Fairbairn, Patrick, *Hermeneutical Manual*. Edinburgh: T. & T. Clark, 1858.

————, *Prophecy Viewed in Respect to Its Distinctive Nature, Its Special Function, and Proper Interpretation*. Edinburgh: T. & T. Clark, 1865.

Farrar, F. W., *History of Interpretation*. London: Macmillan & Co., 1886.

Feinberg, Charles, *Premillennialism or Amillennialism?* (1st edition). Grand

Rapids: Zondervan Publishing House, 1936. (2nd and enlarged edition: Van Kampen Press, 1954.)

Fraser, Alexander, *Is There But One Return of Christ?* Pittsburgh: Evangelical Fellowship, Inc., 1943.

————, *The Any Moment Return of Christ: A Critique.* Pittsburgh: Evangelical Fellowship, Inc., 1947.

Frey, Joseph Samuel, *Frey's Scripture Types,* 2 vols. Philadelphia: American Baptist Publishing Society, 1841.

Fromow, George H., *Will the Church Pass Through the Great Tribulation?* London: The Sovereign Grace Advent Testimony, *n.d.*

Frost, Henry W., *The Second Coming of Christ.* Grand Rapids: Wm. B. Eerdmans Publishing Co., 1934.

Gaebelein, Arno C., *Revelation.* New York: Publication Office *Our Hope,* 1915.

————, *The Olivet Discourse.* New York: Gospel Publishing House, *n.d.*

Graham, James R., *Watchman, What of the Night?* Los Angeles: Ambassadors for Christ, *n.d.*

Gundry, Robert H., *The Church and the Tribulation.* Grand Rapids: Zondervan Publishing House, 1973.

H————, H. W., *The Church and the Great Tribulation.* Dublin: R. Stewart, 1906.

Habershon, Ada R., *The Study of the Types.* London: Pickering and Inglis, *n.d.*

Haldeman, I. M., *The Coming of Christ: Both Premillennial and Imminent.* Philadelphia: Philadelphia School of the Bible, 1906.

————, *The History of the Doctrine of Our Lord's Return.* New York: First Baptist Church, *n.d.*

————, *The Secret and Imminent Coming of Christ.* New York: Charles C. Cook, 1917.

Hamilton, Floyd, *The Basis of Millennial Faith.* Grand Rapids: Wm. B. Eerdmans Publishing Co., 1942.

Hamilton, Gavin, *Will the Church Escape the Great Tribulation?* New York: Loizeaux Brothers, 1944.

Harrison, Everett F., *Baker's Dictionary of Theology.* Grand Rapids: Baker Book House, 1960.

Harrison, Norman B., *His Coming.* Minneapolis: The Harrison Service, 1946.

————, *His Sure Return.* Chicago: Bible Institute Colportage Assoc., 1926.

————, *The End: Re-Thinking the Revelation.* Minneapolis: The Harrison Service, 1941.

Harrison, Norman B., Jr., "The Partial Rapture Theory." Unpublished Master's

Thesis, Dallas Theological Seminary, Dallas, Texas, 1940.

Hodge, A. A., *Outlines of Theology*. New York: Robert Carter and Brothers, 1879.

Hodge, Charles, *An Exposition of the First Epistle to the Corinthians*. London: James Nisbet & Co., 1868.

Hogg, C. F. and W. E. Vine, *The Church and the Tribulation*. London: Pickering and Inglis, Ltd., 1938.

————, *The Epistles of Paul the Apostle to the Thessalonians*. Glasgow: Pickering and Inglis, Ltd., 1914.

Horne, Thomas Hartwell, *A Compendious Introduction to the Study of the Bible*. London: Longman's, Green and Co., 1888.

Hospers, Gerrit H., *The Principle of Spiritualization in Hermeneutics*. East Williamson, New York: Author, 1935.

Hoste, W., *The Great Tribulation Theory*. Glasgow: Pickering and Inglis, *n.d.*

Houghton, Thomas, *The Faith and the Hope of the Future*. London: Sovereign Grace Advent Testimony, *n.d.*

Hubbard, W. R., *Does the Church Go Through the Great Tribulation?* St. Petersburg, Florida: Author, *n.d.*

Huebner, R. A., *The Truth of the Pre-Tribulation Rapture Recovered*. Millington, N.J.: Present Truth Publishers, 1976.

Hurst, John F., *Short History of the Christian Church*. New York: Harper Brothers, 1892.

Immer, Albert, *Hermeneutics of the New Testament*. Andover: Warren F. Draper, 1877.

Ironside, H. A., *Lectures on the Book of Revelation*. New York: Loizeaux Bros., 1919.

————, *Not Wrath, But Rapture*. New York: Loizeaux Brothers, *n.d.*

————, *The Mysteries of God*. New York: Loizeaux Brothers, 1946.

Jamieson, Fausset and Brown, *Comentary on the Whole Bible*. Grand Rapids: Zondervan Publishing House, *n.d.*

————, *Critical and Experimental Commentary*, 6 vols. Grand Rapids: Wm. B. Eerdmans Publishing Co., 1948.

Jennings, F. C., *Studies in Revelation*. New York: Loizeaux Brothers, 1937.

Katterjohn, Arthur (with Mark Fackler), *The Tribulation People*. Carol Stream, Illinois: Creation House, 1975.

Kelly, William, *Lectures on the Book of Revelation*. London: G. Morrish, *n.d.*

————, *The Lord's Prophecy on Olivet*. London: T. Weston, 1903.

Kepler, Thomas S., compiler, *Contemporary Religious Thought, an Anthology*.

New York: Abingdon Cokesbury Press, 1941.

Kimball, William R., *The Rapture: A Question of Timinq.* Grand Rapids: Baker Book House, 1985.

King, William P., *Adventism: The Second Coming of Christ.* New York: Abingdon Cokesbury Press, 1941.

Knapp, C., *Does Scripture Teach a Partial Rapture?* New York: Loizeaux Brothers, *n.d.*

Ladd, George E., *Crucial Questions About The Kingdom of God.* Grand Rapids, Eerdmans Publishing House, 1952.

—————, *The Blessed Hope.* Grand Rapids: Wm. B. Eerdmans Publishing Co., 1956.

—————, *The Last Things: An Eschatology for Laymen.* Grand Rapids: Eerdmans Publishing House, 1978.

Laidlaw, Robert A., *Will the Church Go Through the Great Tribulation?* New York: Loizeaux Brothers, *n.d.*

Lang, G. H., *Firstfruits and Harvest.* Dorset, England: Author, 1946.

—————, *The Gospel of the Kingdom.* London: Oliphants Ltd., 1944.

—————, *The Revelation of Jesus Christ.* London: Oliphants Ltd., 1945.

Lange, John Peter, *The Revelation of John.* New York: Scribner, Armstrong & Co., 1874.

Larkin, Clarence, *The Book of Revelation.* Philadelphia: Rev. Clarence Larkin Estate, 1919.

—————, *The Second Coming of Christ.* Philadelphia: Rev. Clarence Larkin Estate, 1918.

Lenski, R. C. H., *The Interpretation of St. John's Revelation.* Columbus, Ohio: Lutheran Book Concern, 1935.

Lindower, Leslie E., "The Three Distinctive Major Passages of the Prophetic Ministry of Christ." Unpublished Doctor's dissertation, Dallas Theological Seminary, Dallas, Texas, 1932.

Lindsey, Hal, *The Rapture: Truth or Consequences.* New York: Bantam Books, 1983.

Linton, John, *Will the Church Escape the Great Tribulation.* Windsor, Ontario: Hall Printers and Stationers, *n.d.*

Lockhart, Clinton, *Principles of Interpretation.* Fort Worth, Texas: S. B. Taylor, 1915.

Ludwigson, R., *Simplified Classroom Notes on Prophecy.* Wheaton, Illinois: Author, 1951.

MacCorkle, Douglas B., "A Study of Amillennial Eschatology." Unpublished

Master's Thesis, Dallas Theological Seminary, Dallas, Texas, 1947.

Mackintosh, C. H., *Papers on the Lord's Coming*. New York: Loizeaux Brothers, *n.d.*

MacPherson, Dave, *The Unbelievable Pretrib Origin*. Kansas City, Missouri: Heart of America Bible Society, 1973.

————, *The Incredible Cover-Up*. Plainfield, N.J.: Logos International, 1975.

McPherson, Norman S., *Triumph Through Tribulation*. Otego, New York: Author, 1944.

Maas, A J., *Christ in Type and Prophecy*. New York: Benziger Bros., 1896.

Marsh, F. E., *Will the Church or any Part of It Go Through the Great Tribulation?* Glasgow: Pickering and Inglis, *n.d.*

Masselink, W., *Why Thousand Years?* Grand Rapids: Wm. B. Eerdmans Publishing Co., 1930.

Mauro, Philip, *Looking for the Saviour*. New York: Fleming H. Revell Co., 1913.

————, *The Seventy Weeks and The Great Tribulation*. Boston: Hamilton Bros., Scripture Truth Depot, 1923.

McCall, Tom and Zola Levitt, *Raptured*. Irvine, California: Harvest House Publishers, 1975.

McKeever, Jim, *Christians Will Go Through The Tribulation*. Medford, Oregon: Alpha Omega Publishing Co., 1978.

Miles, F. J., *Understandest Thou? Principles of Biblical Interpretation*. London: Marshall, Morgan & Scott, 1946.

Milligan, George, *St. Paul's Epistles to the Thessalonians*. London: MacMillan and Co., 1908.

Murray, G. L., *Millennial Studies*. Grand Rapids: Baker Book House, 1948.

Needham, Mrs. George C., *The Antichrist*. New York: Charles C. Cook, *n.d.*

Neil, James, *Strange Figures: or the Figurative Language of the Bible*. London: Simpkin, Marshall & Co., 1895.

Newell, William R., *The Book of The Revelation*. Chicago: Moody Press, 1935.

————, *The Church and the Great Tribulation*. Chicago: Scripture Press, 1933.

Olshausen, Hermann, *Biblical Commentary on the New Testament*, 6 vols. New York: Sheldon, Blakeman & Co., 1857.

Orr, James, *The Progress of Dogma*. London: Hodder and Stoughton, 1901.

Ottman, Ford C., *The Unfolding of the Ages*. New York: Publication Office *Our Hope,* 1905.

Pache, Rene, *Le Retour De Jesus Christ*. France: A. Coveslant Cahors, *n.d.*

Payne, Homer L., "Amillennial Theology as a System." Unpublished Doctor's dissertation, Dallas Theological Seminary, Dallas, Texas, 1948.

Payne, J. Barton, *The Imminent Appearing of Christ.* Grand Rapids: Eerdmans Publishing Co., 1962.

————, *Encyclopedia of Biblical Prophecy.* Grand Rapids: Baker Book House, 1973.

Pember, G. H., *The Great Prophecies of the Centuries.* London: Oliphants, Ltd., 1942.

Pentecost, J. Dwight, *Things To Come..* Grand Rapids: Dunham Publishing Co., 1958.

Peter, G. W., *Into His Presence.* Fresno, California: Author, *n.d.*, 71 pp.

Peters, George N. H., *The Theocratic Kingdom,* 3 vols. New York: Funk and Wagnalls, 1884.

Pierson, Arthur T., *Stumbling Stones Removed from the Word of God.* London: Richard D. Dickinson, 1891.

————, *The Coming of the Lord.* New York: Fleming H. Revell Co., 1896.

Pollock, Wallace S., "Chiliasm in the First Five Centuries." Unpublished Master's Thesis, Dallas Theological Seminary, Dallas, Texas, 1945.

Ramm, Bernard, *Protestant Biblical Interpretation.* Boston: W. A. Wilde Co., 1950.

Reese, Alexander, *The Approaching Advent of Christ.* London: Marshall, Morgan and Scott Co., *n.d.*

Rimmer, Harry, *The Coming King.* Grand Rapids: Wm. B. Eerdmans Publishing Co., 1941.

Roberts, Alexander, and James Donaldson, *The Ante-Nicene Fathers,* 10 vols. New York: Charles Scribner's Sons, 1899.

Robertson, A. T., *Word Pictures in the New Testament,* 6 vols. New York: Harper and Brothers, Publishers, 1933.

Rogers, W. H., *Things That Differ.* New York: Loizeaux Bros., 1940.

Rose, George L., *Tribulation Till Translation.* Glendale, California: Rose Publishing Co., 1943.

Rosenthal, Marvin J., *The Pre-Wrath Rapture of the Church.* Nashville: Thomas Nelson Publishers, 1990.

Rutgers, William H., *Premillennialism in America.* Goes, Holland: Costerbaan & Le Cointre, 1930.

Ryrie, Charles C., *The Basis of the Premillennial Faith.* New York: Loizeaux Brothers, 1953.

————, *What You Should Know About The Rapture.* Chicago: Moody Press, 1981.

Schaff, Philip, *History of the Christian Church*, 8 vols. Grand Rapids: Wm. B. Eerdmans Publishing Co., 1950.

Scofield, C. I., *Will the Church Pass Through the Great Tribulation?* Philadelphia: Philadelphia School of the Bible, Inc., 1917.

Scott, Walter, *Exposition of the Revelation*. London: Alfred Holness, 1914.

Scruby, John J., *The Great Tribulation: The Church's Suprem Test*. Dayton, Ohio: Author, 1933.

Seiss, Joseph A., *Lectures on the Apocalypse*, 3 vols. Philadelphia: General Council Publication Board, 1911.

Shodde, George H., *Outlines of Biblical Hermeneutics*. Columbus, Ohio: Lutheran Book Concern, 1917.

Showers, Renald, Unpublished "Critique and Objection to *The Pre-Wrath Rapture of the Church.*" Holland, Pa., n.d.

Silver, Jesse Forrest, *The Lord's Return*. New York: Fleming H. Revell Co., 1914.

Smith, Oswald J., *Daniel's 70th Week*. Grand Rapids: Zondervan Publishing House, 1932.

————, *The Book of Revelation*. Grand Rapids: Zondervan Publishing House, n.d.

Strombeck, J. F., *First The Rapture*. Moline, Illinois: Strombeck Agency, Inc., 1950.

Taylor, D. T., *The Voice of the Church on the Reign of Christ*. Peace Dale, Rhode Island: H. L. Hastings, 1855.

Terry, Milton S., *Biblical Hermeneutics*. New York: The Methodist Book Concern, 1883.

Thayer, Joseph H., A *Greek English Lexicon of the New Testament*. New York: American Book Company, 1886.

Thiessen, Henry C., *Introductory Lectures in Systematic Theology*. Grand Rapids: Wm. B. Eerdman's Publishing Co., 1949.

————, *Will the Church Pass Through the Tribulation?* New York: Loizeaux Brothers, 1941.

Todd, James H., *Principles of Interpretation*. Chicago: The Bible Institute Colportage Association, 1923.

Tregelles, S. P., *The Hope of Christ's Second Coming*. London: Samuel Bagster and Sons, 1886.

Walvoord, John F, *The Rapture Question*. Findlay, Ohio: Dunham Publishing Co., 1957.

————, *The Millennial Kingdom*. Findlay, Ohio: Dunham Publishing Co., 1959.

————, *The Blessed Hope and the Tribulation*. Grand Rapids: Zondervan Publishing House, 1976.

————, *The Rapture Question: Revised and Enlarged Edition*. Grand Rapids:

Zondervan Publishing House, 1979.

Warfield, B. B., *Biblical Doctrines*. New York: Oxford University Press, 1929.

Waugh, T., *When Jesus Comes*. London: Charles H. Kelly, 1901.

Winfrey, David G., *An Examination of the Pretribulational Rapture Interpretation of II Thess. 2:7*. Hollywood, Florida: Lighthouse Ministries, 1980.

Wood, Leon, *Is The Rapture Next?* Grand Rapids: Zondervan Publishing House, 1956.

Wyngaarden, Martin J., *The Future of the Kingdom in Prophecy and Fulfillment*. Grand Rapids: Zondervan Publishing House, 1934.

B. ENCYCLOPEDIA ARTICLES

Erdman, Charles R., "Parousia," *International Standard Bible Encyclopedia, IV*, 2249-2251F.

Harnack, Adolf, "Millennium," *The Encyclopedia Britannica*, 14th edition, XV, 495-97.

Kirsch, J. P., "Millennium," *The Catholic Encyclopedia*, 1913, X, 307-9.

C. PERIODICAL ARTICLES

Barker, H. P., "A Partial Rapture," *Prophetic Digest, IV* (February, 1952), 227-32.

Barnhouse, Donald Grey, "Some Questions About Our Lord's Return," *Revelation*, XII (November, 1942), 498ff.

Brookes, James H., "Kept Out of the Hour," *Our Hope, VI* (November, 1899), 153-57.

Buswell, J. Oliver, letter in "Let the Prophets Speak . . ." *Our Hope*, LVI (June, 1950), 717-32.

Cooper, David L., "Will The Church Go Through the Tribulation?" *Biblical Research Monthly*, XIII (January-June, 1948).

David, Ira E., "Translation: When Does It Occur," *The Dawn*, XII (November 15 1935), 358-59.

English, E. Schuyier, "Re-Thinking the Rapture," *Our Hope*, LVI-LVII (October, 1949 through March, 1951).

Gaebelein, A. C., "The Attempted Revival of an Unscriptural Theory," *Our Hope*, XLI (July, 1934), 18-25.

Ice, Thomas D., "Why the Doctrine of Pretribulational Rapture Did Not Begin with Margaret Macdonald," *Bibliotheca Sacra* (April-June, 1990), 155-68.

Kellogg, S. H., "Premillennialism: Its Relation to Doctrine and Practice," *Bibliotheca Sacra*, XLV (April, 1888), 234-74.

Kelly, William, "The Future Tribulation," *The Bible Treasury, IV* (December, 1902; January, 1903), 206-8, 222-23.

Marchbanks, J. B., "The Four Days of Scripture," *Our Hope,* LIV (January, 1948), 421-28.

McClain, Alva J., "The Greatest of the Kingdom," *Bibliotheca Sacra,* 446 (April-June, 1955), 111, 112.

Panton, D. M., "The Removal of the Church from the Earth," *The Dawn, IV* (December 15, 1927), 389-94.

Pieters, Albertus, "Darbyism Vs. the Historic Christian Faith," *The Calvin Forum,* II (May, 1936), 225-28.

Pitt, F. W., "The Great Tribulation: The Church's Supreme Test," *Our Hope, LXI* (October, 1934), 236-42.

Sproule, John A., *A Revised Review of The Church and the Tribulation by Robert H. Gundry.* Postgraduate Seminar in N. T. Theology, Grace Theological Seminary, 1974.

Stearns, Minor B., Book review: "Re-Thinking the Revelation," *Bibliotheca Sacra,* XCIX (January-March, 1942), 124-27.

Thiessen, Henry C., "Will the Church Pass Through the Tribulation?" *Bibliotheca Sacra,* XCII (January-September, 1935), 39-54, 187-205, 292-314.

Trumbull, Charles G., "The Rapture and the Tribulation," *Sunday School Times,* LXXX (May 7, 1938), 329-34.

Van Ryn, August, "Is Jesus Coming Soon?" *Moody Monthly,* XLIX (April 1949), 558ff.

Walvoord, John F. "A Review of 'The Blessed Hope' by George E. Ladd." *Bibliotheca Sacra,* (October, 1956.)

————, "Is the Church the Israel of God?" *Bibliotheca Sacra,* CI (October November, 1934), 403-16.

————, "Is the 70th Week of Daniel Future?" *Bibliotheca Sacra,* CI (January-March, 1944), 30-49.

————, "Millennial Series," *Bibliotheca Sacra,* CVII (January December, 1950), 42-50, 154-67, 281-90, 420-29. CVIII (January December, 1951), 7-14, 153-66, 270-81, 414-22.

————, "New Testament Words for the Lord's Coming," *Bibliotheca Sacra,* CI (July-September, 1944), 283-89.

————, "Premillennialism and the Tribulation," *Bibliotheca Sacra,* CXI, CXII (July, 1954-January, 1955).

Whiting, Arthur B., "The Rapture of the Church," *Bibliotheca Sacra,* CII (July-December, 1945), 360-72, 490-99.

SCRIPTURE INDEX